D0951899

The
Bronfmans

ALSO BY NICHOLAS FAITH:

The Infiltrators: The European Business Invasion of America (1971)

The Winemasters (1978), reissued as The Winemakers of
Bordeaux (1999 and 2005)

Safety in Numbers: The Mysterious World of Swiss Banking (1982)

Sold: The Rise and Fall of the House of Sotheby (1985)

Cognac (1986, reissued 2004)

The Story of Champagne (1988)

The World the Railways Made (1990)

Black Box: Why Air Safety Is No Accident (1996)

Australia's Liquid Gold (2003)

The
Bronfmans

The

RISE AND FALL

of the

HOUSE OF SEAGRAM

Nicholas Faith

ST. MARTIN'S PRESS
NEW YORK

THOMAS DUNNE BOOKS.
An imprint of St. Martin's Press.

Library of Congress Cataloging-in-Publication Data

Faith, Nicholas, 1933–
    The Bronfmans : the rise and fall of the house of Seagram / Nicholas Faith.—1st ed.
        p. cm.
    Includes bibliographical references.
    ISBN-10 0-312-33219-X
    ISBN-13 978-0-312-33219-8
    1. Bronfman family.   2. Seagram Company.   3. Distilling industries—Canada.
    4. Businesspeople—Canada—Biography.   I. Title.

HD9390.C22B718 2006
338.7'66350092271—dc22
[B]

                                                                        2006040391

First Edition: June 2006

10 9 8 7 6 5 4 3 2 1

*This book is dedicated to the memory of Robert Ducas,
most loyal and delightful of friends.*

CONTENTS

The Bronfmans are always great theater.

—DAVID PLOTZ, Slate.com

The
Bronfmans

One

MR. SAM, NO ORDINARY MONSTER

WHEN I TOLD FRIENDS THAT I HAD BEEN COMMISSIONED TO WRITE ABOUT the Bronfman family, many of them muttered about "cement galoshes" and one serious citizen—a leading investment banker—warned me that the Bronfman family would infallibly take out a contract on me. Although this has turned into something of a joke between us, I found that until recently the threat could have been very real. One of his many mistresses had rebuked Edgar, the founder's elder son, when he talked of "knee-capping" someone. He retorted simply, "No, I meant it." And in the 1980s Edgar's son Edgar Jr. told an obstructive television producer that "in my grandfather's time we'd have killed you." Naturally these comments did nothing to dispel the continuing atmosphere of threat and mystery that still surrounds the family and obviously further whetted my appetite for writing a book about this extraordinary dynasty. Such stories still fascinate people several years after the Bronfmans have sold Seagram, the family firm, to Jean-Marie Messier, the French mogul widely viewed as "megalomaniacal" in his overweening empire building and self-aggrandizement, and the name has disappeared from the business scene. Clearly the Bronfman name, and the story behind it, has not lost its capacity to intrigue, and even frighten, the most sophisticated of onlookers.

The attraction is partly based on the family's wealth. This is still considerable. Even after the disaster of the sale to Messier the combined wealth of Mr. Sam's two sons, Edgar and Charles, amounts to over $5 billion, and there are probably several billions more in the hands of the rest of this enormous tribe. But even more important is the reputation of the founder, Sam Bronfman, as "the last bootlegger," the one who went legit so successfully. For the story involves a double fascination, that of the billionaire businessman, combined with the mystery inevitably attached to any survivor of that enormous business, the supply of liquor to the American people during Prohibition. The description "bootlegger" haunted him—and his children and grandchildren—for seventy years after Repeal. One evening his youngest child, Charles, asked him in all innocence, "Daddy, what's a bootlegger?" Mr. Sam dropped the carving knife and said angrily, "Don't you ever say that word again." As late as 2000, sixty-seven years after Repeal, Messier could refer to the family's "bootlegger methods." Yet Mr. Sam, as he was usually called, believed that the mere fact that liquor was illegal in the United States was irrelevant because he felt, with some reason, that he was involved in a legal business, distilling liquor in Canada and exporting it to the US. So he was naturally upset that his trade turned him into a bootlegger and spent his life in an obsessive, and largely unsuccessful, attempt to gain respectability and the respect he felt, rightly, was his due.

This is not surprising, for in reality he was an authentic business genius, undoubtedly the greatest in the long history of hard liquor, indeed the man who really invented the whole industry in the US by exploiting the post-Repeal thirst for decent whiskey and made drinking hard liquor respectable for the first time in American history. He was a major creative force who understood that the key to lasting success was reliable quality, which for him implied blending well-aged spirits. That perception, reinforced by an obsessive perfectionism, proved to be in line with the willingness of ordinary Americans to respond to spirits which were not mere rot-gut.

While this book is about the rise and fall of a dynastic business, the family was so numerous, so widespread, the story of its members so complex, that I have simply not been able to write about the vast majority of the family—Sam's three brothers and four sisters produced innumerable progeny and, over a century, have multiplied into a considerable tribe. So I have had to confine myself to Mr. Sam, his offspring, and, of the third generation, only Sam and Edgar Jr., the sons of his elder son, Edgar.

But even within this apparently limited remit, the story is far more important and more widely relevant than that of a single family who escaped from the frozen poverty of the Canadian prairies to generate immense wealth within a few decades of their arrival from czarist Russia, or of a liquor company, however important, and a single individual, however gifted and fascinating. For the Bronfman saga also involves other, very different worlds, notably those of Hollywood and of the higher reaches of the French business aristocracy.

It also, and perhaps most importantly, shines a powerful spotlight on the fundamental changes in the mindset of the world Jewish community in the course of the twentieth century. Even in the face of the Holocaust, the normally dictatorial Sam, for thirty years the uncrowned leader of the Jewish community in Canada, could never summon up the courage to mount an open challenge to gentile politicians, for he perceived them as fundamentally unchallengeable—an attitude typical of Jewish leaders throughout the world. By the sharpest of contrasts, his elder son Edgar, as the long-serving president of the previously almost completely powerless World Jewish Congress, was able to mount repeated challenges to the most powerful enemies of world Jewry—like Swiss bankers and Kurt Waldheim, previously the secretary-general of the United Nations. He was even bold enough to criticize the leaders of Israel, a group accustomed to treat their brethren scattered throughout the world as what Lenin described as "useful idiots," cash cows without any right to a voice, especially so far as Israel was concerned.

The Bronfman saga starts in the 1890s in the bleak plains of Saskatchewan and ends just over a century later with a disastrous agreement reached in the gilded salons of a French conglomerate. In less than a century Seagram, their family company, first rose to become a dominant force in the world market for spirits, was becalmed for a generation, and then thrown to the wolves in the person of Jean-Marie Messier of Vivendi. The founder had repeatedly warned his children of the oft-repeated motto "shirtsleeves to shirtsleeves in three generations." Whether the fear was genuine, or whether it was simply that he knew that he wouldn't be there to control the activities of the third generation, is open to question.

After a poverty-stricken few years the family established itself as hoteliers, and then, after 1920, started to supply liquor across the forty-ninth parallel into a newly dry United States. Subsequently, as distillers as well as merchants, they continued to supply their thirsty neighbors until 1933, but they became truly, seriously, rich only in the 1930s and 1940s thanks to Mr.

Sam's whiskies, most obviously 7 Crown. Mr. Sam then went on to pioneer, albeit more by chance than deliberate strategy, the totally original concept of a worldwide business producing and selling a wide range of wines and spirits from a dozen different countries. As a result, before Mr. Sam died in 1971 Seagram had become by far the biggest group in the world liquor business and remained a major, albeit declining, force over the following thirty years before its swift demise at the hands of Messier in 2000.

The continuing fascination of the—largely mythical—Mr. Sam begs an important question: why the myth was not attached to other former bootleggers like Harry Hatch of Hiram Walker, famous for brands like Canadian Club and Mr. Sam's great rival in the 1920s, or the appalling Lew Rosenstiel of Schenley Distillers, his archenemy in the United States after Prohibition. But perhaps the most telling contrast is with Joseph Kennedy, in every way a far more disreputable character than Sam Bronfman. While Bronfman was tarred through his associations with bootleggers, Kennedy's far closer relationships lasted long enough for them to be put to good use in ensuring that Illinois voted for his son John in the 1960 presidential elections.

The contrast comes over most clearly in the way Bronfman and Kennedy were regarded by the mighty Distillers Company Limited, universally known as the DCL, which dominated the Scotch business. The hardheaded directors happily went into partnership with Mr. Sam, whom they regarded as an honest fellow with an excellent knowledge of whiskey, but felt, wrote Ronald Weir[1] in the official history of the company, that "Kennedy was difficult to deal with, signing contracts and immediately challenging their interpretation" and expressing himself in language at least as strong as that employed by Mr. Sam. And whereas Bronfman was totally faithful to his beloved wife, Kennedy was the most notorious of sexual athletes—and it would have been unthinkable for Sam to have allowed his daughter to be lobotomized as did Joe Kennedy.

Although Mr. Sam was deeply ashamed of his continuing association with his activities during Prohibition he did nothing to discourage the myths that surrounded his persona. In 1970, the year before he died, he was confronted with the proofs of the official history of Seagram. "This is so much bullshit," he exploded. "If I only told the truth I'd sell ten million copies." The remark has obviously encouraged the notion that he—and the rest of the family—had committed many an evil deed, but probably had more to do with his relentless egomania, the assumption that any story starring him would be of enormous interest to the whole world. I can only hope so.

The flames of speculation have been fed by the fate of attempts by the family to provide an authorized account of their story. Towards the end of Mr. Sam's life the Canadian journalist Terence Robertson attempted to write a biography of Mr. Sam, which was never published but exists in manuscript form.[2] It is based on a number of conversations with Mr. Sam and so can be taken to reflect his own version of events. For Mr. Sam, as is the way with all such successful men, rewrote the family history to exaggerate his—undoubtedly predominant—position in the story. Peter Newman[3] claims that after finishing the book Robertson phoned a Canadian journalist to say that "he had found out things about Sam they didn't want me to write about," and he told another responsible journalist that his "life had been threatened and we would know who was doing the threatening but that he would do the job himself"—a phone call after which the journalist immediately phoned the New York police who found Robertson dying of barbiturate poisoning. Over the years the story has natually added fuel to the Bronfman legend. But none of even the most vociferous conspiracy theorists has ever found any evidence of foul play, let alone anything damaging to Sam, or indeed any member of the Bronfman family.

The next attempt was made by John Scott, a former editor at the Canadian edition of *Time* magazine, who was hired to counter books like that by Newman and the novel *Solomon Gursky Was Here* by Mordecai Richler, both perceived by the family as "anti-Semitic Jews." Scott spent seven years on and off before giving up. He was succeeded, for a very short time, by a journalist, Erna Paris, whose researches were terminated before she had even started. But in the late 1980s the family was lucky in finding in Professor Michael Marrus, a distinguished Jewish historian, an author worthy of Mr. Sam,[4] but one whose interests lay more in the religious side of Mr. Sam's life than in the whiskey business.

Not surprisingly Mr. Sam's sons and grandsons have always employed a team of PRs to protect the family from overmuch publicity. From my experience this has proved counterproductive. When I received the go-ahead for this book I naturally wrote, politely and repeatedly, to each member of the family involved to explain my objectives and my qualifications, such as they were, to write it. Neither Mr. Sam's elder son Edgar nor his grandson Edgar Jr.—normally known as "Junior"—were prepared to see me. Edgar's brother Charles wrote that he saw no reason for another book on the family but was persuaded by a family friend to see me, amiably enough, for an hour-long meeting that he firmly stated did not constitute an interview. Only his sister Phyllis was frank and open with me. Not surprisingly other authors have found the family equally uncooperative. At his first interview with a prospective biographer, the Canadian journalist Rod McQueen, Edgar Jr. agreed to set up a series of interviews, but then canceled them all. This did not stop, indeed may indirectly have helped, McQueen's production of his valuable biography.[5]

This sort of reclusive behavior is partly conditioned by a streak of "control freakery" that runs through the whole history. Nevertheless it—and the adventures of individual members over the years—have merely slaked, without satisfying, the thirst for shocks and horrors regarding the family on the part of the media, and indeed of the general public, and not just in their native Canada. For even today their fortunes remain colossal—despite the collapse of their empire *Forbes* magazine reckons that Mr. Sam's two sons, Edgar and Charles, are both worth over $2.5 billion, and dozens of family members are comfortably millionaires.

The basic structure of this book, however, is the story of three extraordinary figures, "Mr. Sam," the founder of the business; his elder son, Edgar; and his grandson Edgar Jr., although the list of other characters involved is long and picturesque. Their activities and influence spread far beyond their native Canada and the liquor industry on which their fortunes were based. Edgar's story shines a powerful spotlight on the attitude and actions of the world Jewish community in the last twenty years of the twentieth century; while Edgar Jr. personified the great bubble that enveloped the communications industry in the late 1990s. Unlike other business dynasties, nothing they did was predictable or boring.

The comparison often made, most obviously by Peter Newman, between the Bronfmans and the Rothschilds, is facile but misleading—apart from the fact that both were exceptionally rich and in both families the boys, as has been said, "were also Jewish princesses." But they were emphatically not comparable with the Rothschilds, who for two centuries have enjoyed worldwide fame and fortune. Mr. Sam may have been the King of the Canadian Jews but he was of no great importance on the world religious, social, or financial scene. For whereas the Rothschilds have always been numerous—the five arrows on the Rothschild crest indicate the wide geographical spread of the family fortune—the Bronfmans depended on the business genius of one man. Nevertheless, as Mitch Bronfman, grandson of

Sam's brother Harry, put it, "All types of things"—including and inevitably financial generosity—"are expected of you because you're growing
up in the shadow of a literally incredible guy called Sam."

But the real reason for the comparison lies elsewhere, in the psychological need of the star-hungry Canadians for the ideal anti-hero whom they
could loathe—as a rich Jewish bootlegger—while simultaneously craving
for Sam, and probably even more his family, to provide some spice, some
glamour, to a national scene notably lacking in such attributes. For, as
Hugh MacLennan put it,[6] "Apart from the CPR and the mining and forest
industries, from the earliest beginnings of British North America the most
successful and prominent businesses were brewing and distilling," and Mr.
Sam was unquestionably king of the liquor business. Moreover—and unlike virtually all other business empires of Canadian origin—Seagram was
a world force. Yet this was an additional reason why wealthy Jews were not
considered to be part of the fabric of Canada's economic life. As MacLennan writes, "Historically Jewish fortunes were made in areas like retail
trade or real estate, not the traditional sources of wealth and power of the
Canadian establishment of the time."[7] Unfortunately the Canadian obsession with Mr. Sam has rather hidden any adequate appreciation of his business genius.

The Bronfmans were admired, hated, feared. Mr. Sam and his brothers—
with whom he quarreled and systematically sidelined—were loathed for a
variety of reasons, both good and bad. The hatred towards him and, to a
much lesser extent, his family, owed a lot to Canadian puritanism, envy,
anti-Semitism, combined with Mr. Sam's profoundly un-Canadian personality. Nevertheless in a sense the Canadians, not over-endowed with ro-
mantically rich families, needed the Bronfmans over the years as their
fame—and their wealth—spread throughout the country in the thirty
years after 1945 as more and more members of the family spent and invested their wealth and displayed it so lavishly and, in some cases, created
scandals which naturally entertained the great Canadian public.

The close interest paid to the family has ensured that so much mud has
been thrown at the Bronfmans over the past eighty-five years that it is difficult to conjure up any new misdeed of which they could be guilty, apart
from incest. They were Jews in an anti-Semitic social atmosphere, distillers
and bootleggers in a country where the temperance movement was almost
as strong as it was in the United States. The Bronfmans were the richest of
families in a basically egalitarian society. Canadians are traditionally quiet,

and perhaps the worst sin the Bronfmans committed was to be noisy and aggressive in a profoundly provincial society, a totally uncozy element in a cozy world. The self-effacing Canadians hated showing off. As Sam's younger daughter Phyllis puts it, "In Montreal there were no tall poppies," but the Bronfmans, and most obviously Sam, were the tallest of tall poppies. Moreover it was felt that Mr. Sam was not the best the race could offer at a time when Jews were acutely conscious of the need to present only the most honest and respected members of their race to the world.*

Such was the importance of the myth, perhaps even more than the reality, that an important novel by one of Canada's best-known novelists centers round the family. In *Solomon Gursky Was Here*, Mordecai Richler pictured the family—and above all Sam—in vicious and convincing detail. It's a very important book because it provides a poisonous distillation of the myth that the Canadians wish to perpetuate about the family. But in one sense it was merely one example of the author's—usually genial—contempt for his fellow Canadians. He had already deeply offended the French-speaking majority in Quebec through a characteristically rambunctious article in *The New Yorker* before he attacked his co-religionists through a splendid, if deeply libelous, novel aimed largely at the Bronfmans.

Yet despite the obvious and close relationship of his story to the family, Richler furiously denied any connection. In his author's note he claimed that "I made the Gurskys up out of my own head." But, as one close observer put it, Richler "obviously had a thing about the Bronfmans . . . few people in this very polite country bothered to challenge his transparently untruthful statement that *Gursky* was not 'about' Sam." Yet when he was asked about the connection at a reading of the book Richler gave the immortal reply, "I will not have seven years of my work reduced to gossip." To which Leo Kolber, one of the family's closest associates, said simply, "Purlease. . . . I don't know why Mordecai bothered to change the names."

To make matters worse Richler divides Mr. Sam into two characters, Solomon and Bernard Gursky. He could award Solomon with all the positive aspects of his character leaving his brother Bernard with all the disagreeable ones—including the senility that he claimed—totally unfairly—marked

---

* The same criteria applied in post-war Britain. For instance, fellow Jews were proud of the Marks and Sieff families who had built up Marks & Spencer, but were ashamed of a truly ruthless fellow millionaire, Sir Isaac Wolfson. Such was his wealth and his munificence that he was described as "the only Jew since Jesus Christ to have colleges at both Oxford and Cambridge universities named after him."

the last years of Mr. Sam's life. "Solomon" is an imaginative, brilliant businessman, who, for example, plans to distill his own liquor and who disap-
pears during a trial for fraud only to reappear in London in the guise of Sir
Hyman Kaplansky, an ultra-rich international financier. By contrast
Bernard is a money-grubbing horror—the narrator sums him up as a "sly,
rambunctious reformed bootlegger, worth untold millions," but still "a
grobber,* a hooligan who rained shame on Jews cut from a finer cloth."
Richler is also knowingly unpleasant about Bernard's elder son Lionel, a
clearly malicious portrait of Edgar. Another of the Gursky brothers is
clearly based on Allan, Sam's younger, more cultivated and educated
brother—Richler even repeats two real-life incidents, one in which Sam
threw an ashtray at his younger brother and another in which Morrie/Al-
lan begs Sam, vainly, to allow his sons a place in the business.

But his hatred was not confined to the Bronfman/Gursky family. Hard
though Richler was on Mr. Sam, his family, and his associates, he was just
as severe on the book's narrator. This is one Moses Berger, the drunken,
underachieving literary son of the Gursky's court speechwriter I. B.
Berger (in reality the distinguished poet A. B. Klein) and seems to reflect
an element of self-loathing in Richler's own character. But the better
one knows the Bronfman story the nastier the book appears, the more
references emerge, including—inevitably vicious—references to the suicide of one member of the family, and the departure of another into an
Eastern cult. But the whole book could be construed as a hymn of contempt for all of Canada's inhabitants, excepting only the Eskimos in the
far north with whom the founder of the clan, one Ephraim—and one of
his grandsons—lived. As one of the characters in the book remarks,
"Canada is not so much a country as a holding tank filled with the disgruntled progeny of defeated peoples. French Canadians consumed by
self-pity; the descendants of Scots who fled the Duke of Cumberland,†
Irish the famine; and Jews the Black Hundreds.‡ . . . Most of us are still
huddled tight to the border, looking into the candy-store window, scared
by the Americans on one side and the bush on the other." But even today
the novelist occupies a special place in Montreal's folklore, his habits, his

---

* According to Leo Rosten's The Joys of Yiddish, "grauber" is an adjective meaning coarse, crude, un-
couth, vulgar; ill-mannered.
† Notorious for the "Clearances" that devastated the Highlands of Scotland after the 1745 rebellion led
by Bonnie Prince Charlie.
‡ The anti-Semitic gangs of the 1880s.

drinking bouts lovingly recounted. More than a decade after his death Richler remains a greatly loved eccentric in Montreal and not just—or especially—within the Jewish community.

The Bronfmans' close associate Leo Kolber was the source for much of Richler's information about the family. One summer when Kolber was temporarily estranged from his wife he spent a lot of time with the novelist, who picked Kolber's brain mercilessly. Kolber's only reward was to be portrayed as one Barney Schwartz, the family's groveling courtier, in the single most unpleasant personal vignette in the book—and that's saying a lot.[*] But all Kolber says in his autobiography is that Richler was "such a great writer, though not always a great human being. . . . In a certain sense I was flattered to be in it, even if the caricature was highly unflattering."

The novel is picaresque, rambling, kept together largely by Richler's narrative drive and his soaring imagination. Moreover it is full of the romance and sex largely absent in the real-life story. Its framework is seriously preposterous, starting as it does with the creation of Ephraim Gursky, the archetypal wandering Jew, the grandfather of Solomon and Bernard. After many picturesque adventures in Regency London Ephraim had been the sole survivor of the ill-fated expedition led by Sir John Franklin to find a Northwest Passage from the Atlantic to the Pacific through the icy waters north of Canada in the 1840s. The characters are so striking, and if not accurate, express such underlying truths, that they cry out for quotation, though I have been sparing in this respect.

By contrast, in *The View from the Fortieth Floor* the American journalist Theodore White[†] portrays Sam as a minor character, Lou Bronstein, the tycoon behind "Bruno's Liquors." He clearly understood the foundations of Mr. Sam's ethos and indeed his aggressive attitude towards his two sons, the tempestuous Jack, clearly based on Edgar, and the more peaceable Leo, based on Charles: "A business," Bronstein bellows to his sons, "is something living, something you put together with what's in your belly and your heart. It isn't something you put together just with money and brains you hire. Brains like you I can hire anywhere. Business is when you want something to be alive because you had a dream about it. We were triple-A credit

---

[*] Journalists' ingratitude towards their sources clearly has nothing on that shown by novelists.
[†] It was the only novel by a distinguished political journalist best known for his series of books on successive presidential election campaigns, entitled *The Making of the President*. White was clearly ashamed of the book, quite unfairly he calls it "one of the worst novels ever written." How he came across Mr. Sam remains a mystery.

rating before you pissers were able to button your own pants." And the narrator understood that the "theme of his life was that he should need to fight because without the stimuli of challenge, leavened with a little adversity, there could be no joy in victory."

In real life Mr. Sam fitted his elder son Edgar's description of Nikita Khrushchev. "His stature was unimpressive, he was not at all attractive, and he seemed a bit crude—perhaps unpolished is a kinder word—but he had a great command of the facts and figures." For, as with Khrushchev, the force of Mr. Sam's personality did not depend on his appearance. Without descending into psychobabble it is perfectly reasonable to say that Sam's character was affected by his physical characteristics. He was small, physically unimpressive, with a receding chin. Sporting activity was out of the question—when he tried to ski down a small hill he thought that he would generate enough momentum on the way down to carry him up again. He never learned to swim and when his family persuaded him to row he never strayed more than a few yards from the shore. Nevertheless he could occasionally relax, most obviously at the country house the family bought during the war at Sainte Margarite, in the Laurentian hills north of Montreal.

But he did have considerable presence and lots of charm, although he was strangely shy in any crowd that he could not dominate. In later life he resembled a small, round, benevolent grandfather, short and plump—his younger daughter Phyllis would sometimes call his paunch "Mary." At work his presence was such that he did not have to sit at the top of a table. As he once observed perfectly correctly, "Where I sit *is* the head of the table." "Seagram's real head office" said one well-placed observer, "was where Sam happened to be at any given time," which, in the 1950s, could be either in New York or Montreal. And he totally dominated his business. "I should have realized," wrote Edgar,[8] "that Sam Bronfman would always have one more vote than there were people in the room." For he was a world-class egomaniac and control freak, self-centered—everything revolved round him and his wishes—with the demonic streak combining relentless energy and egocentricity and a ruthless capacity to impose his own vision often found in business geniuses. His control was total. Abe Klein, his court poet and speechwriter, called him the "maestro." As Michael Marrus put it, he "not only led several orchestras, he also composed the music, repaired the instruments, and planned the concert seasons as well." In addition, "He was endlessly obsessed with the future, was endlessly curious, constantly probing how things were done, to see if there was a better way."

In 1948, in the first major article devoted to him, *Fortune* magazine wrote that "If there is a whiskey king in America, it is Samuel Bronfman." Not that its journalists were impressed by his appearance. "Seeing him on the street his head cocked back over sloping shoulders . . . one would have no clue to his extraordinary situation as one of the last great tycoons, a vestigial reminder of the gone days when a Vanderbilt or a Rockefeller could actually start from scratch and create a fortune of a hundred million dollars"—as Bronfman had done. "He has a soft voice, an almost natural suavity and casualness, impeccable manners, and a range that extends when required, to indelicate language. His business is his pleasure." His only weakness was "sentimentality. He can lapse into a big and apparently sincere cliché, and is addicted to symbol and ceremony." This is confirmed by Robertson's statement that when in a sentimental mood "he reveals an astonishing addiction for romantic clichés and traditional ceremony."

Mr. Sam is often portrayed—most obviously by his elder son Edgar in *Good Spirits*—as a monster, and of course he did have the monstrous egotism needed to found an empire. Yet most great industrialists, especially those—like Henry Ford or Sam Bronfman—who have built their success on a single brand or a single product, are inevitably obsessive, perfectionist, egocentric, and Mr. Sam was no exception. Nevertheless, as *Fortune* shrewdly noted in a 1966 article, he liked "to encourage such assessments of his personality." For a start, like many self-educated men he was astonishingly well read, apt to quote reams of poetry—a special favorite was Tennyson—as he told Robertson his discovery of suitable retail premises in Montreal was the result of "the skirts of happy chance," a direct quote from the poet.

Mr. Sam had all the capacities required to succeed in business; the flair to understand the product required by the market, combined with the passionate, obsessive temperament to ensure that the drink he had dreamed up reached the drinker perfect in every respect, not only in its contents but also the bottle, the label, the box in which it was packaged. "At times," wrote Robertson, "he seemed obsessed with the phrase 'a silken gown,' which he applied to everything that he personally loved about his business." His perfectionism extended to his private life. He always sought to display himself well, was always smartly and formally dressed, invariably pictured in a well-cut suit and tie which he rarely shed even on holiday. His wife Saidye remembered his unwillingness to dance "because he didn't think he could dance so well . . . and he never liked to do anything he didn't do well." This need for presenting a "bella figura" sprang not only from his obsessive desire for respectability but was also a reaction to the hand-me-down clothes he had had to wear in his youth.

Mr. Sam shone in all the roles required—distiller, blender, packager, salesman, advertiser—as well as possessing a love of, and nose for, a deal, not only in his own industry. He also had an astonishingly retentive memory and an instinctive capacity to seize the financial aspects of a situation, combined with a computer-like brain for financial matters, capable of recalling the smallest detail at a moment's notice. He also had the capacity to do two or more things at the same time. Max Henderson, who worked for Seagram before becoming Canada's auditor-general, told Newman how Mr. Sam "would sniff all the whiskies, have a marketing team in to decide on a run of new labels, then haul off to do a tax problem with me, and in the middle of it get one of his lawyers on the phone, giving him hell for dragging his feet in some upcoming litigation, meanwhile getting ready to receive a deputation from the Jewish community." But he was not impulsive, not in business decisions anyway. He drove his associates (and his family) mad with his apparent indecisiveness—including deciding which train he would take from Montreal to New York each week—a trait which, very often, was merely part of his eternal quest for perfection. As Newman puts it, "Choices that had to be made by any given year-end were usually taken late on the evening of December 31."

He also had a considerable capacity for hiring the right people. As his daughter Phyllis put it, "He picked certain people as partners and felt that his trust in them would be repaid. Not many trust others in this way." Moreover he was colorblind; Seagram was virtually the only major company employing blacks and Hispanics in the 1930s. This was partly because respectable, competent whites steered clear of so disreputable a business, but Mr. Sam genuinely believed that, as he once said, "In three generations we'll all be the same color."

Normally he was soft-spoken, but he was famous for his frequent and explosive bouts of anger. However, the bouts were often merely tactical, usually short-lived; "I bruises easy but I heal quick" was a favorite saying. Marrus quotes one of his key executives, William Wachtel, as saying, "In many ways Mr. Sam was a consummate actor, but every now and then, given the proper provocation, his temper could really flare, and with those sorts of temper it was wise to get out of his way." But most outbursts were means of showing that he was in charge, as he had to be in every aspect of life, personal as well as in business. Moreover even the genuine bouts were often the results of a perceived lack of his own obsessive perfectionism in others.

Temper could, as it were, temper loyalty. As one associate put it, "Sam would sack you one day but you knew perfectly well that he would hire you the next." In fact he hated sacking people and when he did would usually retract the dismissal sooner rather than later—one executive claimed to have been sacked at least three times. But once you had shown you had the "right stuff"—often by standing up to him and putting forward reasoned arguments—you were safe from interference. Once you had survived what was liable to be a pretty tumultuous apprenticeship you tended to stay for the rest of your working life. And this applied to quite a number of associates who could never be described as mere creatures. A senior executive once compared him to a tiger. "If Mr. Sam smelled your fright, he'd jump you. But if you stood up to him, you'd gain his respect and he could be totally charming and most thoughtful." "Nobody can be a friend of mine if I can't call him a son of a bitch" he once expostulated to Sol Kanee, one of his few close friends outside business. In telling the story Kanee concludes, "How could I stay mad at a mad bugger like that?"

When Robert Sabloff, then a junior in the advertising department, showed him some advertisements aimed at blue-collar workers Mr. Sam fell into a rage, to which Sabloff retorted that they "weren't designed to be liked by multi-millionaires." According to Marrus Sam snarled, "You think you're pretty goddamn smart," to which Sabloff retorted, "Well if I weren't I wouldn't be working for you." Mr. Sam smiled and in the next thirteen years of working for him Sabloff claims that "I never had a minute's problem with that man." But men like Sabloff were exceptions, for Seagram under Mr. Sam, and even more so under his son and grandson, increasingly resembled a royal court rather than an ordinary company. But none posed a threat to his authority, for Mr. Sam was so self-obsessed that he simply could not imagine the existence of any rivalry. It did not help that too many employees were hailed at first as saviors before Mr. Sam became disillusioned. As Philip Vineberg, his friend and lawyer, told Newman, this was "not because they were failing to achieve a reasonable standard but because his own standard was so high that the average person couldn't expect to achieve it."

Another famous characteristic was Mr. Sam's use of bad language. In one of the great understatements of all time his daughter Phyllis says that "he had a lively way of expressing himself." Robertson's use of the term "indelicate language" was also a gross understatement for a man addicted to the habitual use of expressions that shocked even men who had served in the army—and it was even more startling when he used the words and phrases in relatively formal discussions. His favorite swear word was "cocksucker." But this in itself was meaningless. As his younger son Charles explained, it mattered only when it went back for generations; to be called simply "a cocksucker" was nothing, but when the invocation was extended, as in "no good cocksucking son of a cocksucking cocksucker," that was serious.* But his language was not unusual at the time. One former employee of Mr. Sam's great rival Harry Hatch of Hiram Walker remarked that his boss's profanity "was something to behold."

Inevitably he was a workaholic. "Those who knew him well," wrote Marrus, "had difficulty identifying a time when Sam was *not* working." Even at home he was apt to write little notes to himself on scraps of paper stuffed into any handy pocket. He claimed that all his children wanted to do was to enjoy themselves, but, as his son Edgar put it, "The great sadness is that he never really enjoyed his own life as much as he might have." Not surprisingly most of his closest friends were also his employees. As a result of his obsession with business, he was lonely, spending many evenings while at home playing gin rummy with Moe Levine, who had married Saidye's sister Freda.

The one truly monstrous aspect to his character was his obsessive need to dominate his three brothers and downgrade their contribution to the business. Two of his brothers, Abe and Harry, were older than him, Abe, born in 1882, by seven years, Harry by three years, while Allan was six years younger. They were the only people who could not to be classed as employees and over whom he could not automatically assert his—to him natural—total supremacy. Not surprisingly his four sisters were not considered a major factor. Robertson got it wrong when he asserted that Mr. Sam "treated his brothers as he did employees . . . to challenge his authority was to invite tirades and trouble." For his more trusted employees were treated

---

* The only person who could stop him swearing was his wife Saidye. One day he used the "C" word at table and she said, "Isn't that a charming word, 'cocksucker,' I'm going to learn to use it." Apparently Mr. Sam went red and never used it again in her presence.

far better than his brothers, who were invariably treated with contempt and rage. Robertson, echoing Mr. Sam, put the case against the three with some brutality, "Abe could be expected to waste money gambling, Harry might have become a builder of white elephants. Allan could hardly demur. He was the youngest brother, had graduated in law on family money earned by Sam and had joined A. J. Andrews's law office through Sam's influence. So Sam could 'resent him without any difficulty.'"

In reality Abe was an amiable, and by no means stupid or incompetent fellow with a weakness for gambling—though Sam refused to let his weakness spoil the family image, preventing the aging Abe from being thrown out of the exclusive, exclusively Jewish Montefiore Club for cheating at gin rummy in the 1950s. Harry would have been far happier in his natural role as a respected provincial businessman, while the youngest, Allan, was a decent, gentle person, the only member of the generation who had gone to university, and who became an excellent lawyer. Robertson alleges that Sam had hoped to become a lawyer, yet another reason for jealousy. So "my brother the lawyer," and a relatively smooth and calm one for that matter, was treated worst of all.

Robertson was reflecting Sam's own views when he wrote that neither Abe nor Harry were "particularly articulate or skilled," while he refers to "Abe's occasional dabbling in real estate investments," which "paid off through sheer luck," a gross libel; for Abe, for all his faults, was able to accumulate a decent fortune of his own through such investments after being excluded from the family firm. Moreover Sam ruthlessly ensured that the brothers' offspring would be eliminated from any involvement in the family business. In his entry in *Current Biography* Sam excused the concentration of power in his hands as a result of the sad example set by the family that had owned Seagram, the distillers he bought in the mid-1920s.

Peter Newman spotted another essential element in his psychological makeup, a search for legitimacy, or rather *yechus*, its Jewish equivalent, that dominated Sam Bronfman's long life and remains the dynasty's major preoccupation to this day. *Yechus* is not merely a craving for respect but rather a state of respect recognized by "something grand"—in his case membership of the best clubs in Montreal and, even more so, of that by no means distinguished body, the Canadian Senate. To him, pathetically, these positions were "the true measurement of success." For as he himself wrote in the introduction to Robertson's book, "If you see *respect* [his emphasis] you are successful. Respect walks hand in hand with integrity. Taken together they, not money, not position, are the true measurement of success." But he remained an outsider in his own country. He felt, writes Marrus, "The cold exclusion of a society that barred his entry into the establishment of the day . . . part of the story . . . was his failure to achieve the recognition he felt he deserved, even though 'for thirty years he was the foremost Jew in the country.'"

His underlying insecurity also showed up in his refusal to spend too much money on himself—though his womenfolk could spend as much as they cared. He had the typical fear of the immigrant that "they," the goyim, whom he knew only too well from bitter experience, were jealous of Jewish success, would deprive him of his hard-earned wealth, as his father and countless other inhabitants of the Czarist Empire had been stripped of their possessions. His all-pervasive and life-long insecurity required balm, and in the last thirty years of his life this consisted of regular banquets and Christmas parties celebrating his achievements, complete with specially written songs and poems, events that were all too easy to parody, and Richler has great fun mocking them.

Nevertheless at least one participant at the celebrations of Sam's official eightieth birthday just before his death remembers them as touching rather than ridiculous. I say "official" because in reality it was his eighty-second birthday, for he had not been born, as he pretended throughout his life, in Canada. It was only after his death that his son Edgar found his father's naturalization papers issued as late as 1937 when he had had to admit that he had been born in Bessarabia, then in Romania, on February 27, 1889, and was not, as he made out, a Canadian citizen born on March 4, 1891, in Brandon, Manitoba. Even Brandon was not the first place the family lived in Canada, they only moved there as one step in their progress up the economic ladder.

His deception has been taken as unusual, as yet another example of Mr. Sam's assumed dishonesty, but it wasn't, for a great many of Sam's generation of immigrants from Eastern Europe turned their backs on their previous existence and retained a profound psychological need to prove that they were truly Canadian. For Mr. Sam's pretense was not due to vanity but to his obsession with being regarded as a loyal Canadian. He did not go so far as Louis B. Mayer of MGM fame, another immigrant from Eastern Europe, who designated his birthday as July 4. But even when he was spending most of his time in New York, wrote Marrus, Mr. Sam never "abandoned his enthusiastic identification with the country in which his career began, and [his refusal to admit to his true place of birth] is perhaps the most significant indication of his obsession with the respectability he associated with Canadian citizenship."

Mr. Sam was not the only member of the family to alter his date of birth. In 1911 his older sister Laura understated her age by three years when marrying Barney Aaron. Nevertheless she did acknowledge that she had been born in Bessarabia, and the change may have been due to a desire to show that she was younger than her twenty-four-year-old husband. This older generation also shared an absolute refusal to tell their offspring anything about their life before their arrival in the Promised Land, or in many cases about their early years of poverty and struggle. For underlying the family's riches was a deep sense of shame as to their origins. When Mr. Sam died the second generation tried to get his younger brother Allan to talk about the early days. But, according to Edgar, "All we got was some philosophical musing. He would never tell us any of the early history." The sense of shame was not confined to the older generation. As late as 1969 Edgar could write—in the *Columbia Journal of World Business* no less—that the family had sold its products exclusively in Canada until prohibition had been repealed. This sort of evasiveness inevitably makes it harder, but even more fascinating, to investigate the family's real history.

Two

YECHIEL AND HIS TRIBE

Oh, I want to go down to the Bal again
Once more before I die;
I want to travel the tunnels once more
And sample Bronfman's rye.
— Phil Redant, Yorkton poet

T HE BRONFMANS WERE MERELY ONE, APPARENTLY UNREMARKABLE, family among hundreds of thousands to come to Canada, as waves of immigration brought 3.5 million immigrants, primarily from Britain and Eastern Europe, into the country in a mere thirty years, spurred on by the construction of the Canadian Pacific Railway (CPR), the country's first transcontinental railroad, which was completed in 1894. It was truly a mass movement and one encouraged by the development of new varieties of grain capable of ripening during the region's short summers. Within a generation the prairies on both sides of the forty-ninth parallel had been transformed into the world's largest granary. But, like so many other immigrants, the Bronfmans had a hard struggle for their first few years in what was far from being a "Promised Land."

They came from Bessarabia, a much-disputed province in the northwest corner of the Black Sea, now called Moldova, a tiny, unhappy, poverty-stricken independent country. When Mr. Sam's father, Yechiel,* was born in the province in 1851 it was under Romanian rule, but in 1878 the Romanian part of the region was returned to Russia. Bessarabia had always been a major center of Jewish settlement—Jews accounted for over a tenth

---

* After the family's arrival in Canada his name was anglicized first to Eichel, the name on his naturalization papers, then to Ekiel.

of the inhabitants—rising to around a half in Soroki, the market town where the Bronfmans lived.

Until 1881 Jewish settlement had been encouraged in many parts of the Czarist Empire—notably by their exemption from military conscription. But in 1881 Czar Alexander II was assassinated, and the new czar promulgated the "May Laws" which, like so much supposedly temporary security legislation the world over, became a permanent fixture. More seriously, in the words of David Vital, "The Jews of Russia" were "admirably suited to the role of institutionalized object of peasant hostility" at a time when the native peasantry were increasingly viewed as the true representatives of Russian values.[1] The result was a series of pogroms—215 by the end of 1881 alone—resulting in few deaths but total economic ruin for many Jewish families. Not surprisingly, the pogroms, combined with the ever more onerous restrictions placed on the Jewish communities throughout the czar's dominions, led to one of the greatest mass migrations in history. Nearly 2.5 million Jews moved from Eastern Europe in the years between 1881 and 1914, among them the Bronfmans, who embarked from the port of Odessa for Canada in 1889.

According to Sam's older brother Harry, before the family emigrated in 1889 it had been "well to do" and had "a large tobacco plantation"—not a surprising occupation in a region where tobacco was a staple crop. Sam expanded Harry's explanation, claiming that his father "owned a grist mill and supplemented its earnings by raising tobacco." This could have involved distillation—some of the production of such mills was frequently used as raw material for making alcohol. At the time Jews were called by their occupation, and in Yiddish "Bronfman" means a distiller of gin or brandy.

The family that left Soroki in 1889 consisted of forty-five-year-old Yechiel, his thirty-year-old wife, Mina, and four children: seven-year-old Abe; Harry, who was nearly three; Laura, who was a mere thirteen months old; and the six-week-old infant, Sam. Proof of the family's relative wealth came from the fact that they were accompanied by their Hebrew teacher, together with his wife and two children. Nevertheless they traveled to Montreal in steerage on the sort of six-week nightmare voyage characteristic of virtually all such family histories. From Montreal they were sped on their way west by organizations run by well-established Jewish leaders, anxious, like the same groups in Britain and the United States, not to be encumbered by their poor co-religionists—though at the same time many gentiles from Ontario also traveled west to seek their fortune. Indeed it took only a single generation for the population of the Canadian prairies to soar from sixty thousand to over a million, thanks partly to a concerted campaign by the government and the railroads.

The Bronfmans ended up at Wapella, a godforsaken spot in southern Saskatchewan, not far north of the forty-ninth parallel on the other side of the border from North Dakota, in the midst of a seemingly endless prairie marked only by a few patches of woodland. At the time Wapella was merely a halt, one of the dozens of groups of huts next to the railroad tracks. It was not even a real settlement—it was incorporated as a township only in 1903. Unfortunately, and notably unlike the majority of Jews who came from the northern, colder, provinces of the Czarist Empire, the Bronfmans were not used to harsh winters, and those on the Canadian prairies north of the Dakotas are particularly long and dire.

For the next quarter of a century the Bronfman story is that of thousands of other ambitious, hardworking Jewish immigrant families the world over. They gradually improved their lot by spotting and exploiting business opportunities, by employing the younger members of the family after only a rudimentary education, and by their willingness to travel—and to move the whole family if necessary. They were lucky—or was it an instinct to be in the right place at the right time? In any event, within twenty years the family's fortunes multiplied exponentially in a series of gambles in which they repeatedly "bet the farm" as they moved from Wapella to two boom towns, Brandon and then Winnipeg.

When they arrived Eichel spent most of his money to set up a proper farm for producing grain—he had brought tobacco seeds with him but soon realized that they would never flourish. Unhappily the late 1880s and early 1890s witnessed unusually dry weather as well as the region's normal short summers and deadly early frosts. In Harry's reminiscences he describes how "the first crop of wheat froze and consequently [Father spent] that winter . . . going into the bush, cutting logs, loading them onto a sleigh and drawing them twenty miles with a yoke of oxen so that when they were sold there would probably be a sufficient amount of money to buy a sack of flour, a few evaporated apples, dried prunes, and probably some tea and sugar to bring back to his family so that body and soul could be kept together."

Two years later Eichel moved a hundred miles east to the much bigger town of Brandon in Manitoba to find work, leaving the family behind in

Wapella. There life was desperate especially for Mina, left alone to cope with her ever-increasing brood—before the end of the century she had had four more children: Jean, Bessie (known as Bea), Allan, and Rebecca (known as Rose). Harry remembered his mother's painstaking efforts to use stones to build an oven—the essential apparatus to avoid starvation, for bread was the family's basic foodstuff. She knew nothing about the process and her first three attempts collapsed, but the fourth was successful after she had learned to let the arch dry for long enough without needing a fire.

While working at a local sawmill Eichel had spotted his chance—to sell the wood wasted in the mill as household fuel. When winter stopped sales he developed another business selling frozen fish caught on Lake Manitoba sixty miles away and peddling it throughout the small towns of southern Manitoba—though his unwillingness to break the Sabbath prohibition on travel forced him to employ a non-Jew to fetch the fish on Saturdays. The horses used to haul the loads of wood led him into another business, natural enough in Brandon, then sometimes called "the horse capital of Canada." Taking the idea from a rancher called Jim McGregor, Eichel would buy half a dozen wild horses from among the many who had broken away from their owners and put them in harness with the better-trained animals in his teams. When they were broken in he would sell them at a profit. But one day Eichel changed his ideas over a drink in a saloon after a deal when he saw how profitable bar- and hotel-keeping could be. (Not surprisingly Sam claimed that he had persuaded his father to switch, though he was certainly too young to have done so.)

In the spring of 1892, only three years after their arrival, Eichel moved the whole family to Brandon, by then known as "the wheat capital of the Prairies"* and by 1900 had accumulated enough capital to spend C$1,000 on moving the family from the former lean-to shack by the railway tracks, which in any case he had steadily enlarged, to a solid brick house on a double plot near the center of town—in fact just behind the town's armory, a site which was also convenient for the children's schools.† It featured a parlor suitably furnished with plush burgundy-red furniture, a sanctuary away from the children. The town was only ten years old but was booming, helped by a train service that brought Winnipeg, 130 miles away, to within

---

* In World War II it became famous as the center for training thousands of pilots from Britain and the British Empire.
† To be precise, to 550 Eleventh Street, Brandon, between Victoria and McTavish avenues.

three hours. By 1892 Eichel was able to be naturalized as a Canadian citizen and in the course of the decade prospered, or rather survived—the children remembered the shame of going to school in torn clothes while Harry,
as a mere ten-year-old, spent his holidays helping with fuel deliveries.

Eichel remained a truly observant Jew, ensuring that his family obeyed
dietary laws and the Sabbath and traveled to Winnipeg for New Year, although he had established a tiny synagogue in Brandon. Nevertheless Jews
were very much a minority—in 1891 there were only 645 even in Winnipeg, the capital of Manitoba, out of a total population of well over
twenty thousand. They were also very low down on the racial totem pole,
only a tad above the much-despised Chinese. Jews—and other immigrants
from Central and Eastern Europe—were lumped together as "Ruthenians"
or "Galicians," and when they were involved in violence their names were
not published, for they were considered as mere "lumpen proletariat" at the
root of local drunkenness, with headlines such as "Mounties Raid Galician
Still"—although these were mostly domestic stills producing only enough
rough "vodka" for domestic use.

Ten years after the move Eichel could afford to help his two eldest sons
to move up the socioeconomic ladder by apprenticing them. Abe was sent
to a cigar maker in Winnipeg, while Harry was to study harness-making.
The only result seems to have been to encourage Abe's drift into hotel-
keeping through meeting undesirables while gambling in the bars he fre-
quented. It was only the youngest son, Allan, who received a university
education, indeed the only one to stay at school after the age of fifteen. As
a result "my brother the lawyer" became the object of great and long-term
jealousy on the part of Mr. Sam. In such a patriarchal society girls' education was not a matter of importance, for daughters were reckoned generally
less desirable than sons. As late as 1927 Sam's mother-in-law sent a wire
saying that "Our hearts are filled with joy even though it is not a boy"
when Sam and Saidye's second daughter, Phyllis, was born before a son had
arrived.

Eichel had always wanted his sons to go into business together and in
1903 they scraped together enough money to lease a hotel from the brewers who were the dominant force in the Canadian liquor business at the
time. The Anglo-American Hotel in Emerson in Manitoba was on the
American border and, more importantly, on the main railroad line to Min-
neapolis. Although Abe was only twenty-one and Harry a mere eighteen
the hotel flourished. Unfortunately Abe's ineradicable gambling habit led

to quarrels and his return home. But he was forgiven. Their next purchase, in 1905, was the Balmoral Hotel in Yorkton, a major center in Saskatchewan northwest of Brandon. The hotel was a substantial establishment, built only a few years earlier, with sixty rooms, directly across the road from the CPR station, leading to a steady stream of travelers from all over Canada. The sign above the door of the hotel—which burned down in 1985—proclaimed "Harry Bronfman, proprietor," though Abe had been its first manager. Robertson says that Sam was running it "with Harry's assistance." But a recent publication[2] talks of Harry as the "whiskey man of the Yorkton and Saskatchewan liquor enterprises."

The hotel—and the symbol it represented of Harry's status within the town—clearly remained important to him and to the town itself. Though Harry probably never visited the town after the mid-1920s he undoubtedly felt some residual loyalty to Yorkton. He did not sell the hotel until 1945, and when he died in 1963 he left C$5,000 to the town's synagogue in his will. By contrast Sam refused even to help replace the synagogue's defective heating system. Abe completely refurbished the hotel and even provided that rarest of luxury in these raw new towns—bathrooms with hot and cold running water. Almost inevitably the Bronfmans have been accused of running brothels rather than hotels. But when faced with the accusation Sam laughed it off, saying, "If they were I'm sure they were the best"—a totally different response from his usual foaming conniption to any accusation with a shred of truth in it.

Harry soon sold the Anglo-American in order to expand his Yorkton empire by buying two other hotels, including the unpretentious Royal Hotel, the Balmoral's main competitor, and put it in the hands of Barney Aaron, who later married his sister Laura and remained employed by the family for nearly fifty years. The only problem was the temptation posed to Abe by the fact that "the Bal" was famous as the home of the biggest poker game in the West, a notoriety that led to eight charges of permitting gambling on the premises in April 1908 alone. But again the Bronfmans had chosen shrewdly. Yorkton was booming, not only as the railroads were built but from its position on both the CPR and a newer transcontinental route, the Canadian National. The town also benefited from the confiscation by the Canadian government of land previously owned by the Doukhobor sect, which had refused to accept federal legislation. Indeed the family was financially solid enough to allow the two eldest sons to marry; Abe to an American girl, Sophie Rasminsky, and Harry to Anna Gallaman, from an ultraorthodox family who came from the Ukraine. The Bronfmans' (relative) wealth also enabled the family to buy a number of undeveloped lots within the town as well as other hotels. These regularly came on the market because mortgage companies wanted immediate cash when, as so often happened, their undercapitalized tenants went under.

Harry moved in with his in-laws in Winnipeg and by 1906 had bought a small apartment block that included a number of stores. The move east was formalized when Eichel moved the family home to Winnipeg—which remained Sam's home till he married sixteen years later. Thanks to his elder sons' successes, Eichel and Mina could effectively retire from the family businesses to manage the new property, a less stressful job for a not surprisingly worn-out couple. Again they had moved at the right time: Winnipeg's population more than trebled—to 142,000—in the first decade of the twentieth century. A local historian described the city as "the strategic center of the Canadian grain trade." In the early 1900s, Winnipeg had a bigger population than the four or five other major towns on the prairies combined. With a Jewish population of seven thousand it became known as "the Jerusalem of the West," complete with a Jewish alderman. In 1913 they had bought an apparently ideal hotel, the Bell, only a few hundred yards from the train station, in what Gray describes as "the heart of Winnipeg's drinking district." But the hotel was bought at the height of the city's boom times; indeed for once the Bronfmans' timing was poor, a real estate collapse was followed by the war, which saw the departure to the trenches of so many thirsty young men.

By that time Harry had taken over the management of the Balmoral. Despite his failings Abe was still considered a competent manager and in 1910 he was put in charge when the family made its boldest move by acquiring the Mariaggi Hotel far to the east in Port Arthur. It was the plushest hotel between Winnipeg and Toronto—even more luxurious than the Balmoral with its elevator, telephones, and en suite bathrooms. Unfortunately Abe again let the family down when his gambling debts sent the venture into the red. But, and this was typical of the family solidarity before Sam took charge, he was forgiven and he continued to manage the venture.

The Bronfmans' move into hotel-keeping had been natural, for "hotel-keeping," wrote James Gray,[3] "was the easiest business anybody with a few hundred dollars in cash could get into"—with immigrants sleeping anywhere they could—although demand dropped in Winnipeg itself as the

CPR started to run through trains farther west. The need was just as great in the countryside. "Before the branch lines were extended from the main-lines," wrote Gray, "many settlers lived fifteen to twenty miles from a rail point." In the extreme climate of the prairie, shelter was essential even in the humblest settlement.

Almost imperceptibly Harry was emerging as the head of the family, and as the putative model for a leading, respected—but limited—provincial busi-nessman. By that time it was clear that Abe was never going to be a reliable associate because of his addiction to gambling, but Harry was the leader in the family's expansion before 1914. By contrast, as recounted by Sam, the story of the family's move into the drinks business naturally makes him the leader. As he boasted to Robertson, Sam claimed that he had been the fam-ily's dynamo even in the period of expansion as hotel keepers.

Of all the Bronfman brothers, Harry was, as Gray says, "The easiest go-ing, most patient, and slowest to anger"—a total contrast to the volcanic Sam. Harry was remembered by one acquaintance in Yorkton as "a nice guy really. You know always pleasant, a real Kiwanian or Rotarian type." But, the friend added, "My God was he sharp, with a mind like a steel trap." During the fourteen years he spent in Yorkton he grew steadily from one of the smallest tadpoles in the puddle to a well-developed frog in a rapidly ex-panding pond. In the small community of Yorkton Harry flourished as what the French would describe as a *notable de province* (a provincial wor-thy). "Time and again," says Gray, "in the hotel business, the automobile business, and as a small-town real estate operator, he had demonstrated an uncanny ability to select the right key to unlock the door to success while his competitors fumbled and failed."

In 1907 he was joined by the eighteen-year-old Sam. For at least a decade—Gray puts the time as twenty years, which is surely an exaggeration—Sam "swung into the role he would play . . . as a sort of util-ity infielder or free safety for his elder brothers." He spent the years before 1914 helping either Abe or Harry at their hotels. But for all their different roles within the family business, it was a joint enterprise typical of Jewish family businesses through the ages, with each member playing a part that was implicitly defined without any formal, let alone legal, definition of their positions. But it was Harry's hotel, wrote Gray, which "grew into something of a social center to which the gentry frequently repaired for Sunday evening dinner."

An active entrepreneur and realtor, Harry demolished the Royal Hotel to build something better, bought the whole block on which the Balmoral stood and built half a dozen stores. He became a motor dealer as the proud owner of the City Garage. He soon developed into a typical auto dealer—an advertisement headlined "Stung" reproduced in the Yorkton booklet claims that he "was so loaded with secondhand cars," which he had "to sell at whatever they will bring" but that he will "continue taking in old cars for new ones."

Harry was a life-long supporter of the Liberal party and even tried to run for mayor. But at that point he came across the deep vein of more or less genteel anti-Semitism that ran through Canada even more deeply than in most of the Anglo-Saxon world until well after World War II. Asking for support from Leo Beck, the richest man in town and one of his major suppliers, he received only the stentorian reply, "Harry, I'd give everything I own to keep you or any other Jew from ever becoming mayor of Yorkton"—though other accounts claim, more convincingly, that Beck actually said that "no damned bootlegger is ever going to run for mayor." "Harry couldn't have been elected dog catcher in Yorkton," as one cynical local explained to Gray, "even if he hadn't been a Jew." The antagonism first seen on the small stage of Yorkton became a national phenomenon over the next decade, further fueled by the family's prominence in the more-or-less legal traffic in liquor and by the abrasive personality of Sam, the increasingly important younger brother. In any event Beck went bankrupt in the post-war slump, a fall rumored to be the work of a vengeful Harry, though such vengeance was not in his nature (by contrast, Sam would have been perfectly capable of such a deed).

Meanwhile Sam was able to exhibit his talents for the first time as an independent member of the family when running the family-owned Bell Hotel in Winnipeg. It was the first venture on which he could lavish the obsessively detailed efforts—in this case including a barber shop and a billiard parlor—so typical of his business style throughout his life.* Newman claims that the Bell made as much as C$30,000 a year and that Sam also made substantial sums in trading muskrat furs. Alas the Bell is no longer what it was. When Marrus visited the hotel in the late 1980s he found that it was "in a seedy neighborhood now part of Winnipeg's skid row and its once tasteful interior scarred by countless renovations undertaken on the

---

* He also learned to play a sound game of billiards, the only sporting activity in which he ever indulged.

cheap. A large square brick building, its battered façade has undertaken too many facelifts to be recognizable as the establishment of which Sam was so proud in 1912."

Unfortunately the family's fortunes depended not on the hotel business as such but on the profits earned in their bars. Already by 1914 the end of the frontier, pioneering period on the prairies reduced the number of lonely, thirsty young laborers. War took the process even further; it reduced traffic on the railroads and removed many thirsty young men—who were voters as well as drinkers—away from the bars and to the front. (Both Sam and Allan were called up but escaped duty thanks to their flat feet, though Harry claimed that they had both undergone at least some military training.) During the war, as prohibition took hold, revenues from the bars literally dried up.

The success of the temperance movement in Canada had been a long time coming. It went back to the 1840s with attempts to block sales to Native Americans, while pressure to shut bars and licensed grocers started in the 1870s. In the thirty years after 1876 government got into the act: Agents had confiscated or smashed over thirty thousand stills and fifty-four agents were killed by "moonshiners." In Canada, as in the United States, the movement involved what might be described as social rather than personal redemption. In the words of Ramsay Cook, it upset the traditional Christian focus, making "society rather than the individual . . . the object of salvation."[4] For, as Gray put it, "in the Kingdom of God there would be no alcohol."

The defining event came in 1907 with the formation of a Social and Moral Reform Council, which united the prohibitionists and transformed them into a powerfully unifying force rather akin to the anti-fascists of the 1930s. "For sheer intensity of conviction and staying power over the long haul," wrote James Gray, "no other prairie mass movement ever equaled the Prohibition crusade." As in the United States the key to the campaign was the general hatred of bars, indeed in both countries they united under the simple, but powerful, slogan, "Ban the Bars." This was not surprising for, as one writer[5] put it: "The most notable thing about a saloon was its stink. It was a fusty, musty odor, damp and clammy, an odor compounded of sawdust, tobacco juice, malt, metal polish, and whiskey, and in the case of Canada horsey smells from the stables next door." "It was dingy and dirty," wrote Herbert Asbury, "a place of battered furniture, offensive smells, overblown mirrors and glassware, and appalling sanitary facilities."[6] But the saloons were "an oasis of good cheer," in the words of Craig Heron,[7] "ideal refuges for the thousands of lonely newcomers, at a time when most children left school at twelve and didn't marry until they were in their late twenties." The hotels run by the Bronfmans were very different from the sleazy norm; they resembled the ornate gin palaces being built in Britain at the time—although they too had a purely male clientele. Nevertheless they, like less salubrious establishments, were bound to be caught up in a wave of temperance propaganda. "Where does the pay envelope go?" screamed the posters, "To the home maker or the home breaker?"—a legitimate cry when a third of all criminal prosecutions were for drunkenness. It ended up, wrote Heron, as a "narrowly focused attack on the public drinking cultures of urban working men."

The cry brought together all the often squabbling prophets of the "social gospel." Temperance—and later Prohibition—was promoted as a major means of achieving social improvement by enthusiasts unaware, as Gray puts it, "of the intolerance, racism, and bigotry that were often the nether side of their movement." Not for nothing was it called the "social gospel." The name was natural enough, for, like most newly settled regions the prairies were rough. It did not help that women had no rights. The synonym for wife was "chattel" and one man appeared in court in Winnipeg for the forty-seventh time in fifteen years charged with drunkenness and wife beating. For drink contributed greatly to the social roughness. As a result the temperance movement blended hatred of the bars with the undoubted social improvement that would be engendered by their abolition.

Canadian prohibitionism, like so much else in the country, owed a great deal to American influence, including speakers and organizations, and was deeply embedded in the country's *moeurs* from day one. But Canada was, and indeed remains, a federal state with much legislation left to the provinces, a country where Tip O'Neill's phrase that "all politics is local" was even more applicable than in the United States. And the pro- and anti-prohibition forces were much more equally divided than in the United States. As a result, apart from the short period of total prohibition at the end of the war, brewing and distilling remained—relatively—legal.

By the turn of the century successive decisions by the final court of appeal, the Privy Council in London, had divided control over alcohol. At the retail level, individual provinces—which were even more powerful than the states, their equivalent in the United States—would be in charge. But responsibility for brewing, distillation, and selling wholesale at home and abroad was left to the federal government. This convoluted formula was guaranteed to create confusion. This was further compounded when it was made easier to organize plebiscites—which would moreover be binding on the legislatures involved. The popular votes involved inevitably exposed a divide: The newcomers in Eastern Canada often came from Scotland, bringing with them a temperance tradition, while those, like the Bronfmans, from Eastern Europe were used not just to drinking spirits, but distilling them at home as well. Moreover home distillation could be profitable. As one Alberta moonshiner put it as he was led away by the police, "Yes, I voted for prohibition, and I'd vote for it again. I went broke farming." Moreover the temperance movement was purely Anglo-Saxon, and did not affect (indeed was opposed by) Catholics, ensuring that the major province of Quebec, dominated by French-speaking Catholics, would always be solidly against prohibition.

The division was not only social and religious, it was also economic. "Prohibition," wrote Heron, "would become one of the most powerful extra-parliamentary forces in Canada outside the business community." As a leading local Conservative put it in 1928, "The Liberal party, at its very inception, entered into an alliance with organized liquor interests"—in the same way the Democratic party in the United States was associated with "Rum and Romanism." Liquor had always been used as a political instrument, with regular accusations that distillers and, above all, powerful brewers like Molson and Labatt, had tried to influence elections through providing their products free to pliable voters. So Canada's attitude towards prohibition was even more tortuous and full of contradictions than in the many other countries that embarked on the same road in the first decades of the twentieth century. Politicians were caught in the middle, and so often employed those useful devices, the plebiscite and the referendum, to avoid having to make decisions that would inevitably anger one powerful lobby or another.

Even when voters went for prohibition, wetter politicians—like Sir Wilfred Laurier, an early Canadian prime minister—could legitimately claim that the vote represented less than a quarter of the voting population. In Saskatchewan in 1906 the provincial prime minister demanded that any referendum would demand a clear majority of fifty thousand votes (i.e., an overwhelming endorsement) to be valid, while additional licenses were issued to saloons. Yet sometimes the referendums in the prairie provinces went into effect with less than an eighth of the population behind them.

However pro-temperance they may have been, politicians were fully aware that the economic fortunes of their state and the finances of provincial and federal government alike were heavily reliant on liquor. A 1928 report quoted by Marrus estimated that "one eighth of all Dominion and all Provincial revenue was derived from the trade in alcoholic beverages" in the form either of excise duties or export levies. Not surprisingly, the "liquor interest" carried considerable political clout. In his history of Distillers Company Limited, Ronald Weir quotes an "internal memorandum" that "the liquor interests are largely involved with both Political Parties, or it may be taken the other way, that Political parties are largely involved with the liquor interest." "I wish somehow," wrote that leading wet, the political scientist and humorist Stephen Leacock, "that we could prohibit the use of alcohol and merely drink beer and whiskey and gin as we used to."

The situation changed dramatically after the outbreak of war in August 1914. Prohibition, or at least temperance, became automatically associated with patriotism; the war undoubtedly gave a final, and in many cases triumphantly successful, boost to the prohibitionists' efforts, not just in Canada and the United States but also in Scandinavia. In Britain, David Lloyd George, the prime minister, restricted pub opening hours in a major defeat for the "beerage"—the previously all-powerful brewers whose fortunes had enabled them to purchase titles. Even in France, absinthe, deadliest of drinks, was outlawed.

Within Canada, historical, social, and religious differences ensured that each province had its own attitudes, reflected in the very different restrictions they applied. Even in the three prairie provinces, Manitoba, Saskatchewan, and Alberta, the rules varied, as did distinctions between theirs and those of the federal government in far-off Ottawa. This multiplicity of jurisdictions was to leave gaps—sometimes large but often temporary—which could be exploited by the brave and nimble. Indeed it was during the four or five years between the imposition of federal prohibition during the war and the uneasy truce of the early 1920s that the Bronfmans showed their entrepreneurial mettle to its fullest in a typical blend of luck, instinct, and preparedness to bet the farm on the next—and invariably bigger—business opportunity.

For prohibition in Canada provided ample opportunities for families like the Bronfmans. Indeed, as Peter Newman put it, "Sometimes it almost seemed that the American Congress and the Canadian federal and provincial legislatures must have secretly held a grand conclave to decide one issue: How they could draft anti-liquor laws and regulations that would help maximize the Bronfman brothers' bootlegging profits." Until Repeal in the United States, Sam and his brothers were living from expedient to expedient, grabbing what opportunities they could. They proved to be many, and increasingly profitable at that.

Three

THE HARRY YEARS

> This book is compiled in friendly appreciation of prohibition in
> the United States, the greatest thing that ever happened—to
> Canada.
> — STEPHEN LEACOCK, *WET WIT AND DRY HUMOUR*

THE FIRST IMPORTANT EFFECT OF THE WAR AND THE ABSENCE OF so many thirsty young voters was in Saskatchewan where all the bars were closed in July 1915—it helped the prohibitionists' cause that a couple of parliamentarians had been found guilty of being bribed by the distillers. At the same time the provincial government nationalized the booze business, replacing the bars with government liquor stores. This greatly improved the quality of the liquor, for that sold in the private sector had often been filthy stuff containing, as Gray says, "all manner of poisonous ingredients." The next year a domino effect ensured that both its neighboring provinces, Alberta and Manitoba, decided in favor of complete prohibition, helped by the miserable way the war was going. Not even a visit by Clarence Darrow, the famous American lawyer, could sway the decision.

Worse was to come. In December 1917 the federal government stepped in for the first time, introducing measures to forbid production and interprovincial trade in liquor until a year after the end of the war—which came to mean November 1919. When it came to longer-term measures introduced by individual provinces, the prohibitionists were counting—not unreasonably—on the votes of women, who had been given the vote during the war. In a series of plebiscites New Brunswick and Ontario, biggest of all, voted for total prohibition, and only Quebec and British Columbia rejected the idea. But the federal government, either by accident, or, more probably, in an effort to placate the country's "wets," had left a loophole, providing that alcohol could still be sold as medicine by registered druggists. And what a loophole! In 1920 five hundred thousand "prescriptions" were filled by druggists even in lightly populated Alberta. As Stephen Leacock put it, all you had to do was "to go to a drugstore . . . and lean up against the counter and make a gurgling sound like apoplexy. One often sees these apoplexy cases lined up four deep." On April 1, 1918, the ban on interprovincial trading came into force. But the regulations left another loophole, providing that "a householder may keep liquor in his own home for private use provided it is not purchased within the province."

When prohibition was introduced Sam tried to run the Bell as a temperance hotel, with little or no success. So he left Harry to "run flop houses or piddle about in land deals if you want," as he put it. Indeed Harry would have been perfectly happy to spend his time investing in real estate. But in reality he was the brother who was the solid lynchpin in the four years from 1918 to 1922 that created the family's first fortune. For a start, it was Harry who arranged a revolving credit of $300,000 from the chairman of the Bank of Montreal to finance their ever-growing business. It was Harry who had immediately bought a license to establish a wholesale drug company in Yorkton. This enabled him to import liquor in bulk and sell it to retail druggists. As Gray says, "The Canada Pure Drug Company* [located next door to the Balmoral] became the vehicle which rocketed the Bronfman clan to fortune." Richler describes the process with his habitual flair: "A girl was provided for the [Liberal Party's] bagman, a considerable tribute was paid, and the necessary license was forthcoming." In reality an abandoned warehouse was acquired and the Royal Pure Drug Company of Canada was born. But Sam could see the broader picture. He promptly went east to Montreal for the first time to "get into the liquor business," taking with him a French-speaking barman from the Bell.

Not surprisingly the authorities were niggardly when issuing the precious wholesaler's licenses required, with only twelve allotted to Montreal. Political pressure ensured that only six were allotted to the French-speaking community in the city, four to the Anglo-Saxons (who formed only a sixth of the population), and two supposedly for the Jewish community. Sam found that the only available Jewish license had been allocated to the French-Canadian wife of his lawyer. But he soon found a way around the

---

* The holding company was called The Yorkton Distributing Company, Importers and Distributors of High Grade Wines and Spirits.

problem. With the help of Boivin Wilson, Montreal's leading importers of wines and spirits, who had supplied the Bell, and one of their associates, Aimé Geoffrion, who was destined to be one of the Bronfman's staunchest legal advisers, Sam was granted a vacant French-Canadian license. Because of the limited competition this was a "license to print money" for Canada Pure Drugs, for it allowed him to import spirits and to sell them to other provinces, as well as giving him the authority to run a retail operation in Montreal itself. The spacious back of this shop served as a warehouse for a mail order operation. This was aimed at the small towns on the prairies which, as John H. Thompson[1] puts it, were familiar with "national mail order houses, which sold everything from yard goods to lumber."

Sam was supported by the giant Hudson's Bay Company, which dominated the liquor business in Canada. They trusted him implicitly after he had refused to make any profit on a couple of thousand cases of Dewar's whisky that Hudson's Bay wanted to buy back from him. To a considerable degree, according to Robertson, Mr. Sam "modeled his activities on the Hudson's Bay mail order company which had been first in the field in 1916. . . . His price lists matched theirs, as did the quality of the brands he advertised. It was virtually risk-free, for the goods were paid for in advance and the initiative enabled the family to run a continent-wide business for the first time. For the first time Sam could demonstrate his flair for packaging and instilling the confidence for drinkers that their requirements would be delivered by the first post."

The family continued to walk a tightrope on the edge of legality right up to the end of Prohibition, for during the years between World War I and 1933 the Bronfmans appeared, rather unfairly, to be the shadiest of operators in an inevitably shady business. Yet Harry Bronfman could claim, as he did in a newspaper interview in 1922, that throughout his time in the liquor business he had operated entirely within the law. Locally Harry was considered to be "The king of the bootleggers . . . who is many times a millionaire" but Sam's wider ambitions had greatly exacerbated the tensions in the relationship between the two brothers. This animosity increased yet further after the death of their parents. Mina died in the summer of 1918 at the age of sixty from what Robertson describes as "influenza and physical exhaustion which had its roots in the freezing winters she had spent in Saskatchewan"—though she must have been pretty tough to have survived that long. Ekiel died a year later even though the brothers sent him to the Mayo Clinic for treatment.

According to Sam, before his father died he had named him rather than either of his two older brothers as head of the family. This supposed blessing set off Sam's systematic denigration of his brothers, which lasted until his death over fifty years later. Typically, and untruthfully, Mr. Sam told Robertson that Harry and Abe had "proved more a hindrance than a help" during Canada's prohibition years because "they had regarded themselves as independent operators." In fact, although prohibition had shut down Abe's establishment in Port Arthur, he promptly moved to Kenora in western Ontario where Sam had managed to buy a hotel that had remained open thanks to local option—though he had to travel by dogsled for six icy days to contact the owner in his successful attempt to outbid the local mayor.

Inevitably the enforcement of the prohibition laws in the prairie states, indeed throughout Canada, was a mix of petty corruption and antics reminiscent of the Keystone Kops. The mess was exacerbated by the near-bankruptcy of the local governments, which had no resources to go after the drinking classes, and of course the local farmers—especially those of Eastern European origin—continued to brew their own hooch. Drinkers and hotel owners were lucky that the honest and effective Mounties[*] were thinly stretched over an enormous area and in any case accepted the idea of "moiety"—a system by which half a fine was paid to an informer, a practice that besmirched their otherwise spotless reputation. So enforcement was at best patchy and in many cases totally corrupt—the first Prohibition commissioner in British Columbia ended up behind bars for bootlegging. For, in Gray's words, "While the Temperance spokesmen were demanding more adequate enforcement, clutches of doctors, druggists, lawyers, and freelance assuagers of the public thirst were conspiring to reduce the law to absurdity." They were helped by Saskatchewan's liquor commission, a notoriously corrupt body—even when it did seize beer some of it was sold back to Harry Bronfman, who made a decent profit by reselling it for four times the purchase price. An added complication was that much of the spirit being sold (350,000 gallons in two years) was imported from the United States and described as medicine, since such exports were not permitted for drinking alcohol. It was then transmuted into "whiskey" and sold by the sales operation Sam had established. This was stopped by a federal law in May 1919—although the ban was to last only until a year after

---

[*] The usual name for the Royal Canadian Mounted Police.

the end of the war. In any event the prairies were, in theory anyway, more or less dry until 1924.

The pre-war slump in Winnipeg and the removal of thousands of thirsty young men to the trenches in Flanders had reinforced the positive effects of prohibition. But even after the war the whole of western Canada was hit by a post-war depression, which contributed as much as legislation to the reduction in consumption after 1920. By November 1919, when wartime prohibition was due to end, new legislation, the Canada Temperance Act, had been passed, making it illegal to ship alcohol to any province that had voted to ban alcohol. But the regulations had to be ratified in individual provinces before it came into full force, and this could not take place until the soldiers had returned home. As a result the referendums would not be held for nearly a year—October 25, 1920. But all the time the tide was turning against the prohibitionists. By 1920 one newspaper could write that "it is rapidly becoming apparent that there are worse evils than moderate drinking."

By then a much larger market had opened up: the United States, where prohibition came into effect in January 1920, an event which provided the Bronfman family with an unmatched opportunity to expand their business. Luckily for the Bronfmans and their rivals, Saskatchewan, unlike Manitoba, allowed an increased number of warehouses, often converted barns, sheds, or stores, nicknamed "boozariums."* But they had one feature in common. In the words of one resident, "They were more secure than the banks." They all had iron bars on their windows, according to Gray, "and enough locks on their doors to protect a mint." They sprang up in most of the small towns to feed the thirst of citizens on both sides of the forty-ninth parallel, which separated Canada from the United States, and were licensed to export liquor to the rum runners and bootleggers† from the south.

For the first two years after prohibition, liquor was supplied to American bootleggers from the boozariums in an estimated twenty-nine small towns, all elevated to the status of "drink capitals," scattered along the railroad line in Saskatchewan near the forty-ninth parallel, towns like Estevan, Bi-

---

* Richler calls them "boozatoriums," the Yorkton booklet calls them "boozoriums."
† According to James Gray, the term originated in the days of smuggling and was adapted to the illicit trade in liquor in the United States in the 1830s when thigh-length boots were the fashion and contraband could be hidden in the folds of the boots. So, in theory if not in later practice, a bootlegger was essentially a small-time smuggler. Their activities also gave rise to such well-known expressions as "getaway cars" and in rougher cases "taking someone for a ride."

enfait, Carnduff, Carievale, Gainsborough, and Glen Ewen. The owners of the boozariums shared a common interest with the excise authorities: to prevent the spirit "leaking" into the local market free of duty. The Bronf-mans took every possible precaution, ensuring that the spirit remained the property of the suppliers until it was sold to the rum runners. Nevertheless Harry's brother-in-law David Gallaman stirred up serious future trouble for Harry when he inadvertently sold liquor to an undercover enforcement agent.

Unfortunately this could never be a major conduit for importing liquor into the United States, for Montana and the Dakotas were hundreds of miles from any major markets, though the Bronfmans and their rivals man-aged to reinforce native supplies by importing three hundred thousand gal-lons from the United States in a single year. Nevertheless the boozariums had several major advantages. The land was dead flat with no obvious ob-stacles to crossing the frontier, and because the plains on both sides of the border were so sparsely settled, customs posts were few and far between. In any event the authorities were more concerned with duty-free imports than perfectly legal exports of whiskey. As a result, wrote Gray, "The mat-ter of duty-paying was one that slipped the minds of many farmers along the border." On the other side of the frontier equally inconspicuous towns also expanded thanks to the liquor traffic. Many of the drivers involved were farmers who enjoyed a detailed knowledge of every track in their neighborhood. For everyone joined in. As Doug Gent, a veteran local— who admits to smuggling liquor in the door panels of cars—told me, "They would cross in farmers' fields, as most farms in the area didn't have a fence, never mind a customs or checkpoint site."

At first the Bronfmans were not the biggest operators in the region. Ac-cording to Robertson, who obviously got his information from Mr. Sam, that honor belonged to one Emilio Picariello, a Sicilian who owned the Alberta Hotel in Blairmore. It was he who made famous the very special vehicles with six-cylinder Buick engines built in Ontario by the McLaugh-lin brothers for use by bootleggers. These "whiskey sixes" came complete with bulletproof gas tanks that were used for transporting liquor. But how-ever big the fleet, they could do little to satisfy Americans' thirst for liquor, for they could carry a maximum of forty cases of whiskey, although the liquor was worth fifty dollars a case. The cars could do sixty miles an hour, though the roads were generally so bad that most of the time they could only drive within the province's speed limit, a modest twenty-five miles per hour.

Harry's first idea was to buy a fleet of cars and trucks to transport the liquor. He even obtained a federal charter for the grandiosely named Trans-Canada Transportation Company Limited. The scheme was clearly totally impractical at a time when there was so little cross-border traffic that the only roads in his native province were dirt tracks running parallel to the border. Nevertheless, apart from showing that Harry could have ideas as grandiose as Sam, this had one beneficial result: in consequence the authorities ruled that interprovincial road haulage was as legitimate as that by rail or parcel post. So Trans-Canada Transportation enabled him to give papers to the bootleggers providing them with immunity, and an insurance scheme to cover the risks the bootleggers ran within Canada. It was at this point that Harry's pride and joy, the City Garage in Yorkton, came in handy. It was described by Robertson (i.e., Mr. Sam) as Harry's "pet project," and he accused Harry, with typical unfairness, of "spending more time looking after the City Garage than the liquor business." Older residents told the authors of the Yorkton booklet how automobiles riddled with bullets often came in for repair. The smugglers' "overworked and often overloaded automobiles were taken to the garage for tune-ups and repairs" and on at least one occasion Harry kept "used cars loaded with liquor on the street outside the garage and [sold] them 'as is'" through a policy best described as "come and get it."

Nevertheless the Americans remained nervous. The rum runners—who included the notorious Dutch Schultz—would arrive in late afternoon and depart at dead of night. There was only one decent road, from Minot, North Dakota, reputedly the gangster center of the West, to Estevan and thence to Regina. But mostly, wrote Gray, "They kept to the back roads and trails and when they saw cars following them they had lengths of heavy chains bolted to the rear axles which they could drop down on the dirt road, creating such clouds of dust that the pursuers were forced to slow almost to a halt." Another route employed the freight trains that ran across the frontier. When a train pulled out of Regina a railroad employee would empty enough sand into the axle of a boxcar to turn the lubricating oily waste into an abrasive. This would cause the axle to stick, creating what was termed a "hotbox," not an uncommon occurrence. It ensured that the boxcar involved would be taken out of service, conveniently just south of the border, as the train was inspected before a long downhill stretch. It was simplicity itself for American bootleggers to get into the car and empty its contents. The histories of Prohibition tend to underestimate the role of railroad freight cars in transporting liquor.

By this time there was a total imbalance in supplies of alcohol. During the war the Canadian government had cut down distillation to encourage production of grain, leaving a shortage that could, however, be relieved by the import of some of the surplus of Scotch that had emerged at the same time. The Bronfmans' friends in the Liberal party were now in power in Ottawa and helped Harry obtain a license for a wholesale bonded-liquor warehouse he had built next to the Balmoral. Seventy years later, when rebuilding the hotel after it had burned down, the locals found tunnels leading from the hotel to the bonded warehouse and shipping railway warehouses on the CPR. The new owner also found "pipes left from the distillery. They were bottling Scotch and brandy and rye there."

Local customs officials allowed shipments which overflowed the warehouses and forced Harry and Sam to work twenty-hour days to unload the thousands of cases of whiskey. The federal customs allowed the Bronfmans to ship the spirit not only abroad, but also to the "export houses," only some of which were owned by the Bronfmans, that were springing up all over western Canada. Within a few weeks, according to Gray, the Bronfmans had shipped over thirty thousand cases of whiskey. It was not a sophisticated product. The market did not demand a branded bottle so around a quarter of the total was shipped not in bottles but in the form of straight alcohol, to be transformed into "whiskey" by the purchasers. The Bronfmans had not yet woken up to the need for quality, they simply supplied their customers' rough demands. But the post-war thirst even in Canada itself was insatiable.

Success at Yorkton led to greater ambitions. The result was to augment their previous role as middlemen between the distillers and blenders such as the mighty Hudson's Bay Company into distillers of drinkable, or at least salable, spirits themselves, in a successful effort to magnify their profit margins through "vertical integration." They didn't have to go far: From the Brewers and Bottlers Supply company in Winnipeg they bought ten one-thousand-gallon redwood vats for mixing their "whiskey," a bottling machine that would account for a thousand bottles an hour, and a labeling machine that would fix two labels to the side of the bottle and another over the cork. And in Kentucky and Ontario they bought carloads of the ethyl alcohol, which formed the raw material—and it doesn't come rawer—required "to launch them," in Gray's words, "into the business of mixing, bottling, and labeling Scotch rye and bourbon whiskey in their Yorkton 'distillery.'"

The acquisition of the license gave the Bronfmans their first experience in blending liquor. Some of the drinks were relatively legitimate. Robertson provides names of "Scotch" like Melrose Special Reserve—although one genius went too far, describing one whiskey as coming from Oporto, Scotland. Presumably neither blender nor buyer knew that Oporto was the source not of whisky, but of port. Mr. Sam defended these names, claiming to Robertson that in Scotland itself "you could get a bottler to make you up a label and make you a blend of Scotch whisky at whatever price you were willing to pay." But many of the drinks were truly awful. A medicated wine turned out to be too impure even for the country's normally unselective drinkers. Robertson describes how: "Raw alcohol was mixed with Jamaican ginger to produce a ferocious spirit called Ginger Spit. The same raw spirit, made from the refuse of sugar refineries, was also mixed with water, sugar, molasses, tobacco juice, and bluestone to make a brew which sold as a patent medicine for five dollars a bottle." But the two that really got the authorities were Sayers Sarsparilla, a so-called blood purifier weighing in at 36 percent alcohol, and "Gely's non-alcoholic wine," advertised as being pure grape juice without any trace of alcohol, whereas in fact it was stronger than ordinary whiskey.

Not surprisingly Richler goes to town when describing the spirits being churned out. They included "Ginger Spit, Dandy Bracer, Dr. Isaac Grant's Liver & Kidney Cure, Raven Cough Brew, and Tip-Top Fixer among other elixirs. The brew was blended by pouring sugar, molasses, tobacco juice, bluestone, and raw alcohol into washtubs and letting it sit overnight. In the morning, once drowned rats had been scooped out with a fishing net, the solution was stirred with an oar, strained, tinted different colors, and bottled." This is not too much of an exaggeration. As late as the 1950s odd bottles of (inevitably awful) pre-Repeal whiskey would turn up at Seagram's offices, including one with the ominous name of Chicken Cock. At the same time the regulations were socially unfair. As one politician—from Quebec—pointed out, "The rich man can have all he wants, but the poor man gets none and is driven to buy innocently all kinds of vile substitutes for wholesome drink."

The capital required for the alcohol itself was greatly reduced by the arcane way in which excise duty was levied. Without the duty ethyl alcohol cost a mere C$1.60 an Imperial* gallon, but the tax was far greater (C$2.00 a gallon) if the spirit was to be converted into beverage alcohol than the 22 cents a gallon it cost if used for making vinegar. In other words the Bronfmans could buy and store the spirit cheaply until the last moment, since the spirit was sold immediately after it had been "blended" in their splendid new vats. As a result none of their precious capital was tied up in tax. The profits were immense; whiskey whose contents cost only a little over C$4.50 a gallon could be sold for five times as much. And given a turnover of over four thousand gallons a week, profits could be over C$4.5 million a year.

Originally the Bronfmans relied on labels supplied by a local printer but they soon grew increasingly ambitious and called in a designer to produce their own. Their finest Scotch was called Prince of Wales, their lower grade Glen Levitt.† Their best rye whiskey was called simply Superior, their second grade Black Knight. Nevertheless there was little question of what we would call distinctive "brands," each with their own qualities. As Gray says, "Accuracy in labeling the bottles was never a long suit in the Regina plant." They were doubly fictitious, being neither brands nor of Scottish origin. But then the customers were not choosy, often preferring to mix their own blends, as they did when rolling their own cigarettes.

This, the Bronfmans' first, decisive step into the spirits business—as opposed to treating the stuff as merely another tradeable product—nearly led to a disaster. The incident, called "the mystery of the discolored vats," required all the family's guts, self-confidence, and stubbornness to overcome—it also provided an opportunity for Sam to prove that he knew more about whiskey, in his own opinion anyway, than Harry. Their very first blend of 382 gallons of water, 318 of overproof alcohol, and 100 gallons of aged rye whiskey had been left for a couple of days in the vats but emerged not the lovely amber color of any proper whiskey but a nasty bluish-black. Such a mistake could have been anticipated given that the young brothers "probably knew as much about chemistry," in Gray's words, as they did "about chiropractic or choreography."

Instead of blaming themselves the brothers went to war, not only with

---

* Twenty percent more than a US gallon.
† A Jewish version of Glenlivet, a famous Scottish malt whisky company they were to buy over half a century later.

the suppliers of the vats—whom they blamed for the discoloring—but also with the makers of the labels, whom they accused of supplying unsuitable equipment. With the almost automatic and impulsive litigiousness that marked their progress throughout life they proceeded to launch— inevitably unsuccessful—lawsuits which provided the press with a splendid opportunity to nail Harry and his family. "Far from being thrown away," gloated *The Winnipeg Tribune,* the contents of the vat were "worked off in lots of 10 gallons to every 100 of other mixture, as what was euphemistically called 'the alcohol content.'" An "expert chemist" rubbed salt, or rather acid, in the Bronfmans' wounds. He testified that the discoloring "could come about by chemical reaction from something such as sulphuric acid. . . . Incidentally . . . there exists such a thing as 'beading oil,' an oil used for putting an artificial 'bead' on cheap liquors, or for artificially aging liquors. It contains a distillate of sulphuric acid according to a high authority on chemistry in Winnipeg"—leaving this particular reader wondering if the "authority" was employed by one of the Bronfmans' rivals. No other vat ever turned the same, and, as Michael Marrus discovered from Mel Griffin, a former Seagram production director, the discoloration was not unusual, and was probably caused by the presence of a tiny piece of metal in the wood.

Nevertheless the Bronfmans did use any number of additives. As Harry explained to a Royal Commission on Customs and Excise in 1927, they— like most distillers throughout the ages—added caramel to ensure that each batch was of the same color. When the blend was to be labeled as Scotch a base of dark-colored Scotch was used instead of rye to give some trace of its proper taste of peat, while at an altogether lower level straight alcohol and water could be transformed into imitation rum by adding rum caramel and blackstrap molasses. Nevertheless the experience was obviously valuable. Even though the Bronfmans would never admit mistakes they had clearly learned a lesson and from then on their whiskey acquired a good reputation—though it helped that their blends were always (a little) cheaper than those sold by Hudson's Bay. Indeed while being cross-examined by the commissioners Sam stated firmly that Harry "had blended whiskey all his life and met with general success," a piece of classic Bronfman *chutzpah* that was not contradicted.

Harry Bronfman had also tried to expand by bringing three other operators into a partnership because he and Sam both knew that it was only a matter of time before their business would be declared illegal. Typically,

Sam (who, as a control freak, would undoubtedly have been consulted about the deal) claimed that he left Harry to run the joint operation and that he wasn't consulted because he "happened to be away on a prolonged trip in the East." But although he told Robertson that Harry "should never have gotten mixed up with these people," he admitted that "if this crowd were willing to ship our stuff south as well as their own I couldn't complain."

The Bronfmans' partners in what was called the Regina Wine & Spirit Company were not, to put it mildly, a well-chosen trio. They were, in Harry's own words, "entirely useless to meet any contingency that arose and [were] of no assistance whatsoever." One, Harry Rabinovich, had jumped bail in connection with the death of a truck driver in a case of liquor hijacking, while the second, Zisu Natanson, was merely the owner of a junkyard in Regina. But most troublesome of all was Meyer Chechik, an inarticulate chicken merchant from Winnipeg who brought the only real asset to the partnership: a C$150,000 open line of credit with Boivin Wilson. They and the Bronfmans formed the partnership to exploit the three months' gap between the October 1921 plebiscite and the February 1922 cut-off date that had been imposed for interprovincial imports. They pooled their liquor supplies and evaded a steep increase in the excise tax—from C$2 to C$33 a gallon. In theory they couldn't sell liquor to each other so they formed Dominion Distributors Company to reexport each other's liquor and turn over the proceeds to their companies.

The trio behaved as might have been expected from their previous record. In October 1921, Chechik found that his "associates had emptied some thousands of gallons of alcohol and filled the vats with water." Of course the excise duty, amounting to C$37,000, had not been paid. Chechik refused to pay until Sam Bronfman persuaded him. When the incident came up before the Royal Commission on Customs and Excise later in the decade Chechik claimed that Sam Bronfman had said merely "it would be better, Meyer, that you should go and pay the duty rather than cause so much trouble." In reality of course, Bronfman's language would have been, shall we say, more colorful. Chechik promptly paid up and a new deal was negotiated between Rabinovich and the Bronfmans increasing their share to 80 percent.

The agreement led Chechik to launch a lawsuit two years later after the partnership had been dissolved, claiming damages for that and other offenses. He failed and was later driven to the edge of bankruptcy when the government of New Brunswick seized a million dollars' worth of liquor for non-payment of taxes. Throughout the 1920s he continued to harass the Bronfmans, and once he was paid, simply started legal actions again. (His son Max continued to harass the Bronfmans throughout his life, sending telegrams to them whenever a member of the family died, blessing the fact that the world now contained one less Bronfman). Natanson fared even worse: The local authorities seized the bottling plant he had installed in his basement after the partnership had been dissolved and he went to jail.

The whole process aroused the opposition of Inspector Percy Dallin, the local customs agent, who, like his fellows, was caught in the middle. One of his worst problems arose when a major shipment of whiskey was on its way to Yorkton, a problem which haunted the whole customs department throughout the 1920s. He consulted his superior in Ottawa who replied, "I'm sorry, you've got to come here. With this thing starting you won't last six months! If you do what the liquor interests want the department will get you; if you don't do what they want they will get you!" Dallin's inability to control the Bronfmans' activities was typical of a situation in which the efforts of conscientious local agents were stymied by Harry's influence with the federal customs department. This was headed by Jacques Bureau, a French-Canadian whose corrupt behavior provided Anglo-Saxon Canadians with fuel for their habitual racist attitude towards the French. In the words of H. Blair Neatby, the adoring biographer of Mackenzie King, the dominant figure in Canadian politics between the wars, Bureau's peccadillos "seemed inconsequential to many French-Canadians who tended to assume that public office was a form of property which entitled the user to some perquisite."

The problems Dallin created were as nothing compared with the long-term consequences of the activities of Cyril Knowles, a former Conservative activist who by 1919 was an assistant preventive officer in Winnipeg. Knowles's job, an impossible one, was to prevent smuggling into the country and to ensure the payment of the full duty on all imports. By then American exporters were adept at employing two invoices, one with the real value and another with a much lower figure destined for the customs authorities. The practice was common enough in every type of trade. One Winnipeg importer made a handsome living out of underpriced rosaries destined for the St. Boniface religious order. The most expensive prayer beads, in particular, were listed as cheap artifacts, not, as they should have been, as jewelry. The fact that such practices were so widespread destroys the notion that the Bronfmans' activities were particularly—let alone uniquely—dodgy.

Knowles himself was no saint, he went along with the moeity system, which greatly boosted his salary. In December 1920, while looking for smugglers, he came across a convoy of three American rum runners who had lost their way and had strayed back into Manitoba. They demanded to go and see Harry Bronfman, who expressed himself willing to pay the deposit of double the requisite duty required (it would be refunded once the goods had returned to the US). The payment amounted to C$3,025, but when Harry went to fetch the cash from the safe he suggested that Knowles take the money but make the receipt out for "C$1,000 or C$1,200 or whatever sum he thought he could get away with with the government." He added that he was prepared to slip an envelope with the same amount under Knowles's front door every month. Knowles responded by refusing to release the liquor, on the grounds that it had been seized in Manitoba—and that in any case he was not involved in dealing with transgressions of the laws on liquor.

This created a problem since the authorities in Manitoba took a very poor view of any transport of liquor that might end up in their own state. Harry flew into a rage worthy of brother Sam, and asked Knowles to go outside for a fight. The incident not only illustrated the Bronfmans' cavalier attitude towards the law, it also grew into one of the most serious judicial problems faced by the brothers in the late 1920s and early 1930s. Knowles also tried to attack the brothers on one of their weakest fronts, for they did not distinguish between the—legal—blending of two whiskies and "compounding" by which whiskey was mixed with water and the many chemicals and fragrances employed to make what was later sold as "Scotch whisky." This process required a special license, which neither of the Bronfmans' establishments possessed. A first attempt to bring Dominion Distributors to justice became public knowledge and all the illicit materials were hidden before the arrival of Knowles and his superior. A second raid was luckier, producing evidence of compounding in the form of jugs of the dubious essences used in the process as well as counterfeit US excise tax stickers and liquor labels.

There followed the oddest single episode in the whole saga. Instead of shipping the material himself to his superiors in Ottawa, Knowles accepted Harry Bronfman's kind offer to dispatch them himself. When the evidence arrived it was found that two key packages were missing. Worse, poor Knowles was left waiting outside Bureau's office for two hours while Sam and Allan Bronfman discussed their problem with the minister. On his return home Knowles was instructed by the top brass in Ottawa to confine himself strictly to customs. His discomfort was as nothing to Sam's anger. Through Robertson's pen Mr. Sam storms that Knowles had an inferiority complex, largely because people like the Bronfmans were earning millions and that "though thin and pinched-looking Knowles had an unfortunate tendency to regard his rather brief authority as giving him the right to be judge, jury, and executioner in his dealings with border violations."

The refusal of the top brass to support Knowles's efforts was made even more obvious in 1923 when he found that the Sairs, another Jewish family of Russian origin who had prospered (largely through using denatured undertakers' embalming fluid as a base) were conducting a trade by which exported whiskey was exchanged for products ranging from automobiles to watches. As first Knowles was congratulated on his coup but after the Sairs had complained to their local senator he was told to shut down the investigation. Knowles remained at work, totally deskbound, until his death in 1932. Nevertheless the whole bitter episode with the Bronfmans led, not surprisingly, to an obsession with bringing them to justice. His anger must have been been intensified by an interview Harry gave to *The Winnipeg Tribune* in the midst of his troubles with the colored whiskey and as part of the series the paper was running on the crimes induced by rum running. Harry presented himself as Mr. Liquor, so far as Saskatchewan was concerned. Notably he regarded "any slap at the liquor business" in the province "as a slap on me." By 1922 he was unquestionably a millionaire, and had moved into 2326 Sixteenth (College) Avenue, the biggest house in Regina. The only two competitors were "two small concerns in Saskatoon which have practically run out of stock." He went on to boast that his was the liquor of choice for bootleggers. Even the Sairs had given up. This was true; of the sixty or more hopefuls scattered over at least twenty-nine towns, many of them tiny whistle-stops on the CPR who had rushed into the business, only half a dozen remained and his was by far the biggest business.

From the start the Bronfmans employed middlemen to handle sales, a foretaste of the distribution system they set up in the 1930s. They also employed Harry Sokol, a former Winnipeg bartender who had smuggled hooch into the US during World War I, as their salesman-at-large. They could also, crucially, guarantee immunity from interference by customs and excise authorities on the Canadian side of the border—and also claim a C$9 a gallon tax levied on alcohol destined for consumption in Canada.

But the Bronfmans' success had left a legacy which has tainted the fam-

ily ever since, for the terms "bootlegger" and "Jew" had become inter-
changeable. In his researches fifty years later Gray "frequently encountered
aging witnesses who still recalled the exporters as 'the Jews.'" At the time
an Episcopalian bishop thundered from his pulpit that "It is time that they
were given to understand that since they have been received in this country, and have been given rights enjoyed by other white men, they must not
defile the country by engaging in disreputable pursuits." A Presbyterian
minister was even blunter. In a letter to *The Saskatoon Star* he stated,
"There are certain Jews in this province engaged in the liquor trade who
could contribute a great deal to Saskatchewan by leaving it at once." The
attacks were not only racist, but served as an outlet for the drys to work off
their frustrations in not getting their way. The split in attitudes was shown
by *The Financial Post* which pointed out, quite correctly, that "rum running
has provided a tidy bit towards Canada's favorable balance of trade."

By the early 1920s Sam had become "one of the most eligible bachelors
in Winnipeg" and had built up his income to a phenomenal C$30,000 a
year. Not surprisingly, his mind—otherwise exclusively devoted to
business—was also occupied by thoughts of romance, or, more precisely, by
one Saidye* Rosner, whom he married on June 30, 1922—even though he
had previously taken out her older sister and Saidye was rather startled to
receive his proposal of marriage by telegram from Vancouver. Saidye is remembered as a tough, impressive, substantial lady with a personality of her
own. Her father had arrived on the prairies at much the same time as the
Bronfmans and had accumulated a substantial fortune and the social standing that went with it. "Gramps," as he was called, had been, wrote Edgar,
"the mayor, chief of police, and captain of the fire department" in Plum
Coolee, because he also owned the general store—and was thus even more
of a "provincial worthy" than Harry in Yorkton. They were married in
1922, just before Rose married Dr. Max Rady, a ceremony where Sam gave
away the bride, a sure sign that by then he had taken over as head of the
family. A few days later Allan Bronfman married Lucy Bilsky, a member of
a pioneer Jewish settler family in Winnipeg, and thus into the Jewish
aristocracy—her sister-in-law was married to Schie Freiman, one of the
country's most prominent Jews.

For nearly fifty years Saidye was the only woman in Sam's life, there

* Allegedly she had changed the normal spelling of Sadie to show that she was different.

never was a hint of sexual scandal connected to him, for Sam was not only faithful, he was an old-fashioned prude. According to Maxwell Henderson, he was inspecting a possible new office with Mr. Sam when they found "a young couple indulging in sex. Sam was shocked but not amused" and refused to consider leasing the guilty building. Sam and Saidye adored and respected each other. She had described him as her "Baby Face" because it was so round—as Harry put it with an elder brother's lack of charity, Sam had "a very young face." Sam returned his wife's compliment by singing the song of that title at the slightest excuse to the end of his life. Moreover he totally trusted his wife—"At any time during our married life," Saidye once said, "I could have signed my name on checks for millions of dollars if I had wanted to do so." Unlike most husbands at the time, he discussed major business decisions with her. Saidye also provided him with some of the social security he so desperately wanted and it was only in her company and that of a few close friends that he was comfortable.

Saidye is remembered very differently by her children; to her elder son, Edgar, she was emotionally distant, but to her younger daughter, Phyllis, she was much warmer, had great good sense, loved young people. Unfortunately their plans for a lengthy honeymoon were interrupted by urgent business matters, including a talk—from which she was naturally excluded—with a "distiller," who was probably a bootlegger, in Louisville. This provided the first taste of a sense of priorities Saidye had to accept through the next forty-eight years.

Such is the peaceable nature of Canadian society that there were few crimes committed by Canadians as a result of the liquor business. Indeed one of the most famous murders was committed by a trigger-happy prohibitionist, the Rev. J. O. L. Spracklin in Ontario in 1920, a crime which greatly damaged his cause. The biggest problem so far as the Canadians themselves were concerned derived from the unusually large sums in cash and cashier's checks drawn on American banks—which could be, and naturally often were, forged. Not surprisingly, too, the American rum runners became notorious as bank robbers and trigger-happy gamblers. The bankers were used to summoning the Mounties from their nearest post by phone, so the criminals had only to cut the phone wires to be left in peace. Hence the shock waves as a result of a single murder, which would have gone virtually unremarked the other side of the border. Corrupt, hypocritical the Canadians and their politicians may have been, but murderous they emphatically weren't.

The exception was the case of Paul Matoff, who was married to Jean, the second of the four Bronfman daughters. Like the rest of the family he was in the liquor business, one of the relatives looking after operations as far afield as Vancouver and Edmonton. Laura's husband Barney Aaron was in charge in Montreal while Harry's brother-in-law Dave Gallaman ran the boozarium in Estevan. Matoff, who was in charge at Bienfait and two other boozariums, fancied himself as the "king" of whiskey operations in the area. He was the only one of the family who resembled the normal picture of a bootlegger of legend, relishing the diamond rings and diamond stick pin he wore in his tie and flashing the large sums in cash he collected.

October 4, 1922, was a typically quiet evening in Bienfait* with the locals gathered to play high-stakes snooker or, if they could not afford the stakes, a more modest poker game. Then, in Gray's words, Jimmie La Coste, "a dapper local sport, pool player, and whiskey runner wandered in" having spotted the arrival of a couple of big cars by the grain elevator, clearly waiting for Matoff to load them. This alerted the regulars that a case or two might fall off the cars—a possibility caused by the routine overloading of the cars and the many potholes on the town's roads, which were sometimes deepened by the locals. The operations should have been routine, with the rum runners waiting until Matoff came along sometime after midnight to unload the whiskey from the elevator. La Coste wandered along to watch the operation, which involved Lee Dillage, an important liquor dealer from North Dakota and sponsor of an outlaw baseball team, two of whose stars had been part of the infamous Chicago Black Sox team which had thrown the 1919 World Series. Then a gun was poked through the station window while Matoff was at the desk of the telegraph operator and he was killed by a single charge from a shotgun from a range of a mere ten feet. The killer (or killers, accounts vary) fled into the night in a Cadillac with C$6,000 in cash and Matoff's diamond pin worth an estimated C$2,000. He, or they, were never found and the motive remains a mystery.

Not surprisingly Harry Bronfman declared that the murder had nothing to do with the liquor business, and had been committed by someone anxious to get his hands on Matoff's cash and diamonds. But inevitably other more or less likely theories abounded: that he had been killed in revenge for getting a

---

* The town, invariably pronounced "Beenfeat," was particularly suitable for smuggling as there were dozens of small open-cast coal mines between it and the frontier, giving those who knew the lay of the land an even greater advantage in outwitting the law.

couple of American hijackers returned to Canada; or that he had been killed by gunmen hired to kill Harry Bronfman, allegedly for supplying inferior booze—the theory favored by Mordecai Richler, but unlikely in view of the brothers' pride in supplying classier products than the competition.

The murder was a decisive turning point. In a sense it marked the end of innocence; it was the first event that singled the family out from the other rum runners in the business, and was the first of many incidents over the subsequent eighty years that hit the headlines. It also shattered Harry. The Yorkton booklet describes how this "painful event . . . sent Harry into a depression." In a memoir he wrote in 1937 he explained how he had "endeavored to adjust myself to relaxation. The strain of the business during this period had been a little hard on me, and the relaxation brought about a nervous breakdown. I endeavored to regain my health for a year and a half." For his part Mr. Sam always tried to disassociate himself from any direct connection with bootleggers. He had, wrote the faithful Robertson, "no taste at all for the gun-carrying bootleggers from the United States with whom Harry had to deal in Saskatchewan."

In June 1922 the federal government had already taken powers to close the export houses if a province requested it. The Saskatchewan authorities effectively put the smaller wholesalers out of business when they limited export houses to cities of over ten thousand inhabitants—which meant simply that the Bronfmans had to operate out of the Dominion Distributors warehouse in Regina and not continue to operate in any of the smaller settlements along the forty-ninth parallel. Matoff's murder, together with the bank raids, led the Saskatchewan government to outlaw exports of all liquor from the province except from breweries and distilleries and thus put an immediate stop to the Bronfmans' business. It also, indirectly and ironically, resulted in the end of prohibition in Saskatchewan, since the prohibition—and not the loopholes in the law—was held responsible for Matoff's demise. Earlier in the year the provincial legislature had passed a resolution asking the federal government to put a stop to the export trade. But Liberal Prime Minister Mackenzie King, ever conscious of the power of the liquor interests, hesitated and it was not until November 13 that the federal government acted, giving the exporters only a month to shut up shop. This led to a gigantic sales drive to meet the deadline for removing stocks of December 14.

Sam's official contacts in Quebec had warned him that all the stocks, amounting to millions of dollars, would have to be handed over to the provincial government's new Liquor Commission, so he hastily shipped the lot by rail to Harry in Regina for sending across the border. Any stock left in Regina was then shipped to Vancouver in British Columbia where they could still store liquor in warehouses for export. Gray reckons that in the two months the Bronfman business exceeded C$300,000—much of it in highly diluted spirits—though on December 15 over a thousand cases were delivered to Harry Bronfman's house.

Not surprisingly, the Matoff murder left as its legacy the dogged, almost obsessive struggle for respectability which marked the Bronfmans' behavior for three generations, while Harry's problems provided the opportunity for Sam to take over. Until then Harry had been in firm charge of the biggest single element in the family's business and had already understood the tension between him and Sam. He began one—ostensibly amicable—letter to Sam with the greeting, "Hello opposition." But after the breakdown he was clearly number two in the business, though his importance was recognized in a family agreement drawn up at the time, the first of several over the following three decades. In it Harry and Sam were both to receive 30 percent of the business: Abe, although the eldest, was to have only 19 percent; Allan had 14 and Barney Aaron 7. The girls received a regular income of C$300 a month—a substantial sum at the time—from a trust fund.

By then the Bronfman operation was not confined to their home province. Abe reactivated the Kenora operation and headed operations everywhere east of Ottawa—including the crucial operations along the Atlantic coast. Sam's role was more mysterious: He was the traveling hustler, moving between the whole of western Canada and customers as far afield as Chicago and Louisville. For after 1922 Canada formed an ever-diminishing element in the Bronfman business even though the Liberal government in Manitoba was defeated and from 1923 on Winnipeg was, as one observer put it, "dripping wet" after the first step to the gradual relaxation of the prohibition laws.

Within a few years the prospect of the enormous tax revenue from licensing drink—a fact which first became apparent in British Columbia—was enough to ensure the triumph of the "Moderationists" throughout most of Canada. But the new, less restrictive, legislation was generally combined with government control over liquor sales, an arrangement that had been around since early in the century and one that has lasted to this day. Quebec had banned private trade in liquor in June 1921, confining it to government-controlled outlets. By 1926 even Ontario, which with its large rural population was one of the driest of provinces, had followed suit after an election in which the Conservatives had swept back to power on an anti-prohibitionist platform, leaving only Nova Scotia to sign up three years later, while tiny Prince Edward Island followed suit only in 1948.

The provincial monopolies, which lasted virtually unchanged for over forty years, naturally reduced the attractions of the Canadian market. The appeal was further reduced when the federal government doubled excise and sales taxes on alcohol, and by 1923 even Quebec had banned exports of alcohol to other provinces, thus eliminating the prospect of inter-provincial sales. With fewer than a dozen customers in a country that had ceased to be hard-drinking, the Bronfmans naturally concentrated on the much bigger American market. This was a permanent move and one that, from a business point of view, largely removed them from the Canadian scene—even though their past did catch up with them later in the decade.

But they had done well out of Prohibition in their native country. Income tax was introduced to Canada in 1917 but Sam claimed that he "had neither the time nor inclination to keep records." Four years later the family, which pooled much of its money, was worth at least a million dollars, indeed Harry had boasted that "you can't buy much liquor for $500,000 and we had a whole lot more." In 1922 the Canadian revenue authorities arbitrarily assessed the family for tax owed for the five years from 1917 to 1921—variously estimated at C$200,000 and C$300,000. It is possible, wrote Robertson carefully, "that had the family submitted individual returns each year the total would have been considerably higher." But this was only the foundation for the much larger fortune they, above all Mr. Sam, accumulated from their American customers in the following decade.

Four

THE PROHIBITION BUSINESS

The Volstead Act will make us millionaires . . . You know we got
it. They ain't got it.
—HARRY HATCH

IN THE DECADE AFTER THE CANADIAN AUTHORITIES CLAMPED
down on the prairie smuggling trade, the continuing thirst of the
great American public for hard liquor saw the creation of two of the
biggest companies in the world liquor business: Mr. Sam's Seagram, and Hiram Walker, dominated by Harry Hatch, less well known than Mr. Sam but
just as outstanding a businessman. The lead these two personalities established in the—inevitable—absence of American competition lasted for
several decades after Repeal.

Since it ended in 1933, Prohibition and the many and various channels
and people employed to supply the Americans with their liquor have been
studied politically, ethically, sociologically, and in more-or-less romanti-
cized accounts in books and, most obviously, in films. But not as a slice of
business history. Yet it was a large and varied industry, albeit a rather unusual one, and one whose history is almost impossible to recount with any
accuracy. Most obviously this is because keeping books was dangerous, indeed Al Capone's conviction for income tax evasion was made possible
only because he employed such a scrupulous accountant, one Jake "Greasy
Thumb" Guzik. But in most cases nothing was written down, and not just
in the United States. "Extreme care was exercised," wrote Max Henderson
about the whiskey being exported from Canada, "not to commit anything
beyond the absolute minimum to paper while always ensuring that the
transactions were strictly legal." Not surprisingly the only reliable figures
come from such indirect sources as the British export statistics, which were

confined to Scotch whisky and thus cover only a small proportion of the total.

Nevertheless most of those involved regarded themselves not as gang-sters but as businessmen. As Harry's son Gerald told Newman, "One of the reasons why Sam and Allan were so successful with the US bootleggers was that they were treated as business people." As a Scotch whisky broker in-terviewed by Ronald Weir in 1968 put it: "Those who acted as bootleggers are now the big names in the US drinks industry as they made vast sums. Bootlegging was done very cleanly, with little gangsterism: Capone was a poacher." Capone was disliked by many of his fellow traffickers for his homicidal tendencies but he emerged as one of the most effective business-men in the country. As he put it: "All I ever did was to supply a demand that was pretty popular," and even his accusers recognized his remarkable qualities as a businessman. By the end of the 1920s Capone had created a true business conglomerate. In *Only Yesterday*, his fascinating description of social life in the 1920s, Frederick Lewis Allen quotes figures of $60 million for Capone's annual revenue from liquor. Capone himself ran an enormous "integrated" business empire that had its own distilleries, breweries, speed boats, and fleets of motor cars and trucks. He and his like in other cities could be selling up to forty thousand cases of hard liquor a month. Not sur-prisingly the liquor business was never so prosperous. And perhaps the con-centration by authors and filmmakers on Chicago is understandable given that the profits from the trade in Cicero, outside Chicago, were $100,000 a week each for Al Capone and John Torrio.

In the words of *The Saturday Evening Post*, prohibition did not abolish the liquor business in the United States. Far from it, prohibition "changed the liquor traffic. . . . It has brought about an organized liquor traffic, clan-destine but effective as to both distribution and profits." Not surprisingly the most successful bootleggers were all highly able businessmen. Meyer Lansky, himself a distinguished example of the type, remarked how an-other, Arnold Rothstein, "had the most remarkable brain. He understood business instinctively." To Lansky, "We were in business like the Ford Mo-tor Company. . . . Shooting and killing was an inefficient way of doing business. Ford salesmen didn't shoot Chevrolet salesmen. They tried to outbid them."[1]

The business was enormous. Estimates of the amount of liquor con-sumed during the 1920s vary between five bottles a head annually to dou-ble that quantity. What is certain is its enormous profitability, with profits grossly inflated because the drinks were so cheap to produce, partly because any idea of quality went out of the window. Beer cost half a dollar to produce half a keg and was sold by the brewer for over fifty times as much— with a similar margin available for the saloon keeper. Jewish prominence in the liquor business was natural. It was a traditional occupation, and moreover Jews have always been ready to seize on new business opportunities. In addition, Jews, although historically "the people of the Law," have had an ambivalent attitude towards laws passed by other races. In the words of Rabbi Arthur Herzberg, "The law had always been the enemy of the Jews; to circumvent it was often the only way to survive, and therefore to outfox authority was a praiseworthy act."[2]

Prohibition agents had very little effect on the trade. As Clinton Howard of the United Committee for Prohibition Enforcement put in 1925, "Prohibition has been enforced half-heartedly at best and with definite intention that it be broken; at worst the law has not been enforced beyond the point where, in the opinion of the enforcers, it would hurt the party in power by enforcing it." Indeed liquor became far more widely available than it had been before. This situation changed towards the end of the 1920s when government agents severely reduced production. Yet as late as 1929 the *New York World* could publish the following staggering list of sources, one clearly lovingly compiled by the paper's journalists:

Open saloons, restaurants, night clubs, bars behind a peephole, dancing academies, drugstores, delicatessens, cigar stores, confectioneries, soda fountains, behind partitions of shoeshine parlors, back rooms of barbershops, from hotel bellhops, from hotel head waiters, from hotel day clerks, night clerks in express offices, in motorcycle delivery agencies, vegetable markets, taxi drivers, groceries, smoke shops, athletic clubs, grillrooms, taverns, chophouses, importing firms, tearooms, moving-van companies, spaghetti houses, Republican clubs, Democratic clubs, laundries, social clubs, newspapermen's association.

But, tactfully the paper left out the doctors' surgeries and drugstores, which were probably the most important outlets of them all. Even before prohibition came into effect 15,000 physicians and 57,000 druggists had applied to sell alcohol for "medicinal purposes." As *The Saturday Evening Post* pointed out, the basis of the traffic was "the medicinal use of whiskey . . . and a nation that has developed enough sickness in eight

months to require 18 million gallons, or thereabouts, of whiskey to alleviate its suffering may be depended on to remain sick indefinitely."

The most important drink in the United States remained beer, for the
legal "near-beer" could be strengthened in a number of ways—since it was
in fact de-alcoholized real beer it could in many cases simply be left in its
natural state. But generally speaking trade remained local, since beer, a
low-value product, was simply too heavy and thus costly to transport any
great distance. It was beer, which needed fleets of trucks to transport,
which led to the ever-increasing sophistication of the bootleggers' operations. Apart from relatively tiny quantities of luxury French wines and
champagne, wine was very largely homemade, thanks largely to sales of the
famous "grape bricks." These were to be dissolved in water, sugar should
be added to taste, and the result "consumed within five days, otherwise,
and in summer temperature, it might ferment and become wine." Within a
few years most gin was homemade, generally in the bathtub, the alcohol
and all-important juniper berries obtainable from their friendly local
bootlegger—a trusted friend to many millions of Americans.

Foreign suppliers of hard liquor—Canadian or Scottish—were a minor
element in the liquor mix. They can be looked at as nimble guerrilla armies
attacking the US market on an enormously wide front—or rather fronts,
comprising a land frontier of four thousand miles with Canada and around
five thousand miles of sea coast. In the official history of the US Coast
Guard during Prohibition, M. Willoughby remarks that "at one time or another liquor was landed on virtually every mile of mainland shore from the
Virginia coast to Maine" and much found its way "between the Virginia
Capes, and also into the New Orleans market."[3] On the West Coast the
single land route south was used quite openly by smugglers who simply paid
a small "levy" to the American customs officials before the liquor went on
its way, usually to San Francisco, supposedly the wettest city in the whole
country.

In this galaxy the Bronfmans' route across the plains was a minor business, if only because the markets were far away and individual loads were
measured in dozens rather than hundreds or thousands of cases. Once they
had been forced to move away from their home territory the Bronfmans
had ceased to be a big fish in a little pond and had to start as a relatively
new, and not enormous, player in a far larger market. Sam was fully aware
of the fact: "We were late starters in the two most lucrative markets—on
the high seas and across the Detroit River," he told Robertson. "What

came out of the border trade in Saskatchewan was insignificant by comparison." Nevertheless he saw the opportunity. "This was when we started to make our real money," for even if the quantities they were shipping were not, relatively speaking, enormous, they were operating at the most profitable top end of the market.

Obviously there was a great deal of leakage along the whole frontier—the border between New Brunswick and Maine was a favorite—but one of the most important routes, dealing in wholesale rather than retail quantities, was the off-shore stretch of the Atlantic Ocean known as "Rum Row." In fact there were several off-shore areas where liquor was loaded from ocean-going ships onto the fast speedboats and schooners employed by the rum runners. Obviously the biggest was off New York, with a smaller one off Boston. But, as Willoughby points out, "A great deal of liquor was run into the country in Florida waters, partly because of the proximity of Cuba and the British-owned Bahama Islands," where imports of Scotch soared from a mere 944 gallons annually to 386,000. Thanks to Prohibition, sales to Bermuda rose, though less quickly, from 958 gallons to 41,000. The tiny French-owned islands of St. Pierre and Miquelon with their ice-free port were favorite spots for loading stocks of imported spirit, and took 116,000. By 1931 enough Canadian whisky was being landed on the islands to provide every inhabitant with ten gallons a week. But Scotch imports were nothing new; before the war 544,000 gallons had been exported annually from Glasgow alone, and Scotch probably accounted for a mere 5 percent of the whiskey consumed in the US. Not surprisingly the customers were not always reliable: One outstanding Glasgow distiller lost so much through bad debts that he committed suicide.

Rum Row was first exploited by Captain Bill McCoy, famous as the carrier of the finest imports—hence the phrase "the real McCoy" given to one of his favorite cargoes, Cutty Sark Scotch. Not that he operated for very long. His first coup, in 1921, was to bring fifteen hundred cases of liquor to the thirsty citizens of Savannah, a major smuggling center, and he had soon increased each load to five thousand cases—worth $50,000 to him at a time when he was clearing double that amount every month. But in 1923 the Coast Guard boarded one of his ships. He went to jail for a short and comfortable stay but then retired. To him, wrote Thomas Coffey, "Rum running should be a free, adventurous, dangerous but profitable sport. There should be some fun in it. Now that it was a cold, ruthless, efficient business he decided he no longer needed it."[4] So the gallant captain retired to Florida, where he made another fortune in real estate. But for all its successes—and its general honesty and devotion to duty—the Coast Guard inevitably faced an uphill struggle, and were often disheartened when the courts dismissed their prosecutions or imposed derisory sentences on the smugglers.

The British government was not anxious to restrict exports: If Scotch ceased to flow to the Bahamas, as Weir pointed out in his history of DCL, "The business would go to one of the more convenient islands belonging to another nation"—like St. Pierre. Moreover the Scots were anxious to block the appalling blends peddled by German merchants operating in Hamburg, a city which had been a primary entrepôt for cognac a hundred years earlier during the Napoleonic wars. Yet by 1924 the Americans had persuaded the British, who then controlled Canada's territorial waters, to extend the existing twelve-mile limit to "an hour's steaming distance," which provided the pursuing Coast Guard boats greater room to chase the smugglers—nineteen out of twenty of whom had evaded capture. At the same time Congress authorized President Coolidge to spend an additional $28.5 million on the Coast Guard, of which $20 million was to be spent on fast boats specially designed to catch the smugglers, and the fleet was reinforced by the transfer of twenty destroyers and two minesweepers from the Navy. Nevertheless in 1925 the official in charge of enforcement reckoned that only one-twentieth of the $4 million worth of liquor entering the country was being seized. As the decade wore on the war became increasingly sophisticated with both sides communicating by radio in code—the smugglers even hired one of Britain's finest cryptographers. While the Coast Guard would follow the supply boats after they had loaded from the "mother ships" stationed outside territorial waters, the smugglers' boats were dispersed.

On Rum Row, Sam was helped by the presence of Abe and Barney Aaron in Nova Scotia where they had been sent to supervise the shipping of whiskey to the East Coast of the United States. According to Robertson, i.e., Sam, the pliant Barney Aaron "did most of the work." But despite Sam's grumbles about his sloppy records, by 1924–25 the pair handled at least $2 million worth of liquor. Sam helped by using his political contacts to ensure that the province's otherwise extremely strict Temperance Act allowed only the family's Atlas Shipping Company to import duty-paid liquor for the purpose of exporting it—lesser companies had to ship direct into bond. So Sam could ship his Scotch to Halifax and then direct to the

Detroit River for shipping to the United States—paying C$700,000 in duty to the customs office in Halifax in two years. Abe even set up his own radio station to keep in touch with Atlas's fleet of boats, which included a vessel called *Mazel Tov*. They later formed the Northern Export Company, a joint venture between Atlas Shipping and local interests and run by Monte Rosebourne, a veteran of their previous efforts. Northern Export had a major warehouse at St. Pierre, its stock valued at between $1 and $1.5 million during several years in the 1920s.

Yet until the late 1920s Sam was by no means the biggest player in the Canadian liquor business. The top man was Harry Hatch whom he hated, not only as a rival, but also because Hatch had once, allegedly, called him "that Jew boy from Montreal." Hatch's father Bill had owned saloons and hotels in the Midwest and had two sons, Herb and Harry. The younger son was five years older than Sam Bronfman and was at least equally talented, though his character was the total opposite—apart from a love of bad language at least as graphic as Sam's. Harry Hatch was reclusive, hating to be photographed or allow the limelight of publicity to fall on him. This—and the fact that he was not Jewish—prevented him from becoming as big a bogeyman as his rival. But perhaps the biggest difference between them was that whereas Mr. Sam was all business, Hatch, by the end of the 1920s, was as interested in his racing stable as in his liquor business, which he left largely in the hands of his trusted associate Bill Hume.

Harry Hatch had served his apprenticeship in what C. W. Hunt describes as "the dingy, smoke-filled and frequently violent atmosphere of the small town Canadian hotel."[5] In 1911 the newly married Harry struck out on his own, opening a liquor store in Whitby, a small town on Lake Ontario near Toronto. He also traveled as a "drummer" or traveling salesman, using the large hypodermic syringe he carried to inject enough caramel coloring into his whiskey to satisfy individual buyers. Like Mr. Sam he and his elder brother Herb cashed in on the lucrative interprovincial mail order trade before it was outlawed. But Harry then did something unusual for so entrepreneurial a character. He went to work for someone else: Sir Mortimer Davis, one of the first Jewish tycoons to be knighted. His Canadian Industrial Alcohol Company operated two major distilleries, Wiser and Corby. But Sir Mortimer, conscious of his position—unique for a Jew—in the highest reaches of Montreal's business elite, was not willing to encourage sales of his firm's whiskies in the United States. So Sir Mortimer hired Hatch as his sales manager, while Herb and his partner, Larry McGuinness,

continued to sell liquor in the United States but had to channel their orders through Harry. Within two years sales of liquor from Corby had multiplied a hundredfold, to fifty thousand gallons a month.

When Sam moved from exclusive reliance on Rum Row, the most obvious route for him, as for other Canadians, was via the Great Lakes, or
more precisely the Detroit River. Even today you can stroll down the carefully tended lawns outside the headquarters of Hiram Walker in the peaceful Canadian town of Windsor, then called Walkerville, and see the office
towers of Detroit across the Detroit River. The "Windsor-Detroit funnel"
was the normal description for this, the narrowest of straits—is not *étroit*
the French word for "narrow"? As Roy Haynes, the National Prohibition
Director, put it, "The Lord probably could have built a river better suited
for rum-smuggling, but the Lord probably never did." The traffic was enormous. In 1929 the Canadian authorities reckoned that twelve boats, each
carrying up to a thousand cases of liquor, were operating across the Detroit
River every day. The Coast Guard's efforts were largely thwarted by a
clause in a Canadian-American treaty limiting the number of armed vessels on the Great Lakes to a mere four—although in 1924 the Americans
prevented the exporters from using American boats.

Hatch's transport problems were solved by an agreement with a relative,
"Big Maudie" Hatch of Whitby, who had lent money to many of the lake's
fishermen, loans on which most of them had defaulted. Thus was formed
"Hatch's Navy," the dominant force in the trade across the lakes—not just
from Windsor to the other bank of the Detroit River. The navy consisted
mostly of open fishing boats, each holding up to twenty-five burlap bags of
booze. In addition a large fish net was slung on each side of the boat, a device allegedly invented by Captain McCoy. The net was loaded with bags
of booze which the Americans retrieved from the sand bars off Olcott in
northern New York State where they had been deposited.* They were
helped by the bags of salt that weighted down the bags. Once the salt had
dissolved in the water the bags floated to the surface. "Commercial fishing," in Hunt's words, "had never been so profitable." Even more so when
the Hatches built "master cruisers," which could outrun—and outgun—
the Coast Guard boats. The Americans were relatively helpless; a drive by

---

* The stains resulting from the immersion of the burlap bags added to the apparent legitimacy—and
therefore the price—of "imported Scotch," so much so that some cunning distillers dipped bottles into
sea water and left them to dry slowly, thus staining and discoloring the label.

the authorities in 1927 resulted in seizures of a mere twentieth of the estimated three million gallons of liquor being smuggled across the river.

Although new picket boats were brought to Lake Ontario in 1925 the Canadian customs officials weren't greatly bothered by the traffic, for they could collect an excise tax of $9 a gallon on spirits destined openly for the US. The Hatches' success enabled them to buy the Gooderham & Worts Distillery, a Toronto landmark on a sixteen-acre site and the oldest commercial-sized distillery in Canada. But by 1923 the distillery had been idle for eight years and carried a mortgage of $500,000. At first William Gooderham,* a difficult man whom Harry Hatch approached through his son Eddie, was reluctant to sell, believing that Hatch was merely acting for Davis, whom he regarded, in Hunt's words, as "a Jew and a Montrealer" and thus "beyond the pale of society." Once reassured he was happy to sell, even arranging the necessary financing from a friendly bank.

To Hatch the distillery mattered less than the name, which allowed him to sell young Canadian whisky to unsuspecting Americans as though it were well aged. Bootleggers used to dilute the—relatively expensive—Canadian whisky with up to three times the quantity of alcohol and water. Hatch then persuaded the federal government to allow an exemption to the rule that Canadian whisky had to be aged for two years by claiming the same exemption as that enjoyed by other distilleries when they had resumed work after the war. As a result, said Hunt, "Gooderham & Worts, a highly respected name in whiskey circles for more than three quarters of a century, could now distill bourbon or rye whiskey on a Monday and export it on a Tuesday"—often through "Hatch's Navy" and Larry McGuinness, who had set up shop at Niagara Falls in northern New York State. Hatch's exemption was signed by the ever-accommodating Jacques Bureau as Minister of Customs. The Bronfmans also had a connection to him through Albercis Gelinas, a Montreal millionaire close to Bureau. He had provided the Bronfmans' Atlas Shipping with the guarantees required for the bonds they issued to cover their stocks. Harry Stevens, a Conservative MP who was an early opponent of Bureau, described him as "the most genial, slapdash, happy-go-lucky chap that one would like to meet." But "he did not

---

* The firm's founder, Sir Albert Gooderham, had been knighted, hence the rhyme: "Gooderham was knighted, Bronfman indicted."

consider that grafting in the ordinary sense of the term was any great political crime."

Hatch promptly started work on a new distillery at Corbyville, destined to be one of the largest in the world, producing ten thousand gallons a month. Soon the company's earnings were running at a rate of nearly C$1.5 million a year—the sum Hatch had paid for the business. Not surprisingly financial analysts began referring to Hatch as "the man who put the dividends into alcohol." Moreover, wrote Hunt admiringly, Hatch knew how "to orchestrate the market for the company's stock like a maestro." Not surprisingly, at one point there were no fewer than thirty-seven "export docks" on Lake Ontario, and this one outlet accounted for four in every five bottles of Canadian beer and three out of five bottles of whisky exported to the United States. Yet the trade was—relatively—peaceful. According to Hunt, "the normal practice for American rum runners was to leave their weapons behind when coming to Canada to pick up a load." The profits were enormous. Hunt calculated that a $3 bottle of Canadian whisky would fetch between $7 and $9 in New York. Moreover prices were lower if the drinker lived anywhere near the lakes—for boat transport was so much simpler and cheaper than overland transport—a thirty-foot cabin cruiser could carry a couple of hundred cases, ten times the amount carried by even the largest of "whiskey sixes."

Sam had a long slog to catch up with Hatch. Two years after the Matoff murder, accompanied by Saidye, he set off on what they called their "two long years" traveling throughout Canada and the United States visiting Sam's customers—years which must have seemed like an eternity to a lonely young bride far from her previous life as a member of a particularly close-knit family. But she obviously helped Sam enormously—her ultra-respectable presence must have been of considerable use in his dealings with his customers in the United States. How much contact Sam had with his customers, the—largely Mafia-led—suppliers of liquor to American towns and cities, is a matter for supposition since, not surprisingly, he left no written records. Sam had obviously hoped to avoid the seriously criminal individuals involved. Nevertheless the journeys enabled Richler to go to town on the brothers' contacts with real or invented hoods. "Or Solomon was in Chicago, consulting with Al Capone's financial adviser, Jacob 'Greasy Thumb' Guzik. Or he was bound for Kansas City to cut a deal with Solly 'Cutcher-head-off' Weissman. In Philadelphia he handled the needs of Boo-Boo Hoff and Nig Rosen and in Cleveland he supplied Moe Dalitz." In reality Sam was influenced by two opposing forces at work: His desire to hustle was tempered by a post-Matoff disposition not to be too directly involved. Indeed the Canadians, anxious to appear honest, probably (but who really knows?) had as little direct contact as possible with the gangsters who controlled the distribution of liquor in the major American cities, who were simply convenient wholesalers. Sam also contacted and befriended dozens of relatively smaller fry, many of whom became his loyal distributors after 1933.

There were only a handful of major intermediaries between the distillers and the final customers who controlled the markets in individual cities—and Sam seems to have been interested in all the country's major markets apart from those on the West Coast. He certainly knew Abner ("Longy") Zwillman, a youngster famous for his friendships with Meyer Lansky and "Lucky" Luciano—and for a passionate affair with Jean Harlow. In 1935, once Dutch Schultz had been eliminated, Zwillman was awarded the honor of being named Public Enemy Number One by the FBI. Sam, aware of his own lack of physical presence, was naturally impressed by the presentable, well-manicured Longy Zwillman. According to one witness Sam kept repeating how "well-behaved Longy is, how studious looking. You'd never guess he was a *shtarker** . . . also had a head on his shoulders, Sam said." Sam also became friendly with Meyer Lansky, the only major Mafia figure from the 1920s to survive unscathed into old age. According to Stephen Birmingham,[6] apparently Sam gave him "lavish dinners" while in return Lansky got him tickets for one of the first "fights of the century," that between Jack Dempsey and Luis Angelo Firpo in 1923.

By the late 1920s much of the Bronfmans' business was being transacted not in the United States but at Seagram's new head office in Montreal. They even had a special office where they could do their business and Sam could rely on a handful of middlemen. The most important were Joseph Reinfeld and Lew Rosenstiel. Reinfeld was described by Michael Marrus as "a jovial, avuncular Jewish immigrant from Poland." According to Terence Robertson, Reinfeld "had been in the industry for longer than Sam and to some extent it was on his advice . . . that Sam began to build up inventory." Before Prohibition he had been running a saloon in a tough, pre-

---

* Yiddish for "strongman."

dominantly Italian neighborhood in New Jersey. He then graduated to act as an agent for a number of well-known brands of Scotch and fine French wine, and was a pioneer in establishing a base in St. Pierre for trans-shipment of imported whiskey through Rum Row. He became a major fig-ure in the industry, a status he maintained after Repeal. It was he who dealt with more famous, if less savory, characters like Waxey Gordon and Dutch Schultz. According to evidence from a former Treasury Department agent he was a regular supplier to the usual suspects. He became one of Sam's best customers, taking delivery at St. Pierre and thus ensuring that Sam did not have to deal with his final customers.

In the early 1950s, James "Niggy" Rutkin, a serious old rogue who had once been Reinfeld's bodyguard and who had spent much of the war in prison for operating an illicit still, accused the Bronfmans and Reinfeld of depriving him of an estimated $22 million profits on an abortive deal. The claims were absurd, but he managed to spread more dirt about the Bronf-mans' early activities in front of Senator Estes Kefauver's committee inves-tigating crime, and clearly hoped to blackmail the family to avoid more revelations. But as usual Sam toughed out the storms involved, despite some embarrassing revelations from other sources about the family's con-nections with Reinfeld and Longy Zwillman. The rumors did not die down finally until Rutkin slit his throat (with a borrowed razor) in 1956, two years after his case had finally been dismissed and he had been indicted for income tax evasion.

Lew Rosenstiel, who was to loom large in Sam's story, was probably an even more important middleman. Rosenstiel, described by Robertson as "loud, opinionated, and domineering," had learned the business at a distill-ery in Kentucky and gone on to be a whiskey broker. He was one of the more unappetizing characters in the whole story. In 1957 he was described as a "hulking figure who favored amber-tinted glasses, which he rarely re-moved, and large cigars to go with his status as one of the wealthiest men alive." In an article in *Esquire* two years later Martin Mayer described him as "intelligent, articulate, and extraordinarily aggressive," a man who "ut-ters his strong opinions with a growl, expressing dislike and contempt for anyone who might disagree. He thinks nothing of calling up an employee at three in the morning." He was, in a way, the mirror image of Mr. Sam. Both were enormously successful distillers, their fortunes based on Prohibi-tion but multiplied many times in the succeeding decades, and both were of a domineering disposition. Rosenstiel was described by *Fortune* magazine as "hair-triggered and scrappy," but "he can be as warmhearted as he can be ruthless." Like Bronfman he was a formidable personality. "He sat there at his desk in his shirtsleeves," wrote Philip Kelly, a senior salesman who had worked for both men, "with his eyeshade hanging over his nose . . . he was a very attractive personality literally vibrating with ideas . . . which seemed to come in figurative waves. . . . Never have I seen an organization that was so affected, rightly or wrongly, by one man."[7]

Before Repeal Rosenstiel had acquired and built up the important firm of Schenley with the help of remodelled distilleries and additional capital raised through the totally respectable banking firm of Lehman Brothers, a connection which enabled him to buy additional stocks. They were close enough for Mr. Sam to have bought a 20 percent stake in Schenley before Repeal but whereas Sam was, in the end, a normal human being, Rosenstiel was a true monster, albeit a most interesting one. In some ways he was a more rounded character than Sam, interested in art, music, psychology. He was a workaholic, needing only two hours' sleep, working seven days a week, impetuous, impatient, unwilling to concentrate for long; a control freak who treated his employees like dirt, sacking them at a moment's notice; going to the toilet to leave them time to compromise themselves by talking in his absence, unaware that he had installed bugging devices in his offices; interrupting a conversation to dictate an advertisement to a newspaper in another state.

Most sensational was the contrast in their sexuality. While Sam was faithful to his "Baby Face," Rosenstiel was married four times and was bisexual—in the office he was known as "Rosie." This side to his character was revealed from evidence given in a bitter divorce suit launched by his fourth wife. If, as is possible, her evidence is true, it guarantees him a place in history as organizer of the parties at which J. Edgar Hoover could frolic in his favorite frocks,[8] parties that featured boy prostitutes for the enjoyment of other guests like Roy Cohn. According to the fourth Mrs. Rosenstiel, at one party she attended Hoover "was wearing a fluffy black dress, very fluffy, with flounces and lace stockings and high heels, and a black curly wig. He had makeup on and false eyelashes." Indeed it was the blackmail potential of the conversations recorded on the microphones Rosenstiel had thoughtfully installed throughout the house that allegedly explained Hoover's refusal to pursue the Mafia. For it was at Lew's place that Hoover met some of Rosenstiel's business associates, truly "usual suspects" like Frank Costello, Sam Giacana of Chicago, Santo Trafficante of Florida, Angelo Bruno (the

Mafia boss of Philadelphia), and Meyer Lansky, a close friend and business associate, not to mention Cardinal Spellman, another Rosenstiel friend.

Sam could see the profits Hatch was making from distilling the whiskey he was selling and decided to go into the distilling business in a more organized fashion than in Saskatchewan. This was to be the Bronfmans' fourth liquor business, following those in mail order, wholesaling, and supplying smugglers. On a trip to Louisville in May 1923, ostensibly to visit the Kentucky Derby, Sam, accompanied by Saidye and Harry, took advantage of the inability of the locals to use their distilling equipment. They bought the Greenbrier Distillery in Louisville, dismantled it, and reconstructed it at Ville LaSalle near Montreal* at a site supplied with plentiful supplies of the clean running water from the Ottawa River required for distilling— though Sam exaggerated both the cleanliness of the water and the importance of its qualities. The choice was deliberate: Montreal was in Quebec, a region whose inhabitants must surely have been the staunchest opponents of prohibition north of the Rio Grande. At the time it was also the biggest port in Canada and the country's business capital.

The LaSalle distillery was the cornerstone of the Bronfman business. As he told his friend Mark Shinbane, "I don't know the first thing about how to make whiskey, but I'll be god-damned if I'm not going to learn." And learn he did with the help of Wathen ("Pop") Knebelkamp, a master distiller from Kentucky, and an engineer, George Abbott. Together with Harry they were instructed to build the most modern distillery in Canada. Construction occupied Sam's entire attention, even when Saidye was about to give birth to their first child, Minda, born in 1925. Sam—and Allan—immersed themselves in all the technical details involved in the production process, including what Sam later described as "grains, water and yeasts, milling, cooking procedures and temperatures, up to the fermenters, the stills and distilling techniques, the barrels used for maturing whiskey, packaging and bottling." All this knowledge was genuine, and indeed for the rest of his life Sam showed a detailed, passionate, and opinionated knowledge of the whole chain of production and marketing of whiskey.

In a classic piece of *chutzpah* Sam had called the company formed to own

---

* Even today the sunken expressway alongside what is now an abandoned distillery is known as the "whiskey ditch."

the distillery Distillers Corporation Ltd., a direct and deliberate echo of the giant Scottish Distillers Company Ltd., the real DCL and universally known as such. At the time he took full advantage of the limited stocks of rye whiskey for sale by the Canadian distillers to the recently established provincial liquor boards. More important than the name of the company was the fact that LaSalle housed the first continuous Coffey still in Canada, which provided the plant with the capacity to produce economically large quantities of the grain spirit required for blended whiskey.

Until 1830 all distillation had been in small "pots" with a capacity even today of only a few thousand gallons, and in the nineteenth century their capacity was even smaller. These produced whiskies called "straight"[*] in North America and "malt" in Scotland. Moreover each batch of fermented liquor—wine in the case of cognac and other brandies, "mash" made from barley or other grains in the case of whiskey—had to be "distilled" twice to produce strong enough spirit. The process was simplicity itself, based on the fact that alcohol evaporates at a lower temperature than water, so the alcoholic fumes from the still could be captured before the water itself started to boil. But this small-scale technique was obviously expensive and the industry was transformed by the development in the late 1820s of the continuous still, called the Coffey still after the Irish customs officer credited with its development. Because the new device allowed continuous distillation the output was greater and fuel costs—a crucial factor before the development of oil or gas heating—infinitely lower. Moreover the strength of the distillate could be varied at will by changing the number of "plates" around which the alcoholic fumes flowed. Obviously the key to "blends" was the ability to mix a majority of the infinitely cheaper, but relatively tasteless, spirit[†] from the continuous stills with a proportion of the more flavorful, much more expensive straight whiskies.

Sam understood the potential profitability of blends. But in addition, unlike Harry Hatch or any of his other competitors, he understood the mysteries of the blending process, which, as he correctly put it, was more an art than a science. He realized that whiskies not only started life differently but, like people, developed differently as they matured in oak casks.

---

[*] Bourbon is merely one special type of straight whiskey, as is "rye whiskey." But rye is inevitably more expensive because it contains less starch than corn, and starch is the raw material which, when converted into sugar, formed the basis of the fermented and distilled liquids.
[†] Neutral grain spirit comes in at 190 proof, only just below "absolute" or "rectified" alcohol without any taste or flavor at all, which is 200 proof.

Moreover he was a brilliant blender in his own right. He also understood and copied the success of the producers of blended whisky in Scotland, in their ability to market brands that could be sold at premium prices, that of the pot-still malt whisky, which was their most expensive ingredient. But, crucially, it formed only a quarter or third of the total blend, the rest coming from continuously distilled and thus much cheaper "grain whiskey." It was a formula that proved the basis of the Bronfman fortune after Repeal.

Five

THE ROAD TO RESPECTABILITY

There was too much overhead in my business anyhow, paying off
all the time and replacing trucks and breweries. . . . They ought to
make it legitimate.
　　—AL CAPONE WHEN ON HIS WAY TO JAIL IN 1931

OING INTO THE DISTILLING BUSINESS WAS PART OF SAM'S SEARCH
for profitability combined with respectability. So his partnership with
the mighty and deeply respectable Scottish Distillers Company Limited
(DCL) was his greatest single coup in the 1920s. It marked an enormously
important step up the social, commercial, and financial ladder and was the
key to the whole of his subsequent career. This was not just because the relationship was unique so far as Mr. Sam was concerned: the only time he
actually accepted anyone as an equal partner and in which he was in many
ways, notably technically, the junior partner. More importantly it was
largely thanks to the association he forged with the Scots that by the end
of the 1920s he had emerged as the largest distiller in Canada. But size was
not all, for Mr. Sam had been particularly struck by the contrast between
the social respectability of the Scots and the disreputability of their Canadian equivalents who, were, after all, selling the same type of products. As
a leading salesman, Philip Kelly, wrote, "In Scotland people in the distilling business represent the best and are at the top of the social strata [sic]."

DCL had been formed in 1877 to produce grain whisky. Before 1914,
writes Ross Wilson, "It was distrusted as a parasitic element of the community."[1] But during the First World War it provided the yeast to help make
the nation's bread as well as "an indispensable munition of war, the spirit
needed for explosives" and other raw materials for the war effort. So DCL
emerged from the war as a newly respectable member of the British industrial community. Nevertheless it only evolved into its modern form in

1925. Until then it had been merely a consortium of grain distillers (using "patent," i.e., Coffey, stills). It was only then that DCL acquired the industry's leading brands. That year, after more than fifteen years of negotiations, Haig as well as James Buchanan of Black and White fame, Dewar's, and Johnny Walker, who called themselves—rightly—the Big Three, joined what became by far the dominant force in the market for blended Scotch, with 60 percent of the market.

The merger was one of the biggest in Britain during the 1920s, and created a board that fully reflected the distinctions earned (or bought) by the heads of the member companies. The directors included Sir John Walker, Lord Woolavington of the Buchanan family, and Lord Forteviot—previously known as Tommie Dewar. Also on the board was Field Marshal Earl Haig, who was not closely related to the whisky-making branch of the Haig family, but had the advantage for publicity purposes of having commanded the British troops in France during the Great War. Not surprisingly Sam became obsessed with DCL as a commercial and social icon, for in the 1920s DCL's directors were a tough and able bunch, and DCL itself was far removed from the sclerotic hulk it became half a century later. As the biographers of Meyer Lansky put it, "The Scottish distillers took full advantage of the demand for their product. . . . Those fine upright men in Britain kept squeezing us for higher prices."[2] The business was so big that Lansky chartered ships to bring their wares across the Atlantic.

For all the social pretensions of the board it was still a relatively new group, and whatever the dates the individual companies had been formed—even today Johnny Walker's motto remains "born 1824 and still going strong"—blended whisky had only begun to be a major seller in the 1880s, above all in export markets, although these were largely confined to the British Empire. Exports became increasingly important as domestic consumption of alcohol in Britain itself declined by more than two-thirds in the first quarter of the twentieth century. After 1918 DCL's priorities naturally switched to the exports which were to dominate the group's activities for the next half a century. So it was looking for partners as well as agencies within the British Empire, above all in the major markets of Australia and Canada, where the need was particularly great because government control had undermined the agency system that had served the distillers so well in the past.

The directors could be choosy as to their associates—they stated firmly, for instance, that "we will not under any circumstances be associated with

Mr. Rosenstiel." In Australia the efforts failed, partly because there was no native tradition of whiskey making, but also because, as Ronald Weir put it in his official history of the group, unlike DCL's investment in Canadian whisky, the country "lacked an indigenous entrepreneur with the capability of Sam Bronfman." Moreover the Scots realized that in Canada the local distillers were naturally so obsessed by the export trade to the US that sales of their native brew were stagnant and there was an opportunity for the more fashionable Scotch whisky.

Despite the obvious mutual interest the road to the partnership between Mr. Sam and the potentates of DCL resembled a slow, circuitous gavotte involving two theoretically incompatible partners. After a first visit to Scotland in 1925 by Sam and Allan, the DCL minutes simply recorded that their prospective partner was merely an "upstart Montreal distiller," although there was no mention of the word "Jewish," for the Scots were less anti-Semitic than the Canadians. Nevertheless Ronald Cumming, who was then a junior director and later (as Sir Ronald) came to dominate DCL, told Robertson that Sam was "quite a persuasive chap in business." In later life Sir Ronald remarked how "It was really an extremely brash kind of thing for anyone to suggest. But Sam had been a good customer for many years and had always paid his bills promptly. That sort of thing counts." (Seagram always had a reputation as a prompt payer.) "Once we met Sam we liked him immensely. Sam put his case quietly, logically, and we were most impressed," though he did claim, not entirely truthfully, that "I send more of your brands to the American market than anyone else in Canada." The carrot he offered was the "opportunity to make Scotch the predominant drink in North America." The Scots were duly impressed.*

DCL's profit margins were greatly increased because although its brands were promoted as being upmarket, three quarters of the blend consisted of cheap, continuously distilled grain spirits with only a quarter of expensive, pot-still malt whisky. The major expense was because even the grain spirit had to be matured expensively in small wood casks for a minimum of three years, a restriction imposed by the British government during World War I. In Canada the minimum was two years—though as we have seen Harry Hatch managed to wriggle out of even this restriction—but most of the

* Later Mr. Sam claimed to his son Edgar that his wooing of DCL was helped when he quoted Tennyson's "To a man love is but a part, to a woman, her whole existence," meaning that to DCL the merger was but a part, but to him the "whole," of his ambitions. Which was, largely, true.

whisky exported from Canada was at least six years old. In 1926 after Sam and Harry's first visit to Britain, the DCL board sent three senior executives to Canada, not in search of a partnership but with the intention of buying control of the LaSalle distillery. When Mr. Sam talked of a partnership they replied, "We didn't come here just to deal with you, or be cross-examined about our intentions," and went off to see his competitors, most obviously Harry Hatch. But this may have been only a piece of bluff, for they had almost certainly already made up their mind. "I think it was a question of trust," Cumming told Robertson. "We liked Sam. He had opened our eyes to wider fields and since we knew him better than anybody else in Canada there was no real point in us seeking to do business elsewhere. We never regretted our decision."

Sam and Allan finally made a breakthrough on their second visit to Britain in 1926 when the Scots approved the quality of a whisky they had produced. After their visit Allan realized the gulf between the two sides. "We thought our distillery was unique," he said afterwards. But "they had fifty or sixty." The approbation was mutual. The Scots thought that LaSalle was superior to its competitors' distilleries; indeed in 1927 one director noted that it was "a first class distillery and is making very good whisky," no small compliment. Indeed the visitors decided that a major advantage of choosing the Bronfmans—apart from their "considerable political influence"—was that by comparison with the four alternatives it had "smaller handicaps in regard to obsolescent plant," for LaSalle was bigger and more modern than their competiors' distilleries. And Sam was prepared to finance the distillery if DCL provided technical assistance.

But during their visit to Montreal the directors had come across the deep anti-Semitism endemic within the Canadian financial community. Bankers the DCL executives consulted admitted that the Bronfmans were "honest, hard-working men who could be relied on to fulfill any financial obligations" but advised the visitors "to have no dealings with the Jews." So the visitors declined the Bronfman offer purely because of their race. The visitors had also objected to "the class of business with which they were associated" but soon found that all five candidates were also involved in bootlegging and in any case DCL had its own subsidiary engaged in selling to the US. Inevitably the negotiations were not simple. At one point Sam offered a half-share in LaSalle for a package including C$1 million, malt whiskies to mix with their grain, the right to sell the blends under the names of DCL's brands, and technical assistance with blending. In the end

DCL created a holding structure which, in theory anyway, kept them at a—short—arms' length from the Jews. As Weir puts it, "If these proposals bear the taint of moral cowardice and hypocrisy, they were based on sentiments prevailing in Montreal's business community"—which were clearly stronger than those prevailing in Scotland, itself not a notably pro-Semitic country. The initial structure involved Distillers Company of Canada, wholly owned by DCL, with a capital of C$2.5 million, which would own the Canadian rights for DCL's brands. It would be the parent for the Distillers Corporation of Canada, which was half owned by each partner, who each nominated two directors. Sam also gained the precious right to buy out DCL's shares for a million dollars, although this had to be based on a handshake agreement since the DCL negotiators were worried about presenting it to their board.

When the agreement was finally signed in Britain on January 13, 1927, a truly red-letter day for the "upstart" Bronfmans, DCL had ceded control of the operating company (the "Corporation") to Brintcan Investments, the Bronfmans' family trust. (Harry's son Gerald claimed that it was his father who insisted on a fifty-fifty split in the course of an acrimonious transatlantic telephone call with Sam.) The deal represented a double triumph. The first was over the Haig distributor, Joseph P. Kennedy, who, as Ronald Weir puts it, "Had an impressive reputation for his selling ability during Prohibition." More importantly the deal represented Sam's first triumph over Harry Hatch, whose approaches had been rejected by DCL, partly because his shares were "grossly overvalued." Hatch was also unable to raise enough money in the city of London to buy DCL, whose shares, he claimed, were largely in the hands of fragile old men.

DCL, wrote Weir, "gave the Bronfmans capital, technology, expertise in blending and marketing, and an appreciation of the product. Sam Bronfman in particular was a fast learner and an extremely good imitator. Far from regarding the Bronfmans as colonial upstarts it is altogether more likely that the men who had given Scotch whisky its international reputation, all past the peak of their careers by the late 1920s, saw them as mirror images of themselves during the pioneering days." Their respect was enough to leave him alone to run their joint venture (in any case detailed control from across the Atlantic was far less practicable before the days of the jumbo jet, let alone e-mail). Moreover the arrangement enabled the Scots to avoid blame should the Bronfmans get into trouble with the Canadian authorities. But even Weir leaves out the biggest contribution made by the Scots—that the partnership gave Sam his first token of re-spectability, one, moreover, granted by the acknowledged aristocrats of the world liquor trade. But then the DCL directors were also Johnny-come-latelies, and had been generally scorned only a few years earlier, so that there was more natural empathy between the two sides than was apparent at the time. From DCL he learned not just about blended whisky but also about negotiating techniques. After dealing with the Scots, he told Robertson, "I adopted a compromise in all my future business dealings. I send executives to negotiate and even if they know in advance what my decision will be in principle they always take time out on the pretext on how to refer to me."

Sam was quick to take advantage of the partnership. Within a year he had snapped up a major prize, the old-established Seagram's distillers. Like many other Canadian whisky companies Seagram had started as millers, producing whisky only as a means of using up surplus grain. It was the founder's son, Joseph Seagram, who had built up the family's liquor busi-ness, notably with two up-market brands, 83, named after the year in which he had become the company's sole proprietor, and VO, allegedly standing for "Very Old," which was launched shortly before Joseph died in 1919 at the age of seventy-eight. He was the very image of the old-established distiller. "Old Joe," wrote Marrus, ended up "looking remark-ably like Edward VII, reputedly pompous and vain." He went into politics, loved racing, and his—often successful—racing colors were also used on the bottles of VO.

Joe's successors took the company public in 1926 but by then it was in difficulties because they scorned the "export trade" to US bootleggers. In the words of *Fortune* magazine it "was foundering under the weight of nepotism and lack of interest." That same year the firm was bought by a firm of Toronto stockbrokers who offered it to DCL. William Ross of DCL was decidedly sniffy, despite the tempting stock of 1.4 million gallons of whisky, rejecting the offer because the distillery at Waterloo near Toronto was such a mess. For the next year Seagram continued to lose money, but the appeal of all that whisky proved too great a temptation and a deal was agreed upon in which the original shareholders took only a quarter of the shares, with the rest divided equally between DCL and the Bronfmans. But the presence of outside shareholders, even DCL, never cramped Sam's style. At the outset the Scottish-based William Ross of DCL became chair-man but the effective manager was Sam as vice president. During his lifetime outside directors were exclusively confined to his friends and associates, for he always treated any liquor company with which he was involved as a family possession. Yet he and the Bronfman family as a whole were still so little known that the *Financial Post* could announce that "Britons secured control at Waterloo." Moreover the decline in Seagram's fortunes because of the dispersal of control naturally provided Mr. Sam with an additional excuse for concentrating control in his own hands and not allowing anyone else, above all any of his brothers, too much, if any, influence.

Sam immediately seized on VO as a promising blend. Like all Canadian whiskies all the ingredients had been aged for at least two years, ensuring that it was smoother than American blends in which the neutral grain spirits could be marketed without any time in wood to remove their asperities. Like all serious distillers Sam was well aware of the old adage: "You put spirits into the barrel, you take whiskey out of it." Canadian whisky had preceded the arrival of blended Scotch on a large scale in the last quarter of the nineteenth century. Nevertheless Canadian whiskies were distilled to a much higher proof and were therefore more neutral, less complex, than an equivalent whisky distilled according to American regulations, especially as Canadian whiskies contained a maximum of 10 percent of "flavoring" whiskies made in pot stills. This meant that the neutral whiskies which formed the vast majority of the blend needed several years in wood to acquire some character. And because many of the casks had previously been used to house bourbon VO had more than a touch of bourbon character.

Harry Hatch remained a formidable rival. By the end of 1926, indeed before Mr. Sam had signed the contract with DCL, he had conducted a lightning raid in which he had captured Hiram Walker, a firm and a distillery as big and as prestigious as Seagram. It was owned by the highly respectable American Walker family. Their natural reluctance to have their business secrets revealed, above all to the American authorities, led them to sell their business. The obvious buyer was the by now elderly Sir Mortimer Davis. When he pulled out it took Harry Hatch only a single day— December 22, 1926—to clinch a deal that gave him the business for only $14 million. This was a bargain, for Walker had a distillery in Windsor just across the river from Detroit, as well as four million gallons of whisky valued at $4 million, part of total assets estimated at $28 million, which included Canadian Club, before Prohibition the biggest-selling imported whisky in the United States, and a brand which is still famous today. Hatch promptly merged his two companies, expanded the Gooderham & Worts distillery, and was proclaimed "King of Canadian Distillers" by *The Toronto Star*—he even set up the Cheerio radio station in Toronto to beam advertisements across the frontier to cities like Buffalo.

To celebrate his newfound status as a partner of DCL, Sam built a headquarters at 1430 Peel Street in Montreal. This is almost invariably described as a "miniature feudal castle . . . a creation of gray granite combining the worst of Tudor and Gothic with early Disneyland."* This is a typical attempt to portray Mr. Sam as a sort of Canadian Citizen Kane, psychologically driven to surround himself with grandiose physical mementos to his greatness. In fact, of course, the only monument he ever wanted to leave was his business. In reality the building is far less pretentious than the grandiose Florentine head office built by the Walker family in a town then called simply Walkerville and now called Windsor. According to *Fortune* magazine the Seagram headquarters "created a considerable to-do in architectural circles at the time." In fact "Peel Street" is not a fully fledged castle at all, merely a narrow, unpretentious office block which today nestles inconspicuously below the office towers of downtown Montreal. It never housed more than sixty employees even when a couple of extra stories had been perched incongruously above the original structure—and was thus totally inadequate for a growing business. But the original façade, smooth like a child's vision of a castle, is indeed a ludicrous tribute to Mr. Sam's beloved Scots, a miniature rather than an imitation castle, complete with tiny crenellations and emblems associated with Scotland—the rose, the thistle, the fleur-de-lys, the coats of arms. The tone is set by a bearded fellow supposedly 152 years old—reminding visitors of the founding of Seagram. The decorations are incongruous, there's even a portrait of Robert Burns, as well as an angelic figure bearing the weight of the world. The Scottish connection was emphasised by the way the words "Distillers Corporation" are picked out in gold and the letters DCL are carved in stone. By contrast the French equivalent, Compagnie Seagram, is tucked discreetly away to one side.

Inside there are solid flagstone floors, a great deal of wood paneling, and carvings echoing the external symbols. Mr. Sam's office, which has been carefully preserved as a memorial since his death, is not that of a megalomaniac. It is reasonably sized, perfectly conventional, with a sizable desk, a

---

* In 2001 it was given to McGill University to house its alumni association.

small table for meetings, and a sofa. The only curiosity is that the desk is glass topped. According to legend, when Sam's brother Allan, who had the office next door, heard his brother slam something—the telephone or any other object within reach—too hard onto the table, he would automatically order a replacement piece of glass, knowing that it was likely to have been broken. The only curious feature of the interior is the number of doors in each office. These were probably designed to enable the many bootleggers who visited Mr. Sam to make an inconspicuous exit.* But the whole setup is best seen not as a sign of megalomania but as part of Sam's eternal drive towards respectability. Rather naïvely, as he told Robertson, he felt that "the older Jewish families were accepted by, and identified with, the English-speaking community" and hoped to be received by "the best people," as he called them, and thus "crown his efforts to bury the family's humble immigrant origins."

With increasing prosperity came greater social pretensions. By 1928, after four years in rented accommodation, Sam and Allan Bronfman felt confident enough to move into two adjacent houses in Westmount. This location was a total contrast to the slums which, in Montreal as in New York, housed most of the Jewish population. The move signaled that the family were now members, if not of the business elite, at least of the group of the city's richest citizens. For Westmount has always been very much the city's most exclusive residential neighborhood, indeed was a separate community until 2002. Its carefully secluded houses are perched on a series of winding streets high on the slopes of Mount Royal with a magnificent view over the city below towards the St. Lawrence River, surrounded by carefully tended gardens without any signs of such vulgar intruders as shops.

Mr. Sam's house was described by Peter Newman as "a turreted Victorian pile of instant medieval splendor." This is a gross exaggeration, for the house, while substantial and with room for a servants' wing over the garage, is otherwise an unremarkable example of Victorian red-brick solidity, less ostentatious than many other residences in the community, and nowhere near as grandiose as those built in Westmount by the most prominent Anglo-Saxon millionaires of the late nineteenth century.† Allan's

---

* I observed the same feature in the office of Swiss private banks, whose clients were naturally also not keen to be observed!
† Today Sam's house is owned by Charles's son Steven, who was married there in the summer of 2004, but it is otherwise unoccupied.

house—which burned down some years ago—was just behind Sam's, with a swimming pool in a space created by pulling down a house between them. To complete the family compound Harry and Abe both bought properties nearby. Here Saidye, far more socially ambitious and aware of her surroundings than her husband, could exploit her desire for a gracious lifestyle—when she visited the homes of the DCL directors with Sam she had taken copious notes the whole time and admitted that she had "learned a great deal from the way that people with different lifestyles and ideas decorated their houses."

"Compound" was a suitable word because by the late 1920s Canada's wealthiest citizens had become terrified of kidnapping. Victims included a member of the Low family, which owned the Carling brewery, but the two names on the top of kidnappers' lists were the brewer John Labatt and Sam Bronfman. In 1931 nine hoods arrived from Detroit aiming to extract half a million dollars through kidnapping Sam. They included one of Capone's close associates, two members of Detroit's infamous Purple Gang, one called Vinnie Massetti, and another, Mario "The Throat Man" Berchello. According to Robertson, Berchello "strangled people with a length of fish gut weighted at one end with a brass crucifix (the victim should not be denied a last sight of the cross) and a bronze St. Christopher medal which guaranteed a safe journey somewhere."

Even though this unappetizing crew got helplessly drunk in Toronto they eventually arrived safely in Montreal. Unfortunately for them Massetti got drunk again, followed an attractive girl to her room in the hotel where they were staying, and raped her. He assumed that she would be too terrified to complain, but she wasn't and identified Massetti. When he was led away to jail the police told his companions to stay put, but they fled—leaving Sam unaware that he had been a potential victim. He was lucky; three years later, after the kidnapping of the Lindbergh baby, these same hoodlums succeeded in kidnapping John Labatt, but were caught and revealed their earlier attempt to get at Mr. Sam. At that point Sam built a security fence round his property and, according to Richler, armed the chauffeurs who took the children to school.

The late 1920s marked a high water mark for the distillers. The peak years for smuggling were 1928 and 1929 when 1.1 million gallons of whisky worth over $118 million were exported to the United States. Throughout the decade the Canadian authorities had been unwilling to help the Americans; indeed Canadian exports of liquor were an important element in forging the country's increasing independence from the United States, which obviously wanted to ban the liquor traffic from its normally pliant neighbor. Canada's fledgling Department of External Affairs was fighting on two fronts: against British domination as well as the influence of the United States. As Marrus says, "Whisky, practically speaking, was extremely important in the achievement of full Canadian sovereignty"— and in the careers of men like Vincent Massey and Lester Pearson, key international officials after 1945. The official attitude was summed up by a magistrate in a smuggling case: "There is no burden cast upon us to enforce the laws of the United States." They were also helped by the slipperiness of Mackenzie King. In the words of J. Bartlett Brebner,[3] "King was a leader who divided least." His course was "marked by natural and by calculated confusion. . . . King lived and moved behind a dense screen of tedious verbiage."

Life became more difficult in 1930 when Mackenzie King was forced to ban exports directly shipped to any "dry" country like the US in an attempt to block American protectionism against Canadian wheat. He hid his volte-face in yielding to American demands by claiming that he "would prefer to go out of office if need be before being dictated to by liquor interests." The U-turn in policy naturally led journalists to wax sarcastic. Typically, the Toronto *Mail and Empire* remarked that "after eight years of sponsoring the rum running business, Prime Minister Mackenzie King has discovered that criminal gangs are engaged in the same business." The blow was worst for Harry Hatch because he could not claim that the small boats in "Hatch's Navy" were capable of exporting liquor across the Atlantic to the usual "cover" destinations. For as a result of the ban all the smugglers were immediately forced to switch nominal destinations to Cuba or other unlikely countries where compliant associates were ready to rubber stamp the documents required. Unfortunately the Cuban customs official chosen by Sam's brother Abe and his brother-in-law Barney Aaron was fired, but nevertheless continued to sign false landing certificates. This got Barney into trouble with the Royal Commission on Customs, although the real culprit was an American "whisky jobber" called August Carillo who bought the whisky on behalf of an American syndicate. But even on Rum Row life was getting difficult; in 1931 the US Coast Guard seized 2,929 vessels, a fifth more than two years earlier. But then the figure declined, for the Depression had seized hold of the liquor business, as of all other businesses.

But in reality it was domestic pressure from Canadian businessmen suffering from illegal imports that forced Mackenzie King and his ministers to tackle the serious problem connected with smuggling from rather than to the United States. This was difficult because by the late 1920s the liquor industry, which would obviously be badly affected by any changes, brought in C$28 million to the federal treasury. But about a quarter of the liquor shipped from St. Pierre was shipped back to Canada and thus avoided excise duty, and as exports slumped with the onset of the Great Depression the smugglers relied increasingly on importing whiskey and other highly taxed commodities back into Canada to avoid duty.

No one minded the export of whisky, but the tax evasion involved in the illegal imports—which resulted in Canadian liquor being cheaper in the US than in Canada—was something else. But the evasion was not confined to liquor, for over $100 million of untaxed goods, not just whisky but also cigarettes, radios, watches, and other high-tariff goods, were being smuggled in, costing the government an increasing amount of money through tax avoidance. In addition the imports also reduced the profits of government-owned liquor stores.* A special "Smuggling Committee" of the House of Commons reported how Jacques Bureau had even ordered the chief customs inspector at Montreal to ship him case after case of illegal samples. The official involved, J. E. A. Bisaillon, the Chief of the Preventive Service of the Department of Customs and Excise, was described by Ralph Allen as "one of the most incredible sitting ducks in the history of public malfeasance." He owned two houses in Rock Island, a picturesque village astride the frontier with the United States, which he used for two-way smuggling, not only of drink, but also of drugs. But the corruption was not confined to the public sector. In late 1929, as a result of a campaign by the *Financial Post*, it became clear that most of the country's leading brokerage firms were in the hands of swindlers and numbers of them went to jail.

In the end Bureau was merely "kicked upstairs" to a seat in the supposedly reputable Senate while several top civil servants in his department were forced to resign following headlines in the normally sober *Financial Post*, like "Weak men in Cabinet allowed sorry mess to fester." The scandal was big enough to require all Mackenzie King's considerable talents as a

---

* Imports included men's suits made in American prisons, and thus far cheaper than their Canadian-made equivalents.

parliamentary operator to avoid defeat. It did not help the government that George Boivin, Bureau's successor, came under such savage attacks that he died a few weeks after his appointment. The Smuggling Committee held hearings that provided a mass of material to increase public understanding of the links between the liquor business and the officials who were supposed to be supervising it. A Royal Commission on the department—always a good way to shunt a delicate subject into the sidings—then held hearings in fourteen cities. It soon became clear that the Canadian government had suffered losses of millions of dollars in sales tax not paid on liquor smuggled out of the country and then back again.

After their hearings in the west, the commission's austere chief counsel, Newton Wesley Rowell, reported on the domination of the Bronfmans and the alleged "reign of terror" they caused along the American border. The situation was not improved by the indefatigable efforts of their former partner, Meyer Chechik, to take advantage of the Bronfmans' awkward situation. But Harry triumphantly survived cross-examination. On his appearance before the commission Sam claimed that he "knew more about the liquor business than Mr. Harry Bronfman," but that he had no connection with Abe's operations—a claim that could not be disputed since the records of the companies involved had mysteriously disappeared.

Eventually the commission, having taken an estimated 15 million words of evidence, merely decided, as so many such enquiries have done over the years, what everyone knew already. Its report was the drabbest and narrowest of documents, concentrating almost exclusively on relatively uncontentious administrative changes. Nevertheless the general commotion led to a major reorganization of the preventive service and its absorption into the Mounties in 1932. DCL-Seagram came out of the report a great deal cleaner than its major competitors, all of which were accused of various infractions of the law—including large, undocumented political payoffs. As the headline in The Montreal Star put it, "Royal Commission gives Distillers Corp clean bill of health"—a headline which cheered Sam for the rest of his days. The biggest victim was Harry Stevens, the courageous Conservative member of Parliament who had initiated the enquiries, and who retired from public life, his career ruined because, as he told friends, "I refuse to submit to the liquor lobby."

The Bureau/Bisaillon scandal exacerbated the general contempt for the French-speaking Québecois, and not only among the Anglo-Saxons. In Richler's novel Bernard Gursky rebukes a friend: "Do not speak the language of the peasantry here, speak Yiddish"—although the French speakers appreciated the fact that Jews were far readier to learn their language than were Anglo-Saxons. For the racism was no joke; as late as the 1950s if anyone spoke French to an Anglophone in Montreal they were liable to be answered with the rebuke "speak white." As Mackenzie King's adoring biographer put it,[4] Bureau's indiscretions "seemed inconsequential to many French Canadians, who tended to assume that public office was a form of property which entitled the holder to some perquisites." This of course was rubbish. Everyone was in on the act when they had the opportunity—in other words the Bronfmans were in no way exceptional among Canadian businessmen, and it was pure anti-Semitism to single them out for blame. Hatch was involved, as was another Roman Catholic, Edmund Burke, who ran Labatt, a leading brewer; and Harry Low, who converted the old Carling brewery into what was virtually an export-only business.

Even before the ban on exporting directly to the US Harry Hatch's business had been badly affected when US agents finally started to crack down on smuggling across the Detroit River, and he was forced to develop a distribution channel through St. Pierre and Miquelon from scratch, which turned the tide against him in his battle with the Bronfmans. Before the clampdowns Hatch was earning 50 percent more than DCL-Seagram, but by the end of the decade the proportion had been reversed, largely because of his move away from the Great Lakes—and from water transport. Even though the use of railroad and cars had been made easier in 1929 with the construction of the Ambassador Bridge between Detroit and Windsor and the opening of a tunnel under the river a year later, only water transport could handle bulk shipments.

The Bronfmans had their own problems. Seven years after the face-off between Harry Bronfman and Cyril Knowles, the confrontation—which was probably not the only one in which one of the brothers had been involved—led to the most humiliating moment ever experienced by any member of the family and a scandal that left a permanent psychological scar on them all. On November 28, 1929, Harry was arrested by the Mounties at home in Montreal, indeed effectively kidnapped, and whisked off to Regina on a charge of attempting to bribe Knowles and of obstructing justice by tampering with witnesses. This was a blatantly political act by a new Conservative government in Saskatchewan. This had been elected with the help of a campaign by the Ku Klux Klan, which had invaded the province in 1926 under the slogan "One Flag, One School, One Race, One

Language," aimed primarily at the province's French-speaking minority but which obviously targeted the Jews as well. As Gray put it, Harry was an ideal scapegoat; "he was rich, he was a Liberal, but most of all he was a 'bootlegger' and a Jew"—accusations that the province had become a bootleggers' paradise had been a major factor in the Conservative victory.

During the trial Harry was saved by a combination of the powerful legal team that surrounded the family like a Praetorian guard throughout their story, and their "connections" with Ottawa. Knowles's evidence was backed up by the two officers who were with him. But the jury preferred to ignore Knowles's accusation of attempted bribery, and to accept the sworn assertion by his superiors in Ottawa earlier in the decade that the agent had never reported any attempt at corruption. Harry was acquitted, as he was after a trial (which had to be held twice) stemming from an incident when two agents tried to buy illegal liquor from David Gallaman, followed by an attempt to recover the liquor seized at the time. The acquittal was inevitable after William Denton, a key, though deeply disreputable, prosecution witness, was trapped by Harry's lawyers into admitting he was prepared to accept a bribe to change his evidence. Harry's double acquittal did not help his relationship with Sam. Far from it; Sam was so horrified that a Bronfman should have been involved in a heavily publicized trial that Harry never even became a director of DCL-Seagram but merely took charge of the LaSalle distillery.

By 1929 DCL-Seagram had grown into a major business with profits to the end of July that year of over C$2.75 million and assets of C$21.5 million, even though it did not handle any of the Scottish group's major brands. By July 1930 earnings had grown by a million dollars, but, in a clear sign of a slowdown, inventory had doubled, for new whisky was going into "wood" (i.e., barrels) faster than older whisky was being taken out for bottling and sale. Not surprisingly profits slumped by more than a million dollars, the following year they fell to little more than a million dollars. Sam was trapped because the family's investment trust, Brintcan, had advanced over C$4 million to expand warehouses to hold the steadily growing stocks of whisky.

The reason was simpler: The Great Depression hit Canada particularly hard. Worst hit was wheat: Canada accounted for a tenth of world production and two-fifths of world trade, but the business was ravaged by protectionism, other countries' efforts to compete and, even worse, the effects of the droughts in the first eight years of the 1930s, which substantially reduced yields. For it was the Depression, rather than governmental efforts, which nearly ruined Canada's liquor business in the three years after 1929. Even worse, the American market was dominated by a small number of "syndicates," which drove prices down by up to two-thirds, to a mere $5 a case for Canadian rye whisky, while Scotch halved in price to $10. Efforts by the distillers to impose a minimum price of $14 a case for "good" whisky proved unsuccessful.

Harry Hatch tried to bypass the Bronfmans by proposing a direct deal with the Scots, but they remained loyal to the man they had once called an "upstart Montreal distiller." Nevertheless even Sam wasn't in great shape. By 1933 the industry was reckoned to hold stocks enough to supply customers for sixteen years, and the Bronfmans' joint venture was naturally hardest hit because LaSalle was the largest distillery in North America, with a capacity of three million gallons a year. The situation was so dire that in 1932 Thomas Herd of DCL started merger discussions with Harry Hatch, whose profits had all but disappeared, falling from C$4 million in 1929 to a mere C$255,000 three years later. But Sam's valuation of the two companies was naturally disputed by Hatch and before discussions had gotten started the prospect of Repeal led to their abandonment. Yet as late as October 1932, a few weeks before the election that seemed certain to bring the ultra-wet FDR to power, Sam played down the prospects of Repeal, writing that "it is too optimistic to hope for favorable governmental action in the US on spirits for a considerable length of time."

Nevertheless, by 1933, thanks to Prohibition, Canada had a major liquor industry—in the previous ten years the number of distilleries had risen by eighteen to number eighty-seven, and officially recognized brand names, a mere five in the early 1920s, had risen to 150. However the Canadian government did not suffer too badly. It received C$152 million in taxes on liquor in the five years before Repeal, a level which had dropped by a mere fifth during the worst years of the Depression. Without the cash from liquor, far higher than the revenue from income tax, the federal government would have had a series of hefty budget deficits and not, as it did, a modest surplus. But that was no consolation to the increasingly desperate Sam Bronfman and Harry Hatch. Repeal came only just in time to save the Canadian whisky industry.

Six

GREAT EXPECTATIONS, GREAT DECEPTIONS

I'm so glad good whiskey has come back again
Don't have to drink no hooch, no more of this moonshine
Now I can drink good whiskey, without being afraid of dyin'
I can walk up and down the street without dodging every cop I meet.
— PEETIE WHEATSTRAW, "GOOD WHISKEY BLUES"

IT WAS REPEAL THAT PROVIDED SAM WITH THE OPPORTUNITY TO emerge from being merely a leading supplier in a relatively small corner of the liquor business into the dominant position he achieved, with astonishing speed, by the end of the 1930s. As *Fortune* put it in 1966, "Mr. Sam's career was the stuff of legend. A few thousand dollars at the beginning of the century became a few million by the early thirties. Then while other men's worth seeped away in the gray depression years, the few million doubled and doubled again." But it was not only the speed that was astonishing, it was the whole story that defied the hopes and expectations of almost all the other participants in the liquor industry, for he was virtually the only participant in the Great Liquor Race who read the runes correctly.

The race had been started on Sunday, March 12, 1933, a mere eight days after the inauguration of Franklin D. Roosevelt. At supper in the White House, following a first week devoted almost exclusively to salvaging the largely bankrupt American banking system, the president remarked, "I think this would be a good time for beer." He had already provided the broadest of hints as to his intentions in a naturally applauded election speech in which he had proposed "to increase the federal revenue by several hundred million dollars a year by placing a tax on beer." The proposal to abolish prohibition was a clear demonstration that the Prohibition lobby was dead.* The next

---

* That same week Congress ignored another seemingly all-powerful lobby when it reduced the pension paid to war veterans.

day, Congress, in no mood to reject anything the president proposed, voted to allow 3.2 percent beer. Prohibition finally expired on the afternoon of December 5, 1933, when Utah ratified repeal. Unfortunately many would-be celebrants were denied their drink. In a foretaste of the problems to be created by the emerging mass of restrictions on the production, and above all the sale of liquor, the police turned out to be far more effective in applying the new laws requiring the licensing of bars than they had been in controlling speakeasies. The excise tax, on which governments, federal and state, were counting, was another impediment to exuberant drinking.

Mr. Sam's achievements in the years following Repeal were the more remarkable considering his continuing legal problems in Canada, based on the accusation that the Bronfmans had been the ringleaders in a vast conspiracy to evade C$5 million in customs duties on liquor smuggled back into Canada. Over fifty other businessmen were also accused but the case was clearly centered on them—they were freed only on bail of C$100,000 each. This was immediately taken—wrongly—as an act of anti-Semitism by the new Conservative government under R. B. Bennett. He had been a successful lawyer and businessman and, writes J. Bartlett Brebner, he was a dictatorial figure: "He treated his cabinet colleagues as subordinates." He was pictured "as talking to himself, that is 'holding a Cabinet meeting.'"

It was Sam's Toronto lawyer, Peter White, who provided the most probable explanation for the prosecution: that it was the Mounties' revenge for their failure to nail Harry a few years earlier. They had been collecting evidence for at least two years and their zeal was also stimulated by anti-Semitism. As one senior Mountie put it, "Our good French Canadian citizens are not going to . . . allow these Jews to sit pretty and make a few more millions." For years Seagram's competitors circulated photographs of the "Bronfman boys" being led from their offices to the Mounties' headquarters. Rumors circulated that the sum in unpaid duties was up to C$70 million—they were taken so seriously that Dun & Bradstreet reduced Seagram's credit rating. The problem was exacerbated by the fact that Sam had neglected to subscribe to the Conservatives. In 1969, when he was eighty, he told Robertson that his only regret was "that he lacked the foresight to make contributions to both major parties, instead of one." Had he helped the Conservatives, "They might have refrained from making Harry the villain of the piece," for, as Robertson rightly emphasizes, all those involved in the liquor business were major political contributors. However

Richler provided another, and equally likely, explanation why Bennett allowed the prosecution to go forward. "When thousands of the unemployed marched on Ottawa, Bennett was convinced that the country was teetering on the edge of a revolution. Unable to provide bread he provided a circus."

The Bronfmans assembled their usual phalanx of lawyers to defend them. Sam naturally hated the whole affair, and not only because it questioned his respectability. Marrus quotes his friend Sol Kanee that "the courtroom was a special torture: It was the one place where Sam knew he was not in control." Fortunately the prosecution failed to establish any connection between the brothers and smuggling into Canada; helpfully all the records of Atlas Shipping and the family's holding company, Brascan, had been mislaid. As a result Judge Demarais threw the case out of court. But the verdict so infuriated the Mounties that they subpoenaed the judge's bank accounts and raided his safe-deposit box, but did not find any evidence. He was soon duly rewarded when he was appointed to the lucrative and undemanding job of chairman of the Quebec Liquor Commission. More mysterious was the fate of David Costley, a former bank manager from Regina employed by the Bronfmans, who hit the bottle after the trials and suffered a serious concussion in a street accident though he continued to work for them. On September 8, 1942, he left home to go to a baseball game but was never seen again. Another case that involved an attempted prosecution by the American authorities for bootlegging was squashed with the help of a fiery politician from the prairies, Aaron Shapiro, who had already acted for the family when Harry was prosecuted.

Before tackling the US market Bronfman had to first sort out his relationship with DCL. Immediately after Repeal the Scots had sent a senior executive to the US. They had hoped to utilize the stocks of aging whiskey in Seagram's cellars, but Sam objected, aware of their importance in the US, a country with inevitably minimal stocks of old whiskey. In the end the directors of DCL honored the handshake agreement they had made in 1926. Sam bought out their half-share in DCL-Seagram for $3.4 million, only $1 million of which was in cash, the rest payable over two and a half years at 5 percent interest. He also acquired the rights to some of the Scots' secondary brands within Canada.

The reason for the split was simple. In Weir's words, "DCL wanted a free hand to select the firm, or firms, that would best advance its interest in the

USA." As Ross told Sam, "After Repeal our brands will enjoy the same widespread acceptance in the United States as they have always done. We even dare to suspect that they may be even more popular than in the past"—as indeed they proved to be, soaring above sales of Canadian whisky. But there was a subtext. As Sir Ronald Cumming told Robertson, "The real reason [for the split] was that Sam's brothers, Abe and Harry, seemed to be accident-prone," and that "continuing association with the Bronfmans might prove embarrassing in future marketing in the United States."

In the short term the biggest single beneficiary from the split was the unlikely figure of Joseph P. Kennedy. He won over the suspicious Scots through his connection to the Roosevelt family. He had ridden on the future president's campaign train in the fall of 1932, and in September 1933 had traveled to Britain with FDR's son Jimmy. The implied close association with FDR so impressed the Scots that they awarded Kennedy's company, Somerset Distillers, the exclusive rights to import most of DCL's leading brands, including Dewar's, Gordon's gin and Haig & Haig, the brand which had accounted for the bulk of his sales during Prohibition. With the help of "medicinal licenses" he had acquired before setting sail for Britain, Kennedy built up a far bigger stock of imported spirits than any of his competitors and became the uncrowned king of Scotch in post-Repeal America. But DCL wavered between direct investment, investment in companies like National and Schenley, and relying on agents, so although sales of Scotch rose from 2.1 million US gallons in 1934 to 7.4 million in 1940, its share of the total whiskey market remained low. DCL's directors have been attacked for the deal they did with Mr. Sam and would indeed have done much better if they had stayed in the partnership, but then no one, not even Mr. Sam, could have dreamed that his success with blended whiskies would have provided them with an even greater reward.

By 1933 Sam was the most entrepreneurial and well-traveled liquor baron in Canada—indeed it was his constant journeyings the length and breadth of the United States that had provided him with the contacts he would need to build up his distribution network after Repeal. Saidye told an interviewer, "At first he had a hard time adjusting to business in the United States. He said that business was more competitive than in Canada." But for all his oft-proclaimed Canadian patriotism, the United States was the only market big enough to satisfy his hunger for success.

The need to spend so much time in the United States naturally created major domestic problems. Saidye was obviously reluctant to leave Montreal, with her family of four small children and her increasing involvement in Jewish community affairs. So Sam commuted by night train, spending four or five days a week in New York, and living in a suite at the Sherry-Netherland Hotel. Typically he made everyone's life a misery because of his refusal to make up his mind until the very last minute as to whether he would travel that night. The result, as his daughter Phyllis put it, was that, "My father does not 'live' anywhere. He was always between Montreal and New York."

In theory the respectable majority of the great American public should have been ready customers for "legitimate" liquor, for one (ironic) consequence of Prohibition was the way it had broadened the market for spirits, previously largely confined to adult males drinking in squalid saloons. In fact Prohibition had slipped through without encountering any serious organized opposition largely because hard liquor, and especially the saloons in which it was drunk, were so generally regarded as totally indefensible. Yet by the early 1930s the members of the Association Against the Prohibition Amendment included fifteen of the twenty-eight directors of General Motors and many other industrial and financial luminaries. In Marrus's words, "Widespread violation of the Volstead Act in the 1920s undercut the stigma against alcohol, turning liquor into an article of conspicuous consumption and a symbol of status." The result was the growing importance of alternatives to whiskey, with all its squalid associations. "Before prohibition," wrote *Fortune*, "gin went into Martinis and Negritas. The alcohol industry of the 1920s turned it into a drink." Gin was not the only one to benefit, so did rum, and even applejack.

The young appeared thoroughly infected with the alcohol virus. "As drink fever mounted," wrote Kenneth Allsop, "the age of initiation proportionately dropped"—with speakeasies clustered round every campus. Indeed during Prohibition alcohol became as fashionable among the young as drugs were to be forty years later, partly because they were a sign of rebelliousness. "Drinking," wrote Herbert Asbury, "became romantic and adventurous, the correct thing for all up-to-date young things to do. The boy who took a girl out during the 1920s and didn't give her a few drinks, or went to a party without a flask of liquor, was considered a poor sport, a clod, a drip."

It was significant that women lined up alongside men in bars when celebrating Repeal. For Prohibition had played a substantial, if obviously un-quantifiable, role in encouraging women's liberation. In 1931 a "dry" infor-mation committee wrote how "since 1920 the changed attitude of women towards liquor has been one of the most influential factors in the encour-agement of lawless drinking. Drinking in 1910 was a man's game, carried on in the saloon or club. . . . Drinking today . . . is a man and woman's game." And the women included the most respectable ones: A league formed by high-grade WASP ladies played an important role in mobilizing the anti-Prohibition forces in the late 1920s.

For the phony glamour around speakeasies, those—usually squalid—premises transformed the social acceptability of public drinking. Roosevelt helped the cause of public drinking when he told Americans to eschew the term "saloon" and to substitute the much less insalubrious word "tavern." As Herbert Asbury wrote in 1950, "there are now no 'saloons' in the United States. Instead there are bars, taverns, grills, and cocktail lounges"—though as he noted, "By and large it is the same old rose with the same old smell." Many of these might have resembled their predeces-sors but nevertheless the setup of a TV series like *Cheers* would have been unthinkable before Prohibition. The trend towards respectability had al-ready become noticeable in Canada, where, as Gray wrote, "Home drink-ing replaced public drinking and . . . excessive consumption and drunkenness became both less noticeable and less common."

It was generally assumed by everyone—including me before I started re-searching this book—that legitimate drinks would immediately replace bootlegged spirits, and that drinking would increase. Both beliefs turned out to be false. Of course, and quite justifiably, "bootleg" spirits had ac-quired an appalling reputation, as demonstrated by the soubriquets that Allsop uncovered. "With a kind of affectionate revulsion it was called cof-fin varnish, craw rot, rot-gut, panther piss, busthead, squirrel juice, horse liniment, razors, tarantula juice, junk, strike-me-dead, belch, sheep dip, and a hundred other horror-comic names." Tales of horror abounded: A Chicago chemist, while analyzing a shipment of bootleg hooch, spilled a little on a sink in his laboratory; it ate away the enamel. Dead rats were found in every one of a hundred barrels of mash confiscated by one Chicago policeman. And there were a great many cases of poisoning, often fatal, through drinking what was called "wood alcohol." This was usually methanol, or methyl alcohol, as opposed to the far less dangerous ethyl va-riety found in proper wines and spirits.

The most common problem associated with methyl alcohol (described as "moderately toxic" in the textbooks) was blindness, and it could easily be fatal. But then all sorts of alcohol, like the antifreeze used in engines, were employed—as it was with Russian air force personnel serving in Afghanistan in the 1980s. After reading a few of the many descriptions of hooch I was surprised that any regular drinker survived. The most telling example I came across was from a distiller called Tony interviewed by Asbury. He had been offered embalming fluid by an obliging undertaker as a raw material. "I knew a guy down on Long Island," said Tony, "put some of that stuff in his booze. He lost some good customers." "They didn't like it?" asked Asbury. "I guess not," he replied, "they died."

Nevertheless, by no means all bootleg liquor was awful. Indeed Prohibition had lasted long enough for most middle-class "wet" households to have their favorite supplier, "their" bootlegger who was as well regarded a supplier as, say, their favorite butcher or fishmonger. As late as 1959 bootleggers were reckoned to control a fifth of the country's spirits market, and naturally financed campaigns directed at ensuring that "dry" states and counties stayed that way. It was the time the song "took my Chevy to the levee but the levee was dry" was a hit, and in the early 1960s Tom Wolfe composed what amounted to a prose ode to moonshiners. (Trust in bootleg liquor was not confined to the United States. When the anise-based drink *pastis* was first legalized in France, bartenders would pour some of it into flasks pretending it was illegal and not the "factory-made stuff," which their customers thought was inferior.)

Unfortunately the shadow of bootlegging hung low over the whole industry for generations, preventing most reputable youngsters from thinking of entering so tarnished a business. The bootleggers' continuing success derived from a variety of reasons. They were helped by the way individual states and the federal government between them took over half the retail price of a bottle of spirits. Bootleggers were also helped by the first whiskeys to hit the streets after Repeal. "The first liquor to appear," wrote *Fortune* in November 1934, "was just as bad as everyone expected it to be." Newspapers gleefully reported that, for instance, "Of twelve alleged straight whiskies each contained large percentages of 'green' [i.e., raw] whiskey; of four blends of 'cut whiskies' each contained large percentages of plain alcohol, three were colored and one was colored with coal-tar dye." The "blends" were worse: "Calmly," wrote *Fortune*, "the repeal distillers took badly made new whiskey, added commercial alcohol and heaven knows what, and sat back to wonder why the ancient and honorable word 'blend' was fast acquiring a sinister connotation." But blends did not have to be so awful. They had to contain at least 20 percent of 100 proof straight whiskey together with whiskey or neutral spirits. Blending agents like sherry or prune juice could form only 2.5 percent of the total volume. Straight whiskies could only be sold after two years' maturation.

The situation was exacerbated by the chaotic licensing situation left by Repeal. Nineteen states—including such populous ones as Texas and Florida—were still dry. But so what? "Dry Florida had a splendidly sopping season last winter," reported *Fortune*. This provided a splendid opportunity for out-of-state suppliers. In 1950 Senator Estes Kefauver uncovered "the workings of a vast bootleg liquor ring operating out of Cairo, Illinois, which is running whiskey illegally into dry Southern states."[1] In nine others, including Ohio, Pennsylvania, and Michigan, liquor could be bought only in state-owned liquor stores, and even in the wettest of states there was a plethora of restrictions. Some were relatively sensible—for instance in Washington, D.C., there was to be no drinking in public parks or vehicles—but others were truly wacky. In Montana the use of the words "bar" or "saloon" was prohibited, in Wisconsin no liquor could be sold within a mile of hospitals for the insane, while in Louisiana no permits could be granted to present or former keepers of houses of ill fame.

The whole muddle made it extremely difficult to organize a national network to distribute liquor like, say, bars of soap—and since the total tax levy varied so greatly between states it was impossible to create a national advertising campaign based on price. In fact the idea of national advertising in so fragmented a market seemed ridiculous. It also made forecasting of likely demand virtually impossible. When *Fortune* published a thirty-page feature on whiskey in its November 1933 issue just as Repeal was finishing its passage through the state legislatures, it proceeded on two assumptions, both of which seemed legitimate at the time but both of which turned out to be false. The first was that demand for "legal" whiskey would rise; the second that the race would be won by older-established firms. What it did get right was that whereas "the first liquor industry was a whiskey business, the second an alcohol business, the third will be both. Its character will be shaped partly by legislation, partly by its own self-conscious character building, mostly by the economic law of supply and demand."

Demand, reckoned *Fortune*, would be at least 200 million gallons, the same as during Prohibition—and thus 45 million more than 1913, the last "normal" year, and over two-thirds of the liquor would be whiskey. Nevertheless *Fortune* pointed out the problems encountered in Britain by DCL, that the war and the depression had reduced whiskey consumption by two-thirds between 1914 and 1932. As a DCL internal memo put it, "Demand was also limited by the obvious shortage of money on 'the other side.'" Moreover the industry had been transformed since 1919. "In the old days," wrote *Fortune*, "there were a couple of thousand companies and individuals in the whiskey business. There were the distillers and the blenders and the rectifiers and the brokers and the wholesalers and the drummers and the rest. The basic commodity was not whiskey but warehouse receipts for whiskey. These the distillers sold as soon as the whiskey was barreled and what came of it afterwards was none of their affair." But, said *Fortune*, "Most people believe that the 1936 liquor business is more likely to be in twenty hands than in 200." The magazine was right: By 1935, according to a report by the US Treasury, a mere fourteen distillers produced 95 percent of all the liquor manufactured in the United States. Repeal had also reduced the number of brands sold in the country. Before 1920 no fewer than a hundred brands of Scotch were available—one of the best-selling was the now-unknown Mountain Dew. Even so, Scotch accounted for a mere 2 percent of whiskey sales. Here the Bronfmans had the advantage that they had been selling bottled whiskey since the mail-order days and had learned all about packaging, a vital element in post-Repeal America.

Not surprisingly the list of big players *Fortune* provided on the eve of Repeal was headed by the distillers who had accumulated stocks of "medicinal whiskey." This had been legal since 1929, but the quotas were based on possession of existing stocks, which provided a further advantage for the old-established. Biggest, with half the country's total stock and such brand names as Old Taylor, Old Crow, and Old Grand Dad, was National Distillers, headed by the improbable figure of Seton Porter, who had nursed the company through Prohibition. Porter was the very image of a Yale-educated WASP—"A gentleman whose best recognized attribute," wrote *Fortune* waspishly, "was his Racquet Club orientation." With the help of some other "Yalies" he had emerged at the head of a group modeled on DCL, which included the leading glassmakers, Owens-Illinois; Canada Dry, makers of the leading mixer; as well as suppliers of the mixers used in cocktails. National owned 1.4 million gallons of "priceless pre-war whiskey" as well as eight million distilled after 1929, but before 1934 was of course dependent on sales through druggists.

Porter was no fool, boosting the price of the stock by offering a "whiskey dividend."* But he was relying almost exclusively on straight whiskey, treating blends as down-market drinks, a policy echoed by all his competitors except Mr. Sam.

Second was Schenley, "Starting from behind, determined to catch up." Schenley had been owned by one Danny Weiskopf, formerly the right-hand man of Julius Kessler, the whiskey king of pre-Prohibition America. Weiskopf had sold out to Lew Rosenstiel. He had managed to build up considerable stocks of "prescription" whiskey, for as early as 1929 he had perceived that Prohibition was not going to be a permanent phenomenon and had proposed that he and Sam merge their businesses, buy out the small distilleries in the US, and thus virtually control the US liquor business. The same year a tentative partnership agreement was formed that would come into force on Repeal, although Sam ensured that he would need the agreement of his Scottish partners before completing the deal.

Harry Hatch, described by *Fortune* as the owner of "the biggest distilling business in Canada," was reckoned to have stocks of 14.5 million gallons in Canada and over C$5 million worth invested in Canadian government stocks. He had anticipated Repeal by building the largest distillery in the US in Peoria, Illinois—known before Prohibition as "the greatest distilling center in the world"—which was capable of turning out 50 million gallons a year. The new distillery was a sign that the Canadian distillers had turned their back on their home market. At the same time Hatch hired the local congressman, William Hull, as his sales director. And Hatch duly flourished, if not on the same scale as Mr. Sam; his profits soared from a measly $250,000 in 1932 to $6.3 million—on sales of $67 million—in 1938. At the time, noted *Fortune*, DCL-Seagram was reckoned to have 13.7 million gallons in stock, but was not thought to be in the race, and the name of Bronfman was not mentioned, in line with Sam's insistence on staying out of the limelight hoping that his past would be forgotten.

But the customers needed to be led, and they weren't. As Philip Kelly wrote, "We found out that there was great confusion in brand identity. People didn't know one brand from another. They didn't know the difference between a bond, a straight, and a blended whiskey. Age seemed to be

---

* A case of pre-Prohibition whiskey on every five shares, payable in late 1934—or when Mr. Porter decided.

important, but nobody knew why."[2] Moreover the purveyors of bourbon and other straight whiskies were living in a time warp, referring to the blenders as mere "rectifiers" or "chemists" who did not even get any recognition for aging the neutral spirits in their better blends. One observer described the old-timers as mere relics who in 1933 "emerged from retirement in frock coats and string ties to preside over 'technical operations.'"

"Selling brands to the American public after Prohibition," wrote Marrus, "was like exploring the surface of the moon: no one had been there before and procedures"—and the brands themselves—"had to be invented from scratch." The only exception was Scotch because such brands as Cutty Sark—the "real McCoy"—had been so hard to get during Prohibition. Scotch took the up-market drinker by storm, with a market share soaring from just over 1 to nearly 17 percent, for a short time anyway. The situation was summed up by Kelly, who had considerable experience of modern marketing methods when he had worked at Goodyear Tire. As he wrote: "Not only were there no 'national' brands in the United States in 1933, there was practically no 'brand identity'—the set of associations carried by particular products that prompted people to choose one over another." When Rosenstiel interviewed him Kelly realized that "Here was a great industry in the making, and as far as I could see, with few exceptions, it was in the hands of merchandising and advertising novices."

After a year it had become clear—in hindsight anyway—just how vulnerable the established companies were to an outsider who could produce up-market blended whiskey and market it in a manner suitable for a post-Prohibition drinking public, with its, so far unsatisfied, thirst for palatable blended whiskies. The thirst for a reputable brand was intensified by several factors. First, of course, the terrible reputation of all types of liquor during Prohibition. Second, the fact that even before 1920 four-fifths of all whiskey was sold in bulk to owners of saloons and liquor stores, thus preventing the growth of any serious brand, and third was the slump.

Virtually all the investment had gone into refurbishing pre-Prohibition distilleries, which were inevitably over twenty years old, leaving very little money for promoting individual brands. Two of the three leaders were from major companies: Crab Orchard, a cheap blend from National Distillers, and Golden Wedding, a pre-Prohibition favorite from a Schenley stable of 127 brands—a number proving a total lack of marketing concentration, though Schenley did spend $1.3 million on publicizing its leading brand. Rosenstiel could justifiably boast that "It's all whiskey. . . . No alcohol or spirits added"—a claim based on the assumption that any blend would contain a majority of mere "alcohol," which would be "hot," (i.e., newly distilled), resulting in an inevitably down-market "commodity brand." But the impetuous Rosenstiel had a scatter-gun approach, for he also imported such drinks as Bacardi rum and Gonzalez Byass sherries. But the biggest surprise was the artificially aged whiskey created by the Publicker Commercial Alcohol Company in Philadelphia. This, they boasted, was a whiskey which was apparently seventeen years old but had in fact been aged for a mere twenty-four hours. Cleverly the makers turned the age into a virtue. "Don't fill your stomach from a nasty old keg," exhorted their advertisements.

Publicker's brazen advertisements did nothing to discourage the idea that blends were inevitably down-market products. Everyone in the industry—including and indeed especially Rosenstiel—simply assumed that blends were inevitably salable only as "commodity" or "fighting" brands, to be promoted purely on price, sold rather grudgingly until supplies of real whiskey were sufficient to allow Americans to return to their old love, straight whiskey. As *Fortune* put it: "One part whiskey to four parts alcohol and water will make a drink that might not satisfy a Kentucky Colonel but will be plenty good enough for you." Rosenstiel showed his scorn for blends by swearing that he would never cut his better whiskies with neutral spirit. So his blends were made with young whiskies, most obviously Old Quaker, which was launched with the motto, "You don't have to be rich to enjoy rich whiskey."

As early as November 1933 *Fortune* had hit the nail on the head when it asserted that within three years, "The whiskey company that is in the lead will be the whiskey company that proves itself most able in merchandising." They would be able to exploit "the business methods developed during the 1920s—national distribution of nationally known brand names, pushed by national advertising." Whiskey was special because it required the additional capital tied up for years in aging stocks—but both Mr. Sam and Harry Hatch had adequate stocks and the requisite funds, thanks to their success as bootleggers.

Hatch could not really understand his success. "Sometimes I pinch myself," he once told a friend, "and ask, is this really Harry Hatch?" Even Mr. Sam was rather daunted by the problems of going it alone. For a time in 1933 he had hopes of going into partnership with Schenley—in 1929 Mr. Sam had invested $585,000 in one of Rosenstiel's major ventures, a distillery producing exclusively medicinal spirits, and had bought a 20 percent stake in Schenley. Moreover the two were virtually the only men in this, the very newest of industries, who had been "in the business before the tables were set" in the words of one veteran. Mr. Sam always claimed—probably correctly—that he was deterred once and for all from going into partnership with Rosenstiel when he visited the Schenley distillery. "I told him from the outside his distillery was a piece of junk and that on the inside it was even worse." The final breaking point came when he saw that Rosenstiel was selling whiskey "hot off the still"—i.e., immediately after it was distilled, and not aged in accordance with Mr. Sam's lifelong credo.

From then on Rosenstiel—whom Sam invariably referred to as Rosenschlemiel*—and the low standards he stood for made him Mr. Sam's number one enemy. "I have no respect or admiration for that man," Mr. Sam once said with unusual reticence. "Rosenschlemiel" retorted by referring to Seagram, still nominally headquartered in Montreal, as an "alien" company. But at the time it took a lot of self-confidence to resist the temptation to make quick profits by selling raw whiskies. In later years, despite Mr. Sam's increasing dominance of the industry, his rival remained an obsession. Old Seagram hands remember how everyone in 1430 Peel Street could hear the sound of his curses when he was talking about the enemy, and Mr. Sam's personal secretary in New York, Golda Morrow, would phone the most fashionable florists in the city to discover whether Mr. R. was in town by finding out if he was ordering any flowers—a habit of his when he had been away. This was not an unusual piece of detection, for she was often entrusted with the mission of finding out, often through a network of other personal assistants, about the plans of Seagram's rivals.

Mr. Sam's failure to agree a deal with Rosenstiel really hit him, for he came down with severe flu, with temperatures of up to 105 and streptococcal throat, unbeatable before the arrival of sulfa drugs. Saidye immediately took the train from Montreal to take care of him in the Sherry-Netherland Hotel, and cook him simple dishes like porridge and soup, suitable for an invalid—after ten years of marriage she confessed that she had never learned to cook. This when her father was in a New York hospital with cancer and her mother was taking care of her four children—Minda, born

---

* In *The Joys of Yiddish*, Leo Rosten provides seven definitions—and four spellings—for the word *schlemiel*, ranging from a simpleton to a born loser, quoting, "no one pays attention to that *schlemiel*."

in 1925, Phyllis in 1927, Edgar (the first, eagerly awaited son) in 1929, and Charles in 1931. At the time all of them had whooping cough. But Sam was strong enough to tell Rosenstiel he wouldn't see him: "We have nothing to discuss." At that point, according to Robertson anyway, Rosenstiel "all but wept as he begged 'for just a minute with my friend.'" After Mr. Sam's recovery Saidye insisted he retain the suite in the hotel, known as the "Bronfman suite," for over twenty years. Rejecting any deal with Rosenstiel left him without any ally in his attempt to dominate the American market. Nevertheless within a year he had succeeded in reaching his apparently ridiculous target.

Seven

_____

CROWNING GLORY

Distilling is a science, but blending is an art.
— SAM BRONFMAN

BEFORE MR. SAM LAUNCHED HIS REVOLUTIONARY BLENDS OF American whiskies in the second half of 1934 he was virtually unknown. Mr. Sam was offering two American blends, 5 Crown, and above all, 7 Crown, together with the imported VO. They were the first brands of whiskey to be promoted nationwide, and the first to demonstrate than an American blend could be a decent drink. They set new standards and greatly helped wean Middle America from its previous dependence on whiskey bought from their favorite bootlegger as the only reliable source of supply. For Mr. Sam persuaded the great American public that a blend produced in North America need not be rot-gut and could compete on almost equal terms with blended Scotch.

Selling an up-market blend was based on his sensible belief that "lower price blends pay a little overhead. Deluxe products are where you make the money." To ensure that his whiskies would be of the right quality he kept out of the market on a large scale until well into 1934. "I let the parade go by," was how he put it, even though "other US distillers were enjoying a sales bonanza"—a claim that rather ignored his attempts at forming a partnership with "Rosenschlemiel." Sam's insistence on copying the Scots by maturing even his neutral spirits in oak further delayed the process. And unlike the rest of the industry he confined his marketing efforts to a mere handful of whiskies. It required considerable courage to go against the assumption that drinkers would want "straight whiskies" as the only ones guaranteeing a genuine product. But in one respect he did hedge his bets,

for his whiskies, unlike American "straights" were mixable: Indeed "7 &
7"—7 Crown and 7 Up—became the normal way his major brand was consumed. Sam had another advantage. *Fortune* noted that "the blending of
whiskies from different batches"—which inevitably varied from barrel to
barrel—"to produce a consistent taste is one of the achievements of the
Seagram organization." For DCL had taught him to "marry" whiskies, not
merely to mix them. He—or someone within Seagram's—even set out a
formal description of the process:

> The art of successfully combining a large number of meticulously se-
> lected, mature, high-quality whiskies, each with its own flavor and
> other desirable characteristics, in such a skillful and judicious manner
> that the whole is better than the sum of its parts and each makes its
> own significant contribution to the final blend without any one, how-
> ever good, predominating. The key was to produce a drink which re-
> mained the same over the years.

Mr. Sam himself was a master blender with a superb palate—which he
protected by ensuring that his lunch consisted exclusively of dishes like
boiled beef or delicately steamed fish that were not going to interfere with
his taste buds. But, in his later years anyway, he was not so fussy about his
breakfast, which, according to Leo Kolber, invariably consisted of a couple
of eggs "fried so hard they could bounce off the floor," washed down with a
gin and tonic "to get rid of the greasy taste."

One of the major problems in going it alone was that because he
couldn't draw on Schenley's stocks he had to buy his way into the whiskey
market. In November 1933 he picked up the historic Rossville Union Distilleries at Lawrenceburg in Indiana, together with its crucial stock of four
hundred thousand gallons of whiskey. Because only he and Harry Hatch
were at the head of quoted companies they could pay largely in shares
rather than precious cash. As a result Mr. Sam could acquire Rossville for
shares worth $3.8 million and only $2.4 million in cash. Sam sent Harry in
to modernize the distillery at a cost of $3 million and a few months later
bought the Maryland distiller Calvert Distilling Company for a further
$1.5 million in shares—craftily he allowed Emil Schwarzhaupt, the experi-
enced whiskey trader handling the deal, to set his own price. The distillery
brought with it Calvert, an excellent brand name.

But even in late 1934, *Fortune* had not grasped Mr. Sam's importance,

noting merely, and correctly, that Seagram had started its campaign by importing high-grade Canadian whiskies, like VO, sold at over $2 a pint, far
more than "domestic" blends. In the US market, VO, always the favorite
tipple of Mr. Sam, and indeed of his son Edgar, was a six-year-old blend—
the "flavoring" whiskies were usually six or seven years old. Helped by what
one old-timer describes as "a teeny bit of Scotch," it was far smoother than
the original Canadian whisky, indeed its smooth style set what *Fortune*
called the "carriage trade tone with which Seagram seeks the middle-class
trade," an appeal which characterized all his efforts. But in talking to *Fortune* for the comprehensive article on the liquor trade the magazine published in October 1934, Mr. Sam had, unusually, hidden his light behind a
front man, Henry I. Peffer, chairman of the Seagram's US distribution subsidiary, Seagram-Distillers Corporation, a reticence probably due to the
family's tangles with the law. Sam was not mentioned by name in the article and the only reference to the Bronfmans is as "four Jewish brothers"
who "shared control of Distillers-Seagram" with DCL. Even the purchase
of DCL's shares in their joint Canadian company was attributed to "a Seagram's syndicate."

Sam, intuitively, had caught the mood of the times. As he told his employees, the demand for light blends was natural: "Today [drinkers] don't
want heavy cloth in their suits; they want everything light and easy. They
don't want stiff collars anymore." For, as he told Robertson, in the 1930s
there were "lighter foods, lighter tobaccos, lighter clothes, lighter shoes,
lighter coffee, and lighter tea. People enjoy things on the lighter side, and
I'll stake everything I've got that they will enjoy lighter whiskies." Philip
Kelly, who had switched allegiance to Mr. Sam after internal maneuverings
had induced him to leave Schenley, understood the point perfectly well.
"Bonded whiskey and straight whiskey were too heavy. They contained too
many congeners, higher alcohols, furfurals, tannins, acids, and so forth.
This had a bad effect on people, because the stuff got in their liver and
gave them a hangover. It was these heavy whiskies that gave the liquor
business a bad name and a bad smell." Sam and his crew "were dedicated to
making a light blended whiskey which, chemically speaking, had one-
twelfth the amount of toxic elements found in the heavier whiskies." But
they weren't cheap, because of a special tax of ninety cents a gallon on rectified spirit.

In fact all the Canadians had a major advantage with the relatively soft,
easy-drinking blends they created—either in Canada or in the US—

blends which included Harry Hatch's highly successful Canadian Club. They were recognizably different from Scotch, and above all light and smooth. In staking his all on light blends Mr. Sam was anticipating the post-war 1945 trend towards lighter Scotch whiskies, a trend exemplified by Cutty Sark and J & B Rare. The public followed. In a later article *Fortune* pointed out that Sam "taught the American companies a severe lesson in merchandising firewater in the modern manner, like a food product. Mildness and uniformity were his formula, following the standard estimate of the American taste developed in the 1920s by merchandisers of ham and cheese and cigarettes."

Mr. Sam was helped by the strict definitions of "straight" whiskies. At the top were the "bottled in Bond" brands, which could only be the product of a single distillery, thus greatly limiting the supply. But even normal rye or bourbon whiskey could not be sold through the sort of national advertising campaign launched by Mr. Sam. *Fortune* noted that "they could not sell much bourbon in the East nor much rye in the West"—though Rosenstiel tried to avoid the problem by advertising the same whiskey as rye in the East and bourbon in the South and West. But not only did Mr. Sam know what was good, but, thanks largely to the intensive study he had made during his visits to Scotland in the 1920s, he knew how to make good whiskey. For him quality began with the humble yeasts used in the fermentation process. "Yeasts," he used to proclaim, "are the workhorses of the distilling industry"—there were no fewer than 240 strains in Seagram's "yeast room." The attention to detail continued with the stringent hygienic conditions throughout his distilleries and was boosted by his obsession with the blending process. He also emphasized the importance of his quality control department which, says Marrus, "dispatched inspectors to Seagram facilities like commissars, responsible only to central command and completely outside the plant manager's chain of command." This led to such apparent extravagances as throwing away hundreds of thousands of bottles every year, for all his products had to be in the right bottles and adorned with the best labels. The logical conclusion of the process was the endless Saturday mornings he spent discussing suitable bottles with his suppliers. Labels were one of his favorite obsessions, designed individually for each product, with VO and Crown Royal decorated with expensive graphics.

His two new American blended whiskies were 5 Crown, and, above all, 7 Crown. The latter made no claim as to its specific age; both the "neutral" and "flavoring" whiskies were four years old. In fact it combined the best features of both American and Canadian whiskies. Like Canadian whiskies all the contents had been aged for at least four years, hence the claim that it contained "fine aged neutral grain spirits," and, like American whiskies, the blends all contained at least 20 percent of "flavoring" whiskey—as against the 10 percent or less in many Canadian blends. By contrast 5 Crown was more ordinary since the grain whiskey was not aged.

The two blends were launched in June 1934 with a fanfare in front of 175 distributors in the ballroom of the Waldorf Astoria. Everything about the launch was revolutionary. It was high profile, it involved blends, and it heralded immediate national distribution of new whiskies. The event was orchestrated by General Frank Schwengel, the newly appointed vice president in charge of sales. He was a real general, having risen through the ranks in World War I, earning numerous medals on the way. After demobilization he worked in marketing and advertising and met Sam when seeking the Seagram account for his agency. Sam, always susceptible to "class acts," was naturally much taken by what Marrus describes as Schwengel's "crisp, no-nonsense military style" combined with a quietly distinguished appearance unusual in the liquor business. Indeed it was by no coincidence many of the men he trusted were "men of distinction," had the bella figura, the suavity, he himself so notably lacked—though they had to perform, whether it be as salesmen or advisers. Sam gave Schwengel an apparently impossible target: to sell five million cases of whiskey, about 15 percent of the total US market. He was up against not only Schenley, but also the combined forces of Hiram Walker and National Distillers, a partnership that gave the Americans access to Harry Hatch's stocks of both malt and grain whiskey. Although he was hindered by a $2-a-case import duty, Hatch had successful brands, above all his premium blend Canadian Club, and by April 1934 was selling one hundred thousand cases a month in the US. But it was Mr. Sam's willingness to concentrate exclusively on blends that put him in pole position.

Even before 7 Crown had proved a winner its success was celebrated in one of the songs written for the major personal events—above all, the regular celebrations of Sam's birthdays—which punctuated the year at Seagram. They may seem embarrassing to us but they were sung with real feeling by the Seagram "family"—especially by the distributors, who didn't feel the lash of Mr. Sam's tongue as frequently as the company's executives. Typical was:

Our Seven Crown's booming
Our VO's zooming
Other brands have fallen away.
Oh, there's fun and there's glory in selling this line
Everyone is saying that Seagram is fine.
Forever and ever, let's all sing together,
Seagram is a grand old name.

By the end of 1934, 5 Crown was the biggest selling brand in the country at five hundred thousand cases a month. Although the advertisements boasted that "the youngest whiskey in the bottle is five years old" it soon faded and virtually disappeared from the market as drinkers realized that it was markedly less smooth than 7 Crown simply because it contained a majority of unaged "neutral" spirit. Within a few years the Seagram blends, principally VO and 7 Crown, accounted for three in five of the bottles of blends sold in the United States. At Christmas magazines were full of advertisements for every type of liquor. Fortunately Mr. Sam understood advertising, in the 1930s at least, just as well as he understood blending. He adjured potential buyers to "Treat whiskey as a luxury"—importantly, one a lot of Americans could afford once in a while. For he had grasped that a country crucified by the slump needed a touch of inexpensive luxury—an understanding he shared with his fellow Jews, the men who ran Hollywood studios with their production of escapist, romantic, funny films—and would pay a little more to get it.

But Mr. Sam was always aware of the danger of a backlash against liquor. He had grasped the need to temper the salesmanship with an appeal to moderation, striving always to transform the image of an industry—and a company—thought of as disreputable and irresponsible. "A pint of [our] whiskey," he pointed out in a 1934 advertisement, "will bring you more enjoyment, more satisfaction, than a quart of whiskey of dubious quality." This was part of a daring pioneering campaign, which, at $100,000 a month, was far bigger than any of his competitors'. Sam went even further by setting a trend followed by the rest of the industry only several decades later. He combined the virtues of quality and moderation in a single advertisement. The first one on the theme had a bold headline: "We who make whiskey say 'Drink moderately.'" Later variations in a campaign that lasted for thirty years included "Drinking and Driving do not mix," and another "One for the road—be sure it's coffee." On Father's Day a year later came a campaign saying that children can never respect "a man who used liquor unwisely." Above all, and in response to the earlier claims by Canadian prohibitionists that drink was bought with money that should have gone to support the family, he proclaimed that "we who make whiskey say 'We don't want your bread money.'" Mr. Sam's attitude was summed up in another advertisement: "If the point of drinking is to get drunk, then you're not our customer." Not surprisingly the advertisements led to hundreds of approving newspaper editorials. All this was part of Mr. Sam's overwhelming objective: to give dignity to products normally maligned as low-class, if not downright dishonorable, to live up to his company motto: "Integrity, Craftsmanship, and Tradition." For the way his whiskies were marketed provided the respectability and reliability lacking in every other product on the market—apart from the very limited quantities of "straight" or bourbon whiskey.

(In Canada, Sam and Allan also pioneered future marketing devices with a whole series of sponsorships, including marathon snowshoe races, a typically Canadian sport, over the nearly 150 miles between Montreal and Quebec City, with prizes of up to C$10,000.)

The sheer speed of the Bronfmans' success was breathtaking. In the two years following Repeal Mr. Sam introduced the products and the people who would make Seagram the dominant force in the American liquor business for two generations—and, incidentally, transform the family from mere millionaires into what would in today's money would have been billionaires. As early as 1936 Seagram's profits were over $60 million in the US and $10 million in Canada. Part of his success was due to his capacity for making speedy, intuitive, and imaginative appointments when he so chose—even though he normally refused to make up his mind until the last possible minute. He was at his best in his treatment of Julius Kessler. In pre-Prohibition days Kessler had headed the Whiskey Trust of Kentucky, a marketing pool of over forty distillers, which, it was said, "sold more whiskey than anyone living." Like Schwengel, the Hungarian-born Jew Kessler had real presence; he was described by one friend as "the handsomest man in the industry, gray curly hair in abundance, a beautiful handlebar moustache, a handsome likeness to Franz Joseph, Emperor of Austria." "Exuding old-world charm and of aristocratic bearing," wrote Marrus, Kessler projected precisely the kind of image Sam wanted for his liquor business. To *Fortune* he "was an exception, a prodigal Jew."

With the advent of Prohibition Kessler had returned to Budapest. Unfortunately his secretary's boyfriend absconded with his savings, reckoned at $2 million, after which she committed suicide. In 1930 he returned from Budapest virtually penniless, largely to pay irregular visits to see his old Jewish friends in the liquor business, to offer his services at $200 a month. "Each of Mr. Kessler's old friends had been sorry for him," wrote *Fortune*. "Each had written a check and pushed it across his desk. Mr. Kessler has torn up all the checks and returned to Budapest." But by 1933 he was back again, an apparently broken seventy-eight-year-old. Sam rose to the opportunity. While Rosenstiel had proposed merely to use Kessler's name on one of Schenley's regular products, Sam set up a new subsidiary, the Julius Kessler Distilling Company, putting the old man nominally in charge and his name in enormous type on bottles of "Kessler's Special." Kessler spent $1.5 million of Mr. Sam's money to produce his first blend, which became an immediate success, selling up to a million cases a year. Mr. Sam would refer to Kessler as "the general of the liquor industry" and naturally Kessler returned the compliment, working for Mr. Sam until his death in 1941. It did not matter that his whiskey was competing with other Seagram brands, for one of the keys to the Seagram system was that each brand had its own distribution system which competed with the group's other brands—a tactic designed, like so many of the aspects of Mr. Sam's operations, to copy DCL's marketing policy of offering several competing blends.

Another key appointment resembled that of Schwengel—although it was not the result of a single meeting but of a prolonged succession of lengthy interviews. Mr. Sam badly needed someone to promote Lord Calvert, a whiskey he had decided would be a suitable counterpart to Seagram's top products as the most expensive blend on the US market. Like Schwengel, William Wachtel was a distinguished businessman, sales manager of a large biscuit company in Kansas City, "With a pencil-thin moustache," according to Marrus, "that made him look like Adolphe Menjou," a film star then considered the epitome of aristocratic charm. Mr. Sam took to him and offered him two alternatives, to head up the sales organization of either the flourishing Seagram or the ailing Calvert brands. Shrewdly Wachtel appreciated that he could gain far more kudos if he chose the Calvert job. He soon discovered that Mr. Sam had already filled the Seagram slot. Wachtel's shrewdness ensured that he became one of Mr. Sam's few friends—most of whom, like Wachtel, were employees who had worked with him since the 1930s.

Wachtel was so successful that, as Mr. Sam put it, the competition he provided "straightened out the Seagram organization and got them off their fanny." Wachtel's first advertising effort for Lord Calvert was a "switch campaign" on why drinkers had switched to Calvert. But his greatest success featured "Men of Distinction" who naturally favored Lord Calvert. Originally they used models, but Wachtel "was nearly knocked off his chair," wrote Kelly, when he heard that the man in one advertisement was also posing for the—by no means fashionable—underwear in Montgomery Ward's mail order catalog. After that shock Wachtel employed real people—including real celebrities, some from Hollywood. The soubriquet entered the American vocabulary—as in the Liza Minnelli song "I heard you were a man of distinction" in *Cabaret* forty years later. Nevertheless, as Kelly wrote, the Seagram disease of corporate politics, "the struggle for power, jealousies at the top, a determination to get even, and the desire for change, killed one of the greatest campaigns Calvert ever had," for Mr. Sam eventually grew to feel that the campaign concentrated too much on the men involved and not on his precious whiskey.

The third arm of the Seagram business was the cheaper Carstairs brand, which he had bought in 1937 and which became part of Seagram's Calvert division. Since it had not been sold in the "monopoly" states where prices were fixed by the state-owned liquor board, he could indulge in flexible pricing to compete with his rivals' lower-priced blends. Within a couple of years Wachtel (with Kelly's help) had transformed the Carstairs brand from a money loser to one that sold over 1.3 million cases of its White Seal in a mere seventeen states. But Wachtel was not just a businessman, he was one of the few (mainly in other liquor businesses) who deliberately employed Negroes in responsible positions—and in 1955 was given the George Washington Carver Award for his work in eliminating racial bias. The lack of discrimination was common throughout the Seagram empire but could be based on sound commercial sense. When Mr. Sam's elder son, Edgar, integrated the previously segregated dining room and other facilities at the distillery in Maryland responsible for Calvert whiskies, one reason was that "Calvert products were big in the then black market." It was also Edgar who went to the White House in 1964 to make an agreement with Lyndon Johnson about equal opportunities in the workplace.

The rivalry was encouraged by the way that, as Philip Kelly wrote, "Each division had complete autonomy. We met together once a month to discuss trade conditions in general; at that time we were supposed to make a complete revelation of any special deals we had pending." The competition was real, for Mr. Sam thoroughly enjoyed "promoting competition amongst executives" as Maxwell Henderson noted, and would play them off each other asking them for opinions of their colleagues. Typically, the national sales manager of the Calvert division once complained bitterly that his top brand, Lord Calvert, was overshadowed by 7 Crown at official Seagram functions, and managed to obtain parallel exposure for his own whiskies.

But the key figure, albeit one whose role was played down or even totally ignored in the official histories of Seagram, was Victor Fischel. The "party line" held that Fischel was merely a salesman who had met Mr. Sam in Montreal when he tried to sell Mr. Sam a sign for the exterior of his building, and had been hired either as a salesman or, in another version, as a guide at the LaSalle distillery. In fact he was a vital element in the Seagram organization as soon as he was hired in 1928 as a rum runner, a middleman between Mr. Sam and his customers in the United States. Previously Mr. Sam seems to have been a one-man band in this delicate aspect of the business, since none of his brothers was suitable for dealing with bootleggers, and in any case he tried as far as possible to avoid contact with them.

Fischel's role was downplayed because he reminded the family of their origins and was the very obverse of the image of respectability so successfully conveyed by other executives. He was the exact opposite of men like Wachtel; a burly, red-headed thug, frankly looking rather a slob even in carefully posed photographs, a man who thoroughly enjoyed telling tall tales of his days ferrying cargoes of liquor round the US and dealing with the bootleggers when they visited Montreal. Yet he was so close to Mr. Sam that he drove Saidye to the hospital when she went into labor before giving birth to Edgar, an episode he recounted frequently and gleefully, and which naturally infuriated Edgar and helped set the stage for the battle between the two in the early 1960s. Nominally Fischel was merely a vice president in charge of sales and distributors, but was so important that both the twentieth and twenty-fifth anniversaries of his arrival at Seagram were celebrated by two of the banquets that formed so frequent a feature of life with Sam Bronfman.

Fischel's language was stupendously vulgar, even by the standards set by Mr. Sam. "You know how to sell liquor," he once enjoined a hundred of his salesmen, "you stick your thumb up the guy's arse and push until he buys." But he was trusted, above all by Seagram's distributors, because he was one of them, a former bootlegger who had gone straight, a poacher turned gamekeeper. For many bootleggers simply could not come to terms with the idea of legitimacy. Even Meyer Lansky, in Robert Lacey's words, "had become accustomed to doing things the crooked way" and preferred to invest in illicit stills. In any case, after Repeal the Mafia had moved on to infest other business sectors as well as trade unions. By 1950 Senator Kefauver's enquiry into crime found that the Mafia were involved in seventy business sectors, with liquor by no means the most important. Nevertheless he also found that "all the major distillers have granted franchises to hoodlums, including some in the top ranks of organized crime."

But Fischel was the ideal person to deal with the distributors responsible for hustling VO, 5 Crown, and 7 Crown, and at the time was generally recognized as the key driving force behind the brands' success. For the final link in the profit machine lay in Mr. Sam's pioneering treatment of the distributors, those crucial middlemen. Fischel took seriously his motto "men make markets." He was backed up by an incomparable setup. Nothing was too good for the distributors—who were after all independent businessmen, perfectly entitled to take on competitors' brands, and if there was no suitable candidate in a state or city, Arthur Edelstein, a Seagram associate, would be financed and installed as a distributor. Seagram also employed thousands of salesmen—"missionaries" they were called—who visited the stores and ensured that Seagram's products got a proper display. Then there were the engineers who would design and build the increasingly sizable warehouses required by the distributors. During the war—when quite a number of his distributors were indicted for black market activities— Fischel increased the respect he enjoyed by the equitable way he carried out the rationing system necessarily imposed on Seagram through lack of stock at a time of increasing demand.

Above all he and the distributors he appointed were virtually alone in being able to cope with the very different situations in individual states; they had an intimate knowledge of the official regulations and regulators and the ways to bend them to their—and Seagram's—benefit. For Repeal had left the control of the sale and distribution of alcohol under state control. The result was an incomprehensible tangle. In seventeen "control" states the state government had a monopoly of distribution, and elsewhere there was a three-tier distribution system in which distillers (or importers in the case of Scotch), distributors, and retailers all took their cut. The complexity involved vastly increased handling charges. It did not help that the distillers' salesmen were not allowed to sell directly to the retailers—all they could do was to persuade them to concentrate on the Seagram brands. This left a lot of power in the hands of the distributors, and here Fischel, whose incomparable contacts with them dated back to Prohibition days, came into his own. A friend remembers a national tour of the United States with Fischel in the late 1960s when they were greeted at airport gates by nefarious figures who would hustle them in a limo to the back room of a local restaurant before discussing business.

Fischel believed in what he termed as "a fair profit to the wholesaler, a fair profit to the retailer, and a fair price to the consumer." He could protect the wholesalers and retailers from ex-bootleggers pressuring them to buy from "friendly" suppliers. Fischel knew all the tricks. He was, for instance, behind the tradition of giving long lavish annual dinners in a famous steakhouse to leaders of the New York police force. There was an astonishingly strong mutual bond between Fischel and his protégés, most of them Jewish ex-bootleggers. He knew them all, he participated in their lives, their family joys and woes. If Mr. Sam was the patriarch of the Seagram family then Fischel was the godfather.

Above all they were loyal, from a mix of greed, fear, and genuine attachment to the firm, or rather, to Mr. Sam personally. Indeed it was not until 1950 that they were given written contracts, a step hailed as "revolutionary" by Seagram's publicists. The next year Mr. Sam ensured the loyalty of the second generation by forming the Seagram Family Achievement Association for their children, a group known to insiders as the "lucky sperm club." The three-day event celebrating its formation was far from being merely a sentimental gesture; it was a way for the Seagram people to judge the worth of the second generation and to be able to weed out those unlikely to survive the consolidation they knew would dominate the distribution system over the next decades—a classic instance of Mr. Sam's long-term vision. The concept of Seagram as a "family" lingered on. As late as 1992 Donard Gaynor joined Seagram as a senior executive and at a dinner shortly afterwards Edgar Sr. asked him, "Do you accept the family? Say you do." Gaynor appreciated the gesture, as emphasizing that he was "joining Seagam at a senior enough level to be taken seriously."

In 1956 fifty-two of the distributors could celebrate twenty years with the company (i.e., since very soon after Repeal), and 108 had been loyal for fifteen years. The Seagram "franchise" was also used as a way of providing a comfortable retirement for senior executives and was much in demand—even the company's leading trade unionist tried to get a distributorship for his son. Until the end of the century they remained the *corps d'elite* of the whole industry, and a remarkably loyal one at that. In 1973 *Forbes* magazine found that over half of the company's 476 distributors had been with Seagram since Repeal, forty years earlier. Mr. Sam was not alone; Lew Rosenstiel did the same, and indeed Southern Liquor, the biggest distributors in the country by the end of the twentieth century, was founded by veterans from both groups.

For "Mr. Sam knew how to inspire loyalty," one distributor told *Forbes* magazine, "but God help you if you ever crossed him. Every time he opened his mouth you shrank four inches. By the time he was through, you felt like a midget under the table." The profits often made them millionaires. It was reckoned that distributors made a net profit of fifty cents a bottle, so that a major distributor, selling five hundred thousand cases annually, would be making $600,000 a year net of all expenses. By contrast, distributors outside the Seagram "family" were squeezed between ruthless distillers and greedy retailers, generally without any guarantee of regular profits. Only Mr. Sam and his team provided them with such a guarantee— helped by a surprise decision by the US Supreme Court in 1935 allowing the Bronfmans to enforce their policy of fixing prices, thus ensuring decent profit margins.

The success of 7 Crown, VO, Kessler, and Calvert led to an urgent need for more top-class whiskey. As a result, within eighteen months of the launch of the two Crowns Sam was planning to build a major distillery in Louisville, Kentucky, the historic mecca of the American distilling business. The distillery was opened with a flourish during Kentucky Derby week in May 1937 in a celebration that drew seventy-one thousand visitors to visit this new wonder. The project, however, had one sad consequence, the destruction—there is really no other word for it—of Harry, who, in theory anyway, had previously been in charge of all Seagram's American distilleries. Harry's exclusion from the business started in 1937 when Mr. Sam hired Frederick Willkie, the scientist brother of Wendell Willkie and a veteran of Harry Hatch's distilleries. When he arrived at the Louisville distillery, which Harry was building, Willkie promptly stopped work and damned Harry's efforts as amateur, and this provided Mr. Sam with the excuse he needed to get rid of him—by the 1930s Abe had already been sidelined, content to run his own, often successful, investments in real estate.

True to his claims of professionalism Willkie became technical director of the whole empire and introduced scientists and scientific standards to Seagram—and thus to the whole industry. He even hired Ph.D.s, available cheap during the Depression, and a quarter of the staff were qualified chemical or electrical engineers. All this was in line with Mr. Sam's aim to create a "seat of learning," a laboratory to study the science of distilling and what was to him the "art" of blending. But Willkie fell from grace after the war since he had allowed papers to be published in scientific journals, and Sam naturally disliked what he perceived as giving away Seagram's secrets and the independence it showed, referring to the scientists involved as "long-haired, short-brained fellows" producing work that was "too scientific." After Willkie's dismissal Sam tried to run production through a committee—an imitation of DCL, a group riddled with them.

Willkie's talents, and his self-serving opinion about Harry's inadequacies, had provided Mr. Sam with the opportunity to get rid of his brother once and for all. He was supported by Allan, an attitude which Harry regarded as treasonable. In 1939 Harry wrote a memorandum explaining his fall from grace, how "the change from the tremendous job I had to relaxation"—i.e., after he had been sacked from the Louisville operation—"showed me that my health had been undermined"—what we would now call a nervous breakdown. He remained nominally in charge of the LaSalle distillery for a time, and retained an office at 1430 Peel Street. Sam's elder son Edgar believes that "Harry, the older brother, resented taking orders, and that Father had to prove in rather drastic action that he was the boss"—a phrase that well illustrates the mentality of both father and son. As Newman puts it, apart from Allan, "Sam treated his family partners as liabilities he had to drag behind him." Asked what his brothers thought of a major business decision, Sam replied, "I don't remember asking them."

Harry's breakdown enabled Mr. Sam—helped by Laz Phillips, the "family lawyer"—to alter the original division of the family's shares. No longer was Harry to be an equal partner. Indeed after the Louisville disaster until his death in 1963 Harry was virtually excluded from the family business. From 1937 on Sam was to possess 40 percent of the shares, 10 percent more than in the earlier division; Harry a mere 22 percent, 8 percent less than before; Allan 19, Abe 14, and brother-in-law Barney Aaron 5. Once he had disposed of Harry, Sam could turn his attention to Allan. In a 1948 article *Fortune* couples Allan with Sam, but hints at his real, subordinate position by describing him as the man who "gathers up the loose ends and centers communication between operating executives and the parent company."

Within eighteen months of the launch of the two Crowns two troublesome disputes had been settled and, for the first time, a serious campaign had been launched against illicit stills. This was due to the transfer of all types of liquor law enforcement to the American Treasury under Henry Morgenthau, Jr., most unrelentingly honest of public servants, determined, as J. M. Blum puts it, to exact "a kind of retributive justice against some of the mighty of the Volstead [era], from such luminaries as Dutch Schultz and bootleggers to Canadian distillers."[1] Morgenthau's attitude was partly due to the fact that he was a charter member of "Our Crowd" and so had little time for more recently arrived Jews from less distinguished backgrounds. Morgenthau started by redirecting his investigators' efforts from winkling out small stills in the mountains to the industrial-sized plants that were still flourishing. "By the end of 1935," wrote Blum, "treasury agents had seized 24,000 stills, many of them large plants, arrested 48,000 persons, and obtained 24,000 convictions. Illicit traffic fell off as the government apprehended a much higher proportion of liquor-law violators than during the period of Prohibition." All this effort greatly increased the market for legal liquor and, in a sense, legitimized the whole industry. At the same time Morgenthau largely succeeded in his efforts to "purify the seas" by virtually eliminating the bootleggers.

But Morgenthau's crusading zeal proved an appalling nuisance for the Bronfmans. A report he commissioned accused the Canadians, encouraged by what he clearly perceived as a sinister Scottish mafia, of having profiteered from prohibition—which was true. So Morgenthau decided to try to collect from foreign distillers—above all the Canadians—the taxes they had evaded during Prohibition and which, he asserted, should have become payable once they could sell the whiskey legally in the United States. Prime Minister Bennett naturally cooperated, but, luckily for the Canadians, in 1935 Mackenzie King's return to power brought in a doughty defender of Canadian interests, and after some Byzantine negotiations Morgenthau's original claim of $17 million was reduced to a mere $700,000. Even worse, Morgenthau's crusading zeal nearly scuttled a crucial free-trade deal between Canada and the United States when he tried to apply an embargo on the Canadian distillers on the grounds that they had not been prepared to submit to US jurisdiction. His first claim was for $53 million but a lot of hard bargaining—and a last-minute intervention by President Roosevelt—reduced the amount to a tolerable $3 million, and the treaty ensured that the duty on Canadian whisky imported into the United States was halved to $2.50 a gallon, an enormous help to Harry Hatch and the Bronfmans.

By 1938 *Fortune* could congratulate Sam on his "first big play" with Seagram, "carrying relatively few, well-liked, well-established brands, on top of the industry." A year later Mr. Sam celebrated his triumphs of the previous five years by creating his masterpiece. This was launched in a breathtaking example of what is known in the business as "product placement," i.e., exposing the whiskey in influential circles.* In 1939 King George VI and Queen Elizabeth (best known after her husband's death in 1952 as the Queen Mother) visited Canada. For the occasion Sam introduced Crown Royal, the result of tasting six hundred samples—and exploiting the Canadian regulations by including 9 percent of bourbon in the blend. Somehow Sam managed to get permission to present the brand to the royal couple before it was launched on to the Canadian market. As a result the royal train carried ten cases of the whiskey across Canada for the delectation of the royal family and their guests. In a typical Sam gesture the bottle was packaged in an Imperial purple velvet bag (made by the family of Saidye's sister Flora) which, for decades, remained a must-have accessory for many Canadians, much favored as a luxury container for women's jewels. As the royal train steamed across Canada, Sam's triumphant rise to respectability as well as wealth was proclaimed the length and breadth of the land.

---

* After the war Frank Sinatra's dressing room invariably contained ample supplies not only of his favorite tipple, Jack Daniel's, but also of J & B Scotch, placed there by its importer Abe ("Abie Baby") Rosenberg.

Eight

A TRULY CANADIAN JEW

A kike is a Jewish gentleman who has just left the room.
— Mr. Sam

SOMEHOW MR. SAM FOUND TIME IN THE 1930S TO COMBINE HIS business success with an ever-deepening involvement in the affairs of the Canadian Jewish community, a role which combined his two roots, as a Jew and a Canadian. Of course Mr. Sam had always been acutely aware of his Jewish heritage but, like many people born into a religion, he was not overly reverential towards religious authority. As Robertson notes, "His attitude towards rabbis generally is about as irreverent as that of the Irish towards their priests." Nor was he particularly observant. He and Saidye maintained a traditional Jewish home and she kept a fully kosher kitchen, at least while her parents were still alive. Nevertheless Sam explained his willingness to eat the crustaceans forbidden to observant Jews by the fact that his mother, living three thousand miles from the ocean, had never heard of them. Fundamentally he was not a devout Jew, he had no real spiritual link with the religion, spending most of his Saturdays in Montreal on business, attending synagogue only on High Holy Days like Yom Kippur, and even then was often observed dozing through the services. He did however punctiliously observe the anniversary of his parents' deaths. As his daughter Phyllis told Marrus, her father believed in religious tradition as "essentially a social sense of decorum and continuity."

This sense of communal rather than religious responsibility ensured that when Eichel died in 1919, all the brothers did their duty and took on the important roles their father had occupied in the Jewish community; indeed Sam, like the others, had first become involved in Jewish activities out of respect for his father's wishes. But his involvement became more important once he had moved to Montreal, where the Jewish population was substantial enough—over one in twenty of the city's total population—to defend itself. They needed to, for the Jewish community, like their French and British equivalents, suffered from what the novelist Gwethalyn Graham explains as an inferiority complex,[1] "The French because they are a minority in Canada, the English because they are a minority in Quebec, the Jews because they are a minority everywhere."

Mr. Sam's motives were accurately pinpointed by his long-term collaborator Leo Kolber: "First a very Jewish sense of responsibility, that sense of philanthropy towards fellow Jews as a Jewish duty; second, a sense of Jewish unity in the community"; and third, what Marrus described as "dignified Jewish standing in the non-Jewish universe, particularly Canada." Until his arrival on the scene, the Canadian Jewish community, though small, was fragmented, and thus relatively powerless. The basic division involved the old-established Jews—the sort of "Our Crowd," generally German in origin—who, as in New York or London, did not welcome the newer arrivals, mostly from Eastern Europe. But Montreal was a city in which any prominent Jew, wherever he came from, automatically became involved in the affairs of the community. As one observer put it: In Montreal "social prestige comes from being a *macher* [leader] in the Jewish community"— and also by not contributing to nondenominational cultural or social civic activities. So his increasing involvement sprang from a sense of racial *noblesse oblige* rather than any spiritual motivation.

Before Sam's arrival on the scene, as Saul Hayes, his key adviser, put it, "There were regional leaders but they seemed to think in terms of provincial interests, and it was not until Sam came into the picture that a national leader was found who was not only willing to bring a national Jewish community into existence but had the ability and energy to do it." By 1939, through a characteristic combination of tact, diplomacy, sheer financial power, and the bulldozing of those involved, Sam had emerged as president of the Canadian Jewish Congress and transformed it into a truly national organization. He arrived at a key moment in Jewish history. As Marrus—himself a distinguished historian of the Holocaust—puts it, "He became head of a tiny, raging, fractious community, just about to face the trials of the Jewish refugee crisis, the Second World War and the Holocaust . . . the darkest moment in the history of modern Jewry." For the next thirty eventful years Sam remained in charge, although it was the only role he ever played in which he was not undisputed monarch of all he surveyed. Moreover his own deferential attitude towards Canadian society and the temper of the times prevented him from having a decisive or even positive influence on the policy of successive governments.

Sam's first involvement in the Jewish community came with the creation of a Jewish General Hospital at a time when Jewish doctors had great difficulty in getting jobs, the sort of cultural racism routine in clubs and restrictive property covenants at the time. While his brother Allan confined his activities to the hospital, as time went on Sam became involved in other philanthropic ventures and was then swept into politics, partly because of his desire to shine but also because of the growing problems faced by Jews in the Depression. This naturally led to increasing jealousy of any apparent business success stories among what was the largest immigrant community in the city. In Montreal, the home of virtually all the Jews in Quebec, anti-Semitism was particularly virulent, as we saw in the story of Mr. Sam's partnership with DCL. Throughout his life Sam was excluded from Montreal's most exclusive clubs and could not enter one of them even as the guest of one of his non-Jewish employees. And despite his willingness to contribute, he became a governor of McGill, Montreal's leading university, only late in life after the death of its biggest—and most anti-Semitic—benefactor. Lavishing money on McGill was not enough to change the policy of "Jewish quotas" in many faculties. Not surprisingly one of his earliest academic benefactions came in 1951 when he funded a Samuel Bronfman Professorship at Columbia University in New York.

In Montreal, but also throughout the whole province of Quebec, the situation was complicated because of the permanent tensions between the French and British communities. As Pierre Anctil put it: "The timing of the Ashkenazi emigration from Russia and Poland had placed the newcomers on a collision course with Francophone aspirations"; they "appeared as a force bent on destroying a political status quo achieved with great difficulty."[2] It did not help that the French-speaking population was largely rural and deeply Catholic. The priests who dominated their lives were vehemently anti-Semitic, though the bulk of their flock was more sympathetic, if only because both they and the Jews were oppressed by the dominant Anglo-Saxon population, and because the Jews were far more ready to learn French than the Anglo-Saxons. But it did not help that as late as the 1930s less than half of Montreal's Jewish population had been born in Canada. All these factors ensured that the Francophone Québecois remained vehemently opposed to any further Jewish immigration until well after World War II. Nevertheless, as Anctil points out: "One Jewish attribute especially appealed to the Québecois, group solidarity in the face of difficult odds!"

Unfortunately in the 1930s the Jewish lobby, which represented only 160,000 people, a mere 1 percent of the country's total population, many of them post World War I immigrants, was not in the best of shape. In 1934, confronted by an—albeit small and evanescent—surge in openly fascist activity, the Canadian Jewish Congress had been reformed under a Jewish lawyer-parliamentarian, Sam Jacobs—the partner of Laz Phillips, for a long time Mr. Sam's favorite lawyer. The general secretary was a former tailor and autodidact scholar, Hannaniah Meir Caiserman. Unfortunately Jacobs was not well and too busy as a politician to have much time for the CJC, while Caiserman, though devoted, was a hopeless administrator, given his excessive emotionalism, a man who, according to one observer, "dealt with problems by bursting into tears."

Enter Mr. Sam, with his willingness—unusual in anyone of his wealth and prominence—to become involved in political as opposed to philanthropic activities, and, what is more, prepared to include the city's Yiddish-speaking Jewish proletariat in the wider world of Jewish politics. His lack of pretension and his genuine concern for people's individual needs were never more evident than when dealing with his less fortunate coreligionists. Throughout his life, wrote Marrus, "He provided a model of how Jews could succeed in Canadian society while remaining intensely Jewish." As always Sam became totally involved, for he struck Avrael Harman, Israel's first consul-general in Canada, as "a community leader who paid attention to minute details of anything that he handled."

In 1938, amid the rising tide of anti-Semitism—and of European Jews clamoring for sanctuary—Jacobs died and Caiserman came to Mr. Sam with an emotional plea for him to take the chair. He did, and even managed to convince the—usually Socialist—leaders of working-class Jews that, despite his wealth, he was the only possible candidate for the unenviable job. Yet he proved an unexpectedly sensible choice, because he, perhaps alone of well-known Canadian Jews at the time, possessed the necessary energy and also because he was a political innocent. He was duly elected, having made clear that there was to be no honorary president above him, no "superimposed authority," as he put it.

Mr. Sam showed his authority when he immediately insisted that Jews had to be united and, above all, good patriotic Canadians. He went further in a speech that showed just how far he, like so many Jews in other Anglo-Saxon countries in the 1930s, felt Jews to be the underdog, still needing to apologize for themselves, to struggle for recognition. "We, as Jews, have a chance to *build up* [my italics] a full position of citizenship and equality which is a privilege belonging to the citizens of the British Empire. . . . We have to be that much better to gain this respect." For, like virtually all Jews of his origins and generation he could not imagine that he could ever be the real equal of an established Anglo-Saxon. According to his son Edgar, Mr. Sam believed "that Canada, the inheritor of English libertarianism, had made it possible for Jews to live as *almost* [his italics] first-class citizens under the Union Jack. . . . Neither father nor any of his friends would ever have dreamed of doing anything that would make the community look anything less than superpatriotic." During the war Sam even commissioned a history of Canada from the greatly respected, but by no means philo-Semitic, political scientist Stephen Leacock. The result, *Canada: The Foundation of Its Future*, became a universally admired symbol of Canada's patriotism.

The war transformed Sam into the unquestioned leader of the country's Jewish community, a role he played virtually until his death thirty years later. His position was helped by a combination of the fear he inspired and his genuine feeling that all the country's Jews, rich and poor, ought to act as a single community. On his fiftieth "official" birthday on March 4, 1941, his role was recognized in the first of many banquets organized in his honor by the Jewish community. It was this position that caused the family to be thought of as the Canadian Rothschilds, their every activity subject to close scrutiny. He was always prepared to put up considerable sums of money to shame his fellow religionists to contribute—and, even more important, backed his financial generosity with hard work, involving innumerable meetings on weekends, even on Saturdays.

Not surprisingly Mr. Sam excelled in the art of fundraising within the Jewish community, and the widely recognized generosity of Montreal Jews dates from his presidency of the CJC. As Kolber puts it succinctly, "Jewish fundraising is to fundraising as military music is to music—loud, brassy, and inescapable . . . the pressure tactics of CJC are legendary in the community. Talk about four thousand years of Jewish guilt—it's all there in fundraising techniques." These—like Seagram's genuflections to its boss—were expressed in the banquets held on any excuse, and were particularly lavish when Mr. Sam's birthday was being celebrated. Not surprisingly Richler went to town in his scorn for such celebrations and those who attended the repeated coronations of "King Bernard."

> Absolutely everybody who counted was there to offer homage. Mr. Bernard's flotilla of lawyers was also there. The ladies—perfumed, their hair sculpted and lacquered, their eyes shadowed green or silvery, outsize rings riding their fingers. . . . The men were harnessed in velvet dinner jackets. . . . At ease in the Ritz-Carlton, they were there to bask in Mr. Bernard's aura.

But Richler did not mention that these events did raise an awful lot of money.

Nevertheless, largely because he shared the subservient attitude of most Jews of the diaspora at the time, Mr. Sam did not lead from the front in dealing with the deeply ingrained anti-refugee mentality of the Canadian political elite. This was summed up by a senior official in 1939: "So long as Canada has an unemployment problem there will be no 'open door' for political refugees here." In early 1939 Sam had badly misread the attitude of his fellow Jews, preaching that "Canadian Jews should be, first of all, Canadians," ignoring their natural concerns not only about immigration policies but also the problems of the Jewish community in Palestine, and, above all, the Nazis' treatment of the Jews. His reaction to the ensuing uproar was typical of the duality of the man. He naturally sacked the PR man responsible for the speech, but he also brought on board two unlikely associates, Abraham Moses Klein and Saul Hayes, who between them greatly increased his capacity to deal with the more complex political world into which his success had parachuted him.

Klein was the most unexpected collaborator Mr. Sam ever had, the very essence of a sensitive, distinguished, troubled Jewish poet—indeed he had so severe a nervous breakdown in the mid-1950s that he could never write any more poetry. He had come to Sam's notice through an equally improbable intermediary, Victor Fischel, when Klein had been engaged as a guide (or spieler) on the tours Fischel had organized in the LaSalle distillery, and was so successful that he was granted an audience with Mr. Sam. Klein had been educated as a lawyer, but he hated the law and was appointed editor of the well-respected weekly *Canadian Jewish Chronicle* in time for his first editorial to express his horror at Kristallnacht in 1938. He soon became the voice of Canadian Jewry—and of Mr. Sam—after he had been engaged at a substantial salary (C$3,000 plus another C$1,000 for expenses) as a part-time employee. Klein wrote not only speeches connected with the CJC but also business speeches and even the long letter Sam sent to Charles on the occasion of his bar mitzvah. Not surprisingly he often rebelled, albeit usually only inwardly, against much of his work. For him the publicity he wrote for a banquet in honor of Mr. Sam was "a humiliation only a philanthropic world makes possible." In one poem he painted himself as one of those who:

> Upon the knees of ventriloquists, they own
> Of their dandied brightness, lonely the paint and board.

Richler provides a convincing explanation of Klein's reasoning in accepting to work for Mr. Sam through the character of L. B. Berger, the poet hired by Bernard Gursky to write speeches about the plight of European Jews: "Me, all I have agreed is to write speeches for Mr. Bernard about the plight of our brethren in Europe. Coming from me, it's noise. From Mr. Bernard *they* [his italics] will prick up their ears. Gates will open, if only a crack. In this country big money talks." Even the author Adam Furstenberg, who attributed Klein's later breakdown at least partially to Mr. Sam, recognized that Klein "elicited an unusual gentleness and consideration" in someone who, like so many undereducated people, was greatly in awe of genuine literary talent.

Very different was Saul Hayes, a lawyer, the type of outwardly impressive figure whom Sam often appreciated as filling in the gaps in his own psychological armory. Hayes, wrote Marrus, "was tall and debonair . . . agile and well connected." In addition, and unlike Sam, he understood the overwhelmingly Christian Canadian elite, allegedly getting along "better with the people he lobbied than those on whose behalf he lobbied." This was a contrast to Sam, whose gut concern was for the worries of the mass of immigrant Jews. Nevertheless Hayes was far more suitable than Caiserman for his successive roles, first as executive director of the newly formed Canadian Jewish Committee for Refugees, and then as executive director of the CJC. Mr. Sam trusted him implicitly, diverting all queries and problems for him to answer, enabling him to avoid any open involvement in attempts to allow the arrival of Jewish refugees.

Hayes's standing was greatly strengthened after a ferocious row with Mr.

Sam where he stood his ground and, as so often happened with him, Mr. Sam was won over. The row enabled Hayes to prevent Mr. Sam from using the CJC as a personal vehicle, in public anyway, when his prominence had caused attacks on the "former bootlegger"—to which was added "gangster, Al Capone's partner." The usual suspicions, the habitual associations, as it were. Hayes was also able to ensure that Mr. Sam was recognized as a major contributor—and not only financially—to the war effort as a member of the obscurely named but powerful War Technical and Scientific Development Committee, which gave him access to some of the war's top-secret scientific information. Nevertheless this was due more to Seagram's technical skills in the production of the industrial alcohol crucial to the war effort than to Sam's own position.

But Sam and Hayes were far from successful in their efforts to get Canada to admit Jewish refugees from the Nazis.* Not surprisingly, given his general attitudes, Mr. Sam made only tentative efforts to persuade the Canadian government to change its policies towards refugees during the war, even though by then unemployment, the supposed reason for their exclusion, had become irrelevant. Mr. Sam's attitude was echoed by the politically savvy Hayes—although at one point he felt sufficiently betrayed by the stubbornness of the government's immigration branch to want to make an open protest and had to be calmed by Sam and Laz Phillips. Even in 1946, when immigrants were flooding into Canada from all over Europe, a Gallup poll found that Jews were considered the second-most undesirable type of immigrant, scarcely more welcome than those hated enemies, the Japanese. Belatedly, from 1947 on, the gates began to creak open, albeit slowly and reluctantly. Mr. Sam's own efforts were concentrated on helping individual refugees, many of whom he employed at the LaSalle distillery, knowing all their names, a fact which greatly endeared them to him. For a year Saidye had to house three members of a truly rich and famous Jewish family, Doris Sassoon and her two children. Edgar remembers Doris as a snobby, condescending "bitch on wheels," but, fortunately, Saidye's sufferings lasted only a year.

In 1938 Sam did manage to get two hundred refugees settled on farms in

---

* The Bronfmans' only encounter with a Nazi had been in the early 1930s when they met von Ribbentrop, later Hitler's foreign minister but then selling champagne (and the appalling German imitation *Sekt*) on behalf of his father-in-law. According to Saidye their host assured them that when Adolf Hitler came to power they would find that his attacks on Jews were meant purely for show and would not be carried out in practice.

Quebec and to gain permission for twelve hundred Jewish orphans to enter the country. But between 1933 and the end of the war a mere five thousand Jewish refugees were admitted to Canada, proportionately only half as many as were allowed into the United States, itself by no means a welcoming refuge. Richler explains Canada's exclusionist policy through the mouth of a character who explains that Canada "is not so much a country as a holding tank filled with the disgruntled progeny of defeated people . . . now that we are here prospering, we do our damned best to exclude more ill-bred newcomers because they remind us of our own mean origins in the draper's shop in Inverness or the *shtetl* or the bog." As Mr. Sam's younger son Charles recalled much later, after his father's trips to Ottawa to lobby the government during and after the war: "He'd come back thinking he'd really accomplished something. It's amazing in today's world to think how powerless they were. They were nothing." Charles was being rather harsh. The far bigger and more influential Jewish community in the United States also proved largely futile in its efforts to help their fellow Jews.

For the war had not stopped the flow of anti-Semitic feeling—one church leader even asserted that Sam was reaping huge profits from monopolizing the production of penicillin. As a result it was Saidye, not Sam, who received official recognition in the form of the Order of the British Empire, a relatively minor decoration, for her war service, a decoration which Mr. Sam greeted with apparently wholehearted joy: "The King thinks as much of you as I do," he is said to have remarked as he knelt before her. The children took an altogether less reverential attitude, referring to the OBE as the Order of the Boiled Egg. She had indeed deserved the award, her Jewish branch of the Canadian Red Cross grew into a factory with four thousand women putting together medical kits and other necessities. By contrast, Sam, who had done even more for the war effort, got nothing. As David Sim, a senior minister who was involved in the awards process, told Robertson, "It was generally accepted that both he and and his wife should be recognized," but that any award to Sam "would receive considerable political opposition" and that the OBE was in a sense their joint reward.

Sam had been an early—though not very active—supporter of Jewish settlement in Palestine. "Those of us who live in a free country like Canada," he told a banquet in 1938, "should express [our] gratitude by making it possible for other Jews to find freedom and security in Palestine." And in 1945, rather surprisingly, he attended the meeting in San Francisco to organize the fledgling United Nations to plead for the establishment of a Jewish state. There he met the leaders of world Jewry like Rabbi Stephen Wise and Nahum Goldmann, head of the World Jewish Congress, establishing him as a figure rather more considerable than as merely the leader of a relatively small national Jewish community.

The complex story of the Bronfman family's involvement with Israel and the larger world Jewish community is really about very differing ideas of Jewish identity as expressed in the attitudes and actions of Mr. Sam and his sons. The establishment of Israel in 1948 forced Mr. Sam to look at the world far more closely than ever before. He had not been a keen Zionist, though Goldmann had become a friend, and in 1948 Mr. Sam issued a cautiously worded welcome to the new state, as a means of rectifying "the age-old wrong done to our people." After 1948, for Sam himself and to an even greater extent Charles, this meant supporting—and investing in—Israel, while remaining physically and psychologically at a distance through a desire to remain patriotic Canadians. But, as we shall see, for Edgar it represented a far more ambitious—and indeed unprecedented—challenge.

Sam was speaking for the mass of Canadian Jews when he assumed that the future of Canadian Jews lay in Canada rather than Israel. To him, as Marrus writes, "Israel was not central to his Jewishness"—though of course he led the way in providing financial support for the fledgling, struggling nation and was treated like royalty when he first visited the country in 1956, a visit which enabled him to sound off subsequently on geopolitics. His importance was recognized with his promotion to be a vice president of the World Jewish Congress. His motives were mixed. Chaim Bermant explains them as "the residual adhesion to Judaism, inherited from his father . . . but what was probably more important was the memory of his frantic pre-war efforts to rescue Jewish refugees, when he found almost every door closed."[3]

But Canadian Jews were not that important; even within their own country, they had far less influence on their favorite party, the Liberals, than did their American counterparts on the Democrats. More important were Sam's financial contributions. After the war he had organized and helped finance the flow of arms to Haganah, the underground Jewish army in Palestine. Once the new state was established he gave large sums through the Combined Jewish Appeal—most of whose funds went to Israel—money reckoned as running at around $1.5 million annually in the late 1970s. When the Six-Day War erupted in 1967 he summoned other Jewish leaders to Montreal and set a target of the unheard-of sum of C$20 million, which succeeded after he had given C$250,000 of his own money.

Within Canada the Bronfman family, as is normal with successful Jewish people throughout the ages, had always been major contributors to charities. The beneficiaries ranged from Boy Scouts to universities (including those where Mr. Sam hoped his sons would study) and hospitals and medical institutions—particularly those with which Saidye was associated. In Israel the most obvious result was the Bronfman Biblical and Archaeological Museum, part of the great Jewish museum being built in Jerusalem under the city's inspirational mayor, Teddy Kollek. The museum was a seventieth birthday present for Sam in the form of an institution named after him. They had the choice: spend $2 million to have the whole museum named after him, or half that amount in return for a wing named after Sam housing the archaeological and biblical artifacts. Kolber spelled out the case for the smaller donation, on the grounds that if the whole museum were named after a single person, potential donors would be less likely to give to the institution. Sam also fell in with a program started in the 1950s when donors could have a village named after them in return for a donation of $500,000. But the aid was spread wide. As David Plotz put it: "I defy you to find an American student who studied in Israel and received no Bronfman aid."

Charles for one always believed that the best way of helping Israel was to invest in it. Indeed Israel remained a favorite for what the family considered "semi-philanthropic investments." The "capitalist" investments included orange groves and a major chain of supermarkets called Super-Sol (the Hebrew for superstore) of which Charles became chairman while still only thirty-three. But it took all the family's financial and managerial muscle to save the group when it went broke after a series of frauds involving a leading member of the Canadian Jewish community. Sam even tried to produce an Israeli liqueur, which, according to Chaim Bermant, "looks and tastes like a chocolate mousse which has failed to set." To be fair it still sells well enough in Israel.

But Sam's staunch Canadian patriotism ensured that his attitude clashed with that of David Ben-Gurion, Israel's first and greatest prime minister, who believed that Jews ought to try to return to Israel. To him they could remain elsewhere in viable Jewish communities. As Edgar wrote, Ben-Gurion could not understand that the United States—and by implication Canada as well—was a special case where "American Jewry had found its Zion." There is even a Hebrew word, *noshira*, describing the sin of not wanting to migrate to Israel. As a result, for the Israelis the Bronfmans fell into the category of what Lenin called "useful idiots," their contributions, especially financial, obviously welcomed by successive Israeli governments, but their influence minimal or nonexistent. When the Israeli prime minister opened the Samuel Bronfman Museum in Jerusalem in 1962 he told Charles bluntly that "with all his money—I don't know how much he has, but it's certainly more than I have—he cannot get a real personal share in Israel unless and until one of his children or grandchildren lives permanently in this country." None of them have ever done so.

Nine

THE REGAL ROAD TO SCOTLAND

This year quality came back to its own.
— *BUSINESS WEEK,* 1947

APART FROM ALLAN, WHO JOINED THE CANADIAN ARMY, THE
Bronfman brothers were too old to be called up in 1939. From a business point of view war naturally resulted in a surge in demand for liquor and a simultaneous shortage of supply. *Fortune* provided the explanation: "More money around and fewer things to spend it on, and a great many uprooted people finding sociability in bars." During the war the acute and growing shortage of mature whiskey—distillation for civilian uses was forbidden for two years and greatly resticted for two more—ensured that the market share of blends soared from under a third to seven-eighths of the total. To help alleviate the shortage, during the war Seagram absorbed twenty-four independent distilleries, mainly for the stocks they brought with them. In 1941 Sam bought the British Columbia distillery, his first major plant on the West Coast, but most of his purchases were in the United States. In 1942 he mopped up a number of less-well-known distilleries—Bedford Distilling, Blair Distilling, Old Colonel Distillery, William Jameson, Dant and Dant, Majestic Distilling, and Kasko Distillers. The result of similar activities by his rivals meant that by the end of the war the Big Four distillers—Seagram, Schenley, National, and Hiram Walker—accounted for three-quarters of whiskey sales in the US.

Sam's most important wartime investment came in 1943 with the purchase (for a seemingly expensive $42 million) of a famous business, Frankfort Distilleries in Louisville, the country's fifth largest liquor business, which included two major brands, Four Roses and Paul Jones. He bought it from family shareholders who had only recently inherited the business and were anxious to avoid paying income tax, preferring to pay the much lower rate of capital gains tax by selling up. In a move which showed his obsession with blended whiskey Sam converted Four Roses from a straight whiskey to a blend. More relevantly so far as Mr. Sam was concerned, Frankfort had one of the most important stocks of aging bourbon in the whole country—twenty million gallons. Mr. Sam's credit rating was good enough to enable him to raise $75 million—well above the $42 million he needed to buy Frankfort—from two major banks in the form of a revolving credit line. Such finance was crucial in what *Fortune* described as a "banking and inventory business" with the need to store whiskey for four or more years and then to pay a tax of $9 a gallon to the federal government when it was taken out of bond to be blended and sold.

As a result, by 1946 Mr. Sam controlled the whole production chain from raw material to the bottle in the liquor store. The whiskies, grain and straight, came from fourteen distilleries in Canada and the United States, the whiskies they produced were matured in sixty warehouses and bottled in ten bottling plants. The result was 25 million gallons of whiskey, enough to produce over 10 million cases a year. Sales of $400 million— overwhelmingly in the United States—produced profits of $14 million a year. Immediately after the war he frustrated a plan by National Distillers to build a distillery in Quebec to produce rye whiskey—soon buying it up himself together with two other distilleries, which brought in eighty thousand barrels of old bourbon. By 1948 Seagram owned three of the top ten brands: 7 Crown, Calvert Reserve, and Four Roses. Five of the leaders— including 7 Crown, which alone had held 20 percent of the total market before the war—now accounted for half of total sales.

In 1940 Mr. Sam had taken his first major step outside the narrow world of whiskey when he bought Browne Vintners from Joe Reinfeld, his old friend from Prohibition days. Browne brought with it substantial stocks of whiskey as well as a number of import agencies, most notably those for White Horse Scotch, Mumm Champagne, and Martell cognac. It was run by one Oscar Weil, who reported directly to Mr. Sam. Mr. Sam's first venture into the wine business had been the purchase of a couple of Canadian wineries, Jordan and Danforth, which had brought Noah Torno, a skilled negotiator, into the Seagram orbit. But this was a minor investment. The creation of what became a major wine business was triggered by his desire to help two refugee wine merchants, Alfred Fromm and Franz Sichel. The latter was a member of one of Germany's leading family-owned wine mer-chants whom Mr. Sam already knew as his importer in Berlin. Typically, Sam remained very loyal to Sichel and his family. After Sichel's death Sea-gram bought total control of the company but for the following thirty years his widow received a case or two of whiskey every Christmas. Mr. Sam re-fused to give the refugees a loan. He preferred to create a partnership, and his attitude towards his investment—and the loans he guaranteed—was simple: "As long as you don't lose money I won't interfere." This proved the model for many other such agreements over the following thirty years.

The new partners then bought a majority stake in a company that was the sales agent for the Christian Brothers, a religious order in Calfornia who were also important producers of sherry and other fortified wines, sold mostly at Christmas. At the time wines like these were far bigger sellers than table wine. With some difficulty Franz Sichel persuaded the monks to increase production of table wine and to take advantage of the way the government was buying up surplus grapes, which were then distilled. Hence the creation of a brandy that dominated the American market for several decades. They also owned a business called Mount Tivey, and legend has it that Mr. Sam was disturbed to find that the company's winery was in a val-ley, so told Fromm to find him a mountain. In that way Seagram acquired the prestigious Paul Masson vineyard, high up on the Santa Cruz hills above Saratoga. By the mid-1960s the business was selling $100 million worth of wine annually, probably second only to the Gallo family.

In March 1946 his great Canadian rival Harry Hatch died, worn out by running what amounted to a one-man business, for Hatch's partner Bill Hume had died in 1938. His relatives hired a private train to carry his body back to the little town of Desaronto where he and his brother Herb had spent their youth. There this most unassuming of business geniuses was laid to rest beside his father and grandfather, and his tombstone gave only his name and dates of birth and death. Nevertheless, another rival re-mained, apparently stronger than ever. Mr. Sam's steadfast refusal to dilute the quality of his precious brands meant that he lost ground to the hated Rosenstiel—by 1943, and despite the acquisition of Four Roses, his market share was 17 percent below that enjoyed by his rival. Later Mr. Sam claimed that "I let him go for a few years, yes it was bad whiskey, I sat and let him take it." Unlike some of his claims, this was true. For, in an un-canny parallel with the situation immediately after Repeal, his rival was prepared to use inferior spirit in his blends, in this case alcohol distilled from potato and sugar cane, to replace neutral grain spirit, of which he held very small stocks. Sam preferred to maintain quality at the inevitable cost of reducing sales, trumpeting that his whiskies were based on "superb neutral spirits" and simply stopped selling some of his cheaper brands, thus, albeit accidentally, moving further up-market. Schenley's reputation naturally suffered because cane spirit inevitably carried overtones of rum, then considered an inferior spirit, while the public distrusted the potato spirit–based blends (even though they were perfectly good). The result was a catastrophic fall in sales of the all-important Three Feathers brand.

During the war Fischel played a crucial role by soothing distributors who could never get enough whiskey. He was helped by the fact that while sales decreased, the distributors—and Seagram—could expect greater profitability. Moreover Sam's distributors were selling only whiskey and were not being pushed to sell less-favored drinks like rum and wine. Indeed while sales decreased by 18 percent between 1944 and 1946 profits rose by 8 percent. Cannily, and thanks to his knowledge of distillation techniques, Sam had also reinforced his stocks of aging whiskey by retaining and storing in casks some of the by-products—the heads and the tails*—left after the distillation of the high-proof alcohol required for munitions production. After the war these stocks gave him a head start in the production of his light whiskies.

As soon as the war ended Bronfman came into his own. Between 1946 and 1948 sales of bottled whiskey fell by a quarter but Seagram's sales rose by over a half while profits more than doubled. Mr. Sam's reliance on up-market brands proved triumphant. In 1947 profits amounted to nearly $54 million on sales of $738 million as against Rosenstiel's $425 million. By 1950 net profits after tax, at $42 million, were more than four times higher than their level ten years earlier. Seagram accounted for over a fifth of the US liquor market, selling seven million cases of 7 Crown every year, about the same as its three closest rivals—which included VO—combined, while its other brands were also top sellers. But, once the post-war boom died down drinkers started to opt for other spirits, and for the next fifteen years sales stagnated and profits never again hit their 1948 high.

That year too, the business world outside Canada first realized that the

---

* The heads are the first, high-proof spirit off the still, the tails the lower strength alcohol deemed too weak for use.

Bronfmans were among the seriously rich of this world. This was thanks to an article in the September issue of *Fortune*, which, more than any credit rating, provided the family—above all Mr. Sam—with its legitimacy.

Sam was greatly helped by his policy of "divide and rule." By the end of the war he had established three separate and competing sales subsidiaries, each with their own president: Seagram-Distillers, selling mainly 7 Crown and the imported VO; Frankfort, with Four Roses; and Calvert/Carstairs. Seagram accounted for a half of sales and the other two a quarter each, for the purchase of Frankfort had proved a major help. Competition extended even to the distilleries, which were completely separate from the sales companies. "Let them fight like hell," he said, referring not only to the sales companies but to individual distilleries. He, the "President of Presidents," as he called himself, could thus reinforce his dictatorial status.

Mr. Sam had always gambled that he could reinforce his stocks of straight whiskey on the open market, and by the end of the Korean War in 1953 he had accumulated sufficient stocks to redistill them to make them into the base whiskey for blends. The hated Rosenstiel had always accumulated far larger stocks of aging whiskey than Mr. Sam but came badly unstuck when he calculated that the Korean War would last longer than it did and as a result accumulated enormous stocks of whiskey that would be subject to a new tax of $10.50 a gallon. Nevertheless he retained enough political clout to lobby Congress to compensate him for a major business mistake. Congress obliged, passing the Forand bill freeing liquor companies from the punitive taxes due on whiskey stored for over a dozen years, giving him ample time to rid himself of his stocks.

Unfortunately Seagram's managerial "system" remained totally personal and thus unsuited to any task more complicated than producing, blending, and marketing a handful of brands of blended whiskey. As secretary-treasurer, Max Henderson was in a good position to observe how "Mr. Sam directed practically every facet of the business. Everything was decided on the basis of emotions and family interests. There was no such thing as an organizational chart or definition of lines of authority. You got approval of what you wanted to do directly from Mr. Sam or you went to his brother, Mr. Allan, who appeared to possess authority in certain understood areas." These were never very clear and grew ever fewer over the years until they comprised mainly the company's extensive charitable activities.

It did not help that Sam treated titles as mere indications of the appropriate financial rewards suitable for specific executives, for he operated an extreme example of what the founders of Hewlett-Packard called "management by wandering," he would simply pick up the phone and talk directly to the person involved and not go through any chain of command. Habits developed during Prohibition ensured that neither Sam nor Allan ever put anything on paper, relying solely on telephone conversations—"mail answers itself," Sam would say. Not surprisingly Edgar lamented that he "couldn't learn much about that [organization] from such an unstructured man." Attempts to rationalize management were infrequent and ineffective. For instance training schemes and plans were supposed to ensure that executives moved between technical jobs and line management every couple of years but these ideas were recognized more in the breach than in the observance. The chaos in the office was not helped by the presence of Barney Aaron, who, like Abe and of course Allan, had an office in the building. Barney was the only member of the family prepared to reminisce about life under Prohibition. One veteran remembers how he "was always making idiotic suggestions, like introducing a blind taster."

Even in the early 1950s Seagram remained very much a family organization, not only because of Mr. Sam's total control but also through his genuine paternalism, which remained a feature of the company to the very end and greatly helped to retain the loyalty of the group's employees as well as of its distributors. Henderson noted how Harry Hatch had behaved extremely meanly to employees who joined the armed forces during World War II. By contrast, "Mr. Sam simply told each employee that his salary or wages would continue to go to his family while he was away, that his job would be there when the war was over, and wished him good luck." In 1960 four hundred American employees—the majority of the workforce—could celebrate a quarter century of service with Seagram. This was not surprising, for once you had survived the first few months and had got used to Sam's tempestuous management style you tended to stay—as late as the 1950s one of the men in the post room had been one of Sam's rum runners in the 1920s. Employees already enjoyed what were then the unusual benefits of health plans and pension schemes and a sort of Jewish-mother type clucking over their problems. Edgar continued the tradition, helping an employee with the cost of transporting his family from the West Coast of Canada to Montreal, a gesture which was unusual in the 1950s—and as late as the spring of 2004 he took the trouble to phone the same employee, by then long retired, to commiserate with him on the death of his wife.

Out of all this muddle came a jewel, the product of the fusion of all Mr.

Sam's qualities, as a visionary, a practical businessman—and a blender. He had always dreamed of having a world brand—for sales of VO and 7 Crown were almost exclusively confined to North America. And he succeeded with Chivas Regal, a premium blended Scotch whisky. It also provided Sam with a brand that proved a direct, and successful, challenge to his old mentors, DCL. They owned, but had never properly exploited, Johnny Walker Black Label, the older and more expensive version of Red Label, and Chivas Regal's only real competitor in the then-tiny market for premium brands of blended Scotch. Like 7 Crown, Chivas arrived on the world's markets at precisely the right moment; this time in the post-war boom years of the late 1950s and 1960s, just as drinkers the world over were acquiring a taste, which they could now afford, for little luxuries that enjoyed a certain prestige and set them apart from the normal run of drinkers. It helped, especially in the United States, that Chivas was an import, not a domestically produced drink. "It was," said *The Economist,* "a completely new up-market brand aimed fairly and squarely at an affluent, increasingly international, business elite." It was naturally hugely profitable, as was Johnny Walker Black Label, which by the 1980s accounted for a quarter of the total profits made by DCL, owner of over a hundred brands of whisky as well as Gordon's, the world's top-selling gin.

Mr. Sam's first investment in Scotland had come as early as 1935 when he bought the Glasgow firm of Robert Brown through a remarkable broker, Jimmy Barclay. He had met Sam while traveling in the United States under a variety of assumed names selling Scotch. Sam's purchase was partly designed to prevent Brown from exploiting "Four Crown," a brand name it owned. But Brown also brought with it a stock of aging Scotch, a hoard to which Mr. Sam gradually added over the next decade without revealing any specific outlet for it. Harry Hatch had already gone further, buying two Scottish distilleries, followed in 1936 by James Ballantine, a well-known blender. Two years later he built a proper production complex, the basis of the growth of the best-selling Ballantine's Scotch after the war.

Just after the war Sam had visited Scotland but had concluded that the outlook was unpromising. But in 1949 Barclay came to him with the offer of Chivas Brothers, grocers* and whisky merchants in Aberdeen. (Until

---

* The original grocers' shop is now a Chinese restaurant.

1945 much of the best Scotch was blended by up-market grocers). The firm had all the qualities Mr. Sam was looking for: It was old-established—indeed founded in 1801—and had an excellent reputation. Above all since 1843 it had had a Royal Warrant, supplying whisky as well as groceries to Balmoral Castle near Aberdeen, summer home of Queen Victoria and Prince Albert. So the Chivas Brothers had supplied the whisky which Queen Victoria habitually used to strengthen her claret. The founders and their successors had pioneered the idea of up-market blended whiskies, for James Chivas had seized on two key concepts, reliability and continuity of quality, supplemented by an age statement—and mention of the royal connection. Their finest blend was a Royal Glen Nevis twenty-year-old whisky. Chivas Regal, introduced in 1909 as a blend containing exclusively whiskies aged twenty-five years or more, was a natural extension of the firm's long-term policy and until Prohibition was successful in the United States. But after World War I stocks had been so depleted that the age claim had been made less specific, stating that the whisky was merely "of great age," although by 1938 a little was being sold to the United States as twelve years old. So Mr. Sam, who paid a mere £80,000 (then $192,000) for the firm, the name, and its stocks, got a bargain, for he also acquired the unique Chivas combination of an up-market blend containing an age statement.

Combining his stocks and his newly acquired brand name Mr. Sam created his masterpiece. He had a very clear idea of the taste he wanted. The key was not the grain whiskey, which formed over half the blend, but the malts, lovingly twice distilled in pot stills at distilleries scattered all over Scotland near suitable sources of pure water. Mr. Sam had decided that he would continue with a twelve-year-old blend—making it the first major brand ever to make an age statement on the label, though it is now a routine claim. So he needed to find whiskies that would reach their peak at that age. He kept asking for samples to be sent to New York and soon found that there were half a dozen relatively gutsy whiskies that needed the time to mature into a round and satisfying blend, and these accounted for half the total malt content. The rest came from up to a hundred different grain distilleries from continuous stills.

He had largely avoided the peaty whiskies from the Isle of Islay, concentrating for the most part on the deep but elegant malts from Speyside, west of Aberdeen. In 1950 he bought Strathisla near Keith in the heart of Speyside, a distillery with a history dating back to 1786.* Over the past fifty years it has provided a high proportion of the malts required for Chivas. Jimmy Lang, who was to remain a key figure in the blending of Chivas for thirty years, becoming chief blender in 1966, describes it as "the heart of Chivas, a hell of a nice Speyside malt." Over the following decades Seagram built two more distilleries nearby, Glen Keith in 1958 and Braes of Glenlivet in 1973, to cope with ever-increasing demands for malt whiskey. Lang remembers how "we always had problems getting more of the best malts. Sometimes we had to go round pubs which often had casks of old malts." To make the final blend he called on the services of Charles Jullian, head of an old-established London firm that also blended tea. Indeed in 1775 they had sent a cargo of their finest blend to Boston. The rest, as they say, is history. Charles had already blended two best-selling whiskies for two London wine merchants† J & B Rare and Cutty Sark, which were lighter than those created by Scottish-based blenders. But it was Sam who set the style of the whiskey when he presented Jullian with the "palette" of malts he was to use. Inevitably Mr. Sam continued to take a close interest in the blend, which, as Jimmy Lang says, "should combine quality and consistency. Over time the formula changed but the style didn't." Not surprisingly, "No one dared interfere."

Sam naturally exploited the coronation of Queen Elizabeth II in June 1953 as he had her father's journey to Canada in 1939. Sam and Saidye were two of the handful of Canadians invited to attend the event—when he found that their seats were behind a pillar in Westminster Abbey he arranged to exchange them with those allotted to two other Canadians. Sam celebrated the event with Royal Salute, a twenty-one-year-old Scotch, an age chosen to accord with the twenty-one-gun salute reserved for royalty. Amazingly his team managed to find enough whisky of the proper age to produce a few hundred cases within seventeen months. Royal Salute was packaged in a porcelain bottle and came complete with a dark green bag, echoing the ones used for Crown Royal but in a color the British associate with classiness. The whisky duly received the Royal Warrant, albeit only for coronation year.

Over the years as sales grew Seagram had to build ever larger premises to

---

* The date was naturally exploited in 1986 when Edgar received supplies of a specially blended thirty-five-year-old Strathisla single malt to celebrate the distillery's two hundredth anniversary.
† Justerini & Brooks and Berry Bros. & Rudd.

hold immense stocks of Scotch—at one point they were the second largest in the world, since all the ingredients in Chivas, including the grain whisky, had to be matured for three or four times as long as an ordinary blended Scotch. With his usual foresight—or, if you prefer, obsession—with "inventory," Sam had arranged for associates whom he financed to build up their own stocks on which he could draw if required. One was a man called William Whiteley; another, Haim Irving, is remembered by old-timers as a "typical film gangster" who also owned four brands, including, improbably, one called House of Lords. Nevertheless Sam's foresight did not help the blenders, for they never received any idea of the amount of Scotch likely to be sold, and when, later, they did, the forecasts tended to be unreliable, far too pessimistic for a couple of decades, and then in the 1980s and 1990s ludicrously overoptimistic.

The stocking and blending of Chivas was concentrated in Paisley on the outskirts of Glasgow. The design of the offices and warehouses—the architect, Lothian Barclay, was Jimmy's son—was more harmonious than that of 1430 Peel Street. The appearance of the offices was modeled on elegant eighteenth-century Scottish architecture, while Mr. Sam insisted that they should be built from the same type of stone as that used at Strathisla. Typically he also made detailed changes to the design: The coynes at the corners of the building were rebuilt on his instructions and he insisted that there should be a portrait of the poet Robert Burns, because of his supposed connection with Aberdeen, as well as a plug in Gaelic and the date 1801, when distilling first started on the site.* Barclay based his design for the warehouses on the "Ctesiphon style" the, very suitable, Persian idea of a series of elegant arches. Within twenty years Keith also housed a sprawl of warehouses on a hundred-acre site. And with the purchase of the Glenlivet company in 1978 came five more. All these were key because the Chivas blend originally contained over a half of malt whisky.

To market the new wonder whisky he turned to Philip Kelly who had moved into advertising after leaving Seagram, tired of the political nature of the organization. Kelly's first reaction to the packaging was, "Well Sam, this is so bad it's good. You must have done it on purpose. It looks like it's a hundred fifty years old"—precisely the image Sam was trying to promote. He was immediately rehired. He knew he was lucky: "We had age, tradi-

---

* Locals claim that distilling at the spot dates back to 1208.

tion, and the Royal Warrant. We had everything, including a wonderful product." He recruited a small team of other "refugees from a powerful political scramble." They decided to set a high price, $8.40 for a fifth,* giving enough room for profits for everybody down the chain. The exclusive distributors specially chosen for every major territory were not allowed to grant discounts. The sales campaign started in New York on the grounds that "any time you can get a brand of anything going in New York, you can sell it at any place." Later Victor Fischel did his bit by "persuading" the distributors in Chicago not to cut prices.

In devising the marketing campaign Kelly naturally concentrated on tradition. The Scottish hero Sir Robert Bruce served as a trademark and the label had a "beautiful tapestry effect that breathed Scotland and all its tradition and glory." As Kelly pointed out, Seagram were the first people to exploit the "Americans' deep and abiding interest" in the fact that "the business in Scotland is deep in romance and tradition." Even the bottle was old-fashioned—Kelly arranged for two hundred thousand copies of a "classic, stuffy Scottish letter" on Chivas Brothers stationery specially written by him, and signed by Jimmy Barclay to be sent out. The letter insisted that the recipient was known to be a connoisseur and should act quickly to be able to buy his share of this precious liquid. It was a classic element in the launch of a brand designed to be up-market, without in fact being too exclusive. Edgar did a great deal to help. When sales in the United States stalled in 1960 he relaunched the brand, making it lighter by bringing down the proportion of malt whisky from the previous 65 percent to 40 percent. He also ensured that the bottle was lightened. But, most important, he persuaded his father to hire the advertising genius Bill Bernbach. He produced advertisements whose text was a model of aspirational yet tongue-in-cheek copy summed up in one of the captions: "Of course you can live without Chivas, the question is how well?" (Mr. Sam had wanted to simply place bottles on a pedestal.)

Nevertheless at one point Mr. Sam rather lost his nerve, thinking of exchanging the brand for a substantial, though by no means controlling, stake in the DCL group, which, by the early 1950s was clearly already stag-

---

* It had become customary for prices not to be in round dollars. If they were, Kelly explained, "The clerk could easily slip the dollar into his pocket without being noticed. If a price were at ninety-eight cents, the clerk had to ring up the ninety-eight cents in the cash register and get the change, the customer saw the price in broad daylight."

nating. He had to be persuaded out of the idea by Edgar though neither of them ever dreamed that Chivas could end up selling over four million cases. For at first sales of Chivas grew only slowly. This was partly because of the need to accumulate ever-growing stocks of aging whisky. Indeed it was not until 1958 that Chivas sold a hundred thousand cases and another five before sales topped the 250,000 case mark. But from then on, helped by Edgar's changes to the blend, they leaped ever upwards. By 1971 Seagram was selling 1.2 million cases of this highly priced whisky, seven hundred thousand in the United States and another five hundred thousand in the rest of the world, and sales reached over two million by 1976. From the beginning Chivas was a truly aspirational drink. Sam and Edgar realized this during a visit to a working-class bar. "A construction worker comes in and he wants a drink," said the bartender. "For ten cents more you can ask for Chivas Regal and be a big shot." Chivas became a cult drink; if you drank Chivas you were, by definition, a "man of distinction." By the 1980s Chivas was a bestseller in markets from Belgium, France, and Italy to Japan and Mexico, with the US accounting for only a half of the total. Seagram was lucky because during the 1960s and 1970s DCL had become increasingly sclerotic, never adequately promoting Johnny Walker Black Label. Well before he died in 1971 Mr. Sam knew that he had his world brand.

Ten

NOT JUST DYSFUNCTIONAL,
DISINTEGRATING

The Bronfmans are monsters. We are all monsters.
—MINDA DE GUNZBURG TALKING TO LEO KOLBER

SEAGRAM'S EMPLOYEES MAY HAVE BEEN ONE LARGE, MORE-OR-LESS happy family, but by contrast the split within the Bronfman family itself, which had started thirty years earlier, had widened and deepened by the early 1950s. By then Sam was able to ensure that the company was his personal possession, to be handed down solely to his two sons, Edgar and Charles, with his brothers reduced to ciphers, legally as well as managerially. Not surprisingly his two daughters, Minda and Phyllis, were assumed by their father to be as irrelevant to the business as his four sisters had been. It was still very much a family company, with the eight family members holding 53 percent of the equity. The estimated nine thousand, inevitably small, shareholders, holding 47 percent of the equity, were not of much concern in Peel Street.

It was already clear that the other members of the family and their offspring would no longer have any say in running Seagram. It was in 1942 that Sam first started to impose his solution to the dynastic problem. It was simplicity itself. As Robertson put it, "There was room for only one dynasty in the House of Seagram." In one sense this was reasonable, after all he had seven siblings who produced two dozen offspring, and power did need to be concentrated. Abe had five daughters, Harry two daughters and two sons, and Allan two sons and a daughter. Mr. Sam told Robertson that "Harry and Allan seemed confident that their sons would inherit part of Seagram's on a more or less equal basis with my own sons. I could never allow this." The reason he gave was plausible but only marginally accurate. It was mainly "because I don't believe that anybody should clutter up his business with relatives." The result could already be seen in the 1930s when Harry's second son, Gerald, realized that he would be cut out. The crucial moment came when Wachtel introduced him at a sales conference as "the heir apparent." "Both my uncles [Sam and Allan] were there and I knew my days were numbered"—though his brother Allan, the only exception to the exclusion of other members of the family, had been put in charge of the enormous LaSalle distillery until his early death in 1944 at the age of thirty-seven.

But a definite separation was reached only in 1951, after a "family conclave" dominated by Mr. Sam. By then the family had around $20 million in assets apart from their shares in Seagram. A trust called Cemp was set up in succession to earlier holding companies called Brintcan and Brosis (brothers and sisters) designed to shield the family from inheritance taxes. The assets were divided, with Sam getting $8 million, Allan $3 million, Abe and Harry $2 million each, while the four sisters received a mere $1 million each. Sam received an even greater proportion of the family's holding in Seagram, 70 percent, the remainder shared between his siblings. Moreover Sam would be in total control of the business. Not surprisingly, the proposal led to a furious row. Sam claimed a considerable reward for his cleverness in steering clear of the family's problems with the law, enabling him to charge that had Harry and Abe steered clear of trouble they would have been as much use as Allan, who, as so often, supported him. But it was Rose, speaking for the sisters, who clinched the argument when she said that "Sam is being modest about his own share, and generous to all of us. I for one am very proud of him." Harry, at least, had anticipated the new arrangement, for he had already pulled most of his money out of Seagram and started his own investment fund called Grahsom, named after his four children.

The shares in Seagram were placed in a holding company, Seco Ltd., which itself was owned by two groups of trust funds, Edper for Allan's three children (Edward, Peter, and Mona) and Cemp (Charles, Edgar, Minda, and Phyllis), which owned 70 percent of Seco. But Sam's four children had four unequal holdings in Cemp. Charles had a stake of 33 percent, Edgar 28 percent, Phyllis 21 percent, and Minda a mere 18 percent.* Typically, Sam said that he was sure that the girls would find husbands rich enough to

---

* The percentages within Cemp changed over the years. When any of the four wanted to draw money out of the trust, as Charles did to buy the Montreal Expos or Phyllis to set up the Canadian Centre for Architecture, their share was naturally diluted.

make up the difference. As soon as the eldest child in one branch of the family reached twenty-one the trust would be split in two and half the income diverted to the younger generation—who would inherit the assets when the eldest child reached his or her fortieth birthday.

In the mid-1960s Cemp paid $16.6 million for Edper's 32.2 percent of Seco, thus consolidating Sam's control. Earlier the finest legal brains in Canada, most notably Laz Phillips, had created a tangle of holding companies (Econtech, Grandco, Rampart) which actually owned the stock in a manner so tax-efficient that the tax man has never been able to touch the income or gains enjoyed by the trusts. Under Canadian law dividends paid by one company to another are free of tax, and they could also carry their investments at cost rather than their—invariably far greater—market value. They were also organized to withstand the death of individual beneficiaries and left the family in control of over half the shares. By then several members of the family, including Harry, Abe, and their sister Laura, had already sold some of their shares to Sam and Allan. Although Sam treated his siblings appallingly, they all ended up rich, only partly because of their own talents.

Sam had ensured that he and Allan pooled their interests in a way that prevented Allan from ever joining together with his brothers and the next generation to oppose Sam's policies. The fact that Allan was a partner of Sam's within Cemp naturally encouraged him in his—mistaken—belief that his sons would be actively involved with Seagram. In fact, by handing over his stock, he had relinquished his power as a substantial direct holder in Seagram, for Sam would have been in a minority if all three brothers had been able to gang up on him.

The sidelining of Allan was the final episode in Sam's systematic downgrading of his brothers that had started in the 1920s when he downplayed Harry's contribution to the family's success and, as we saw, continued in the 1930s when Harry's second son, Gerald, was excluded. The situation with Allan was more complicated. According to Edgar, Sam started feuding with Allan in the mid-1950s, most obviously because Allan would use the word "we," implying that he was an equal partner, "and that galled Sam to no end." According to Robertson Mr. Sam had told Allan, "The business is mine. You must understand that the words 'we' and 'us' no longer apply." Yet Allan remained a danger; charming, well educated, the only member of the family to have gone to university, and naturally Sam was jealous of him. Indeed Henderson describes Allan as the very opposite of

Sam, as "a person of considerable dignity, well educated, suave and urbane, and infinitely patient and tolerant . . . never once do I recall Allan losing his temper." As Leo Kolber put it, "Theirs was never an equal partnership, and Mr. Sam was very unsparing, and often cruel, in his tirades against his brother." Richler provides a pretty accurate description of Bernard's younger brother, a character modeled on Allan. He "never forgot a cleaning lady's name, a secretary's birthday, or the illness of a filing clerk's wife" and was adored by all the employees. A pattern had been established that was to be repeated over the generations, with a hustler—Sam, Edgar, and Edgar Jr.—and a much-loved brother—Allan, Charles, and Sam Jr.

From the late 1930s Sam's unchallenged dominance was obvious from the way that Harry, Abe, and Barney Aaron were allocated inconspicuous offices on the third floor of the Montreal head office, well away from the seat of real power, Sam's office on the first floor. But Allan was a different matter and remained a challenge. When he turned up in the office in the uniform of a private in the Canadian army, smartly saluting Sam, he exploded with jealous rage, "Ah look at the fucking hero, you'd think he'd just won the war. Christ, they get a few more like him and Hitler's got a chance." Worse was to come at the end of the war when Allan donated a boatload of flour to the stricken French city of Le Havre and was promptly awarded the *Légion d'honneur.* Sam exploded, asking, "How come he didn't send the flour from both of us?"—and continued to steam whenever he saw Allan wearing the little scarlet ribbon of the Legion in his buttonhole. But the worst insult came when Allan led them to make their first diversification outside the drinks business through the successful purchase of a stake in the Canadian oil company, Royalite Oil. "If Sam was angry with those who gave him bad advice," observed Newman, "he was downright enraged at anyone whose counsel he opposed and who later proved to be correct."

One day an argument over some of the trusts their father had set up and of which Allan was a trustee exploded when Mr. Sam threw a glass at his brother. "With an unerring eye for weakness," wrote Marrus, "Sam punished Allan for not living up to his own standards. Allan, for his part, slipped deeper and deeper into dependency. . . . Mild mannered and courteous, Allan deferred gently to his fiery brother and the very deference seems to have irritated Sam, confirming his sense of his brother's weakness and timidity." For, just as Harry would have been happier as a provincial worthy, Allan would have been far happier as a lawyer than as Sam's punching bag.

Edgar was just as harsh as his father, attacking his uncle as "essentially weak," while Sam was attacked as "jealous for having the education he so desperately felt he lacked." Nevertheless "as time went on Father realized that he really didn't need Allan." In his autobiography, *Good Spirits*, Edgar claimed, too, that the frequent calls Allan made to the office when the family went on fishing holidays were designed purely to impress his family—he even sneered that Allan did not dare tell his other children that his daughter Mona had committed suicide, saying merely that she had died from a heart attack.

As time went on Allan was increasingly shunted aside, remaining a senior vice president until 1975 but by then charged almost exclusively with looking after the family's many philanthropic activities. His sons were excluded even more completely even though they had assumed that they would be part of the business. According to Edgar, Allan did not dare tell his children that they had been excluded. But in reality when Peter graduated from Yale in 1952, Allan told Newman, "He started to cry and asked me, 'How is it that I can't get into the company?' So I told him." Sam had indeed ensured that, contrary to their expectations, neither of Allan's sons, Edward and Peter, would be involved in the business. But earlier he may well have been ambiguous in his dealings with Allan.

The final showdown had involved a shouting match between Sam and Allan. "Sam was really mad at me," Allan told Newman, "and when Sam gets mad he goes back four generations." The break was complete; Sam stopped talking to Allan for a whole year, even though they occupied adjacent offices, and the families stopped crossing the lawn between the brothers' houses. The final break came in 1969 when Sam threw Edward and Peter out of his offices after their investment company, Edper, had made its first major independent financial investment, for Sam's jealousy extended across the generational divide.

By 1970 the situation had deteriorated so far that none of the brothers were mentioned in *From Little Acorns*, the official company history, which otherwise included such crucial figures as the company's chef, saluted for making "the best boiled beef in the world." Two years later the British-owned Canadian Marconi Company, which owned a televison station and three radio stations in Canada, had accepted a bid of C$18 million from Cemp, even though Edper had made a counteroffer that included a larger cash element. Edper's eminent lawyer Jacques Courtois—who fulfilled the same role for Edward and Peter as Laz Phillips had done for Sam—complained to the regulatory commission which oversaw radio and television licenses that Cemp was guilty of shady dealings, stock manipulation, and of trying to acquire the television station merely to make a tax loss. The two families now had in common only their names—and the money they had acquired, either from Seagram or from their own efforts, which were far less unproductive than Sam made out. The profound schism within the family left scars on everyone involved—except Sam and Edgar. As Harry's son Gerald lamented, "The closeness of the family was once a wonderful thing. All the children and the children's children are being denied that. They've lost a lot."

The younger generation went on to make their own fortunes; within a couple of decades their investments were scattered throughout North America. Newman's sample, taken in the late 1970s, included Barney Aaron's son Arnold Aaron, who was in plastic cups, while Rose's son Ernest was in real estate in California, and Jean's family ran the Seagram distribution company in Boston. As for Gerald, he inherited some of the family financial talents. He invested in *The Institutional Investor*, a highly successful international financial magazine, and ensured that his holding company, Gerin, went public to ensure that he received its dividends tax-free—one year it even received a tax refund. Most members of the family retained the almost regal haughtiness inevitably associated with great wealth. In the words of the chairman of Ranger Oil, a company controlled by Edper, "Edward demands special treatment, and he gets it. He's extremely gracious but occasionally expects the deference due to a financial aristocrat."*

Sam was a ruthless brother but he wasn't a very satisfactory father either. He was away the whole week, generally in New York. On Saturdays he went to the office, while, from the late 1930s on, he was busy on Sundays because of his deep involvement with the Jewish community. Nevertheless, as Marrus says, through sheer force of personality, "Physically distant though he certainly was, Sam was a constant presence" in the family. Not

---

* The most extraordinary recent phenomenon is an ecological activist called Jeffrey Bronfman. He is deeply involved in a small religious group founded in Brazil in 1961 that apparently blends traditional Christian theology with indigenous beliefs, including the drinking of a tea called hoasca. Unfortunately the American authorities regard this beverage as hallucinogenic and thus a controlled substance. Bronfman has sued the American government and the case, which he won in every lower court, went to the Supreme Court in 2004.

only was he largely absent, he could be as terrifying at home as he was in business—though this never occurred to him, because he did love his children in his own way. He tried to educate them through weekly talks, which he liked to call "lessons in life." But the children were more affected by hearing Sam's periodic outbursts of rage, after which, wrote Robertson, "Four pairs of innocent young eyes would nearly pop out of four little heads as the sound and fury of these eruptions blasted through the shut door." They were not to know that his associates were used to such eruptions and that they died down as quickly as they had arisen.

Like many old-fashioned fathers, Sam was too nervous to hold his children when they were young, afraid that he might drop them. But he was strict and Victorian—Minda* vividly remembered being banished from the family table in tears when she once appeared wearing lipstick. Victorian too were the written contributions, the diaries and poems, they would present to him. Like most self-obsessed tycoons—and many other fathers then and now—Sam left virtually all the upbringing of his four children to his wife. As Saidye told Terence Robertson, "I was pleased at what he was achieving but not particularly happy at being father as well as mother to the children." As Edgar put it, "Business was one of his children—his first child." Not surprisingly Edgar once claimed that he was closer to the family chauffeur (for they were driven everywhere, even to school) than to his father—or even to his mother.

But perhaps the story which best illustrates Mr. Sam's total unawareness of family life—possibly mythical but still typical—concerns the children's baths. When he was in New York he would phone every evening at about the time the children would be having their baths. Once, hearing the noise, he asked what it was all about. Told that they were in the bath he exclaimed, "Baths? At this time of day? Why can't they have their baths in the morning like ordinary people?" On another occasion he phoned after 10 P.M. and was astonished to be informed that the children were asleep. Nevertheless his children were not the only ones to suffer from such a privileged upbringing. Allan's son Peter told Newman how he "grew up in a castle on a hill, sensitive but not fully aware of what was going on. I had no friends and no real relationship with my parents. I had a nurse from when I was about five to about ten and felt so strongly about her that when we met

---

* The name by which she was universally known, even though her real name was Mindel.

in Ireland eighteen years later, we just fell into each other's arms and hugged and hugged."

Edgar, for one, did not feel that he received sufficient motherly love to replace his father's absence. In contrast to his father, "Mother, while physically present, to me she was remote and inaccessible." Typically, when the eight-year-old Edgar threatened to run away her only reply was to ask, "What will you do for money?" Edgar clearly did not appreciate what was intended to be a jocular remark. Indeed he does not mention his mother's death in his autobiography, he merely remarked that when he visited her three months before she died "she was awake but not quite up to eating."

The young Bronfmans lived an almost royal existence, largely confined to their compound in Westmount. There was even a track between the two houses so that the children had somewhere to ride their bicycles. They enjoyed, wrote Edgar, a lifestyle consistent with the Bronfmans' status as by far the city's richest Jewish family. "We had a large staff: a butler, a cook, a kitchen maid, a parlor maid, a 'lady's maid,' a laundress, a gardener, a chauffeur, a 'madamoiselle' for the girls, and a nanny for the boys." They also had a deeply intimidating butler, a veteran of the Danish Royal Guard. Life inside the compound was isolated, encouraging a lack of contact with external reality similar to that experienced by the Rothschilds, or the British aristocracy for that matter. To emphasize the point the children were dressed like young British aristocrats and led a totally sheltered life, their social circle limited to the tiny Jewish plutocracy in Westmount. Not surprisingly Sam's children were also very close, in their childhood anyway, though later there were strains, especially between Edgar and Minda.

The children realized how different they were only when, as Robertson puts it, they started "bringing home friends who would run about the place, count the number of bathrooms and talk in awed whispers." These children generally came only as guests to the family's famously lavish children's birthday parties. Richler was not exaggerating—much—when he wrote of one such event, featuring the "enormous swimming pool. A heated, multilevel tree house, designed by an architect and furnished by an interior decorator. A miniature railway. A hockey rink, the boards thickly padded. A corner candy store with a real soda fountain tended by a black man who laughed at everything."

Mr. Sam, as the ultimate Victorian patriarch, naturally believed that daughters were destined purely for marriage and children and that his two sons would automatically inherit his qualities as well as his business. Indeed, in those far-off days, the fact that Sam's daughters, Minda and Phyl-lis, were to inherit shares in the business and not cash, represented a rela-tively liberal attitude. He was by no means alone in his dismissive attitude towards girls, which extended to the smallest gestures. When Edgar's first wife, Ann, showed her grandfather, the banker C. M. Loeb, the sapphire and diamond bracelet Edgar had bought to celebrate the birth of their first son she asked him what would have happened if the baby had been a girl. "The stones would have been a little smaller," said the old man. The girls were not even given Hebrew lessons—which makes one wonder if Mr. Sam secretly hoped that they would "marry out." He would also harangue them about the uselessness of going to college because too much education was not good for girls, and the resulting independence might ruin their chances of a good marriage. Ironically they were the only members of the family to even get first degrees, Minda at Smith College followed by a masters at Co-lumbia (her thesis was on the influence of Darwinism on French thought in the last sixty years of the nineteenth century), and Phyllis at a number of universities, whereas neither of their brothers had remotely distin-guished academic careers.

Minda, who died of cancer in 1986, seems to have been deeply frus-trated, a reaction natural in an intelligent, strong-minded woman doomed not to have a worthwhile job. For most of the time she managed to present a much appreciated, elegant, gracious face to the world. Robertson de-scribed the thirty-four-year-old Minda as "amongst the most poised of women"; her "dark hair which one can never imagine windblown or ruffled frames pale sculptured features which one can never imagine to be any-thing but wholly composed. Her slenderness creates the illusion of tallness and natural grace gives the impression of lithe economy of movement." But even Robertson noted "slips" which revealed "some part of her father's inner turbulence." For, as Robertson puts it, "If her appearance is that of physical fragility, she is intellectually tough and uncompromising." Behind the façade was an appalling temper reminiscent of her father. "In some ways," wrote one observer, "she was the most like her father. . . . She was ambitious, she was able, and she was angry her entire life." At times, too, she could appear the very model of a Jewish princess. Her cool contemptu-ous stare daunted even her father. "That girl," he would mutter, "sometimes she infuriates me." Indeed Sam was so frightened of her that he would hide, claiming that he was in a meeting to avoid seeing her, while later she would intervene loudly and emphatically in the twice-yearly meetings of

The "Old Bal," Harry's pride and joy, in Yorkton *(Yorkton Archives)*

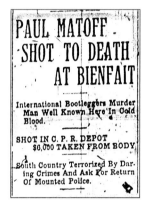

Harry was just as interested in selling cars as in hustling liquor. *(Yorkton Archives)*

The murder of his brother-in-law Paul Matoff traumatized Harry—but didn't greatly interest the local press. *(Yorkton Archives)*

Harry Hatch of Hiram Walker, the Bronfmans' great rival *(Fortune)*

William Ross (on left) and Thomas Herd (on right), the hard-nosed Scots from DCL who organized a partnership with Sam and Allan Bronfman *(James Bacon and Sons / Fortune)*

To *Fortune* magazine in 1948, Mr. Sam was America's "whiskey king."
(Edward Burks, Scope / Fortune)

Seagram had been a major business for over half a century before the Bronfman brothers took over. *(Yorkton Archives)*

The Bronfman clan (from left to right): Abe, Harry, Sam, and Allan; sisters Laura, Rose, "Bee," and Jean *(Fortune)*

Sam's formidable wife, Saidye, with the children: Edgar (standing), Charles, Minda (center), and Phyllis *(Fortune)*

Sam's key executives (from left to right): Frank R. Schwengel, a real World War I general; William W. Wachtel, the Alphonse Menjou look-alike; the crucial but unmentionable Victor A. Fischel; and Frederick Willkie, the scientist-distiller (*Myron Ehrenberg / Fortune*)

Seagram's laboratory was not for show but an essential element in Mr. Sam's obsession with quality. (*Hugh Frankel / Fortune*)

Allan Bronfman, Sam's civilized, persecuted younger brother (*Fortune*)

Philip Beekman, who went on to have a successful business career after leaving Seagram (*Laurence Barnes / BusinessWeek*)

Charles Bronfman, the younger brother who was too meek for his—or Seagram's—good (*Christopher Morris / Maclean's*)

Happy families—at the time anyway:

Edgar and his first wife, formerly Ann Loeb, with Sam Jr. and Edgar Jr. (standing), Matthew, Holly, and Adam *(Fortune)*

Phyllis Lambert, architect and visionary *(Fortune)*

Charles with his first wife, Barbara, and their son Stephen *(Fortune)*

Minda, "my daughter the baroness," with husband Baron Alain de Gunzburg and their sons, Jean-François and Charles Samuel *(Fortune)*

Edgar's three glamorous Englishwomen: Sue Lloyd (above left), long-time mistress whom he ditched, here with Michael Caine in *The Ipcress File*; the Lady Carolyn Townshend (above right) at a charity event at St. James's Palace with a client, Queen Elizabeth, the Queen Mother; and his third wife, née Rita Webb (left), also known as Georgiana
(Rex Features, the author, istockphoto.com)

Edgar (center) with his eldest two sons: his chosen successor, the younger Edgar Jr. (on left), and his unlucky older brother, Sam Jr. (on right)
(Duane Michaels / Fortune)

Edgar Jr. and Sr. in search of
investments away from the
liquor business, as portrayed
by *The New Yorker*
(*Robert Risko / The New Yorker*)

Barry Diller, nicknamed—
not without reason—
"Killer Diller"
(*AP Photo / Tammy Lechner*)

Michael Ovitz, the super-agent
who was too greedy for his own
good (*AP Photo / Chris Gardner*)

Ron Meyer, the unassuming
ex-Marine who made a surprising
success of Universal's film
production business
(*AP Photo / Dean Cox*)

Edgar Bronfman, Jr., (left) and the French megalomaniac Jean-Marie Messier of Vivendi (right) who absorbed—and nearly destroyed—the Seagram empire
(AP Photo / Laurent Rebours)

Messier's nemesis, Claude Bébéar, the insurance tycoon nicknamed "the Crocodile"
(AP)

The iconic Seagram building in its glorious isolation from its surroundings *(Emory Library)*

Sam Bronfman's house in Westmount, comfortable but not grandiose *(Montreal Star Gazette)*

The Seagram head office, a picturesque
building now nestled among Montreal's
skyscrapers
(Andre Forget / CP Images)

Chivas Regal as a status
symbol—advertising genius
Bill Bernbach at his most
fanciful
(Author)

"Men of Distinction,"
a slogan so successful for
Lord Calvert whiskey
that even *The New
Yorker* could assume
its readers knew all
about it
*(Tee and Charles
Addams Foundation)*

the trustees of Cemp, the family's investment company. Not surprisingly Edgar claims that she was always jealous of the attention paid to the first-born son, four years her junior.

From her adolescence on she was only too aware that she was an heiress. When she was nearing thirty—relatively late for a Jewish princess—Minda married Baron Alain de Gunzburg, a member of what the French call *la haute Juiverie*—the Gallic equivalent of Our Crowd. Mr. Sam was naturally proud of her alliance, referring to "my daughter the baroness," while Minda was fully aware of their pretensions, calling them the "Ginsboigs." The Gunzburg family was loosely connected with the Rothschilds* while Alain, the son of a much-decorated general, was actively involved in merging the family bank, Louis Hirsch, with the financial interests of the Seligman family and those of the Louis Dreyfus family, the biggest French grain merchants.

Alain naturally assumed that his wife's family would welcome a scion of such a distinguished family into their inner counsels. But Alain was much disliked by the Bronfmans as a pretentious, lightweight fellow and by Seagram executives as an arrogant, bad-tempered, and fundamentally useless person. This was rather unfair; he was by no means stupid and could relax driving his Mini Cooper round Paris with a splendid disregard for traffic lights—"Red is French for green," he would say. Despite his—and Minda's—efforts he was never allowed to play any active role in the business. This does not seem to have worried him too much, he was happy hunting in France, Spain, or Scotland, although it obviously greatly affected his wife's ambitions and thus damaged the marriage. He and his brother François had to content themselves with managing the group's investments in France—which were considerable for they included Barton & Guestier, leading Bordeaux merchants, as well as Mumm and Perrier-Jouet champagne. And neither of Minda's two sons, Jean and Charles, was allowed anywhere near Seagram.

Minda's uptightness continued until her final illness, for while she was suffering from the liver cancer that killed her in 1986 when she was only sixty-one, she refused to tell anyone that she was ill except her husband and her two sons—hoping above all that her mother would die before her

---

* Alain's grandmother was a first cousin of the mother of Guy de Rothschild, the dominant figure of the French Rothschilds in the decades after the war.

and not be preceded into the grave by one of her children. She was even more tax-oriented than the rest of her family. In 1985, when she was near death, she consulted two of the family's senior advisers, Leo Kolber and the lawyer Paul Vineburg, to ensure that her affairs were rearranged so that her heirs would pay the minimum amount of tax.

But to Sam neither of his daughters was remotely as important as his two sons, for the total exclusion of his uncle and cousins left Edgar and Charles as the heirs to the business. His eldest son, Edgar, seemed doomed to go down in history as an Edsel Ford figure, ground down by a domineering father, unable to change the company he inherited from the pattern set by Sam, who kept a tight control until his death. Edgar had the sort of physically spoiled, psychologically rough upbringing typical of sons of monsters. So it is greatly to his credit that, whatever his faults, he was able to preserve the business and later, as we shall see, make a considerable contribution to world Jewry as the president of the World Jewish Congress. But throughout his life Edgar has always carried with him the burden of his inheritance. As he says: "I never got credit for being me, it's just that 'You were Sam's son.'"

From his youth Edgar was fully aware of his future, or if you prefer, his destiny. In a letter to his father when he was only sixteen he referred to himself as "the future President of Distillers Company-Seagrams." In *Good Spirits*, one of three books he wrote in his late sixties, he leaves a disagreeable taste in the mouth through a blend of whining, especially over his father; compulsive self-justification; and bitchiness about almost everyone else. A characteristic piece of ruthless contempt was his comment on the news that Oscar Weil of Browne Vintners had been run over and killed in London. He was, wrote Edgar, "probably looking the other way." His insecurity was just as profound as his father's but concentrated rather on a failure to appreciate his father's love for and pride in him—as Phyllis put it: "He never realized just how much his father adored him—despite the permanent obstacles he put up to any change." Typically, when Edgar asked for a new warehouse as a birthday present Sam remarked to Saidye, "A good son asks for such a birthday present."

Even now, in his mid-seventies, Edgar presents a striking figure. Newman provides an amazingly gushing—but not entirely inaccurate—description of him in the late 1970s when he was approaching his fiftieth birthday, a panegyric which clearly corresponded to the image Edgar was trying to convey of himself. "He stands there, looking through one of his two office windows, and he is beautiful, the body supple and relaxed, the fingernails manicured but not polished, the face graced by just a touch of tan. . . . He is beautiful and he knows all the tricks: how to invite attention by deliberately reducing the tempo of his limb movements," and so on and so on, but "it was his star quality rather than good looks that set him apart."

As his first wife put it, "Other people don't always like someone to be right handsome, bright—all these things, and a rich father too." Not surprisingly, throughout his life his appearance, wealth, and charm have brought women flocking. He has been married four times, first to Ann Loeb, by whom he had five children: Sam, Edgar Jr., Matthew, Adam, and Holly. She left him in 1971 and two years later he was married, very briefly, to a British aristocrat, Lady Carolyn Townshend, then to another English girl, Rita Webb—whom he called "George"—by whom he had two more daughters, Sara and Clare. Soon after Clare was born they divorced after only five years of marriage, though they came together again for a short time. But in the late 1980s he married for a fourth time, to painter Jan Aaronson, who had hesitated for a long time before she agreed.

In contrast to his father he has always been very aware of the bella figura that he deems essential for someone in his position. His father's attitude towards personal expense had always been deeply ambivalent. Sam was quite happy to let Saidye spend all the money she wanted on houses or her clothes but, as is so often the case with men from poor backgrounds, could be ludicrously penny-pinching, turning off all the lights in an office even if told that the cleaners were about to arrive. By contrast Edgar has always enjoyed a lifestyle far above his father, albeit one perfectly appropriate for a billionaire. He bought a 4,400-acre estate (called the VO Ranch) and commuted to it in the biggest of the company jets, later exchanging it for an estate in Virginia. As he took over so the lavishness extended to Seagram's own offices. In London they owned two charming townhouses, useful for conducting deals and for ensuring that Edgar's liaisons remained out of the public eye.

Richler provides what is only a slight parody of Edgar's office with its "Antique desk. Leather sofas. Matching wastepaper baskets fashioned of elephant's feet"—in reality his office was festooned with trophies from his African safaris, the heads of wildebeest, antelopes, and Cape buffaloes. "Thick creamy carpet. Silken walls. A framed *Forbes* magazine cover of Lionel. . . . Photographs of Lionel shaking hands with President Nixon, bussing Golda, embracing Frank Sinatra, dancing with Elizabeth Taylor, presenting a trophy to Jack Nicklaus." Edgar admits to a regal attitude:

"Like my father, I enjoy being 'somebody,'" he once said, for his style has always been far flashier than that of his father. With the figura went the address book. Richler also gives a—not greatly exaggerated—example of Edgar/Lionel's name-dropping: "I used to schmooze with Bobby [Kennedy]. I know Teddy. Sinatra has been out to our place in Southampton. You know who sang at Lionel Junior's Bar Mitzvah? Diana Ross. . . . Rocky was also at the Bar Mitzvah. So were Elaine and Swifty [Lazar the legendary Hollywood agent] and Arnie Palmer. We golf together." Nevertheless, friends attest that his door was always open to them or to their offspring in need of help or advice.

Edgar's style has always been most obvious when he travels, invariably in a company jet, requiring a helicopter for a journey of more than a few miles and of course a limo for the last few hundred yards to his destination. Early on he bought a company airplane without telling his father, who had never thought of owning one. At first Mr. Sam pretended to be shocked but from then on refused to travel by a "commercial" airline even when it took longer by a Seagram jet. In time the habit grew and senior executives thought nothing of using one of the company's fleet for even the most routine journeys, even though a flight to Paris would cost over $10,000, forty times that of the most luxurious commercial flight.

As time went on Edgar became obsessed by the status conferred by the ownership of what became a small fleet of jets, including the very latest Gulfstream executive planes, capable of flying higher, faster, and farther than mere "commercial" airliners. As late as 1988, by which time one would have thought that the "Seagram Air Force," as it was called, had become merely a convenience rather than a status symbol, one executive being interviewed for a senior position remembers that all Edgar talked about was how he had been the first to fly in a private plane from Moscow to Tel Aviv.* The Russians, he grumbled, were "abysmally ignorant of how to deal with private aircraft." As chairman he was also given to taking holidays in a company jet with a group of friends in sometimes outlandish places— once as far as Tashkent in Central Asia, visited after a business trip to Moscow. On these trips an advance guard would ensure that all was prepared, obviously including a plentiful supply of Seagram products in any bar he might visit or the minibar of any hotel suite he might occupy.

---

* A flight, Edgar proudly recalls in his autobiography, listed in the *Guinness Book of Records*.

Throughout his life Edgar has been capable of arrogant and insensitive behavior. When Julius Kessler, by then well into his eighties, showed him an ornate musical watch and told him it would be a present for Edgar's Bar Mitzvah, Edgar's prompt reply was "Thanks. But you're an old man now. And you may not be here for my Bar Mitzvah." Kessler, it is said, merely shrugged and handed over the watch immediately. In his book he dwells in detail, almost gloatingly, on how in the 1980s the son of Phil Beekman, his COO, developed AIDS, badly affecting the father's performance. And his arrogance came through in his remark that David Sacks, a lawyer he hired as treasurer, had a "strong intellect," citing the fact that "he does crossword puzzles even better than I do."

Edgar's education did not help. Both sons went to school in Montreal where Edgar showed early signs of disobedience—he became known as the boy who was caned the most. This stroppiness was not confined to his school days. Robertson summed up the difference between the two brothers in the contrast between their attitudes to bullying at school. "Edgar reacted by meeting the challenges of his tormentors head on and forcing them to back down. Charles, often thwarted when he tried to make friends, tended to either suffer in silence or become angry and petulant." At the age of fifteen Edgar was the first Jew to attend Trinity College School, a high Anglican (Episcopalian) establishment whose headmaster was the first not to have been a bishop. Not surprisingly Edgar failed to understand that it was normal for ambitious Jewish fathers to try to insert their offspring into non-Jewish society hoping that they would assimilate— he has never mentioned that while there he had a "nose job" that replaced the handsome hook found in the rest of the family with a rather unappetizing blob, a step clearly designed by his parents as part of a process to integrate him into non-Jewish society. At Trinity College Edgar first encountered anti-Semitism—as well as academic tests, resulting in a claim that one of them showed that he had enormous potential as a lawyer. He naturally complained about the way he was sent to such a school.

Two years later the by-now rebellious adolescent went to Williams College in Massachusetts. His behavior was typical of many rich men's sons who are unable to cope with the discipline, the intellectual rigor, involved in studying at an elite university. He behaved with the sort of recklessness typical of a spoiled billionaire's son—even getting engaged one weekend. But, as he put it, "What's the use of having a rich father if you can't spend his money?" With the help of James Linen, a Williams graduate and pub-

lisher of Time, Inc., a group in whose publications Seagram was obviously
a major advertiser, his father managed to have him allowed back. But, following a motorcycle accident, his father hauled him back home after the
authorities had suggested, in Robertson's delicate words, that his "diversified talents and interests might be more suitably cultivated elsewhere,
preferably outside the state of Massachusetts." As a result he returned
home to study at McGill, Montreal's finest university, and duly graduated.

As soon as he decently could, Edgar had moved to New York, the headquarters of the American business that accounted for four-fifths of Seagram's turnover—largely to get away from his father. He became an
American citizen in 1955 as soon as he was twenty-six and no longer eligible for the draft. His move did have one side effect, for it enabled him to
behave like a dutiful son, in one important respect at least. His first marriage was an entirely suitable one, to Ann Loeb, whose family, as partners
in the investment bank Loeb Rhodes, were charter members of the Wall
Street branch of Our Crowd. As such they retained an unappetizingly
snobby attitude towards co-religionists who, like the Bronfmans, had arrived in the late nineteenth century, mostly from Eastern Europe. At the
wedding, according to Marrus, Mrs. Albert Lehman, a charter Our Crow-
der, sighed that "those Bronfmans have just come down out of the trees."*
This was an echo of the condescension that had greeted the Bronfmans on
an earlier occasion when they "brought out" their elder son as though he
had been a debutante. The wedding was a Jewish one although the attitude
of the Loebs was very different from the Bronfmans' (at one time, according to Edgar, members of their Emanu-El synagogue were told to remove
their yarmulkes in what religious Jews referred to as "that cathedral").
Edgar was only too conscious of the racism involved: "Being a Russian Jew
in New York is worse than being black," he would say. And he went to extreme lengths to "pass for white" as it were, matching his blue eyes by dying
the hair on his head—and his chest—blond.

By contrast, Charles, wrote Newman, "is the most appealing of the
Bronfmans," the only one of Sam's children who could not remotely be described, in Minda's words, as a "monster." "There is a gentleness about

* Though his in-laws did at least enable him to join the Westchester County Century Country Club,
home-away-from-home for Our Crowd.

him," wrote Edgar, "humor in his eyes, and a sense of goodness when he speaks." Above all, Charles, like his uncle Harry, wanted a quiet life, but his brother also stood in the way. Charles had the attitude of British aristocrats throughout the ages, that money was a zero sum game, that they weren't making the stuff anymore and that all you could do was to preserve your inheritance. Charles, the peaceful one of the family, took more after his uncle Allan than his father and throughout his life he has been marked by the scars resulting from the terrible rows between them, scars that were to prevent him from opposing his brother's and nephew's sale of the family company. The trauma induced by the rows was so great that he would never move into an office that had previously been occupied by his uncle Allan, even if it was the most convenient one available. Charles's problems started in childhood when he suffered from a rare streptococcal infection that confined him to bed for six months and brought him to death's door. In the end he was cured only when his father pulled enough strings for him to be the first Canadian civilian to be treated with penicillin.

But, added Newman, "Mr. Sam could make boys out of men—and with Charles he almost succeeded" though his story was for a long time a happy one in which he got out of his father's shadow slowly, but far more effectively than his brother. But, as Michael McCormick, a long-time Seagram employee who had chaperoned Charles in his first years with the family firm, pointed out, Charles's main trouble "is that he's at least five times as good as he thinks he is." Nevertheless, despite an outwardly serene character he could be just as competitive as the rest of the family. "He's a terrible loser," a friend told Newman. "It's inbred that a Bronfman can't lose." Later in life he rejoiced when Hiram Walker's key brand, Canadian Club, started to cut into the sales of Seagram's whiskies. As he told Newman, when his employees wondered why he looked so happy he replied simply, "It's about time somebody really threw us one."

Not surprisingly Charles was never happy, either at TCS, where the anti-Semitism which he had encountered for the first time greatly upset him, or at McGill, where he encountered similar problems. He also found that although he could write essays, "When it came to exams, I'd get panic attacks"—a vital clue to the combination of indecisiveness and inability to respond positively to stress which was to haunt him throughout his life. Much later in life he asked Sir Martin Gilbert, the Jewish historian and authorized biographer of Sir Winston Churchill, to interview him with the object of publishing a book provisionally entitled *Conversations with Charles*. But Charles was so horrified by the frankness and honesty of his own replies that the project was aborted.

When his father allowed him to leave college in the middle of his third year he claimed that "it was like being let out of jail." He immediately went to work for the family firm. He soon won his spurs when put in charge of the newly acquired Thomas Adams Distillers, the new name for a British Columbia business called United Distillers Limited—its brands known to local drinkers as "U Die Later." He designed a new label for the leading Adams whiskey that his father dismissed as a "fancy design" but he persuaded Mr. Sam to allow him to go ahead, increasing sales fivefold in a mere two years. "I liked running Adams," he once said, "I guess that's because I enjoyed the challenge of selling." In 1958 he was given charge of House of Seagram, the Montreal-based company responsible for sales in Canada, the Caribbean, and Israel. He proved an excellent chairman, willing to delegate—an unusual quality in the family—and running a devolved, relaxed, successful business.

Charles seems to have been content to live within the relatively closed world in which he, like the rest of the family, had been brought up. Charles was still so timid that, allegedly, his father offered a friend's daughter several million dollars if she would marry him. In the end she preferred to marry "out"—a non-Jewish industrialist called Bill Green, rich and independent enough to become one of Edgar's few real friends. In the end Charles continued to live in the house on Belvedere Avenue until he got married at the relatively late age of thirty-two to a woman he had met on a blind date in New York; Barbara Baerwald, the daughter of a Wall Street banker.

Sam could claim that he'd set his sons up better than the Rothschilds: "They spread the children, I kept them together"—notably by excluding any of their uncles or cousins from the company. His boast was justified by the peaceful way the two sons soon divided their inheritance, both choosing a path which suited their very different temperaments. A possibly apocryphal story tells of the way they reacted when a bartender ran out of a particular brand of whiskey at a reception. When Edgar said "I'd fire him," Charles reacted, "Too bad you can't condone one mistake." To which Edgar replied, "Why should I?"

When Edgar was only twenty-three and Charles just twenty-one they settled their respective roles in the business. Charles was clearly content with a secondary position, or rather chose to be a major fish in the relatively small pond that was Montreal. "I don't like New York and the throat cutting, the tremendous competitive drive that goes on there. . . . I don't particularly want to run this empire," he said, happy to remain number three in his father's lifetime and then number two. Both Edgar and Charles were also only too conscious of the misery inflicted by their father on his three brothers—above all on Allan, a saga of sadism that was still being played out before their eyes. Edgar wrote, "He and I were equal partners, and he wanted to be treated as such," though the nominal equality slowly evaporated over the years. Nevertheless, however ridiculous Charles's loyalty to his brother may seem, he could point to the example of the Mondavis, a family-controlled wine business. It had been founded by Robert Mondavi in 1966 after a blazing series of rows with his brother. Thirty years later, as Julia Flynn put it,[*] Robert's sons Michael and Timothy, "following the example set by their father and uncle, had paralyzed the business by fighting over details large and small, from whether Mondavi should go public to the design of its labels."

Phyllis, two years Minda's junior, managed to escape her sister's fate and has led a thoroughly fulfilled life. According to Edgar, Phyllis had started rebelling at the age of two and a half. When young "she would hold food in her mouth for hours rather than swallow something she didn't want to eat." Her major interest was her desire to play ice hockey with her younger brothers. She always got on well with Edgar, never interfered with the business, feeling that "if the clock works don't fix it . . . ," and rarely displayed in public her notorious temper or impatience—character traits that reminded Edgar of their father. "Money," wrote Robertson, "had little meaning for her except that it could serve her aggressively independent spirit by enabling her to concentrate upon her own creative ambitions without interruption or interference." Like her elder sister she had insisted on a proper education—in her case at Vassar.

In 1952, at the age of twenty-five, she emigrated to Paris, largely to escape from her father. There she married Allan Lambert, a scion of a distinguished Belgian banking family. The marriage was clearly designed to escape from her family—and the name—rather than provide matrimonial bliss. As she told Newman, "The marriage was just a way of winning my

---

[*] In *The Wall Street Journal* under the delightful headline "Blood and Rosés."

freedom; it hardly seems to have belonged to my life"—especially as neither of those involved seems to have been interested in a physical relationship with the opposite sex. She remained very close to her mother, but she
never felt family-minded. "I don't really identify especially one way or another with the Bronfmans," she told Newman. Lambert was clearly a fortune hunter, indeed whenever he entered the room Edgar would go to the
piano and pick out "I've come to wed it wealthily in Padua" from Cole
Porter's *Kiss Me Kate*. On hearing of her proposal to divorce him a couple
of years later Sam is said to have exploded, "What, my pretty little
daughter?"—she was twenty-seven at the time.

However she soon returned—temporarily—to New York to supervise
the construction of the Seagram Building, the family's greatest single
legacy. To her a monument like the Seagram Building even has a moral di-
mension. "The moment business or professional organizations decide to
build," she has written,[1] "they claim responsibility and take a moral position affecting all those who walk by or who enter their building, affecting
the larger area around them, and the city as a whole." And it was thanks to
this ethos, and the force of Ms. Lambert's personality, that the Seagram
Building on Park Avenue remains a fine monument to the best, imaginative, forceful, generous side of the Seagram heritage.

The scale of the achievement of Mies van der Rohe, the architect whose
dream was fulfilled through Ms. Lambert's support, can best be understood
by comparing the Seagram Building with two other landmark buildings in
midtown Manhattan, the Empire State Building dating from the late 1920s,
and the Lever Building, constructed only a few years before the Seagram
Building, and so close that the three can easily be compared. The majesty,
the grandeur of the Empire State Building cannot be properly appreciated
because it is largely invisible from the street. Twenty-five years later the
Lever Building, designed by the legendary Gordon Bunshaft, the talent behind Skidmore, Owings & Merrill, was recognized as setting a splendid precedent for the redevelopment of Park Avenue, one of the broadest and
most dignified of New York's thoroughfares and one previously lined with
dignified residential apartment buildings.

The Lever Building was sponsored by Charles Luckman, architect
turned soap salesman, and by the early 1950s the chairman of Lever Brothers. As Vicky Ward put it,[2] "Lever House, the first all-glass International
Style office building in New York City," looked "as if it had dropped from

the sky across from the grand old Montana Apartments." It was indeed elegant but the cleanliness of the lines of the tower was spoiled because it stood on top of a low-rise base, which extended to each corner of the city block on which it was built, even though the building covered only half the space allowed by zoning laws. "The Glass House," as the press called it, was so different from the sooty brick and limestone ziggurats of New York's previous architectural generations that it became an instant icon. Naturally, in such a competitive city Lever quickly became the standard by which other office buildings were judged, but soon became a model too often imitated, but reckoned to be as far as a commercial building could go in terms of what might be termed "profitable elegance."

Only the Seagram Building, which, like Lever, occupies a whole block on the same avenue, stands proudly clear, surrounded as it is by a plaza generous enough to allow everyone to appreciate the nobility of the architecture. And if the architect was Mies van der Rohe, the totality of his design could only be fully realized thanks to Phyllis Lambert. By sponsoring and shaping the building Mr. Sam's rebellious younger daughter showed her father's qualities of vision and obstinate determination to the full. For the building is not only a superb architectural achievement, it is also an object lesson in city planning, showing the way that even the most monumental buildings can enhance the cityscape, especially when the layout involves the sacrifice of valuable office space. Curiously the same key element—allowing a building space in which to breathe, as it were—applied also when designs were submitted for the Centre Pompidou. The design submitted by the eventual winners, Enzo Piano and Richard Rogers, was one of only two—out of eight hundred—built only on a small part of the site with the rest left as a piazza.

The project for the Seagram Building had started unpromisingly in 1953 when Mr. Sam charged the improbable figure of Victor Fischel with finding an architect for a building in New York that would house the company's growing number of employees in a city that had replaced Montreal as the center of the group's operations. Fortunately Mr. Sam had already abandoned the need to ape historical models—as he had done in the head office in Montreal and the Chivas Building in Paisley. The most obvious idea was to imitate—or rather surpass—the Lever Building, in a structure that would include three separate entrances for the three sales companies. Fortunately Phyllis had been alerted by reports in the press and was thus aware of the plans to build what she described as a "very mediocre building." "I was boiling with fury," she told *Time* magazine. "I wrote to him [Mr. Sam] that he wanted a really fine building, and he was lucky to be living in a period when there were great architects." She promptly returned from Paris when he invited her back to New York to help.

No one, including and especially Mr. Sam, had any idea what they were letting themselves in for. Like her father, Phyllis is a perfectionist, formidable and autocratic, with a temper worthy of her father. Thirty years later when she felt—unfairly—that the Centre Pompidou was not going to provide her with proper space to mount an exhibition of architectural photographs and drawings,* she thought nothing of enlisting the help of the Canadian prime minister to lobby the French prime minister to protest. But, like her father, she is bursting with creative energy, which throughout her long life has been devoted to improving the environment, saving buildings, enabling the construction of worthy new ones, and, in the last two decades, creating a major center for the study of architecture. In her mid-seventies—though looking a decade younger— with her close-cropped, gray-black hair and severe tailored pinstripe suits, she remains a formidable guardian of all that is best in the urban environment, clearly unwilling to suffer fools at all, let alone gladly, but nevertheless far more affable than her reputation would suggest. Again, like her father, throughout her life she has shown herself willing to respect the opinions and abilities of others, provided only that they provide adequate proof of their qualities.

Phyllis was perfectly aware that her father called her in largely to lure her back from Paris. "He thought," she said, "isn't our little girl nice to come and help us choose the stone?" But she was never going to be content with anything that was not perfect and forward-looking. "The question to be asked," she said, "was not who should be the architect, but who was now going to make the greatest contribution to architecture?" She was lucky that her father had called in a friend, Lou Crandall, head of a major construction firm, who suggested that she do the research to find an architect—we will never know whether he was merely placating the boss's daughter or had already appreciated her qualities. Through the

---

* In fact the curator of architecture at the center was mounting his own major exhibition and had kindly arranged for her to have a gallery of her own.

Vassar mafia she met Philip Johnson, chairman of the Department of Architecture at the Museum of Modern Art, but finally came to the conclusion that her ideal was Mies van der Rohe, a sage of the modern movement. In the event Johnson did much of the work—even though in the 1930s he had quite open fascist sympathies, a fact that did not seem to disturb Mr. Sam.

Originally Phyllis had "not intended to do more than help choose the architect" and then return to Paris but, as she says, "it became increasingly clear to me that the person who had chosen the architect must stay with the job to fight for the concept." Indeed it was only her fierce willpower that prevented financial considerations from cluttering the awesome simplicity of van der Rohe's dream. Fortunately and at first sight improbably, the architect had got on well with Mr. Sam as well as with her; largely, I suspect, because all three had in common a fierce desire for perfection in everything done in their name. As Phyllis Lambert wrote, "My father simply told Mies that his building was to be the crowning glory of everyone's work—his own, Crandall, and Mies's." And, she could have added, hers. As a result it was a girl—a mere twenty-seven years old at the time—working in a totally masculine environment, who took on what she called the "keeping of the concept . . . making sure that Mies could build the building he wanted to build." The results of her beady eye and the powers her father had given her were many, varied, and sometimes costly—typically she ensured that the ceilings were to be nine feet high rather than the normal eight and that the stairwells were made of "good brick" rather than cinder blocks.

Thirty years earlier van der Rohe had dreamed up the idea of monumental glass-walled skyscrapers, long before the idea had become technically feasible. But after the war technical advances had meant that this ideal could be transformed into reality, and they were, first by Gordon Bunshaft, then, more completely, by van der Rohe himself. The result was emphatically not what the distinguished architectural critic Lewis Mumford calls "the now standard thin, slab-sided building" like Lever House. Rather, it was "a single shaft of bronze and glass, thirty-eight stories high, set well back from both Park Avenue and the surrounding streets." It was "everything that most of the office buildings that have been going up in the midtown area in the last few years are not. . . . Out of this stalled, rush-hour clutter of new structures, brightly sordid, meretriciously up to date, the Seagram Building has emerged like a Rolls-Royce accompanied by a motorcycle escort that gives it grace and speed."[3]

Over the past fifty years this "proud and soaring thing"—the term Louis Sullivan had employed for the first skyscrapers in Chicago in the 1890s—has formed a challenge to other clients, other corporations, other architects, daring them to surpass its grace, simplicity, and its unique blend of cleanliness and warmth. As a result, not only is it a magnificent building in its own right, but it has also helped ensure that a handful of the dozens of skyscrapers built in Manhattan since 1953 at least strive for some form of architectural quality, though none of them comes near van der Rohe's achievement. And unfortunately the sheer scale of the many inferior towers built since the 1950s has physically overshadowed 375 Park Avenue.

Van der Rohe had escaped from his earlier dreams of "almost surgically aseptic designs," the result of the way that his famous motto "less is more" had come to mean "nothing is even better." As a result there was, noted Mumford, a "certain warmth and fantasy in the decoration"— including the narrow vertical bronze fins that soften the otherwise stark appearance but seem perfectly attuned to the idea. The central structure, he continued, "is a shaft and nothing but a shaft, straightforward in concept, solemn in color"—dark green and bronze—"sober in execution. It was not just another business building but a singular monument, [so] that its aloof aristocratic qualities are not likely to be often repeated where . . . 'money does not look ahead more than five years.' Such purity and dignity are completely lacking in most contemporary metropolitan architecture." As Lambert herself wrote, "The bronze of the skin improves as it weathers." A few years earlier Bunshaft had had to use green glass, the only color available at the time, for the Lever Building, but van der Rohe could use glass of a warm pink-gray color. Even the entrance had a "becoming massiveness and dignity" thanks to the luxury of allowing greater space than would have been possible if it had been a truly commercial building. (Mumford was so awestruck that he even liked the display of a range of liquor bottles, which he found "both an honest symbol and a handsome one.")

The lack of commercial pressure was most obvious outside, on the plaza that surrounded the building. Phyllis Lambert and Mr. Sam ensured that they did not respond to the urgings of banks anxious to occupy satellite buildings next to the tower, which would have ruined the spaciousness of the architect's vision. As Mies van der Rohe told Mr. Sam, "If I were you I wouldn't do it." He didn't—and despite the fears of realtors Seagram was able to compensate for the loss in income by getting premium rents for the floors of the building the company did not need for itself.

To ensure that the new structure would not jar with its surroundings the architect had made a cardboard model of the whole area. Mumford found the space "open without being formidable," where "again the clients showed themselves ready to sacrifice rentable space to achieve an aesthetic effect that does more to set this building apart than the most lavish murals or the most exuberant horticultural display." The luxury of not crowding the ground plan, ensuring that most of the space was free, provided the building with what Mumford calls its "ambiance" through an "act of detachment from the surrounding buildings." He felt that the setup was a lesson to other developers, for "small plazas like this, if repeated often enough about the city, would accomplish more for recreation than thousands of distant wild acres hardly worth the effort of a crawling Sunday journey." This opinion reflects Phyllis's idea of "the social responsibility of a building." Complementing the office building were the—ever-fashionable—Brasserie under the tower and, to one side, the Four Seasons Restaurant—another architectural masterpiece, complete with shallow pool as its centerpiece—the whole offering a coolness, a spaciousness and elegance rare if not unique in restaurant design. (Fortunately the cuisine lives up to the architecture.)

At Vassar in 1947 Phyllis and her friends had been persuaded to mount an exhibition on the relation of paintings and sculpture to the buildings we live in and exploited to the full the knowledge she had gained. She kept iron control over the interior decor of the building, insisting, for instance, that a graphic designer develop a standard lettering, which was also used in the murals. "I bought and commissioned prints, posters, tapestries, paintings, and sculpture for the offices of the Seagram company, the public areas and the restaurant. These procedures involved every part of the building, from desk handles and bathroom tiles to the bronze extrusions, the glass, the plaza."

The result was a major and well-chosen collection of modern art—plus some seven hundred photographs featuring names like Edward Steichen and Walker Evans, all "images of the City" in Lambert's words. Every executive was entitled to two, and only two, works of art for their offices (though at least one cheated by choosing a pair of pictures as one of his choices). The star of the fourth floor executive suite was Rothko's masterpiece *Brown and Black in Reds*. But the artist rebelled and bought back another masterpiece, an enormous mural that was to be the crowning artistic glory of the Four Seasons Restaurant. Rothko, born in Russia into a poor Jewish family, had strong feelings about the commission. As he told John Fischer,[4] through the intensity of the black gloom they conveyed he hoped that the murals would "ruin the appetite of every son of a bitch who ever eats in that room," making "those rich bastards feel that they are trapped in a room where all the doors and windows are bricked up." After his first (and probably last) meal in the restaurant he told his studio assistant that "anybody who will eat that kind of food for those kind of prices will never look at a painting of mine." He promptly withdrew the paintings and sent the money back. They ended up, a miracle of sensual, meancing, almost occult art, in a special room in the Tate Modern museum in London. In any case Rothko's work was a total contrast to the favorite painter of the whole family—apart of course from Phyllis Lambert—Jean-Paul Riopelle. He was a pioneering French-Canadian abstract painter, interesting enough to have been chosen by Baron Philippe de Rothschild to paint a label for one of the vintages of his precious wine from Chateau Mouton Rothschild. The brothers both had one of his paintings in their offices, though his second son, Edgar Jr., defiantly went for more modern works. In the end the building cost $40 million, far more than forecast, but the cost came "from the cash box" without any borrowings, as one Seagram executive put it. But the building more than achieved Phyllis's aim that it should enhance "Seagram's good name."

Eleven

THE GENERATION GAP

Father scared people—and he scared me too.
—EDGAR BRONFMAN, SR.

I N THE LAST QUARTER OF A CENTURY OF SAM'S LIFE HE EXPANDED his empire in two quite distinct directions. By the time of his death in 1971, Seagram included a worldwide wine and spirits business as well as an increasingly successful portfolio of investments, owned either by Seagram or by the family. For by the 1950s the whiskey business had become a money machine on a gigantic scale and the biggest problem was how to invest the cash it spewed out. At the time whisky, principally VO and Canadian Club, was the biggest fully manufactured product exported by Canada. But in the fifteen years before Sam's death in 1971, the principal feature of the Bronfman landscape was not financial but the continuous battle between Sam and Edgar. As Leo Kolber notes: "Whereas Charles was always deferential towards his father, Edgar did a pretty good job of standing up to him." The defiance could show up in relatively petty ways. After Israel and Germany exchanged ambassadors in the 1960s Edgar deliberately bought a small German liqueur company as a gesture aimed at his anti-German father. But there were limits to his defiance.

Unsurprisingly until his dying day Mr. Sam could never hand his baby over to anyone else. For, although each subsidiary had a "president" who was nominally in charge, until the day of his death Sam remained, as he used to say, "president of the presidents"—including the Seagram Overseas Corporation when it was created in 1962. But Edgar refused to accept that. As Charles put it in 1962, "The company belongs to Father. Edgar and I only administer our parts of it," in the face, he could have added, of their father's interference. The results were inevitably unhappy. As *BusinessWeek* noted in 1962, Mr. Sam's "personal style of intuitive management is already becoming more and more a thing of the past. Morale was poor, personnel procedures varied from division to division or were totally lacking." For, "until Mr. Sam died," wrote *Fortune*, "Sam's sons rule with his advice and consent." Yet to outsiders Mr. Sam's pride in his sons was obvious. In the firm's official history (*From Little Acorns*) published in 1970, the old man wrote, "Well done, Edgar and Charles."

In 1951, to ensure that he could continue to supervise his ever-spreading empire, Mr. Sam had bought a large estate at Tarrytown an hour's drive north of New York, where he and Saidye started to spend more of their time—though he moved back to Montreal fourteen years later after he had been disturbed by a burglar. The Tarrytown estate was also useful in the game he and Allan played to reduce their tax bills. Max Henderson told Newman how "They were strictly Canadian when there was trouble in the States and vice versa . . . when the US Internal Revenue Alcohol Tax Unit came up to Montreal complaining about the unfair competition Canadians were giving American distillers. So Mr. Sam spent two whole months living in Westmount, very much the Canadian resident. When the situation changed, they were all down in Washington. Arguing the other way. Oh they were fantastic!"

Over the years the intergenerational problems grew steadily worse. As *Forbes* magazine put it, in the late 1950s, "The trouble was that Mr. Sam grew old and increasingly out of touch with his industry. Like many a strongman-founder, he overstayed his time, either not listening to the unwelcome truth or not being told it by his fearful managers." Theodore White understood the problem very well. Accused of not understanding America anymore the aging Lou Bronstein, the tycoon behind "Bruno's liquors" in White's novel, roars back to his sons, "It's *you* who don't understand America anymore. . . . You come into business behind desks, so you don't know what people want, you have to hire experts and specialists to tell you. With organization charts. It's a bureaucracy they got there, not a business. It's *you* who got to run your own business."

According to Henderson, Mr. Sam, although "quick enough to pick up a bargain, had a childishly annoying habit of procrastinating for weeks, sometimes months, on decisions that he either did not want to make or was uncertain about. . . . He would ask everyone for their advice, thoroughly enjoying the tensions he created and then managing to pin the blame on some unfortunate individual if the final decision went wrong." Jimmy Lang was a witness to the tensions this could create when Sam and Edgar started to blend two new Scotch whiskies. The search for a blend was not helped by arguments between Sam and Edgar—who had just as good a palate as his father. Lang remembers one telex from Edgar saying that father and son were trying "to be consistent in the constant changing of our minds." And he and his colleagues got used to separate letters from father and son giving different instructions.

Blending was one of the few aspects of the business for which Edgar had been properly trained before he took charge of the company. His apprenticeship had involved a long spell working with Roy Martin, the chief blender at the Villa LaSalle distillery, and at the early age of twenty-three had an early test of his ability to taste and blend when he was left in charge after he had forced the obviously sick Martin to go home. He found that a batch of twenty-five thousand cases of VO wasn't up to its usual standard. Bravely Edgar closed the plant and spent a weekend detecting and remedying the fault.* That bold step proved—even to his father—that the son's palate was up to his, and indeed throughout the next forty years Edgar could be relied on to ensure that every whiskey that went out under the name of Seagram was what it should be. In the mid-1990s he caused chaos when he insisted on reblending A Century of Whisky, an ultra-premium blended Scotch with, as the name implies, one hundred different ingredients. One of the constituents, he insisted, was flawed. It was, and it was removed.

As heir apparent, Edgar took over, nominally anyway, as president of Seagram in the United States in 1957 at the age of twenty-eight. But his rise had always been inevitable. The previous year James Friel, the treasurer of the US company, died suddenly and Henderson felt that he had the experience to take the job. But no, it went to Edgar, "Notwithstanding his very limited experience and training. It soon became obvious that the younger son, Charles, was to head the Canadian operation with Edgar to become top man in the United States." Not surprisingly Henderson refused to "resign myself to becoming a bookkeeper for the rest of my time with the Bronfmans" and left to become Canada's auditor-general. Edgar himself put it with characteristic bluntness when he said that, "Nobody comes

---

* They had left some used casks out in the rain, allowing acetic acid to develop.

to work here thinking they're in line to be chief executive." As one former executive told *Business Week* only a little unfairly, "The Bronfmans think of themselves as royalty . . . as an employee you feel like household staff. They give orders and don't expect to be talked back to."

Edgar inherited an administrative mess including three separate brand empires, each covering production, sales, and marketing, but was exaggerating when he claimed that Seagram "was a company that was absolutely the worst managed in the business." Edgar tried a giant reorganization that brought all the previously fiercely independent companies together in one company, the House of Seagram, with Victor Fischel controlling forty brands, including the Chivas Brothers Import Corporation. Inevitably the move simply made matters worse. Instead of—often creative—chaos you had a situation where, as Kelly said, "all of the companies lost their autonomy, their identity, their sales momentum, and their spirit." Fischel's iron determination to make "all the companies replicas of Seagram" merely led, if not to their destruction, at least to the removal of any growth prospects for the other brands. The sales of Seagram's blends rose to 7.5 million cases as well as 2.5 million of VO, all immensely profitable brands. But as Kelly points out, in the process "it sacrificed the Frankfort company with Four Roses, and the Calvert Company with Calvert Special and Lord Calvert."

The resulting struggle gave Kelly appalling eye problems and while he was in the hospital recovering from an operation he was sacked by the marketing boss of House of Seagram. Edgar was given the task of telling Kelly on his return to work. He copped out by telling Kelly that he didn't agree with the decision but "it's my job to tell you." He was given a mere two weeks' termination notice—although this was rectified when Mr. Sam heard about it. Things had changed. "In the past," he wrote, "if you were right you would win and be quickly rewarded for having enough guts to tell the truth." But now "the House of Seagram had been set up as a hierarchy of supermen"—headed, he didn't need to spell out, by Victor Fischel— "whose judgment was supposed to be infallible." Of course it wasn't and the setup was later abandoned, but the damage had been done.

For Edgar, gaining control over Seagram's American subsidiary, Joseph E. Seagram & Sons, proved a lengthy business. In 1957 he and his father had a major row before Mr. Sam finally gave in—though not before consulting Saidye. That same year Edgar lost the first battle against his father—and Victor Fischel—when he hired Robert Bragarnick, a marketing executive from Revlon. Bragarnick lasted less than two years, his doom sealed the day

Mr. Sam looked down the boardroom table and said to Edgar, "Why is that guy still with the company?" But it was Bragarnick, said one insider, who had "introduced the concept of change. He was the first to suggest that Sam's concepts weren't necessarily eternal. He wanted to market liquor like soap"—an eternal delusion in an industry that is inevitably different from FMCGs.* One observer said simply, "He got into a battle with Fischel and lost."

Not surprisingly Edgar's biggest problem came with the executives, above all Fischel, who had helped Mr. Sam build the company in the 1930s and who were now aging. "Sam," one veteran told *Fortune,* "ran Seagram's like a little duchy where the lord of the manor took care of the serfs. Nobody was fired and as long as you avoided trouble, nothing happened." Not surprisingly these executives grew increasingly risk-averse as they approached retirement. Edgar's manner did not help his attempts to change the company. In *Good Spirits* he dismisses Schwengel, who was still president of the American company, as "an elderly figurehead who did little more than represent the company to trade associations and such groups as the American Legion." Worse was Jack Owen, a long-serving advertising executive who "had become a crony of Father's" in Edgar's bitter words, by "spending time with him, especially on weekends in my parents' Tarrytown house where he was more than willing to schmooze while artfully kissing Father's behind"—the son shows no sympathy for an increasingly lonely old man, whose whole life had been devoted to business and who therefore found himself at home only with long-term business associates.

Predictably his biggest battle was with Victor Fischel. "In a masochistic way," Edgar wrote, "I probably enjoyed taking on Father." For it is obvious that the ferocity of Edgar's lengthy attacks on Fischel in *Good Spirits* were a clear indication that Victor Fischel acted as a substitute for the untouchable father—or rather Father, for in his book Edgar invariably employs a capital letter when referring to Mr. Sam. The result was a titanic five-year battle: "I became president," Edgar used to say, "de jure in 1957 and de facto in 1962." Edgar hated Fischel, not only because he headed his father's old retainers, but also because he was the most obvious link with Prohibition, bootleggers, and the old ways of doing business. Indeed Mr. Sam had refused to allow Edgar to become president for some time because he

---

* Fast Moving Consumer Goods, like soap, or in Bragarnick's case, cosmetics.

"would have to consort with all sorts of people, distributors who were once bootleggers." It did not help that Fischel was personally closer to Mr. Sam than Edgar himself. Fischel even hoped to succeed Mr. Sam, which he must have known was a ridiculous dream. Mr. Sam had often screamed at him that, in Edgar's words, "This was his company, it was being built for his two sons and don't you ever forget it." But to write, as Edgar does, that this "strong, unattractive red-haired man . . . knew how to spend money, but not how to save it or make it" was grossly unfair. Even Edgar had to admit that "he was very good with distributors and retailers, and had wonderful interpersonal relationships with many of both. He was a great hero during the years of shortages—which didn't end until the late 1950s—because he was fair and trusted."

The battle covered many fronts. When, for instance, Edgar simplified the supply of bottles, Fischel wanted the savings to go to his beloved distributors, but Mr. Sam backed his son in ensuring that the money went straight into Seagram's profits. The crunch came when Edgar sacked Fischel's brother, a notably incompetent sales manager. Following the inevitable screaming matches, it was a senior executive, Jack Yogman, who found a compromise. A number of minor brands, like Wolfschmidt, were hived off into a separate company housed in the Chrysler Building and thus away from head office. The arrangement enabled Fischel to continue his sales efforts which, according to Edgar, consisted mostly of "schmoozing and drinking with his chums." But then Edgar could be as unforgiving as his father. In the late 1970s, after he had sacked Yogman, another of his father's favorites, any mention of the "Y name" would produce an explosion worthy of his father. By contrast Charles in Montreal, far from the action, had imposed his authority quietly over a couple of executives who could not believe that Mr. Sam was no longer in charge, but for Charles too the sidelining of Fischel was the key moment when his brother assumed effective control.

It was entirely appropriate for Yogman to have played a crucial role in the Fischel drama. A chemical engineer and former naval officer hired by Mr. Sam in 1957, Yogman, who is remembered by some as a tough character, acted very much as a buffer between Edgar and his father, first as Edgar's chief of staff. In 1965 he was promoted to the job of Seagram's executive vice president—whatever that meant—and three years later acquired the real title of Chief Operating Officer—of course Seagram never had a CEO who was not a member of the family. His rise seemed unstoppable—indeed at one point Mr. Sam said that if this had persisted Seagram would become Yogman's company—an unthinkable concept. But Edgar treated him as an employee, not an executive partner. "At one time I was close to Jack Yogman," he wrote, "but not to the point of joint holidays, or even dinners with our wives." Because his father had tended to blur the line between business and friendship he had "avoided such relationships and have never developed an intimate friendship with anyone who works for me"—this was not entirely true; he became and remained firm friends with Ed Mcdonnell who took over as COO in the late 1980s.

But the key relationship remained that between the thirty-something Edgar and his septuagenarian father. Despite the eternal shouting matches they did manage to work together, notably in the introduction of younger blended Scotches to give Chivas pole position as the top brand within a range of whiskies. As Chivas's sales grew Seagram needed an ever-increasing supply of younger whiskies, some of which, they assumed, could be used to launch one or more less-expensive blends. But they found that the malt whiskies Jimmy Lang had in stock were designed to be ready to drink at twelve years of age so were often not suitable for younger blends. Mr. Sam had tried to solve the problem by buying Berry Bros. & Rudd, the venerable London wine merchant that owned the best-selling Cutty Sark brand. But when Mr. Sam arrived for lunch at the company's venerable head office the chairman greeted him with the discouraging greeting, "Mr. Bronfman, I have something you want, but you have nothing I need." Mr. Sam turned on his heels and left without staying for lunch.

The whole process of defining and creating the new brands inevitably involved lengthy and frequent arguments and discussions, mostly between a father and a son equally proud of their tasting skills. They thought of a name, Cairngorm, after the Scottish mountain range, but found that they couldn't buy the name,* so they settled on 100 Pipers, a name owned by none other than Jimmy Barclay. Edgar's aim was to make it the Scotch equivalent of VO, indeed complained that an early blend resembled its Canadian equivalent too closely. An estimated $100 million was spent on promoting it in the United States to no great purpose. It was simply another ordinary Scotch in a market saturated with well-established brands. The failure demonstrated clearly the inability even of the fabled Seagram

---

* Nevertheless it was used on a brand sold, successfully, in Argentina.

sales force to succeed with a me-too brand. More successful was Passport, another Scotch introduced in 1968. This was Edgar's idea, blended to compete with other "commodity" Scotches imported in bulk from Scotland and bottled in the United States because transport costs were reduced and import duties lower for bulk than for bottled imports. Although, as one insider puts it, "they were successful in different markets, they did not have any great impact on the market for standard blends of Scotch, since, unlike Chivas, they were 'me-too' brands." They did try one original idea, The Keith, a "vatted malt," that is a pure malt whisky but not a "single malt," i.e., one from only one distillery. This was introduced at the same time but was a failure, partly because of its appalling label of a fierce—and inevitably kilted—Highland warrior.

All Edgar's strengths, his knowledge of blends, his self-confidence and willingness to take a risk, showed at their best in 1962 when he transformed the prospects of Calvert, a brand that had slipped badly over the years. With the help of the legendary advertising genius Bill Bernbach he totally changed everything about the brand. The name was changed from Calvert Reserve to Calvert Extra, the packaging was revamped, the whiskey itself would be aged (and Edgar successfully challenged the authorities to allow Seagram to give a precise age on the back label). Moreover Seagram agreed to take back every unsold bottle of Calvert Reserve from the retailers at no cost and replace them with bottles of Extra. In a final step worthy of his father's beliefs, discounting would be forbidden.

Edgar had understood that blends were gradually losing market share to "straight" (i.e., unblended) whiskies like bourbon and also to other spirits. So he tried to reintroduce Four Roses as a straight whiskey as it had been before Seagram had bought the company, but all Mr. Sam would do was confuse the potential buyer by launching it as a "blend of straight whiskies"—i.e., without grain spirit—an idea similar to, and just as unsuccessful as a "vatted malt," while sharing the disadvantage that the whiskies in the blend did not come from a single, promotable distillery. The only success came in Germany where Seagram built a major distillery to serve the American forces stationed there, who were great consumers of Four Roses.

All the time the US spirits business was changing dramatically. In 1947 86 percent of all the liquor sold was blended whiskey, by 1960 its market share was down to a mere 30 percent, a figure never to rise again. A dozen types of liquor—white spirits like gin, vodka, and Bacardi rum, as well as brandies, rums, and straight whiskies, above all Jack Daniel's—all started an inexorable rise that has continued for the fifty or more years since Mr. Sam's prejudices had prevented him from buying the brand. These same beliefs blocked any serious venture into the vodka business—Mr. Sam had cheered when Schwengel tipped a case of the neutral spirit into a swimming pool. By contrast Rosenstiel understood the potential of vodka clearly, noting to a visitor in 1967 that sales of a spirit which, unlike whiskey, did not require capital tied up while the spirit aged, had already surpassed those of domestically produced gin. His son-in-law Sidney Frank obviously took note: in 2004 he sold Grey Goose, the ultra-premium vodka he had concocted, for $2 billion to Bacardi.

Fortunately for Seagram Mr. Sam showed greater foresight when it came to expanding outside North America, which had accounted for all Seagram's business until 1945. Between the end of the war and his death he accumulated the first all-round, worldwide group of liquor companies, covering not just whiskey but also champagne, claret, and, especially, rum. It was always said that the British Empire was acquired in a fit of absent-mindedness, and it has to be admitted that virtually all the purchases and investments that transformed Seagram into the first[*] worldwide wines and spirits business empire came in a most casual fashion; it was certainly not the result of any great master plan, but rather a series of opportunistic investments. Sam, it was said, "felt he had to buy whatever was on offer" throughout the world, and he became a compulsive dealer, buying company after company in wines and spirits, without much regard to any sort of overall plan, for Sam was not greatly interested in the management of these new subsidiaries. For his part Yogman loved wheeling and dealing, indeed it was said that at one point he was negotiating fifteen deals simultaneously. Above all he was largely responsible for creating Seagram's worldwide network of wholly or partially owned distributors and agents, for whereas in the US distribution had to be separate from production, elsewhere vertical integration was perfectly legal. As a result he had sales forces in place throughout the world producing native products as well as blends, hence the creation of the Seagram Overseas Corporation in 1956 and the Overseas Sales Company that followed nine years later.

So by the time of Sam's death Seagram's interests ranged from the Paul

[*] Rosenstiel had diversified first but relied on agencies and had never bought foreign businesses.

Masson vineyards in California to Barton & Guestier, one of the most re-spected names in Bordeaux, half of which was already owned by Browne Vintners when Seagram acquired the company in 1941. He gained com-plete control by issuing masses of new shares that the Barton and Guestier families could not afford to buy. More profitably they also acquired three brands of champagne: Mumm, one of the biggest; Perrier-Jouet, one of the most prestigious; and the cheaper Heidsieck Monopole.[*] All, in theory anyway, were supervised by Mr. Sam's son-in-law Count Alain de Gunz-burg and his brother François, a great favorite of Charles's, but whose man-agement techniques left something to be desired—he sacked Anthony Barton, the brand's most successful salesman, by telephone, even though Barton was a member of the founding family and had served loyally for six-teen years.

But, not unexpectedly, Mr. Sam's greatest success came through another blended spirit, dark rum. After the war, at a time of acute shortage of whiskey, Seagram imported large quantities from Puerto Rico and—for sale in Canada—from Jamaica. By the 1960s, and despite the ready availability of whiskey, rum was the second favorite spirit in Canada and Seagram soon became the first company for generations to distill rum in Canada itself. He also bought Long Pond Estates on the north coast of Jamaica, giving him a distillery. In 1954 Sam bought Myers's, the world's leading dark rum, based in Nassau, and the Puerto Rican white rum Ronrico, and as a result of a friendship with a local importer and distributor he set up a distillery in Venezuela. The rum business was greatly boosted by his invention of Cap-tain Morgan's Spiced Rum, named after a famous pirate figure. So he went a fair way to achieving his aim of becoming the "rum king of the world"—though he never succeeded in his ambition to buy United Rum Merchants, makers of another bestseller, Lemon Hart. Unfortunately, and typically, he was thinking only of dark rum and not of the then virtually unknown white rum called Bacardi.

But these ventures paled into insignificance compared with the results obtained through investing the gigantic sums thrown up through the divi-dends earned since the mid-1930s. Mr. Sam had always dabbled in other investments, for he was not one to neglect pure financial advantage. Asked

---

[*] Yogman also acquired Mumm's German subsidiary whose appalling *Sekt* was a domestic favorite. It also used the Mumm name for the excellent sparkling wine Seagram produced in California.

what was the world's greatest invention he unhesitatingly answered "interest." By 1966, when *Fortune* first worked out the the size of the family fortune, the shares in Seagram itself accounted for less than a half of its—admittedly conservative—estimate of $400 million, while real estate alone accounted for $165 million. Ten years later Amy Booth could write in the *Financial Post* that "Cemp, which controls the world's major (and most profitable) distillery, was able to turn up a loss of C$2.4 million and let it be known that 'future income for income tax purposes may be reduced by the application of losses approximating C$1.2 million reported income in prior years' income tax returns.'" More simply, in the modern version of the old adage: "He who has, gets tax losses too."

Previously Mr. Sam had always been ultra-cautious with his investments, putting his surplus capital into low-yielding bonds. But he—and above all Edgar—had been introduced to what would now be called "insider" stock market dealings by the Loebs and the Gunzburgs. For the two examples of "hypergamy"* provided the family not only with the social distinction denied to Sam in Montreal but also with many joint investment opportunities. It helped that the Bronfmans had the same criteria as the Gunzburgs and the Loebs; they were looking for long-term capital gain rather than dividends or quick trading profits. In France the Gunzburg connection with the Rothschilds enabled the Bronfmans to get in on the ground floor of such successful ventures as the innovative holiday group Club Mediterranée. In the United States the investments included a highly successful speculation into Polaroid—made after Edgar had taken a picture of Mr. Sam and showed it to him a mere sixty seconds later. In partnership with Loeb Rhodes, the family took its first steps into show business. The first investment was in 20th Century Fox before the families tried to take over Paramount Pictures. "We thought we wanted to own the business," said Kolber, "but too many others also did." Nevertheless, as in most of the other joint investments, they came away with a substantial consolation prize in the shape of a healthy profit.

The family's first serious venture into show business came in the late 1960s, for Edgar's first marriage was breaking down and he was looking for excuses to visit Europe, and more particularly London, where much of his extramarital sex life was conducted. He found an excuse through his per-

---

* Marrying above your social station.

sonal involvement in show business with the formation in 1967 of Sagittarius Productions, in partnership with a "minor" film producer called Claude Giroux and an equally "minor" television executive called Henry White. Sagittarius produced a number of Broadway hits including *The Apple Tree*, with Stuart Ostrow; *1776*, a successful musical; and a handful of—generally well-regarded—films. Some of these were profitable, like a film version of *Jane Eyre*; an animated version of E. B. White's classic children's book, *Charlotte's Web*, about the friendship of a pig and a spider; and *Joe Hill*, which won an award at the Cannes Film Festival. But, in a giveaway aside Edgar remarked how the venture provided him with "a great excuse to spend time in England" and "partake in such indulgences as attending the Cannes Film Festival."

The family entered the big time when Edgar and Leo Kolber decided to invest some of Cemp's money in MGM—Edgar had already committed Cemp to buying $40 million without telling anyone, not even Kolber. Eventually the family accumulated 15 percent of the stock, with the vague intention of merging the studio with Time, Inc. Mr. Sam was furious: "I don't want you in the goddamned movie business. We have got whiskey. We have got real estate. What the hell else do you want?"—an unanswerable question. He also suspected that the investment was due to Edgar's desire to meet possible mistresses. Edgar's response has become a classic: "Nobody," he retorted—according to his version anyway—"needs to spend fifty-six million to get laid." More to the point, Edgar admits that he knew nothing of show business and had no reply to his father's query, "Why are you spending all of your time for 15 percent of the stock?"

Edgar's plan failed when a Las Vegas high roller, Kirk Kerkorian, moved in. Mr. Sam was relieved: "I'm just goddamned glad that someone else besides you thinks it's interesting." The family overruled Edgar's wish to battle it out. Cemp sold its shares at a loss estimated at $10 million, although Sam—and Kolber, who remained on the board—kept their own shares long enough to sell at a profit after Kerkorian had created the enormously profitable MGM Grand hotel and casino in Las Vegas. But the episode was bruising—when Edgar walked into a Hollywood night club the comedian Don Rickles spotted him and remarked, "Hey, there's Edgar Bronfman! He was chairman of MGM for five whole minutes." Nevertheless the experience merely served to whet Edgar's appetite for involvement in show business.

But many of the Bronfmans' greatest successes resulted from their backing of Leo Kolber. His background was similar to theirs, for his grandparents had also migrated from czarist Russia towards the end of the nineteenth century. But Kolber's dentist father had died young and Leo had to find his own way in life. At McGill he had befriended the younger Charles Bronfman, to whom he remained particularly close. As he told Robertson, "I knew I fulfilled some need in Charles." His lifelong ambition and self-assurance matched Charles's desire to be liked for himself. Saidye was worried because Kolber was—relatively—poor and thus could have been merely a sponger, but Sam welcomed what he called "a touch of poverty around the place," which "wouldn't do the children any harm at all," and Kolber was soon perceived as a "necessary adjunct to the family."

As he portrays himself in his autobiography,[1] Kolber is an inveterate name-dropper, and a close friend of Danny Kaye and other showbiz luminaries. More helpfully he was close to every Canadian politician of note in the last decades of the twentieth century—and a genuinely close friend of Pierre Trudeau, whom he and his wife would take on holiday. Not surprisingly he became a senator as financial "bagman" to the Liberal party. He thought of the senate merely as "an interesting place to spend part of my time," and regarded it as "taskless thanks" for his efforts. This was a marked contrast with Mr. Sam's obsession with membership of a body that he clearly took to be of the highest importance, a desire parallel to that of many British businessmen over the generations to acquire—in many cases to buy—a title.

From the start both Charles and Edgar were prepared to back Kolber's investment judgment, although he did not make a propitious start—in particular a shopping center in the French-speaking part of Montreal was described as "a national disaster," but he learned from his mistakes. By 1956 he was doing well enough for the brothers to ask him to come into Cemp against the advice of the family's lawyers Laz Phillips and Phil Vineberg—life in the narrow Bronfman circle sounds exactly like that in a royal court, full of mutual suspicion and jostling for the ear of the monarch. Their jealousy continued: When Kolber brought in Wood Gundy, a new and perfectly respectable investment banker, on a deal, Phillips tried to get Kolber sacked because he was sullying the Bronfman reputation.

But Mr. Sam shrewdly saw that Kolber was a "little Jewish boy on the make" and liked the way "he knows how to squeeze a dollar. . . . That's the best kind to have handle our money" and treated him as his "third son"— an implicit rebuke to his spendthrift real sons. In return Kolber regarded

Mr. Sam, whom he always referred to as Mr. Bronfman, as a father figure. And he liked to think of his relationship with the family as not only that of a surrogate son but also of a *consigliere* to Canada's leading Jewish family. Originally Kolber was allocated 10 percent of all the profits from deals he initiated, but Edgar soon reduced the figure to 5 percent, a cut that Leo felt he had to accept because his wife was pregnant. For Kolber remained insecure, psychologically if not financially. Even in the early 1970s he kept C\$2 million in the bank—and no debts, for he invariably paid cash—he reckoned only that he could survive for twenty years even if he didn't earn any more money.

Until Charles and Edgar sold the real estate operations in 1987 they went from strength to strength. The success was due to the opportunities offered by the growth of major shopping malls and office buildings thrown up by the post-war expansion of the Canadian economy—and above all of Toronto as a financial center. As Kolber wrote, "It was pure luck that shopping centers were the next big thing in the late 1950s, just as we were looking to spread our wings at Cemp and branch out into real estate."

His first coup came in 1958 with the purchase of Principal Investment, a company built up by three reclusive brothers named Bennett who had overstretched their resources. Kolber was able to cherry-pick their portfolio and place the properties involved in Fairview, a real estate company controlled by Cemp. Their first major building was the Toronto-Dominion Centre, the landmark building that was the first declaration of the increasing importance of the city in Canada's financial life. While the great American realtor Bill Zeckendorf had pioneered large-scale property developments in Canada with the Place Ville Marie in Montreal, Fairview outbid him when the Toronto-Dominion Bank was looking for a new headquarters. The result was the tallest office tower in Canada. Thanks to Phyllis Lambert's influence it was designed by Mies van der Rohe. Fairview was an equal partner with the bank, and Kolber became closely associated with its long-serving chairman, Allan Lambert, marking an unprecedented degree of acceptance by the city's Anglo-Saxon establishment. They went on to build the enormous Pacific Centre in Vancouver—and bought back the giant Eaton Centre in Toronto, again in competition with Zeckendorf. Fairview went on to follow the American pattern and build further malls in the suburbs round Toronto and to develop malls and major office buildings in American cities as far afield as Dallas and Atlanta. Indeed, according to his own account, Kolber became the first point of call for many would-be developers. He admitted that he was "not a detail man," he left the actual construction to a brilliant builder, Neil Wood, claiming that his only instructions were, "Neil, here is the deal, invite me to the opening." In 1968 Fairview merged with Cadillac, a major residential developer, thus providing the company with an even wider spread of interests.

Perhaps inevitably, Allan's sons, excluded from Seagram, imitated—successfully—their cousins' efforts, by founding Edper, named after and controlled by Allan's two sons Edward and Peter. They were guided by Jack Cockwell, their equivalent of Kolber. Edper often followed Cemp's example, at one point controlling Place Ville Marie through their Trizec Corporation as well as other major real estate holdings in Los Angeles, the Peachtee Center Tower in Atlanta, and the Clearwater Mall in Florida. They also bought control of Noranda Mining, the pride and joy of one of the historically dominant sectors of Canadian business, and over the following decades Edper became a financial empire that at one point controlled C$100 billion of assets. This reinforced the impression that they were at least as able as their cousins Edgar and Charles. They even thought of bidding for Hiram Walker but were dissuaded by fear that the creation of what would effectively have been a Bronfman monopoly of the Canadian liquor business would arouse considerable official opposition.

But Sam's biggest success had nothing to do with Kolber or the *haute Juiverie*. It was in oil, in the form of investments owned, not by a family company, but by Seagram itself. Fortunately for Seagram's shareholders Mr. Sam approved of the oil industry: "If it's good enough for the Rockefellers, it's good enough for me," he would say to Edgar (he was thrilled when David Rockefeller paid a courtesy call on Cemp, even though it was just normal banking practice for the head of Chase Manhattan to visit an important client). Following their investment in the shares of Royalite, Sam and Allan bought the small Frankfort Oil company, leaving a veteran oil executive in charge because they were fully aware of their ignorance of the industry. In 1963 the brothers went one further when they bought a small, but old-established oil producer, Texas Pacific. Fortunately Edgar had spent a short time working for a trust company in New York where he had learned to value small oil companies, basing his estimates on the value of their reserves, and Texas Pacific had reserves bigger than appeared from its production level—or its stock market value.

The deal, probably the most successful in the family's history of financial success, was masterminded by Mark Millard, a brilliant banker of Hungarian Jewish origin at Loeb Rhodes. He invented what would later be called a "leveraged buyout" to pay the $276 million price. Seagram invested a mere $50 million in cash, and even that was borrowed through a twenty-five-year loan, even though Seagram had ample cash. The rest of the purchase price was to be paid over a twelve-year period as a fixed percentage of the revenue Texas Pacific received from sales of oil—and Seagram even received the 22 percent "depletion allowance," a tax break designed to help oil companies. As Raoul Engel, of Canada's leading financial newspaper, the *Financial Post*, wrote, it was "the next best thing to self-levitation, or lifting yourself off the ground by your own shoelaces." Sam had to be reminded of the deal when he was with Seagram executives, but one day was prompted to announce proudly that "gentlemen, we're in the oil business." Over the following seventeen years the company expanded enormously, exploring (and finding oil) the world over, from Thailand to the North Sea. By the late 1970s analysts reckoned that 40 percent of Seagram's earnings came from oil.

The investment in so well established an industry as oil was part of Sam's continuing desire for respectability, which remained a permanent feature of his personality. It emerged most obviously in his obsession to become a member of the Canadian Senate, not by any means a distinguished body—remember how Jacques Bureau had been "kicked upstairs" after facing disgrace as a minister in the 1920s. But while general anti-Semitism declined after the war it was replaced by "anti-Samism"—for the next generation found it easy to slip, quite naturally, into establishment institutions. Indeed Charles recognizes the irony of the fact that he was awarded as a matter of course the recognition within the Anglo-Saxon business community for which his father had fought so long and so unsuccessfully. "I became a director of the Bank of Montreal," he said, "as a totally unqualified thirty-five-year-old." But Mr. Sam was denied any such recompense. Indeed Sam's generosity was exploited by the Anglo-Saxons to whom he gave generously. Henderson remarks indignantly how he "received little in return for these benefactions. My gentile friends were quick enough to come after him for his money, but giving him thanks in the form of the public recognition he so ardently longed for came slowly indeed."

The failure was more obvious because he continued to make lavish contributions to the Liberal Party.* "Sam Bronfman's main problem," wrote Peter Newman, "was that he never learned to appreciate the subtlety of the process in which he was involved." Any number of candidates had purchased their appointment to the second chamber by contributing to party coffers. But while seats in the Senate might be for sale, they could not appear to be bought. And when Mr. Sam directly approached C. D. Howe, the intermediary between the Liberal party and Canadian business, the response to Mr. Sam's threats to cut off funds was simple. "We'll just raise the excise tax on liquor by ten percent and get the money that way." But Mr. Sam never understood. When David Croll, a well-respected Jewish provincial minister, was appointed the country's first Jewish senator in 1955, Sam allegedly erupted: "I'm the King of the Jews! It should have been mine. . . . I bought it! I paid for it! Those treacherous bastards did me in!"

The depth of the hurt was shown by his behavior towards Laz Phillips, his old friend, legal adviser, and intermediary with the Canadian establishment over the years. It was Phillips who had, for instance, ensured that enough funds had been unfrozen by the Canadian Treasury to finance Mr. Sam's wartime expansion in the United States, and he had helped draw up the regulations governing alcoholic beverages in the early 1950s. But in 1949 Phillips blotted his copybook when it became clear that it was he, rather than Sam, who was destined to be appointed as the—token—Jewish senator. This was the result of an unfortunate mess. According to Edgar, a deal had been arranged years earlier that Phillips would enter parliament for a safe seat and do his utmost to ensure that Sam was appointed a senator. Unfortunately Phillips was defeated by an opponent who showed his largely working-class constituents photos of Phillips's mansion in Westmount. So the deal was frustrated and Phillips determined that it would be he rather than Sam who would be appointed to the Senate. And in due course he was.

But the Liberals wouldn't make the appointment if it offended Mr. Sam, their biggest contributor. Mr. Sam not only refused to allow the appointment, he didn't talk to Phillips for years, claiming that he was ungrateful after he'd made Phillips "rich beyond the dreams of avarice." Mr. Sam's

---

* The money was distributed by Max Henderson, who demanded a signature for every cent, a habit which created curious situations when he left Seagram and had to deal with the recipients of Mr. Sam's largesse as Canada's auditor-general.

only consolation came when he was nearly eighty when he was named as one of the fifteen Companions of the newly created Order of Canada after he had helped Montreal stage Expo '67. The next year the now-aging Phillips was finally made a senator. Even so, Phillips joined Sam's brothers in being excluded from the official history of Seagram's.

In the late 1960s Sam's health began to trouble him, and the sheer size and worldwide spread of the empire ensured that he could no longer do more than interfere in individual aspects of the business. He began to drink more—the sips of his beloved VO and water started earlier in the day—and he spent much of his time playing gin rummy with old friends. He often appeared to sleep in meetings—though the somnolence could have been deliberate and not real. Even so his attention to detail remained undimmed. When overseeing some new packaging he asked the designers if they had looked at the bottle with whiskey in it. Of course, they said, to which Mr. Sam replied: "Have you looked at it half full?"

For Sam never gave up. As Kolber says, "Mr. Bronfman was always looking forward," and even in his seventies his ambition was still unsatisfied. Moreover his instincts were still sound enough for him to try to repeat his success with up-market Scotch with cognac. Having failed in attempts to buy major firms like Martell, Courvoisier, or Bisquit, he turned to the tiny firm of Augier, basically because it was the oldest firm in Cognac and thus a natural vehicle for launching a new up-market cognac. The partnership he formed to exploit the name was an unlikely one: The late Jacques de Varenne of Augier, a delightful, wry, aristocratic figure, was related to most of the leading names in the town's history, including the Hennessys, Cognac's leading family. But he and Mr. Sam got on like a house on fire. Bronfman wanted quality; Augier was happy to sell control of his firm and to spend five years buying enough old brandies to launch the cognac equivalent to Chivas Regal. And Augier fully understood a crucial point that "money is only real when it's in the bank"—a truism that was especially applicable to the enormous stocks required to launch an up-market brand of cognac—or Scotch for that matter. The new Augier could have had as beneficial an effect on the whole cognac market in the 1970s as Chivas had had on Scotch in the 1960s. But, sadly, Mr. Sam died before the launch, and the idea was abandoned. The stocks were dispersed, and while Seagram kept Augier, it lost interest and, for a time preferred to launch, disastrously, a cognac bearing the name of Mumm.

In March 1970 Mr. Sam was diagnosed with advanced prostate cancer.

Even so, a year later, when celebrating his—official—eightieth birthday he was still able to croon "Baby Face" to his beloved Saidye:

> You've got the cutest little baby face
> There's not another one could take your place.

The occasion was the first at which he was honored by a major contingent of Canada's "Best and Brightest," including four cabinet ministers as well as the bosses of the five largest distilling companies in the world—headed by his old partner Sir Ronald Cumming of DCL who presented him with a decanter. Sam died on July 10 that year. His last words were, "I'm afraid to die but it pains too much to live." An even more distinguished group attended his funeral, when, as Newman puts it, "Sam Bronfman joined the establishment at last. And he made them pay for it. A downpour had washed all the numbers off the limos in which the great and the good had arrived at the funeral." The resulting chaos proved, wrote Kolber "a kind of revenge for all the snubs he had endured from many of these establishment figures."

It was his daughter Minda who best summed up the character of this extraordinary man. "There's no pretense, no sham about you, Father. You always state your position succinctly and clearly. Your words and your actions are one. This is the sturdy fiber of your inner core—this your heart of oak. Your courage, your vitality, your consistency, your plain thinking and plain living—these are the qualities that make you such a whole man."

Twelve

CROWN PRINCE

It is the misfortune of princes never to hear the language of truth and sense. They have men about them whose business it is to bow and smile and agree.
—CHARLES GREVILLE WRITING ABOUT PRINCE ALBERT, QUEEN VICTORIA'S HUSBAND

EDGAR FINALLY INHERITED HIS LEGACY IN 1971, FOR IT HAD never occurred to him, or to anyone else for that matter, that he would not automatically take over from his father as chairman. Edgar confesses that, "When Father died I thought I would inherit the mantle and more—I thought that his persona would pass on to me. In other words I thought that I would become Sam Bronfman. Eventually it occurred to me that I was going to have to prove myself through deeds, and I really wanted to be Edgar." Following his father's death he needed to reinvent the company, but for nearly five years seemed psychologically incapable of decisive action, leaving the company to be run very largely by Jack Yogman, who felt so confident that to insiders his attitude to Edgar often appeared contemptuous. Indeed during one Monte Carlo Formula One motoring Grand Prix it was Yogman and his cronies who took a suite at the glamorous Hotel de Paris while Edgar had to be content with lesser accommodation. Edgar could leave the management to others since he didn't have the problem with relatives normal in the second generation of family-controlled businesses. Underlying the agreement he had made with Charles nearly twenty years earlier was an assumption largely unspoken, that, as Edgar put it, "My brother Charles and I are in charge of the company and as long as we agree that's it." Inevitably this was going to limit the firm's ability to retain ambitious employees.

But Edgar seemed to have found his new responsibilities impossible to cope with. "He couldn't escape from being Mr. Sam's son," wrote Newman. Moreover his father's death removed the prime excuse for his own mistakes. As Newman notes, his ability to exercise untrammeled and absolute power of Seagram "prompted Edgar to act as if he alone mattered in the universe"—just like his father in fact. But, adds Newman, "he appeared for a time to be acting from that rarely diagnosed disease that infects so many offspring of the very rich: a terminal case of immaturity." Indeed after his father's death, the forty-two-year-old Edgar suffered what can only be called a midlife crisis. The shock of his father's death was compounded a year later when his wife Ann left him. This was not surprising, for his notorious, often-public infidelity had given her ample reason to leave. But it was he who sued for divorce.

As a result the four years following his father's death were dominated by his personal life, culminating in 1975 in the kidnapping of his eldest son Sam. In the preceding four years he had become deeply involved with three beautiful Englishwomen, two of whom he married, while he abandoned the third after she had accepted his proposal of marriage. His problems were not helped by the fact that he was drinking heavily—his preference, like his father's, was for VO and water. He was so sodden with drink that it required only a few sips to make him drunk—and three Coca-Colas to relieve his morning hangovers—though he was not generally aggressive or disagreeable. But it was only the ever-powerful Bronfman legal machine that enabled him to escape relatively unscathed from successive imbroglios, and even then they left behind a trail of queries. The most dramatic demonstration of the ruthlessness of the Bronfmans, and above all their advisers, came with the amazing story of Edgar's second, brief, marriage, and above all an annulment that would have destroyed someone less gutsy than the woman involved, Lady Carolyn Townshend.

She is the daughter of Marquis Townshend,* an enterprising aristocrat from one of Britain's leading families who had created Anglia TV, a very successful commercial television company in East Anglia, northeast of London. The family's estate in Norfolk was near the royal family's estate at Sandringham; indeed, the family had known the royal family for nearly two hundred years. Some of the family met Edgar while hunting—for their estate was famous for its pheasants. They also met in Spain where the Bronfmans, members of the Townshend family, as well as Alain de Gunzburg all

* Their ancestor, "Turnip" Townshend, was a distinguished agriculturalist who pioneered the idea of crop rotation. More relevantly he was the Chancellor of the Exchequer who introduced the Stamp Tax that played such a big part in fomenting the demand for American independence.

went to hunt. Curiously, Edgar found it much easier to relax with British aristocrats than with the German-Jewish aristocracy into which he had married and so he could show his charming, thoughtful side, which endeared him to the Townshends and their like.

When she met Edgar, Carolyn, a beautiful and independent-minded girl, had already had an adventurous professional and family life. She had married Antonio Capellini, a member of a distinguished Venetian family, but he had taken to drink and she had felt forced to flee, virtually kidnapping her young son. While still in her late twenties Carolyn had carved out a successful career in PR with clients like Bob Hope and Jerry Lewis, and these contacts attracted the attention of Seagram, for all liquor companies are keen on "product placement," associating their products with glamorous figures in show business. For two years she worked on Seagram's public relations in London. Among the successful events she organized was the spectacular launch of the 100 Pipers brand with "The Night of a 100 Pipers," held at London's biggest venue, the Royal Albert Hall. Even after meeting Edgar she avoided any personal relationship with him for some time, largely because he had behaved so badly to a number of girls close to her, including her sister, who had been among his innumerable women in the late 1960s. But in the course of time she came to appreciate his charm and attentiveness; it helped that she was on the rebound from a shady financier, Roy Johnson, to whom she had become engaged. Edgar obviously enjoyed the fact that she stood up to him, and of course marriage into so distinguished a family would trump his sister Minda's social pretensions. As she put it: "He chased me round the world for two years asking me to marry him." For several months they had an on/off affair, although they always lived in separate apartments, and eventually she accepted his proposal of marriage.

Her acceptance meant that he had to ditch another beautiful Englishwoman, the actress Sue Lloyd, a classic glamour girl of London's "Swinging Sixties" who had starred in a number of pictures, including *The Ipcress File* with Michael Caine. She was deeply in love with the man who had been her lover for four years when, according to her account[1] he told her, "Darling, I just wanted to tell you that I'm getting divorced. I've had enough of living like this. I love you and I want to marry you." Not surprisingly she accepted. A few weeks later she bumped into him in the street. He blurted out simply that he was engaged to her friend. "To do what?" she said. "To be married," he replied, and that was that. But then she should have remembered Alain de Gunzburg's remark: "Remember, American men don't marry their mistresses."

(This was not the only case where Edgar was unable to be honest with those close to him. He was godfather to Katie, the daughter of Joan Collins. Her husband, Ron Kass, worked for Edgar at Sagitarius Films and organized a successful twenty-first birthday party for his son Edgar Jr. The following week came a cold, impersonal letter sacking him.)

Lady Carolyn was already a close friend of the Gunzburgs. And they, and Edgar's family, welcomed her with open arms, for she seemed to be the ideal, strong-minded bride who would enable Edgar to settle down. He even bought a house in London's Belgravia—for £500,000 ($1.2 million), an enormous sum at the time. He almost certainly did not take seriously her genuine protestations that she wanted to continue her career, and assumed that she would be a dutiful Bronfman bride. But Yogman and the Bronfman court, especially Edgar's ultra-loyal secretary Maxine, felt threatened by someone who had worked for the company for several years and therefore knew too much about it, them, and their open contempt for Edgar in his absence. Their fears were exacerbated when Edgar quoted her opinions in board meetings, and they naturally assumed that she could wield enormous power. "I suppose you're going to get us all sacked," was a typical reaction after they believed, wrongly, that she had caused the dismissal of an incompetent senior executive. The courtiers preyed on Edgar, emphasizing that she was certainly only after his fortune. Convincing him was relatively easy, for like many very rich men he could be very mean and was always worried that he would be taken for a financial ride. But she was not interested in either power or wealth—she had sent back a number of expensive baubles he had sent her and at the time was earning £30,000 a year (equivalent to over $300,000 in today's money), from her PR agency.

At that point they persuaded Edgar that she presented a danger, ostensibly to his fortune, but in reality to their power—as one close observer put it, "The whole affair was not on his initiative, he was a victim of his own advisers." They were afraid that if he broke off the engagement she could claim enormous sums in a suit for breach of promise. Their fears were reinforced in the summer of 1973 when she did break off the engagement for a while. So his lawyers set to work, led by David Sacks, a future CEO of Seagram and someone on whom Edgar relied to solve every type of problem, personal as well as corporate—associates remember the frequent cry to

Sacks over the phone, "It's not my problem, you deal with it or I'll sack you." For on leaving Canada Edgar had abandoned his father's long-standing Montreal-based legal advisers for Sacks's firm, Simpson Thatcher, who handled both personal and corporate business for him over the next thirty years. The firm, now Simpson Thatcher Bartlett, is a large and generally reputable corporate firm.

The result of Sacks's efforts was a plot worthy of a bad thriller, one designed to remove the danger Carolyn was supposed to represent—though she claims, probably rightly given her career record and notorious independence, that she wasn't going to claim a substantial chunk of a fortune that Edgar himself estimated at $600 million, a considerable sum in the mid-1970s. Edgar's tactics, or rather those of his advisers, for he appeared rather shamefaced, as though merely carrying out instructions, proved successful. They were to ensure that the breakdown of the marriage would be swift and could be blamed on her non-consummation and that as a result Edgar would escape with neither his pride nor his purse suffering any serious damage. His lawyers insisted on a prenuptial agreement, which seems minimal by the standards of today's prenups involving men far less wealthy than Edgar, but even at the time it was by no means excessive—indeed Lady Carolyn's lawyers advised her that she should ask for more. It involved $1 million in cash, a $4,000-a-month allowance for "pocket money," and the deeds to the family's "baronial" estate in Yorkton. But all these assets were placed in escrow so that Edgar could reclaim them if anything went wrong.

The black comedy of the "marriage" started in the weeks preceding the wedding. Carolyn had kept insisting that he could, if he wished, cancel the marriage, but he firmly refused. Indeed he gave her a Cartier box containing a nose plug to emphasize his frequent advice that she should "hold her nose and jump in" to the marriage. He even pressured her by organizing phone calls from his family and his children, urging her to become their stepmother—in which their feelings were probably genuine. Yet he had found a new girlfriend, which led to a farcical occasion at a fashionable New York restaurant. Carolyn had gone there with a client but a terribly embarrassed headwaiter apologized that she couldn't have her usual table. When she passed it she was naturally surprised to find Edgar ensconced there with another lady.

The wedding—naturally organized by the bride—was celebrated at the St. Regis Hotel in New York on December 18, 1973. During the wedding dinner the groom casually announced that he wouldn't be staying the night in the bridal suite because "it might upset my son Adam." In fact Adam was playing happily with Carolyn's son Vincenzo, who was always suspicious of his potential stepfather, telling his mother that "Edgar keeps trying to buy me" through the lavish gifts with which he was showered. Mysteriously, the photographs taken of the wedding were never released and are still not available.

The wedding was followed, not by a proper honeymoon, but by what can only be described as a giant family holiday at the famous Las Brisas resort in Acapulco. Edgar owned a house on this exclusive estate set in 110 acres of grounds by the bay, and although its hotel is publicized as "The honeymooners' paradise where you can enjoy privacy and sophistication at its best," so far as the Bronfmans were concerned privacy was the last feature of the week the newlyweds spent there, since the guests included a dozen or more members of both the Bronfman and Townshend families, with the bride doing virtually all the organizing. This included looking after Edgar's children, who had been sadly neglected in the two years since their mother had left, and Carolyn was a welcome potential stepmother. But such was the neglect that she even had to find new clothes for them.

Edgar spent every evening drinking hard and playing backgammon until the early hours. One night when he came to the bedroom declaring that he "felt horny" she had to leave the room because he was frantically chain-smoking Camel cigarettes, leaving trails of ash throughout the room, knowing that it would trigger off her allergy to tobacco smoke and her tendency to asthma. Only later did she realize that his behavior would provide proof of "non-consummation." Not surprisingly she fled to her sister's room. After the "honeymoon" the bride immediately returned to London to prepare a ball at the fashionable Inn on The Park hotel for three hundred people, all in Russian costumes—including the waiters—an event involving all London, five bands, and lashings of caviar. But Edgar refused to join the wedding reception, and when she went up to the bridal suite she found it locked, with Edgar inside occupied with yet another girlfriend. He left the next day to attend a sales conference in the Caribbean. She never saw him again after a "marriage" that had lasted a mere ten days.

Carolyn then returned to New York, not to his apartment, for they never lived in the same home together, but to the company apartment in the St. Regis Hotel to see the architect about the house Edgar had bought for her in an idyllic spot by a lake in a forest north of New York. But the first morning after she returned she was shocked to read in the gossip column of "Suzy Knickerbocker," a friend of Edgar's, that the marriage was over, and when she tried to phone her husband he was too drunk to make any sense. Within a few days she received a totally unexpected missive from the State Department, no less, informing her that she was to leave the country immediately since her husband was no longer prepared to be responsible for her debts (not that she had any) and that, consequently, she no longer had any visible means of support. Fortunately, Allan Kalmus, Bob Hope's manager, rallied round and offered her a—notional—job entitling her to a green card certifying that she was gainfully employed. But she had to leave the St. Regis, largely because her lawyers had warned her that her telephone was probably tapped.

At that point—if not before—the Bronfman legal machine took over and ensured that she was banished, like a traitor, from her husband's kingdom. Carolyn had a nervous breakdown and remained bed-bound for several months suffering from severe gastric pains. The family's doctor—who was also hers—had provided the obvious diagnosis before the wedding; "Not marrying Edgar is the only way to cure you," he had said. Carolyn was also impoverished because she could not touch the assets in the prenuptial agreement. On August 8, 1974, Edgar's lawyers filed for the marriage to be annulled. The date was, as the British saying has it, "a good day to bury bad news," for it coincided with the announcement of Richard Nixon's resignation from the presidency. Matters came to a head in December that year at a court hearing in New York. The suit for annulment was based on the bride's refusal to sleep with her new husband. Unfortunately only Edgar's side of the argument seems to have been heard in court, and even today the actual documents remain unavailable for anyone not directly involved in the case.

Edgar's lawyers had spared no expense in preparing their case. They had even flown to Rome to try to interview her ex-husband, presumably on the assumption that all Italians lived in the capital. After they had driven the three hundred miles to Venice where he lived, he literally threw them out of his apartment when he learned of their intentions to blacken the reputation of his ex-wife. It did not help her case that the judge was one Jacob Grumet, an immigrant's son made good and thus perceived as hostile by Lady Carolyn. Moreover he was not a divorce lawyer but a former head of the New York Homicide Bureau and later a district attorney.

She was confronted by a mass of largely indirect evidence. The most extraordinary, which would have been farcical if it had not been taken so seriously, was that she had slept with the family doctor, and had phoned her "lover" from Acapulco. Indeed she had phoned him, but only to consult him because Saidye had suffered a slight stroke. But by far the most serious damage was done by Roy Johnson. That summer he had turned up for no apparent reason in Switzerland where Carolyn was on holiday with her mother, and at the hearings perjured himself in providing some direct evidence. For he claimed that he had merely "met her on a number of occasions" even though they had first met when they were teenagers and later had lived together for months. But Grumet was quite prepared to believe her alleged statement that "it gives me a lot of satisfaction to screw him without having to deliver." Her reply was far more convincing. "He chased me round the world for two years asking me to marry him . . . finally when I agreed he just didn't want me anymore," she said, "frankly I didn't want his money, and that isn't the reason I married him. But an agreement is an agreement. I shall fight the annulment as vigorously as I can." In the end the judge accepted Edgar's case that Lady Carolyn "had fraudulently induced him to marry her." Some years later Johnson was murdered in Cental Park under mysterious circumstances, possibly because he was involved in a drug deal.

The decision was legally laughable, particularly as it relied heavily on the alleged non-consummation. Normally this reason for annulment is only valid when the period involved is at least months, usually years, and not the mere ten days which had passed before Edgar disappeared from the marital scene forever, and even more unusual where the ruling is made against someone who, like Lady Carolyn, had slept with her husband before their marriage. But Grumet's decision, a result of Edgar's toughing it out, cost him only some temporary embarrassment and enabled him to get back the $1 million and provide his ex with a paltry $10,000 annually for eleven years. And although in these cases it is normally the husband who pays the legal costs, his lawyers argued, successfully, that the two had never been married because of the annulment.

Not surprisingly Lady Carolyn had been dropped by the Bronfmans immediately after the separation and all her clients had vanished into thin air. She spent nearly seven miserable years living in France, allegedly to avoid the tax of up to 93 percent then levied by the British tax authorities on unearned income like the $10,000 a year she was receiving from Edgar.

But there's a curious subtext to the decision. Edgar's advisers were clearly very scared that they might meet if she lived in London—for he was clearly still fond of her, sending her friendly notes—so they arranged for her to obtain a resident's permit in France, a process which normally takes months, within a few days. As she says, "I became anonymous, another person, if it hadn't been for my son I don't know what would have happened to me." Fortunately in 1980 she plucked up enough courage to go back to work, first on the Britain Salutes New York arts festival where she was so successful that she was hired by Lord Forte, owner of a number of high-profile hotels, and this ensured her return to her old profession of up-market publicist. In recent years her most high-profile events have included several premieres of *Lord of the Rings* and she also organizes regular events for members of the royal family, including a concert at Windsor Castle to celebrate Prince Charles's fiftieth birthday.[*] In 2003 she was entrusted by Queen Elizabeth II with the organization of the party for children at Buckingham Palace that formed part of the celebrations for the Golden Jubilee of Her Majesty's Coronation.

Almost exactly a year after the announcement of the proposed annulment came a dramatic episode that contained a substantial helping of uncertainty and even farce. On August 8, 1975, Edgar's eldest son, the twenty-three-year-old Sam, was kidnapped, the ultimate nightmare for a family as rich as the Bronfmans, and made worse by the fact that it came the year after the Patti Hearst drama. Not surprisingly the case attracted enormous attention from the public—and the FBI, which mobilized five hundred agents, moving twenty of them into the Bronfmans' house. The kidnappers demanded a ransom of $4.6 million, the largest ever such request, although within a few days it was reduced to half that sum. Further excitement was added to the event by an alleged statement by the kidnappers that they had buried young Sam with enough air and water for a mere ten days. On August 16 Edgar complied with the demand and $2.3 million—drawn from Seagram accounts—was bundled into oversized plastic bags, which were to be handed to a lone stranger. But by that time one of the kidnappers, Dominic Byrne, who ran an airport limousine service and had provided the kidnap vehicle, had grown nervous and tipped off the FBI. They duly arrested Byrne—but only after he had mistaken the

[*] It was the first event held at the castle after a disastrous fire six years earlier.

agents for hit men employed by the Bronfmans—and the supposed master-
mind behind the plot, Mel Patrick Lynch, a New York fireman. After the
arrest Sam—who had emerged wearing a clean shirt, not normal wear during a kidnap—thanked Byrne for his help.

The trial exposed some weird aspects to the case, including allegations
that Lynch had been involved with the IRA, for whom the money had supposedly been destined, and that Sam had been sympathetic to the Irish
cause. Moreover, as Newman explains, when one of the jurors picked up
the rope with which Sam had been tied "and tugged at its knotted ends, it
broke in three places." Such an inadequate restraint seemed unlikely to be
enough to hold Sam, an athletic lad—though he claimed that had he broken free, the kidnappers would have killed him. The tape of a telephone
conversation between Sam and his father did not help. After emotionally
begging his father to pay the ransom before, he regained his composure and
was heard remarking to his captors, "Hold it, I'll do it again."

The oddest element in the story was the fact that a car had been spotted
at the scene of the kidnapping with the driver apparently acting as observer. The car's registration number was traced back to the owner of a gay
bar in New Jersey. Nevertheless no attempt was made to follow up the clue
and when the police arrested Lynch and Byrne they stated firmly that they
were the only people involved. The presence of the car chimed in with the
defense's claim that the whole affair had been a setup by Sam and Lynch,
his alleged homosexual lover. In the end Lynch and Byrne were acquitted
of kidnapping—partly because the "Lindbergh law" was aimed only at in-
terstate kidnapping—and, much to the family's disgust, Lynch and his associate were convicted only on the lesser charge of extortion.

But in reality Sam has never shown any trace of homosexual tendencies,
then or since. A clue to the puzzle had come during the kidnapping when
his close friend Peter Kaufman had muddied the waters with his comment
that "we've done a lot of wild things but never a kidnapping . . . you'll do
anything for publicity." But then the case left so many unanswered questions that it inevitably aroused a storm of speculation. It was even suggested that Sam was desperate to get the attention of a father who had
neglected all his children and was, as we shall see, hopelessly besotted by
Sam's younger brother Edgar Jr. They were aching for parental love, though
they got on well enough with their father, whom they called "tree" because
of his repeated threats to tell them "get out of my tree" whenever he was
with them.

The drama surrounding Sam's kidnapping delayed Edgar's third marriage, which was due to take place the day after the kidnapping. But on August 20 he married one Rita Webb, who had been renamed Georgiana Eileen—or more often simply "George"—by her future husband, as being more suitable for a Mrs. Bronfman. "George" was a beautiful English rose, who looked uncannily like her predecessor, although there was a vast gulf between their respective backgrounds, for George was the daughter of a restaurateur in the little village of Finchingfield in Essex, forty miles northeast of London. She had followed a Spanish lover to work as a receptionist (some say she was a barmaid) at the ultrasmart Marbella Club in southern Spain. But her lover had ditched her and, like Carolyn Townshend two years earlier, she was on the rebound when she was spotted by the head of Seagram's UK operations. Edgar immediately fell head over heels in love with her. "She was twenty years younger than him and made him feel young again," as one executive put it.

After the marriage—at the house by the lake originally bought for Carolyn—the couple produced two more children—both daughters—to add to the five children born to him and Ann Loeb. Edgar and George then divorced and then, temporarily, came together again—they did not need to remarry because they had never been through a Jewish divorce. But their final breakup was not without incident. When Edgar returned to his estate in Charlottesville in Virginia he found that Georgiana had removed all the furniture to add to the substantial divorce settlement she obtained. Over the past thirty years the settlement has been enough for her to enjoy a relatively lavish lifestyle in both Britain, where she bred horses, and in Kenya, where she reportedly had a long relationship with Richard Leakey.

By contrast Charles seemed to find it easier to escape from his father's shadow. Until 1968 he had not shown sign of any real initiative, fitting unobtrusively into Montreal society. That year came a transforming event. He was persuaded to participate in a scheme put forward by Montreal's megalomaniac mayor, Jean Drapeau, for the city to bid for a major-league baseball franchise, the first ever to be awarded outside the United States. Most of the other sponsors dropped out and after a lot of heart searching— and forceful opposition from Kolber—Charles agreed to put up C$4 million to buy 45 percent of the proposed team, the Montreal Expos—named after the 1967 World Exposition. In the end the other members of the syndicate dropped out and Charles had to provide all the finances required. The purchase, taken only after much agonizing, was his first independent act, and a brave one. For the first time, he said later, "I felt in command of my own life," for the team looked like, and for many years was, a bunch of no-hopers. His cousins Edward and Peter went one better, buying the Montreal Forum ice arena and the franchise of the Canadiens ice hockey team, which won Canada's prime championship, the Stanley Cup, four times.

Drapeau did his bit by spending C$3 million on extending the team's first home, and although the Expos ended their first year in last place in the league, the game caught on with Montrealers, especially when the team started to win a few games and became known as *Nos Amours*. As Kolber shrewdly points out, "At some level . . . owning the Expos gave Charles a comfort level with becoming a public figure and a community leader." And when he sold the team in 1993 to a group of Montrealers he realized C$100 million—a sum that would have been far larger if he hadn't insisted that the buyer should be local and not a carpetbagger who would have taken the franchise back to the United States. The money went to the Charles and Andrea Bronfman Foundation he had established with his second wife, for he was always happier in his role as a philanthropist than as a businessman. Despite Charles's efforts, in 2004 the franchise ended up in Washington, D.C., which had been deprived of a baseball team decades earlier.

Two years after buying the Expos, Charles grew even bolder, setting out his idea for a grandiose new house in a twenty-page booklet entitled "My House in the City." It was an imaginative idea, a sprawling modern house clinging to the slopes near the ancestral home in Westmount. In any event it cost C$2 million, a record, including a huge swimming pool complex and a sweeping canted glass roof that rolled down into the ground in summer. By the early 1970s, as Peter Newman puts it,[2] "There was only one leader of Montreal's Jewish community." More broadly, "Bronfman *was* [his italics] Montreal at a time when the Jews had taken over the leadership of the province's non-francophone population." Charles "was the touchstone Montreal Jews looked to, to be there when money was being raised or the community needed some quick advice. He was not only a good Jew but an avid Canadian."

But in 1976 Charles ruined his image with an act that was totally out of character. In the last week of the provincial election campaign he burst out in bitter opposition to the Parti Québecois, which was stridently advocating independence, or at least greater powers, for Quebec, and a party that by then had emerged as a racing certainty to win the election. The Jewish elite, of which Charles was so prominent a member, had been long-term supporters of the PQ's great rivals, the Liberal party, but also felt quite sincerely that a triumph for the PQ would be disastrous for their province and indeed the whole country. As an Anglo-Saxon character in Richler's book puts it, "All their head offices [were ready] with contingency plans, prepared to sneak out of town tippytoe if the Parti Québecois ever rode into office. The Gurskys, I hear, are already abandoning the sinking ship, shifting key personnel to Hogtown [Toronto]. And they know those boys, those clever semitic mice, they can feel balance sheets in the seats of their pants." In reality Charles was motivated by his genuine love of Montreal and was so fearful of the results of a PQ victory that, for once, he burst out in public. "If we turn our backs on the Liberals," he orated the night before the election, "it will be suicide. The moment the PQ gets in, folks, it's all over." He also threatened that this would be the last annual meeting to be held in Quebec—a hollow threat since the firm's head office and that of Cemp had been transferred to its major distillery at Waterloo near Toronto five years earlier.

Charles was so naïve, so enclosed in his own world, that he had not anticipated the hatred he had aroused after the PQ's triumph the next day—at one victory party each table carried a card proclaiming that "Seagram's Liquor Not Being Served Here." However he was not the only prominent Jewish personality appalled by the onset of Québecois nationalism. At a gala evening organized by Leo Kolber in 1977 involving the Canadian prime minister Pierre Trudeau and a guest list headed by Danny Kaye, the Premier of Quebec turned to Kolber remarking, "You know, nobody contributes as much to the cultural life of Montreal as the Jews." To which Kolber shot back: "So why are you scaring such hell out of them that they're nearly all thinking of leaving?" And they were right, Big Business—Christian as well as Jewish—fled to Toronto and by 1978 a mere 4 percent of Cemp's assets remained within Quebec.

Thirteen

TIME FOR BUSINESS

The whiskey marketing the distillers have been practicing is
basically inept . . . They just walked away from the challenge that
white goods raised.
— MARVIN SHANKEN IN *IMPACT* NEWSLETTER

IN THE EARLY 1970S LEO KOLBER WAS NOT THE ONLY ONE TO NO-
tice that "Edgar's management of Seagram was rather unfocused, to say
the least." On taking over Edgar did, however, take the opportunity to re-
vamp the Seagram board. Under Mr. Sam this had performed a purely dec-
orative function. For Mr. Sam had a total contempt for all the apparatus
surrounding a quoted company, what we would now term "corporate gover-
nance," a phrase unheard of in the Seagram boardroom—as in that of most
other companies at the time. "They were there to declare a dividend and
have a drink," he said of the board, and when one director, the French
Canadian J. Alexander Prud'homme, compared Seagram's dividend policy
with that of Hiram Walker, Mr. Sam simply threw a glass of water at him.
It missed. Prud'homme promptly resigned.

The new structure was more businesslike, in theory at least. But Edgar
had to deal with Minda, who wanted her husband to be appointed in Sam's
place on the board of directors—and thus, in a sense, take Sam's dominant
position instead of Edgar—while the rest of them wanted Leo Kolber, "So
that was one more thing I owed to Mr. Sam," wrote Kolber deferentially,
"his own seat on the Bronfman board." The new structure looked orthodox enough, with an executive committee that included Edgar, Charles,
Leo Kolber, and the company's financial whiz, Harold Fieldsteel. The outside directors included four of Canada's leading businessmen, but in reality
all this was mere window-dressing, the board remained a cozy setup, involving Seagram's commercial and investment bankers, and none of them

was going to challenge the brothers' domination. The outsiders felt part of the Seagram family, and while the family remained united they were not going to argue, however much they disagreed with a move, even the most important.

During his quarter of a century at the helm Edgar preserved the business intact, but introduced few innovations, continuing along the path laid down by his father, a formula for relative stagnation in what had become a fast-moving industry. The trend was away from the blended whiskies on which Seagram was still so heavily dependent, and the statement made about—and possibly by—him in the *American Jewish Biography* that "under his aegis" he was "following American drinking habits closely" was simply not true. He was unable to grapple fully with trends within the industry, he could never break with his father's basic ideas, could never get away from his inherited obsession with blends. This was not surprising given his great palate. The signs were already only too visible during the later 1960s when sales of blends were already starting to decrease. But Sam and Edgar never escaped from blends, for them the rest was either unprofitable—like bourbon—or mere nothings like gin and vodka. And Edgar shared his father's views, although when Robertson had asked Mr. Sam about mistakes he had made he was surprisingly hard on himself. He worried about his failure to invest earlier in Scotland or in Bourbon, and admitted to three errors, one of which, and perhaps the most important, was his inability to take vodka seriously, largely because of his insistence on the aging and quality involved in his beloved blends.

In the early 1970s Edgar's one initiative—and a successful one at that—was an improbable one, a major venture into the world of fine wine. For some years he had been wooing Abdullah—universally known as Ab—Simon, a Jew of Iraqi origin but British upbringing who had built up a business buying fine wines, above all classed growth clarets—for Austin Nichols, a long-established importer of fine wines. Unfortunately Edgar and Yogman had insisted that he be based in San Francisco as part of the Seagram wine division. Simon had insisted on staying in New York, nearer the action—and the restaurants that are the crucial launching pad for serious wines. When Austin Nichols was taken over by Liggett & Myers, a tobacco group markedly less sympathetic to the wine business, Simon decided to leave, once Edgar and Yogman had agreed to allow him to stay in New York. Their timing was perfect; they were out of the market when prices of, and demand for, claret crumbled in 1973–74 as a result of the first oil crisis and the ridiculous prices paid for the wines in the early 1970s. So for a couple of years Simon relied on sales from a handful of agencies from other regions while the market for claret slowly recovered, a recovery hampered by the way his former employers dumped their wines on the market. As a result Simon was able to achieve some remarkable bargains, often buying back for his new employers wines at half the price he, acting for Austin Nichols, had paid a few years earlier.

For the following twenty-five years the company, Chateau and Estates,* became the biggest single purchaser of claret *en primeur*—i.e., in the spring following the harvest. Alone among such buyers they—or rather Simon for it was a totally personal business—could rely on the considerable financial resources Seagram could pour into a venture where the wines were drunk at least five years, and usually longer, after the producers had been paid. It helped that Simon, as he says, "treated the money as though it was my own," and he was, of course, working for a group used to financing slow-maturing stocks. Key to his success was the way he was prepared to buy wine from every single vintage, even the bad ones—like 1984 and 1992—thus ensuring that he obtained substantial allotments of the most fashionable wines in the best years. But the requirement to buy lesser vintages, combined with the cost of holding stock during years of high interest rates, like the late 1970s and early 1980s, meant that profits could jump to $20 million one year and down to nothing the next.

But Simon's greatest single success came in the 1980s and 1990s when he took over distribution of Perrier-Jouet, the best brand of champagne in the Seagram stable. Such was the lack of coordination within the group that it had been selling only a few hundred cases a year through a New York distributor. Simon marketed it through his nationwide network of specialized salesmen, and the brand—particularly its premium fizz Belle Epoque, in its delightfully floral art nouveau bottle—became a must-have item on the wine lists of the country's best restaurants. Within a few years a single outlet, Sherry-Lehmann in Manhattan, was selling ten times as many cases in the runup to Christmas as the previous distributors had sold in the entire country in the course of the year. Moreover Barton & Guestier was maintaining its position as the best-selling range of branded claret in the United States and boasted Bordeaux's most up-to-date production facilities.

---

* It was later renamed Seagram Chateau and Estates to help support the parent group's image.

Nevertheless these were relatively minor successes and within a few years of his father's death Edgar's neglect of the business had become so obvious that Minda approached Kolber to help him persuade a majority of Cemp's trustees to oust Edgar as chairman. Since this would have involved three of the family's most loyal retainers—Laz Phillips, Phil Vineberg, and Kolber himself—the idea was clearly impractical and Kolber told her so. Nevertheless it was the first breach in the wall of family solidarity that was to become a gaping chasm over the following twenty years.

In the later years of the decade when he had recovered from his personal problems Edgar had an unpromising business situation to sort out; above all he had to cope with the inexorable fall in sales of 7 Crown and VO. Consumption of blended whiskey dropped by nearly a third between 1965 and 1977, but, as so often in declining markets, the leading brand, in this case 7 Crown, emerged as increasingly dominant, its market share rising from 27 to 40 percent. Nevertheless, as sales dropped, the stock market was increasingly treating Seagram as a stagnant stock, worth a mere ten times earnings, only two-thirds of the value placed on it a few years earlier. Charles understood the problem. In an interview at the time he complained that "we were over-inventoried. There wasn't strict enough control. We had a multiplicity of brands and were losing money on many of them. We weren't working hard enough. The heart had gone out of the business." Typically, he was too tactful and too loyal to his older brother to pin the blame on Edgar's personal concerns. Nevertheless in what was, in many respects, his absence from the business, Yogman had done a great deal to expand the group's international operations. Moreover, sales of Chivas were taking off. Between 1969 and 1977 sales rose from 681,000 to over two million cases, largely in the United States. Nevertheless, by the early 1970s Seagram's position, if not disastrous, was clearly wobbly. Edgar and Charles were also unlucky in the timing of their inheritance: In the years after the first oil crisis in 1973, as I wrote some years later,[1] "A high proportion of the world's surplus disposable income was diverted to teetotal followers of the prophet Mahomed" and, "In the past decade a disturbingly high proportion of the drinking classes in the industrialized world have become increasingly obsessed with their health"—a trend that has never ceased to intensify since then. During Prohibition drink accounted for 4 percent of Americans' net disposable income. By the mid-1980s the figure was down to a mere quarter of that.

Seagram suffered severely from what I like to think of as "Faith's Law," that children never drink the same alcoholic products as their parents. This meant that adolescents had abandoned the previous generation's thirst for "7 & 7" (7 Crown and 7 Up) for new mixes, most obviously Bacardi and Coke, and, later, Jack Daniel's, which had been below the waterline in the 1960s and was to prove the star performer among whiskies in the following years. It was, and still is, marketed as made by "good ole boys" in a picturesque rural corner of the South and not, as it is in reality, in an ever-expanding industrial distillery; a drink, moreover, that could be sipped like the best bourbon or mixed with Coca-Cola. Its owners, Brown-Forman, were one of the elite firms who—together with Bacardi, and Heublein, owners of Smirnoff—cashed in on the habits of new drinkers, especially the younger ones who did not really like the taste of spirits and were looking for the most neutral alcohol possible—most obviously vodka, but also that eminently mixable rum Bacardi. Not surprisingly the profits of all these companies rose at a compound rate of over 10 percent in the years around Mr. Sam's death. Unfortunately Edgar, despite his superb palate, seems not to have understood the quality factor in the success of individual brands. "The only difference between Chivas Regal and something else," he wrote in Good Spirits, "is the creativity of the advertiser and the aura about it. That's what marketing is all about."

During the 1970s the situation grew ever grimmer, for by then blends accounted for a mere fifth of the market, a drop of two-thirds in twenty years. Joseph E. Seagram & Sons, the American subsidiary that accounted for 85 percent of the group's total sales, saw its market share fall to less than a fifth, against a peak of 30 percent. As one observer told Forbes, Seagram, like the other whiskey producers, had been too "arrogant and complacent." Above all they had ignored the climb of vodka to an eighth of the market from a standing start twenty years earlier. Seagram was doing well enough with its Canadian whiskies—principally VO—where sales were less affected, for, as is so often the case, serious, habitual, adult drinkers were consuming less but better. Chivas was making great profits—one magazine compared it to the position of Cadillac within General Motors—but was too small a brand to save the group. But the key statistic was that in 1968, 7 Crown sold nearly eight million cases, two-thirds more than the combined sales of Smirnoff and Bacardi, and the second brand in the United States was VO with 3.5 million. By 1983 sales of 7 Crown were down by over a third and it was running a bad third behind Bacardi and Smirnoff.

Drinking habits also became increasingly civilized; the way in which liquor was being consumed was far less as "shots" at a bar but sipped as long drinks at home or at parties. "Americans have moved away from their traditional pattern of hard, purposeful drinking," noted *Fortune* in 1977. "More people are drinking and they are drinking a greater variety of alcoholic beverages." The much cherished and reliable "category drinker" was being replaced a new "eclectic" drinker who varied his—or increasingly her—choice depending on mood, the time of day, or the occasion. People were no longer faithful to a particular drink, increasingly they experimented with a variety of spirits depending on the season and the occasion, a fatal development for single-type distillers like the Bronfmans.

Some of the (relative) newcomers managed to occupy the high ground, even in the vodka market. How, asked one salesman, "can you have a premium brand in a market whose major asset is its tastelessness?" Well you could, first Smirnoff and then Absolut showing just how. At the premium-end straight whiskies were climbing fast with Jim Beam outselling VO, and so was Jack Daniel's. To make matters worse all the traditional whiskey distillers wasted the early years of the 1970s amassing vast stocks to try to compete with the new lighter spirits by launching "light" whiskies that they had matured in old barrels (not, as previously, exclusively in new ones) to soften their taste and lighten their appearance. National Distillers described its offering Crown Light—the only one to survive more than a year or two—as "lighter than Canadian, smoother than Scotch," a perfect example of "head in the sand" marketing. At the same time the distributors were having to change their habits. Previously their absolute priority had been sales volume, "selling boxes" in the jargon of the trade. This involved hard selling, discounting, and "loading up," forcing a distributor to take on slow-moving brands to be allowed enough of the drinkers' favorites. But these tactics were, if not stopped, at least reduced by campaigns mounted by the BATF,* and even the SEC got into the act.

Obviously the biggest gap in the Seagram range was vodka. Allan Bronfman had bought a minor brand, Wolfschmidt, but Edgar had never thought through the threat posed by vodka. In *Good Spirits* he wrote how "the rule in those days [the 1960s]—and except for imports such as Absolut, Stoli, and others, it hasn't changed much in almost forty years—was that there were two vodkas, Smirnoff and price." And Wolfschmidt was very much in

---

* The Bureau of Alcohol, Tobacco, and Firearms, which regulated the industry.

the second category, known in the trade as a "commodity brand." But then Edgar's attitude to these newcomers was profoundly defeatist. "You really can't improve on the taste of these products," he wrote, "and by the time we got into those arenas, we were playing catch-up against giants like Smirnoff and Bacardi"—which was outselling Seagram's white rum, Ronrico, by a margin of ten to one. Thus spoke the son of an—honorable—father for whom perceived quality was all, and image had to be associated with superior quality, which meant aged, blended spirits.

The accounts, however, concealed the long-term problems. The build-up in the stocks of Chivas required to sell a twelve-year-old whiskey had reached a plateau and those required for 7 Crown were actually diminishing as ever-decreasing sales meant that stocks could be reduced. But both sales and profits were skewed for the three key brands, 7 Crown, VO, and Chivas, which accounted for two-fifths of sales, and contributed three-fifths of profits. Yogman did make a minor cull of five of Seagram's fifty brands but that was not enough. The long-term problems were also hidden by an increasing exposure to sales outside the United States and to wines, which were far more socially acceptable than hard liquor. It helped that Mr. Sam had ensured that Seagram's steady flow of investments in wine concentrated on premium products—in the early 1970s Seagram had one-twentieth of the total American wine market in volume terms, but half the total for premium varietal wines with United Vintners, and in the early 1980s Seagram strengthened its position further by buying up Coca-Cola's wine interests, though by then Seagram had fallen to a distant third to E & J Gallo and to Heublein.

Its overseas subsidiaries also flourished. Throughout the world they operated on a similar pattern to that established in the United States. It involved either agents/importers in whose businesses Seagram had invested or its own subsidiaries, a pattern unique in the world's liquor industry at a time when other distillers failed to profit from the fortunes their agents were making with their brands. But by going into partnership with its agents, and investing in their equity, Seagram was able to absorb them over the years when the original owners wanted to sell up. And when the arrangements were unfair the partners could be bypassed. So it was in Japan, where access was both difficult and expensive and taxes ludicrously high. Nevertheless in 1971 Seagram had established a partnership with Kirin, the biggest brewers in Japan.

Everywhere else drinking patterns continued to evolve, with many markets throughout Europe and then in the ever-expanding Far Eastern markets slowly abandoning their traditional thirst for purely locally produced spirits in favor of imported luxuries. But these trends demanded a continuous flow of novelties. These were not only "mixables," for the market was also open to totally new confections, most obviously Baileys Irish Cream, as well as pre-mixed cocktails, wine coolers (for a time at least), and dark rum—where Seagram had its only major success, Captain Morgan's Spiced Rum, the leader in its category.

The only other consolation was that Seagram's Gin became a bestseller, with sales that peaked at 3.5 million cases, thanks to the abandonment of Mr. Sam's idea that gin, like his beloved blends, should be aged in wood (drinkers didn't like the golden tinge this imparted). But unfortunately this was not a premium brand at a time when the market for any spirits was increasingly separating into two, commodity and premium, and to most American drinkers "domestic" gin remained too closely associated with the horrors of "bathtub gin" to be regarded as other than a low-priced drink. Only imported gins, like Tanqueray and Beefeater, could command the sort of premium prices to which Seagram had been accustomed in the past. Squires, Seagram's other "commodity brand," was never a great success. Edgar had had a battle with his father, who refused to allow their brand Sir Robert Burnett's London Dry Gin—typical of the snobby echoes he so admired—to be produced in London. They had tried a compromise featuring the slogan, "British gin at an American price," but it never enjoyed the cachet of gins bearing the magic word "imported." And when he did try to market a premium gin named after Boodle's, a distinguished London club, it failed, partly because the name was unknown to anyone in the United States apart from a handful of WASPs.

The situation in the United States should, in theory, have been more favorable to firms like Seagram with powerful distribution networks. As I wrote in The Economist, "Wholesalers and retailers enjoy even greater power because the distillers cannot easily go over their heads directly to the drinking public, for spirits cannot be advertised on radio or television. The ban inevitably reduced the number of new products and the effectiveness with which they can be promoted. So the life cycle of drinks is slower, and the half-life of older, declining brands infinitely longer and more profitable, because they are not being promoted to any great extent. Inevitably, too, new introductions depend far more on word of mouth and fashion than they do with other consumer products."

But fashion could prove more important than the strength of existing distribution channels—the purveyors of Baileys knew that they were on to a winner when they saw air hostesses schlepping heavy bottles of the stuff home after coming off duty. Nevertheless Edgar continued to believe in the idea of blends, arguing that they should be advertised as a category rather than as individual brands even when sales were sliding. In 1977 when he authorized a hefty increase in advertising, most of the money went to shore up the declining sales of the blended whiskies—twenty years later his son Edgar Jr. had realized, rather belatedly, that "the real future is in brands. People tend to consume brands rather than categories." Seagram's attempt to market an ordinary Scotch in the form of 100 Pipers had proved a disaster, and Edgar blocked an attempt to introduce an eighteen-year-old Chivas, a type of "brand extension" normal in the spirits business, saying, "You don't screw around with a brand like Chivas Regal." (In the late 1990s an eighteen-year-old was, successfully, introduced.) Moreover prices of blends had been stagnant for far too long with the blame laid squarely at the door of Seagram, the market leader, but when prices were increased it was only slowly even though the price of Four Roses, for instance, had risen by a mere thirteen cents in fifteen years.

Yogman became a victim of Seagram's problems, exacerbated by the economic downturn following the first oil crisis in 1973 and combined with the fact that Edgar was jealous of the way he had taken effective control of the whole business during his troubled years after his father's death. Yogman's fate was sealed by his boast that he could bring in $100 million profits by the end of 1976. He fell far short of that ambitious target and in 1975 the company was saved largely by the dividend income from the oil business. He was duly fired in July 1976 with a generous payoff—provided that he stayed out of the liquor and oil businesses for ten years. So he went on to run companies producing a major ice cream (Dolly Madison) and chocolate bars (Oh Henry). Because Edgar had been rather jealous of Yogman, he became an unmentionable name after his departure, likely to induce displays of temper similar to those his father had evinced at the mention of Lew Rosenstiel. For in Edgar's mind Yogman, his father's protégé, had come to occupy the same role as a reminder of his father as had Victor Fischel.

By this time Edgar had recovered from his father's death and wanted to take a more active role and after some hesitation decided to take control of Seagram as CEO. Nevertheless even in the period of his most active involvement with Seagram, by his own admission, and notably unlike his father, he was never totally involved. As he confessed to a trusted employee, "I'm not a detail man." So successive COOs found themselves in an unfortunate position, for they had the responsibility of running the business, but without the power associated with the title of CEO.

In 1977 he found a suitable candidate, Philip Beekman, who had previously been in charge of all the non-American operations of Colgate-Palmolive, confirming Edgar's taste for executives from FMCG companies rather than the liquor business. He was awarded a lavish employment contract, involving stock options, an unusual element in an employment package at the time. His timing was impeccable; profits rebounded and in his first year debt was reduced by over $100 million, thanks to stock reductions and revenue from the oil business. He followed many others in the drinks trade at the time by trying to bring Seagram's management up to date. To get away from Mr. Sam's scattergun approach to management he relied on the FMCG techniques to which he was accustomed, and on executives he brought over from his former employers. In the words of one former employee, what was once "a casually managed business had become more structured, with more formal systems and procedures and neat, precise organization charts." He even tried to ensure that every senior executive came up with a "succession plan" to cover his departure. Unfortunately the new formality damaged the precious relationship with the distributors. As one put it, "There's been a subtle change at Seagram. There's a toothpaste mentality at certain levels. We're all prima donnas, but Seagram's new marketing men don't see us in the same fashion"—as their predecessors like Yogman had done. But Beekman was used to dealing with intermediaries who did not have egos that needed to be pampered.

Part of Beekman's problem came from the extraordinarily high margins Seagram had historically enjoyed on its whiskies. As a result he is accused by fellow executives of botching the introduction of a new and warmer style of vodka using lower-strength spirit by marketing it at too high a price. A need to achieve exaggerated profit margins may also have been behind his refusal to match price cuts introduced by Baileys Irish Cream, the wonder of the last quarter of the twentieth century, even though the Seagram product, Myers Original Rum Cordial (known as MORC) was a superior beverage* and even though Seagram would have made a very decent profit even at a lower price. Moreover drinkers found that Seagram's bourbon, Benchmark, was too smooth, in line with the Seagram tradition but not what drinkers wanted.

The new regime did take one major initiative. In 1978 Seagram bought Glenlivet, makers of several of Scotland's finest malt whiskies, a market where Seagram had no major brand. Glenlivet also brought with it some useful stocks of malt whiskies. Mr. Sam had twice offered to buy it, but had failed, though Seagram remained their agents in the United States. Charles worried that his father would have complained that they had overpaid, for they had to pay $70 million, many times the price Sam himself had offered. The takeover did not go altogether smoothly because Phil Beekman tried to break the agreement between Edgar and Ivan Straker, the managing director, that Glenlivet's other foreign agents would remain and that no one would be sacked. After a blazing row Edgar agreed with Straker, and although Seagram failed to exploit Queen Anne, a successful blended Scotch owned by Glenlivet, they did make Glenlivet the best-selling malt whisky in the United States. With Glenlivet came Longmorn, one of the greatest of all malts, as well as Glen Grant, which became a great success in Italy thanks to an unusually young malt-whisky, a five-year-old Glen Grant.† Later the deal brought Seagram into the big league sponsorship business when Ivan Straker persuaded Edgar to pay £700,000 (then $2 million) to save Britain's most famous steeplechase, the Grand National, after the owner of Aintree, the course on which it was run, had gone bankrupt. This was the first time the British public had become aware of the Seagram name. (Later it became the Martell Grand National, though in reality the "brand name" of the race itself was so strong that no one used the sponsor's name, and after Pernod-Ricard took over the Martell business in the early years of the twenty-first century it promptly abandoned the race.) And in 1979 Seagram paid £17 million (then nearly $40 million) for another venerable family business, Sandeman, a leading producer of ports and sherries, which again benefited from Seagram's incomparable distribution network.

---

* Because it didn't separate into its individual components as Bailey's often did when it was first sold.
† They appealed to the Italian palate by blending it so that it tasted like grappa.

By the early 1980s two new stars were rising at the court of King Edgar, neither members of the legal mafia that had done such sterling service for the family over the generations. One, Steve Herbits, was particularly un-usual, openly gay, much of his experience had been in Washington, latterly as troubleshooter for Donald Rumsfeld when he was Secretary of Defense in the Ford administration. For nearly a quarter of a century until he re-turned to help "Rummie" in early 2001 Herbits took on the same position with Edgar, as a trusted troubleshooter and unusually frank friend. Herbits was also able to put his experience in Washington to good use when he was largely responsible for promoting "equivalency," a major campaign that ex-ploited research showing that a glass of beer contained much the same quantity of alcohol as a shot of whiskey. This provided an effective, and logical, argument against the excessive taxes paid on liquor, imposed, as Herbits puts it, because "wine was considered as a food and beer as just an-other soft drink." To the great annoyance of Adolph Busch and other lead-ing brewers, in the 1990s the argument also enabled Edgar Jr. to exploit the way that spirits came to enjoy the same freedom to advertise on television and therefore compete on a level playing field as beer and wine.

The second recruit, Ed Mcdonnell, was a more orthodox appointment, a bluff, confident, effective Boston Irish Catholic, with considerable experi-ence in the international side of the food business. Without much of an interview—Edgar spent most of the time strumming at the piano—Mcdonnell was hired and immediately sent to London as head of the inter-national side of the business, to reorganize, or rather organize it for the first time. Not surprisingly the process involved removing a substantial number of notably incompetent managers and replacing them with competent ones—notably Hubert Millet who replaced François de Gunzburg in France. This went directly against Seagram's historic paternalism—indeed Edgar had told him, not entirely truthfully, that he had never sacked any-one. Inevitably after Mcdonnell's first year in the job the financial results were poor, badly affected by the redundancy payments involved in the re-construction. This provided the opportunity for some of the courtiers to try to persuade Edgar that Mcdonnell should be sacked. Fortunately Her-bits came to his rescue and a number of senior courtiers were shown the door. When Mcdonnell arrived, over four-fifths of Seagram's profits were derived from North America, but within a decade the majority came from his division. This was partly due to the continuing fall in the sale of the—

purely domestic—"old" brands but greatly boosted by sales outside the United States of Chivas Regal.*

But Edgar's biggest contribution to Seagram came, not in the liquor business at all, but in his masterly handling of the situation that arose in 1981 when Sun Oil made a bid for Seagram's stake in Texas Pacific. The Bronfmans accepted with alacrity. They had been afraid that a major oil company—Mobil was the rumored favorite—would buy Seagram itself purely to get their hands on Texas Pacific's reserves at a time when the industry was suffering as a result of the second oil crisis of the 1970s, and would simply sell off the liquor business. The Bronfmans received a staggering price, $2.1 billion, after Mark Millard of Goldman Sachs, Edgar's friend and trusted investment banker, had persuaded Sun to pay an additional $200 million. This was four times their valuation in Seagram's books and forty times the amount Seagram had paid twenty years earlier. Edgar's decision was made, as he wrote, on the excellent principle that "the right time to sell anything is when everybody thinks the price is going to keep going up, as was the case with oil in 1981. In fact the price of oil soon started to drop."

As Edgar points out in his book, at a time of soaring interest rates the Bronfmans did not have to be in any sort of hurry to make another major investment. For their "fighting fund," in cash and credit lines, had increased to $3 billion by the time they reinvested the money. There was clearly an internal argument as to what they should do with the money in the longer term. Naturally Beekman, as an alumnus of Colgate-Palmolive, was keen on buying a company in the FMCG sector—there were even abortive merger talks with his old employers—but in the end the board preferred not to go for a consumer-linked company. Their search was wide ranging—it was even rumored that they might bid for that mighty symbol of American capitalism, the Union Pacific Railroad. But their first bid was for St. Joseph Lead, a major and well-diversified mining company. Seagram's offer of $48 a share was well above the market price, which was in the low thirties. It was predicated on the—false—assumption that the price of gold would rise to $500 an ounce. In the end, and luckily, Edgar re-

---

* Sales rose so fast that Jimmy Lang, the blender, grew short of stock and it took some nifty trading in the informal, and totally secret, market operated by the master blenders of the major Scotch companies to satisfy Seagram's requirements.

fused to increase a bid that had been rejected by a board that was profoundly anti-Semitic. In any case the argument became academic when the Fluor Corporation offered 75 percent more than Seagram, leaving the company with a $10 million profit on the shares it had bought.

As Edgar acknowledges, it was Mark Millard who spotted what proved to be a magically successful opportunity. When Dome, a minor Canadian oil company, made a tender for a small proportion of the stock of the much larger Conoco, a company with oil fields the world over, the offer was hugely oversubscribed, proving to Millard that Conoco's stock was very loosely held and that the company would be very vulnerable to a bid. Edgar and Millard met Conoco's CEO, Bill Bailey, and proposed that Seagram would bid for a quarter of Conoco's stock, promising to act as a passive investor. Bailey prevaricated and Edgar soon found out why. At Westchester Airport, home of the "Seagram Air Force," they discovered that one of Conoco's planes kept flying to Wilmington, Delaware, and, as Edgar pointed out, "what else is there in Wilmington except DuPont?" Who, to everyone's surprise except the Bronfmans, turned out to be a rival bidder for Conoco. (There was a third bidder, Mobil, but everyone knew that this bid was doomed from the start for antitrust reasons.)

The DuPont bid appeared to be in the form of 51 percent in cash, with the rest in DuPont stock. Millard reckoned, rightly, that much of the Conoco stock was held by arbitrageurs who would prefer cash if the price was right. But it was Edgar, not the bankers, who had read the small print and found that Seagram could get the whole payment for its 20 percent stake in Conoco in the form of DuPont stock, thus removing any need for paying capital gains tax, and, moreover, providing the Bronfmans with a significant 5 percent stake in the combined group. So Seagram bid a hefty $90 a share, providing only that they received offers of 50 percent of the outstanding stock—i.e., a quarter of the whole. The danger was that they would receive bids for a much lower percentage, leaving them stranded with a meaningless minority of the stock. But the existence of the 50 percent safety net frightened the Conoco stockholders, afraid that the Seagram conditions would not be met and they would be left with unwanted stock in DuPont.

So, against the advice of his distinguished investment bankers, Edgar dropped the condition as to how much of the stock they would be able to buy. He won his gamble and Seagram ended up with 20 percent, not only of Conoco (itself representing far more oil in the ground than Texas Pacific had possessed) but also of the rest of DuPont, then as now a major force in the world's chemical industry. Moreover the size of the holding was over the 20 percent level, which enabled Seagram to consolidate that proportion of DuPont's profits in those of Seagram itself, instead of treating the dividends as investment income. It was Edgar's finest hour. Even the normally grudging Kolber wrote how it "was entirely due to Edgar's instincts and leadership." Yet at the time the reaction to this, the greatest deal in the history of Seagram, was by no means favorable. *BusinessWeek* even quoted a DuPont executive claiming that "Seagram was on the rocks." The only disadvantage was that over the years many sophisticated investors tended to treat an investment in Seagram as one in DuPont, with the returns from the liquor business merely as non-core income. Such investors would naturally treat any attempt to sell the stake in DuPont as a highly destructive step.

By the early 1980s Edgar had decided that wines and spirits offered limited growth prospects—and, though he didn't admit it, this was largely due to his failure to diversify the company. But while diversifying he had to ensure that control remained with the family. Hence an ill-fated scheme launched in early 1985 to create a new class of "high-powered" common shares, with each share entitled to ten votes, while shareholders who did not convert to the new stock would receive a higher dividend. There was the natural outcry at what was perceived as a blatant attempt to strengthen the family's position if and when new capital was required, and, unexpectedly, a number of major investment institutions decided to convert, thus foiling the Bronfmans' ideas. The move clearly showed that Edgar was determined to have his cake and eat it, to ensure that the family retained control of Seagram while at the same time steadily withdrawing from active involvement in the management of the empire. His aim was clearly to hand over the reins as soon as possible to one of his sons; not to the eldest, Sam, but to his second son, Edgar Jr. The reason was very simple. In the last years of the 1970s he had rediscovered his Jewish identity, and the result was a second career, and one, moreover, that had the unique advantage of showing that he could make a greater success than his father had done, albeit politically rather than financially.

Fourteen

KING OF THE JEWS?

In the early 1960s my father said that if I thought anti-Semitism
was dead, I was fooling myself.
— EDGAR BRONFMAN

T̲HE REASON EDGAR BRONFMAN BECAME STEADILY LESS INVOLVED
in Seagram's management was simple: As president of the World Jewish Congress for a quarter of a century after he took over in 1981 he became an increasingly important figure on the world political stage, which
enabled him to become the only member of the family who will be remembered in the history books. For he may have been merely the custodian of
his father's business heritage but by contrast he was a mold-breaking leader
of world Jewry. In this role, crucially, he not only escaped from his father's
shadow, he far surpassed the achievement of a father who had merely been
the leader of a relatively unimportant element of the Jewish diaspora.
Where the father, as head of the Canadian Jewish Congress, had been almost a provincial figure, Edgar could, and increasingly did, strut the stage
as one of the unquestioned leaders of his race outside Israel.

The presidency of the WJC seemed a totally unlikely role, for one major
aspect of Edgar's revolt against his father had taken the form of turning his
back on Judaism. "As a young man growing up, Judaism had meant little to
me; in fact, much of my life had given secularity new meaning," he wrote.[1]
Even after his marriage to his first wife, the only one born Jewish, "My Jewishness all but lapsed . . . there was absolutely no religion in our home
whatsoever . . . there was ham in our house on Yom Kippur . . . I had rejected not just Judaism, but religion in general." Before he became involved
in the WJC, "I followed the path of least resistance. I made no effort to
have our children learn anything about their traditions as Jews. I joined

neither a synagogue or a temple. My Jewishness all but lapsed. . . . But never for a second did I forget that I was a Jew. . . . The creation of the state of Israel affected me as it affected other Jews." He was "active for Israel . . . but in my heart and head it had nothing at all to do with the Jewish religion." Indeed he rarely if ever even contributed to any of the numerous Jewish charities supported by many Jews far less wealthy than him, a lapse that made him extremely unpopular in the upper reaches of Jewish society at the time. His escape from his Jewishness was emphasized by the string of anti-Semitic jokes that regularly punctuated his conversation before he "saw the light."

Yet the presidency not only enabled him to rediscover, and indeed flaunt, his Jewish heritage, it also proved an ideal outlet for the aggressive and arrogant elements in his character. At the WJC he helped ensure that Jews ceased being supplicants or subservient. He simply brushed aside the old reluctance of Jews, in the diaspora at least, to draw attention to themselves for fear of retribution. Indeed he acted as a bulldozer against anti-Semitism the world over, for his attitude to the relationships between Jews and gentiles was the total opposite of that of his father, and indeed of previous Jewish leaders outside Israel.

On a personal level his involvement with the WJC finally liberated him from his father's shadow when he was already over fifty, and created a sense of self-worth for himself. He became, as one observer put it, "his own man for the first time." For while Mr. Sam had been merely the King of Canadian Jewry, Edgar has been called King of the Jews—though a substantial number of Jews sneered at the description. He is obviously at ease in his role, as he seems never to have been before in his life. In his second autobiographical work, *The Making of a Jew*, he traces his gradual discovery of his heritage, of the Bible, and of his ancestral religion—"The more I learn, the prouder I become of my heritage," he wrote. The book is a vivid contrast to *Good Spirits*, in which he describes his family and business life in a mean, bitchy, vindictive, defensive-arrogant work. By contrast *The Making of a Jew*, though full of his characteristic bluster and egotism, is a sympathetic, naïve, and sometimes moving account of his role as president of the WJC and of his conversion—there really is no other word—to Judaism.* Moreover

---

* His other book, *The Third Act* (with Catherine Whitney, New York: Putnam, 2002) can most charitably be described as a tired collection of clichés about retirement.

the presidency also obviously helped cure the previous turmoil of his private life. In the 1980s he calmed down, his only mistress a distinguished New York neighbor who repulsed his advances for some time. But she refused to marry him and in 1988—as a much more secure personality—he finally found emotional stability with his fourth wife, Jan, a feisty independent-minded artist.

Oddly, Edgar became a Jewish activist before converting himself into a private, religious Jew. Indeed it was his official position that seemingly did more to make him a believer than any private conversion—and even afterwards, as he admits, he kept the Sabbath only when he was acting as a representative of the Jewish people. Touchingly he writes how on a trip to the Soviet Union he saw his mentor and colleague, the orthodox rabbi Israel Singer, "take a little book from his pocket, study it for ten minutes, close it and replace it in his pocket. Out of curiosity, I asked him what he had just read. 'That was the daily portion of the Torah' came the answer. . . . That's how my Jewish education started." It was not until 1990 that Bronfman, at the age of sixty, who had already been the nominal leader of world Jewry for nearly a decade, started any systematic study of the basic text of the Jewish religion and read the Bible through for the first time.

His father had been chairman of the Western Hemisphere Section of the World Jewish Congress and after Mr. Sam's death in 1971 Edgar was lured back into the fold, largely because of his pride in Israel, first in money-raising, then, as an indirect result, into the World Jewish Congress. The WJC had been established in 1936 as a sort of "organization of organizations" by Nahum Goldmann and the leading American cleric Rabbi Stephen Wise to bring together the world's scattered and very diverse Jewish communities. Within a few months of his father's death Edgar had been approached to be co-chairman of an international advisory body, a request clearly designed to involve Mr. Sam's heir in world Jewish affairs, at first very largely financially. Once allowed to be in charge of the powerful North American branch, he naturally agreed, but as he admits, neither the job—nor indeed the WJC itself—were at all important—especially as the headquarters was in Geneva and Goldmann himself was based in Paris, indeed used to write in French. But Goldmann, generally considered a rather ineffectual figure, had one major success to his credit, for he had persuaded the West German chancellor Konrad Adenauer to make enormous reparations to the Jewish people, amounting to $73 billion in all, to go some way in expiating the Germans' responsibility for the Holocaust.

In 1977 Goldmann, by now an octogenarian, was eased out of the presidency by a leading American figure, Phil Klutznick, but when he was appointed Secretary of Commerce by President Carter, he could no longer act as an executive president of the WJC, so the organization urgently needed what they called a "convener," someone who would actually organize the meetings. There was also an element of public relations in the appointment, as Edgar's *consigliere* in these matters clearly wanted to provide an antidote to the unpleasant image he had conveyed during the hearings that led to the annulment of his marriage with Lady Carolyn Townshend. The WJC also needed a wealthy Jew, for it was virtually broke. By 1981 after the politicking inevitable in any such organization, Bronfman was appointed president, a total contrast to Goldmann, who was a typical European Jew, and so had been rather wary of his brash American co-religionists.

Edgar inherited an institution which, typically of most such Jewish bodies throughout the world at the time, was timid and reactive. Mr. Sam had always behaved like the traditional Jewish leader, refusing to risk a surge of anti-Semitism by appearing too aggressive. He was, said his official biographer, "wary of activism." During the war Mr. Sam did not go seriously into battle against a Canadian government deaf to the demands of the thousands of European Jews trying to escape from Hitler and until 1948 was no Zionist. By contrast—and to distinguish himself from his father—Edgar immediately made it clear that he was going to be far more positive, far bolder, even free to continue to criticize the leaders of Israel—as he had just done in a series of articles. He was even prepared to tackle President George H. W. Bush, to help secure American backing for the removal of the United Nations' declaration that Zionism equaled racism.

But Edgar had neither the knowledge of the WJC or of Jewish life, nor indeed the temperament, to lead without the help of a man who would be at once a guru and a negotiator. He was lucky in finding Singer, who became the WJC's secretary-general in 1985. Singer came from a family of Austrian Jews that had escaped to the United States thanks to forged passports issued by the Chinese consul-general in Vienna. One of his first memories was of his grandmother lighting 113 candles during a festival supper to commemorate the members of the family put to death by the Nazis. Even before his arrival at the WJC Singer had enjoyed an impressive career. He had started working in the family construction firm—personally responsible for building over seventy thousand dwellings—before becoming an Orthodox rabbi, going on to teach politics in New York and in Israel. He met Goldmann in 1969 when the WJC president was trying to make contact with the Russians. As a result Singer became an expert on East-West relations in the WJC's office in New York—its headquarters moved from Geneva only in 1983.

Singer recruited one Elan Steinberg, a brilliant publicist, as executive director in charge of external affairs. None of the trio was exactly quiet or deferential, as Tom Bower says, both Singer and Steinberg possessed "aggressive energy and the courage to shout when others might shy away out of embarrassment. The level of noise generated by these two men suggested an enormous organization, but in reality the two were the complete executive staff of the WJC."[2] Fortunately the WJC's organizational structure, was, unbelievably, based on the Soviet model, so it could be directed by a strong president. Singer and Bronfman shared a single aim. As Singer put it, "We wanted to show people that we weren't going to be victims, and that we were not going to allow other people to make us victims."[3] But Singer clearly felt that he was the real leader. "Throughout the resolution efforts," he said,[4] "WJC President Edgar Bronfman was my greatest supporter. In a rather uncomplicated way he believes in justice and the transparency of history"—an attitude totally opposed to the reticence of any member of an earlier generation of Jews—including Edgar's father. For the relationship is totally interdependent. As one observer put it: "Bronfman sees Singer as his ticket to redemption . . . having been a secular Jew most of his life, he decided rather late that Judaism mattered to him, and Singer has, if you will, koshered him."

For Edgar, guided by Singer, led from the front in tackling anti-Semitism throughout the world. For the first time the world Jewish community became proactive, indeed aggressively so. Singer put it bluntly: "There is often criticism about the aggressive methods we've used. A small organization confronting powerful, unyielding governments cannot be soft if it wants to achieve anything. If I had listened to all the good Jewish advisers who said we shouldn't scream, the survivors would not have received anything. Fighting for the truth cannot be done in a nuanced way." The two worked surprisingly well together, although, not surprisingly, they each claimed the major share of the credit. But there was enough success for both of them, notably in their—highly effective—campaign to get Russian leaders to release Jews under the emotive banner "Let My People Go," their hassling of the ex-Nazi Kurt Waldheim and their campaign against the Swiss banks that had hoarded Jewish funds. As a "non-Jewish Jew" of a younger generation Edgar lacked the instinctive caution ingrained in his father and other members of an older generation. It was not an easy role, for it required considerable courage. As Abraham Foxman, national direc- tor of the Anti-Defamation League put it, "Edgar Bronfman is the most powerful Jew in the world," a status that, he added, "fulfills the fantasy of every Jew—and every anti-Semite." For, as president of the WJC he in- creasingly became the spokesman for world Jewry, behaving, in his own words as "Jewish ambassador to the world."

In Edgar's new role what were character flaws in any other context were transmuted into enormous assets in dealing with an—only too often hostile—world. It helped that he had been brought up and had lived in a largely non-Jewish environment and could thus understand the position of the people he was dealing with far more easily than someone whose world had been exclusively Jewish. His arrogance, his insensitivity, his what one can only call bumptiousness, proved invaluable in his success in becoming the first Jewish leader in modern history to act aggressively, to lead from the front, and not be deferential in the face of external authority. Tom Bower puts it politely, writing how he was "accustomed to compliance and obedience from others. It even helped that his attitude was not that of a re- ligious Jew, but of someone wanting power, wanting to assert himself to be seen to have influence and authority." The fact that Edgar could, and in- variably did, descend from the skies in his own plane was a curiously im- portant aspect to his—implicit—claim to be a head of state, for the welcome accorded to a dignitary arriving in his own plane was inevitably more impressive than if he had descended from a "commercial" flight.

In this context even the perpetual name-dropping only too visible in his book was useful, for Edgar relished the way he could treat prime min- isters and president as equals, was able to criticize and advise them freely. "As with other leaders," he wrote of Helmut Schmidt and Helmut Kohl, both chancellors of Germany, "as the occasion warranted I've criticized them and I've applauded them." Indeed after German reunification he challenged Kohl in a speech "to build a Germany firmly rooted in peace and respect for universal human values." Later he rebuked Kohl for pro- posing to visit an SS cemetery at Bitburg. His gutsy attitude extended even to Pope John Paul II. At a private meeting Bronfman reproached His Holiness for allowing nuns to erect a twenty-two-foot cross on the site of Auschwitz and to live in a building previously used to store the deadly gas Zyklon B—shortly afterwards they left. And he even managed to "hold my own" in an interview with Mikhail Gorbachev, who "loves to lecture."

Edgar was also prepared to stand up to Israeli leaders. In 1982, after Ariel Sharon's incursion into Lebanon and a mere couple of years after he had taken on the presidency he said firmly that "out of this war Israel must finally face the Palestinian problem. It must look for new openings to make peace with the Arabs rather than war on them." Israeli prime ministers were not spared either. Bronfman was especially fierce when he compared the Oslo accord with the infamous pact the British prime minister had brought back after a meeting in Munich with Adolf Hitler. And in 2003 he enraged the Israelis—and many American Jews as well—by denouncing the security fence the Israeli government was building to separate the Israelis from the Palestinians.

It helped that, as one of his associates put it, Bronfman "didn't carry any emotional baggage . . . he was not obsessed with the shadow of the Holocaust." For in the first decades after 1945 European Jews and gentiles alike tended to underplay the appalling nature of the Holocaust, to forgive and—so far as many European countries were concerned—forget as well. By contrast, Edgar was quite prepared to exploit the Holocaust as a means of persuasion. Throughout his presidency he has acted as part of an "anti-forgetfulness" movement. His refusal to forget, let alone forgive, played a major part in their first major international public relations triumph, the WJC's pursuit of Kurt Waldheim, the former secretary-general of the United Nations, a campaign carried through in the face of accusations that he was interfering in the internal affairs of a sovereign country.[*] In January 1986, just as Waldheim was starting a six-year term as president of Austria, the leader of Austrian Jewry informed the WJC of stories concerning Waldheim's wartime career—which, he had insisted, consisted merely of early wounds on the eastern front, followed by continuing law studies in Vienna. By March 25 the WJC's researchers had proved that he had not—as he had subsequently claimed—been merely an interpreter, but a senior intelligence officer in occupied Greece responsible for prisoner interrogation. It soon emerged that he had even

---

[*] The WJC was greatly helped by Benyamin Netanyahu, the future prime minister who at the time was Israeli ambassador to the United Nations.

been involved in the arrangements for the deportation of Jews to Auschwitz.

During the year further evidence piled up, culminating in the WJC's revelation in November that Waldheim had been responsible for planning the German army's reprisal measures in the Balkans. As a result, the WJC declared that he was "a war criminal." In early 1988 Bronfman had enough evidence to state at a press conference that Waldheim had been "part and parcel of the Nazi killing machine." The WJC's campaign—which was later joined by the Americans—ensured that throughout his presidency Waldheim was treated as a pariah outside his native country. The only exception was Pope John Paul II, who made him a papal knight. Bronfman naturally wrote to the appropriate Vatican official, Cardinal Cassidy, protesting that the reward was "like giving a rotten structure a fresh coat of paint." He received no reply. Typically of the prevailing pre-Bronfman attitude, many other Jewish leaders believed that the attacks would create ill will, a dramatic demonstration of their continuing timidity. But Bronfman found that ordinary Jews in the street were far less timid and applauded his attitude. It was a major triumph. The WJC had "single-handedly destroyed the politician's reputation," as Bower put it. He had also gone a long way towards destroying the picture that Austrians had successfully foisted on the world of their country as "the first victim" of Nazism, and not as enthusiastic supporters of the Führer.

Bronfman and Singer were prepared to go on the attack throughout the world, remaining on the alert for insults to world Jewry, like their campaign against Helmut Kohl's 1995 initiative to honor dead SS officers at the Bitburg cemetery. Their efforts were not confined to Europe—Singer was particularly concerned to take the fight to any country with a Jewish community. He and Bronfman were quite prepared to rebuke such leaders as General Videla in Argentina and General Pinochet in Chile over the lack of human rights in their countries, and in 1983 they refused to meet the South African president Botha. Wherever they went they looked out for Nazis. In Argentina, for instance they inquired about the Nazi criminals who had fled there in the 1940s, with particular reference to the way the Vatican had helped them to escape. And, naturally, Bronfman acted as the representative of world Jewry when confronted by a couple of anti-Jewish outrages in Buenos Aires.

Singer had perceived that the Cold War had prevented Jewry from helping their co-religionists in Russia or, more especially, Eastern Europe. Singer called these people "double victims." "The Nazis had persecuted them," he said, "thereafter the Communists wronged them." Goldmann's legacy included a commitment to freeing Russian Jews. "He often said," wrote Edgar, "that we had lost six million Jews to Hitler and he was not going to lose another three million Jews in the Soviet Union"—though no one had any precise information on just how many there were. At the time, wrote Edgar, "I had made no attempt to learn anything about Soviet Jews. I had not heard of refuseniks. I did know that the practice of religion was proscribed, but I felt that it was not particularly anti-Semitic, since that proscription applied to all religions." Both sets of Edgar's grandparents had been born in regions that became part of the Soviet Union. So had Israel Singer's. Goldmann had—unsuccessfully—tried a soft approach in trying to gain access to the Kremlin. But Bronfman and Singer devised a double strategy. First they used students who could be expected to rally at the slightest opportunity. They were to "create plenty of noise—chaining [themselves] to embassies and general *shraying*." They felt that this sort of activism, combined with Edgar's brashness, would create a better atmosphere for negotiating with the Soviet leaders, whom Goldmann had been too timid to approach directly. Yet in a sense their attack on the leaders of Russia was indirect, for Singer and Bronfman approached them through Eastern Europe, in countries that acted in a way as pilot schemes, before tackling the Soviet Union.

Curiously, they found that some of the Communist leaders in Eastern Europe were—relatively—benevolently disposed to the Jews, who, after all, had been fellow fighters against fascism. The first success was with Erich Honecker, the East German prime minister, who was, says Singer, "eying a kind of most favored nation status with the US." Honecker was not alone in believing that the Great Zionist conspiracy was alive and well (and living in New York) and that Jews were all-powerful. The Hungarian Janos Kadar was another, though Bronfman had to show considerable tact when Morris Abram, the head of the US/Soviet Jewry movement, made what Bronfman describes as his "typical 'let my people go' speech," for not all Jewish leaders could understand the diplomacy required when dealing with foreign politicians. Even the Polish leader General Jaruzelski—whom Bronfman found honest and sympathetic—asked why the Jews, who he was convinced controlled the banks and the media, weren't helping Poland. By contrast he found at first that Lech Walesa, the hero of Solidarity, was a typical Polish anti-Semite, though Bronfman later managed to extract from him a declaration condemning anti-Semitism.

In the early 1980s the atmosphere was far from promising. In the 1970s the emigration of Jews from the Soviet Union had become a regular and well-publicized item on the international human rights agenda and Jewish emigration had continued at a steady pace, though fewer and fewer Jews stayed in Israel. At the same time there had been a gradual loosening of the previous constraints on Jewish life in the Soviet Union with occasional visits abroad by one or two of the handful of Russian rabbis—although they were refused permission to take part in the deliberations of the WJC. But the Russian invasion of Afghanistan in 1979 brought an end to the thaw, with the Americans cutting down trade and cultural relations. In 1980 Zionist activists were arrested on a number of trumped-up charges, and that same year Jewish emigration was cut back by 60 percent. According to Zvi Gitelman, "From 1983 through 1986 the average annual number of emigrants was just above 1,000 whereas in the 1970s it had been over 25,000. It seemed that, once Soviet-American relations turned sour, Soviet leaders no longer saw any point in playing up to American opinion by permitting emigration."[5]

Bronfman and Singer were undeterred even in the do-nothing atmosphere that marked the last years of Brezhnev's reign and that of his senile successor, Chernenko. But they were lucky that in the mid-1980s the atmosphere changed dramatically with the arrival first of Andropov and then of Mikhail Gorbachev. Their objectives, however, remained the same as Goldmann's: to achieve the release of the "Prisoners of Zion" whose only crime had been their openly expressed wish to migrate to Israel, and to allow Soviet Jews to reclaim their religion, lead Jewish lives, eat kosher food, and educate their children as Jews. This last objective was one of the many occasions when Edgar found himself in conflict with the government of Israel, which naturally assumed that the only objective in such negotiations was to get Jews to migrate to Israel—although most of them preferred to move to the United States.

Bronfman and Singer's timing was perfect—although they deliberately refused to go to Moscow after Georgiy Arbatov, the all-powerful director of the Institute for the United States and Canada, had insulted Singer. This proved their independence of spirit, showing that they were not as desperate for an agreement as Goldmann had been. But not only was Gorbachev emerging as the dominant force in the Soviet Union, but, more importantly, his foreign minister in the late 1980s was Eduard Shevardnadze from Georgia, virtually the only country within the Soviet Union without a tradition of anti-Semitism. They were also helped by that fact—of which they only gradually became aware—that Arbatov's father was Jewish as was the mother of his deputy, the ex-KGB general Radomir Bogdanov.

In 1988 Gorbachev amazed the WJC leaders by accepting—off his own bat—all their demands excepting only free emigration. As a result, by early 1989, the Jewish population of the Soviet Union was suddenly free to come out of the closet, as it were, and celebrate its Jewishness by teaching Hebrew in Jewish schools. Nevertheless Bronfman and Singer did not show any gratitude: They still fought—successfully—against granting the Soviets Most Favored Nation status because of the continuing refusal to allow Jews to leave. Once this was granted they went on to press—again successfully—for Soviet recognition of Israel and direct flights from the Soviet Union to Israel. Edgar used the same weapon against President Ceauşescu of Romania, even though Israel Singer was frightened they might be shot, but "sometimes," wrote Bronfman, "you have to bully a bully to get results."

After Gorbachev's departure Singer and Bronfman helped ensure that his successor, Boris Yeltsin, announced his protection of all the many minorities within the Russian Federation. And after the collapse of communism Bronfman was recognized as the leading figure in world Jewry when he was asked to chair the World Jewish Restitution Organization by the many bodies involved—including the state of Israel—in the inconceivably complicated task to try to return the property, personal and communal, confiscated from Eastern European Jews in the previous fifty years. (Singer headed the Claims Conference, which organized the distribution of the reparations granted by the German government to world Jewry.)

But these campaigns were as nothing compared to the longest, most bitter, and must public argument in which they were involved—the battle with Swiss banks to try to secure restitution for the money deposited by Jews from all over Europe in the 1930s. Thirty years later the Swiss had, grudgingly and inadequately, claimed to be helpful, but had found only a handful of Jewish accounts. In 1994 Bronfman and Singer apparently both read a novel, *The Swiss Account* by Paul Erdman, that linked the Swiss with Jewish funds* and this inspired them to return to the attack. The word "at-

---

* They could have discovered this obvious fact twelve years earlier if they had read my book *Safety in Numbers* (New York: Viking, 1982).

tack" is not too strong, for after the event Edgar would refer to it as a "corporate war story." The time appeared propitious since the Swiss were—belatedly—beginning to come to terms with their appalling behavior during the war.

After six months' negotiations Bronfman and his colleagues were finally granted a meeting with the Swiss Bankers Association, where they were confronted by a typically Swiss blend of condescension and smugness. "We were ushered into a small room with no furniture and left standing. That was enough to irritate me," wrote Edgar. "I don't treat people that way and I don't expect to be treated that way," he told a later audience. The delegation was nominally from the WJRO but was backed by the Israelis. They were graciously offered a mere $30 million on a take-it-or-leave-it basis, an offer due largely to the SBA's newly appointed "ombudsman," Hanspeter Hani, who believed that they wouldn't find much for the heirs of the Nazis' Jewish victims. The Swiss were shocked when Bronfman said that he didn't like the take-it-or-leave-it attitude, and that he "hadn't come here to discuss money. I'm here to discuss a process." For he was conducting a crusade. As he said, "As long as I draw breath I will see to it that nobody profits from the ashes of the Holocaust." He would have to consult banker friends before replying, a statement that set off a lecture on how small the Swiss banks had been in the 1930s. But they agreed to hold discussions, which, Bronfman emphasized, would have to remain strictly secret.

Even then they were hampered by the narrowness of the Swiss attitude; the Swiss simply could not understand the depth of Jewish feeling and the possible repercussions throughout the world, for they thought exclusively in domestic Swiss political terms. Heinrich Schneider, the deputy secretary-general of the SBA, broke the silence by announcing the result of the association's survey of the banks' research into Jewish accounts, which demonstrated their seemingly inconsequential amount. As Tom Bower says, Schneider thought the Jews "were powerless." But the Swiss position was undermined when the researcher the WJC had employed to hunt through the voluminous American archives found a list dating from 1945 showing that 182 Jewish clients had entrusted substantial sums to a single Geneva-based notary and trust company specializing in the Balkans.

By then, with the help of Hillary Clinton—who may already have been thinking of running for the Senate—Edgar and Singer had recruited an unlikely and powerful pair of allies, President Clinton and Alfonse D'Amato, the senior senator from New York and, crucially, chairman of the Senate

Banking Committee, even though D'Amato was a sworn enemy of the president and in the midst of investigating the Whitewater real estate scandal in which the Clintons had allegedly been involved. "As a street fighter with a rottweiler's compassion for his target's sensitivities," writes Bower, "he was the ideal politician to challenge the Swiss banks." Singer and D'Amato naturally played rough. With the help of Alan Hevesi, the comptroller of New York City, all the state organizations indicated that if the Swiss did not resolve the issue, they would no longer do business with them.

After the Swiss bankers had made their derisory offer Edgar summoned them and declared that "we want an accounting." The Swiss merely offered the setting up of a commission that would report in five years' time. "It's the old game," Edgar apparently snarled. "Delay, delay, time, time. We're not satisfied with that," language normal in Edgar's business world but totally alien and indeed barbaric to Swiss ears. D'Amato went on to summon witnesses who told the committee terrible stories of their families' fates and recounted how British and French banks had handed over their relatives' funds but that the Swiss had demanded a death certificate—for victims of Auschwitz!

But there was one banker who did understand, Hans Baer, whom the SBA had chosen to represent them at the hearings of the Senate Banking Committee. The Baers were Jewish and as a result their family's bank, Julius Baer, was virtually the only bank in Switzerland not to have the Nazis as important clients—indeed was used by the OSS to handle its financial transactions. But Baer was helpless given the intransigence of the majority of his fellow bankers, even when confronted by further tragic stories and Edgar's testimony. He put the hearings in the widest possible context. "Our collective mission here is nothing short of bringing about justice," he told the committee. "We are here to help write the last chapter of the bitter legacy of the Second World War and the Holocaust." He condemned the Swiss banks for "their repeated failure of integrity," for earning a "profit from the ashes of man's greatest inhumanity to man." He went on to accuse the Swiss of breaching their supposed neutral status during the Nazi period in ways that cost "a staggering [number] of American lives," and finished by demanding "a proper accounting." D'Amato took up the theme. "We cannot rest," he said after hearing Edgar's evidence, "while unnamed individuals profit from the deaths of the six million."

Baer had proposed a bilateral commission, but all his work was undone by Edgar's appeal to a higher court, President Clinton. He was granted immediate audience after bending Hillary Clinton's ear at a lunch in New York. The president supported D'Amato and appointed Stuart Eizenstadt, already his envoy for seeking restitution for Jewish losses, to coordinate the government's research efforts. The Europeans had already been convinced by what Bower calls Steinberg's "terror by embarrassment," which covered not only accounts in Swiss banks, but also the appalling story of how literally tons of gold extracted from the teeth of Holocaust victims had been melted down and sold to the world through the Swiss National Bank; "The greatest robbery in the history of mankind," as Steinberg put it. But the Swiss still did not understand, and their position was further weakened when the chairman of the Union Bank of Switzerland, the country's biggest, dismissed the sums in the official Swiss position—$32 million—as "peanuts." The bank further fueled the flames when it sacked a security guard who had revealed the existence of a stack of wartime ledgers beside a paper shredder in the bank's basement.

By the end of October 1996 there were no fewer than five investigations either under discussion or under way. Nevertheless the atmosphere heated up even further. D'Amato urged the Swiss to establish a "truth commission" similar to that in post-apartheid South Africa, while in New York and Washington lawyers organized class actions against the country's three leading banks, an initiative that frightened the Swiss, especially when three thousand more claimants arrived on the scene. D'Amato and the WJC fed fuel to the flames and in December 1996 it was found that over $2 billion of Nazi loot had passed through Switzerland on its way to Latin America. On a visit to the US Edgar told one of the investigators, Thomas Borer, an ambitious official from the Swiss Foreign Ministry, that "we need an interim fund to compensate the survivors . . . so far the pace has been slower than a snail. Not one franc has passed hands." Borer was badly mauled at a hearing of the House Banking Committee. Worse, his visit to the Holocaust Memorial Museum, like the rest of his trip, proved counterproductive when it emerged that he had spent only fifteen minutes in the museum for a photo opportunity. The Swiss still continued to treat the pressure as a Jewish conspiracy until a senior Jewish official pronounced the dreaded cry for a total boycott of Swiss banks by American institutions. The Swiss were fully aware that this was the nuclear option, a threat already raised by Avesi and D'Amato, for withdrawing the banks' licenses to operate in the United States would have removed their single biggest source of income.

On January 22, 1997, the continuing denials of responsibility, and the delays in the production of any of the various reports, finally broke the unity of the Swiss establishment. That day Rainer Gut, the chairman of Credit Suisse, one of the Big Three, proposed the establishment of a "well-endowed compensation fund," eventually offering the sum of $72 million from his bank alone. But the WJC wanted more money and, above all, official recognition by the Swiss of the assistance they had provided to the Nazis. The final act of the drama was played out at the World Economic Forum at Davos the following month where the world's leading financiers told the Swiss that their attitude had proved self-defeating.

The next month Edgar Bronfman welcomed all the people involved to finalize a deal in an atmosphere far cooler than had been the case in the previous two years. A $250 million fund was established, but as Bronfman pointed out, "The issue is the truth. The issue is morality." But by then the Swiss had surrendered; even he was satisfied by an announcement the following month by Arnold Koller, the president of Switzerland, that a fund would be established, financed through the revaluation of Switzerland's massive gold reserves. This would provide $250 million annually to compensate victims of catastrophes including the Holocaust. He went on to admit the country's "moral lapses" during the war.

But the success merely fueled the WJRO's ambitions, which were extended to a list of twenty-four countries that had given fuzzy answers about what happened to the assets of exiled or murdered Jews. One result was that the WJC led the Jewish delegation to the London Conference on Nazi gold attended by delegations from over forty countries. Edgar's efforts were recognized not only within the world Jewish community, but also within the United States. Eizenstadt thanked Bronfman for forcing the human rights issue onto "the conscience of the world and of countries who would never have opened up this dark chapter in their histories," and in 1999 President Bill Clinton awarded him the Presidential Medal of Freedom.

Fifteen

CLOWN PRINCE

He was everything Edgar wanted to be but felt he couldn't be.
—SEAGRAM FAMILY FRIEND

𝕋HE JANUARY 1986 ISSUE OF *FORTUNE* MAGAZINE CARRIED A LONG interview with Edgar Bronfman, Sr. He told the interviewer that he had decided that his successor would be his thirty-one-year-old second son Edgar, Jr., and not Sam, his elder by two years. After the interview and before the magazine went to press Edgar's associates made frantic efforts to persuade the magazine to remove the remark, for the very simple reason that Edgar had not then got around to telling the two people most closely concerned, Sam and his own brother Charles, though Edgar later claimed that he had told Sam of his decision the previous year. *Fortune*'s editor refused, saying that not only had Edgar made the statement, he had repeated it under further questioning. As for Edgar's five other children, who included two boys, Matthew and Adam, both grown-up sons of Edgar and Ann Loeb, Edgar Sr. put it bluntly, "They are not involved in the business, but follow their own paths instead"—as did Charles's only son, Stephen.

Uncharacteristically, Charles reacted both angrily and publicly. In an unprecedented break with the tradition of total family solidarity he told *The Montreal Gazette* that "Both my brother and I realize that any succession is determined by the board. Not by Edgar, and not me." He even said that the next chief executive "ought to have lengthy experience and may not be a family member." Whenever Edgar did get round to telling his eldest son of the decision, the reasoning was the same. "You're good," he's reported as saying, "but you'll always be compared with your brother, and as my successor he's better." Edgar particularly admired Edgar Jr.'s toughness as against what he perceived correctly as Sam's gentle nature. In *Good Spirits* Edgar tells the story of a tennis match against a couple where, as he writes, "The man had a slight disability, making it difficult for him to shift positions easily. Noticing this I said to Sam 'you can afford to poach at net.' Sam replied 'Oh Dad.' If [Edgar Jr.] had been playing he would have noticed immediately and moved nearer the center of the court." According to Edgar Junior's biographer[1] this story seems totally improbable. For Sam was by far the better player and had driven his brother out of the game in his teens. Junior, unwilling to admit defeat, had taken up golf instead.

Edgar's dramatic decision, and his subsequent support for Edgar Jr.'s every action, however disastrous, was based on grossly exaggerated compensation for his continuing belief that his own father had not loved him. The extent of Edgar's worship of Edgar Jr. is breathtaking, his description (in *Good Spirits*) unbelievably gushing. "He's blond and very handsome, with a straight Roman nose," goes the panegyric. "His stride is purposeful, his manner that of both a leader and a lady-killer. As he was growing up, there was always something special about Edgar Jr.—his calm in a crisis, his ability to deal with his mother's problems, his sense of responsibility for his siblings. He is one of those rare individuals who instinctively understands the business world and always has his priorities in order. . . . Charles and I agree that he is clearly the ideal leader to take us into the twenty-first century." It was this attitude, combined with the absurd assumption that Edgar Jr. could run two world-scale businesses, Seagram and MCA/Universal, simultaneously, that led to the downfall of the House of Seagram. Kolber got it right when he wrote that "Edgar was mesmerized by his son. There is no other way to describe it. Edgar Jr. is a very nice man, very diffident, a good listener, and not a show-off in any sense of the word. He is anything but stupid. But he had no business running Seagram, and if he hadn't been named Bronfman, he wouldn't have been . . . he was playing with other people's money, not just his own or even the Bronfman family fortune, but money that belonged to the shareholders. Bottom line, he had no business running the business."

The reaction of the two brothers to this announcement goes some way to explaining Edgar's decision. "Jealous?" Sam is supposed to have said, "That's not the right word. Chagrined. But I wish him good luck." "If it had been the other way round," commented Edgar Jr. "I'm not sure that I could have handled it." But in fact he may already have been preparing himself for a long time. He once told a business friend that just before his grandfather died the old man had physically laid his hands upon the teenage Edgar Jr. and anointed him as the successor to his father and grandfather. His elder brother Sam was partially compensated when he was put in charge of Seagram's wine interests, which included not only the California brands but also Mumm and Perrier-Jouet. Sam was ideally suited to run the firm's wine interests, for he knew and loved wine. But he remained marginalized, never even consulted beforehand about the sale of the group fourteen years later. Yet some former Seagram executives believe that he could have proved a perfectly acceptable chairman, for like his uncle Charles—and his great-uncle Allan—Sam is the quiet charming one; he remembers people's faces, and the subject of his conversations with them, for years after a meeting. He thanks people with handwritten notes and is able to delegate, without the arrogance of his father and brother—who had refused even to take press conferences after Seagram board meetings in Montreal in French, the sort of gesture guaranteed to infuriate the city's proudly Francophone media.

This typically arrogant gesture was typical of the behavior that has ensured that over the past twenty years Edgar Jr. has had a bad press. In early 2003 *New York* magazine called him "possibly the stupidest person in the media business," while *BusinessWeek* named him as one of the worst managers of 2002, no mean accolade in a year full of the noisy crashes of so many former titans of the business world. This is not surprising. In a mere five years he led his family's firm first into Hollywood by selling the Seagram stake in DuPont and using the proceeds to buy MCA/Universal and Polygram Records for a total of $15 billion, with dubious results. Then in 2000 he negotiated the sale of what was by then Seagram-Universal to the French Vivendi group, led by the magnetic megalomaniac Jean-Marie Messier, who destroyed the Seagram empire, resulting in one of the biggest losses ever sustained by a single family. As a result he has been generally regarded as a spoiled, self-indulgent adolescent who never even tried to attend college. In fact he was a curious mix: totally selfish, willful, totally self-confident, and determined to go his own way, disregarding the interests of his family—or his employees for that matter—and at the same time famously helpful and supportive of his siblings. In 1991 he moved to California for a time when Sam's wife Melanie was dying of breast cancer. He once said that when he and his second wife Clarissa lost a child "everything changed for me."

The positive case was put by Jean-Marie Messier; indeed Edgar Jr. was the only member of the family for whom he has a kind word to say. His description was lyrical. "Rebel or romantic. In any case cultivating the difference [with the rest of the family]. Appears soft and conciliatory. Hiding a great capacity for indifference to others with a difficulty in making up his mind." In Hollywood "he left the memory of someone who forgets to come and support his team during difficult times but never missed a plane to share in their successes." Nevertheless "he chose well in Hollywood, was a shrewd analyst of a situation, and someone worth consulting for his advice."

The complexity of his character was not in itself surprising, and was due both to his basic character and his personal history. To start with, as a close friend of the family puts it, he was "ashamed of being Jewish, of being Canadian [and thus in danger of being considered a provincial hick by sophisticated Americans], and of being in the liquor business." Perhaps more importantly he had had to grow up too quickly. His brother Sam, who had every reason to be bitter with his younger brother, emphasized that "Edgar was always older than his years. . . . He wanted to be grown up. He liked doing things adults did. I always enjoyed being the age I was." To Edgar Jr., "being grown up" had two consequences: He didn't have to do anything he didn't like, but it led to very genuine concern for his family. According to McQueen, "Junior" as he was usually called, was already considered as the peacemaker in the family. Sam Jr. felt the pressure of being the oldest while, not surprisingly, Holly, fifteen months younger than Junior, was a typical Jewish princess. "I was generally the facilitator or the peacemaker," said Junior. All this amounts to saying that family problems forced him to grow up too early.

In 1971 his mother, Ann—who remained a staunch supporter—had left his father when he was in his teens after a period in which his father had paid little or no attention to his family. As Sam put it, his mother "was unjudgmental" but his father's tumultuous life following the separation meant that the children "had sometimes felt neglected"—and even when he was around Edgar was "much more standoffish." This inevitable lack of stability must have made Junior extraordinarily self-sufficient, but the cost was that he never properly grew up. He seems to have suffered throughout his life from a problem which Newman shrewdly defines: "He appeared for a time to be acting from that rarely diagnosed disease that infects so many offspring of the very rich, a terminal case of immaturity." His family history led him to be totally self-sufficient, concerned exclusively with his own opinion.

An old friend, Porter Bibb, told McQueen that Junior had been "a roly-poly, cherubic, big teddy-bear-like teenager." But he soon transformed himself, to present an image that was at once sophisticated and totally unlike that of any other member of his family. He became—and remains—the epitome of cool: slim, handsome, unruffled, six feet three inches tall, generally Armani-clad, complete with designer stubble. The whole image was obviously deliberately designed to be the total opposite of anything worn by his father—let alone his grandfather, never seen without a jacket and tie. But occasionally another, less sophisticated side peeped through—as in the really filthy jokes he told or the life-size painting of his first wife, nude and very pregnant, he displayed in his living room.

"From his early teens," his father noted, Edgar Jr. "managed to avoid what he didn't want and get what he did. We sent him off to camp, and he made it clear that it wasn't for him. Nor was he going away to preschool. Nor to college. And when he wanted something he worked that out too." At school he was notably arrogant, refusing to accept the teachers' authority, aware of the power he represented from the amount of money his family had given the school. Inevitably he lacked any intellectual training or discipline, any willingness to learn in any orthodox fashion. By contrast he was quite prepared to attach himself to, and learn from, father figures like Barry Diller—who empathized with him because "as a teenager I always acted older than I was. You see that in someone else and gravitate to it." His precociousness impressed a Broadway producer called Bruce Stark who found him "an amazing kid. He has a language facility that's really quite amazing. He often made me feel like I was kind of incompetent." Stark also noted his capacity to exploit his undoubted charm to get his way and proved a sympathetic supporter when Junior would turn up at night in tears, fleeing the dramas attendant on the breakup of his parents' marriage, for in his teens the "coolth" was skin-deep, though it had become a thick armor against the world within a few years.

In any event he left Collegiate, an exclusive Manhattan day school, at the age of fourteen—although he did return, later and reluctantly, to graduate. But he had already avoided summer camp by taking on the script of a film called *Melody*, persuading his father to invest $450,000 in the project. This was a precedent for his years in show business, his projects invariably oiled by family money. Unfortunately, as Stark put it, "Both of us had one fatal flaw: We couldn't pick a show that people wanted to see." Junior took the idea to London and worked as a runner, tea boy, and general gofer on the film. It was the first effort of a former advertising filmmaker, David Puttnam, who went on to become a major force in the film world—and to be created Lord Puttnam.

Clearly Puttnam found the connection with the Bronfmans potentially helpful but he was obviously genuinely fond of Edgar Jr. whom he nicknamed Efer after a contemporary advertising campaign featuring giant posters saying "E for B"—Eggs for Breakfast. So Edgar Bronfman became EB and, by affectionate extension, Efer, a nickname often used by his intimates since then—though Seagram insiders preferred to talk of him as "Junior," an implicit if not-so-subtle comparison with his father. Puttnam, who has said that "my success is very largely due to Efer"—or, more probably, the financial support provided by his family—remained a father figure when Efer returned the following year to work on another film and to live with the Puttnam family, "washing dishes and idolized by our kids" in an environment he clearly found more relaxed than that in his own family.

The newly christened Efer was obviously a most attractive adolescent. As *Time* magazine put it, "he was very bright, incredibly tenacious, and learned very fast," while Puttnam found the fifteen-year-old "a very decent kid who has never been short of his opinions . . . he was absolutely determined to do things on his own"—as he was later to do, invariably after the very shortest of apprenticeships. Moreover at the time everyone agreed that "he showed absolutely no interest in getting into the Seagram business" and was seemingly bent on a career in show business, or, even better, music. He had already developed a haughty attitude towards the world outside his immediate family. When he arrived for an interview at a new school at the age of twelve the head asked him whether he had come with his father. To which Efer replied, "No, with my pilot," for he is alleged to have boasted that he had never flown other than in a private plane. His lofty attitude extended even to the Four Seasons, the widely respected restaurant on the side of the Seagram Building. "I have my own kitchen," he once said, "The Four Seasons is good, but it doesn't compare with my cook"—although in October 2002 he spent $4.3 million to buy control of the restaurant and still has a regular table there.

Efer's greatest problem in life—and more especially in business—was his aristocratic, almost regal hauteur, his lack of contact with external reality, his obvious disdain for the "little people." As a result he has proved to be an effective and cold-blooded butcher in successive businesses. He was however fully aware of the importance of his name, as he explained his success to a group in New York, "You just have to be real smart and choose the right father." It did not help that, like the Prince of Wales, he had, according to many who worked with him, "the attention span of a gnat." Like Prince Charles, "he was," says one associate, "perfectly pleasant but tended to agree with the last person he had talked to." All this inevitably led to a lack of follow-through, the assumption—among their entourage as well as themselves—that they were somehow above the fray.

To many people Efer came over as a surprisingly modest individual—"He never swung his weight around," said James Walsh, producer of *Soon*, a rock opera in which Efer had invested and on which he worked as a gofer. But his lack of antenna applied not only to individuals but also to potential customers, for he proved to have a total lack of understanding of what the public was prepared to pay to see. As a result his own ventures in show business were inevitably unsuccessful. The first film he produced—at the age of seventeen—was *The Blockhouse*, a grim drama about Poland during the Second World War, featuring Peter Sellers during one of his low periods. As Ken Auletta puts it, "Absolutely nobody wanted to see a movie that took place underground with seven men slowly starving to death."[2] Indeed it was literally unwatchable, so poor was the lighting. Later Efer himself described it as a film "nobody's ever heard of." The play *Ladies at the Alamo*, which he produced when he was twenty-two, was also a disaster.

Even when Efer was given a three-year contract with Universal Pictures he could not come up with a viable project. Not surprisingly he expressed himself frustrated with the film industry, his excuse at his failure explained by his father as "from his standpoint it wasn't a 'business.'" For his first love, his life-long obsession, has been music, largely because it was the only business arena in which he was, rightly, convinced that he had anything creative to provide; he did not, as one insider put it, "have to rely on other people's operating and creative abilities." His interest in music led him to meet Dionne Warwick, who recorded one of his, typically romantic, even erotic songs, like *Whisper in the Dark*, which included lines like:

> I want to hold your body close to mine
> I want to hurry love and take my time

and reached number seven in the charts. Through her he met a beautiful black actress, Sherry Brewer. They lived together for three years and even then he avoided a formal marriage, which, he knew, would offend both sets of parents, by "eloping," as he put it, to New Orleans. "Mom closed ranks immediately," said Junior, "it took Dad a little longer." In fact Edgar was furious. His then-wife Georgiana persuaded him at least to give the newlyweds a cocktail party but, as Efer says, "I could see that he was not happy. We remained estranged." It did not help that Edgar is not an expressive man. As Sam says, "Dad doesn't really like to talk about stuff, he wrote letters." They came together at a private screening of *The Border,* a film about illegal immigrants trying to enter the United States, which was made by the well-known British director Tony Richardson and starred Jack Nicholson, a film that had proved a critical, if not a commercial, success. It was an agreeable evening, with Efer saying that he was thinking of returning to New York to produce plays rather than films. (The only tension came when the check for dinner arrived—at which point Efer had to pay, having waited in vain for his father to do so!)

In 1982 Edgar Sr.—who had just been appointed president of the World Jewish Congress and was clearly anxious to start to reduce his committment to Seagram—startled his second son by asking him to come and work for what he described as a "publicly held family business" with a view of taking it over. "It was always important to me," as Edgar put it, "and I'm not quite sure why, that one of my children would take over this company from me." The son's acceptance of the offer was clearly influenced by the fact that his show biz career was not getting anywhere, but he probably also felt his tribal roots. "There is an incredible pride in this company and in the family," he has said. In reality he was caught between being a businessman and an impresario, and he was an amateur in both these roles. So, after consulting Sherry—who, he was convinced, would be implacably hostile to the idea but in fact agreed—he embarked on a move which he, and everyone else, assumed would lead to the top. Those who had known him in his previous life were cynical, an attitude summed up by David Freeman, who had written the script for *The Border.* "I thought, this guy will be back. He loved movies and theater and music." "He was an artist," said Bruce Stark, "he didn't have a corporate attitude."

As "special assistant" to Beekman he quickly demonstrated his dual character. "He was always very respectful," said Beekman, "even when questioning my decisions. And question he often did." Nevertheless, as

Beekman told McQueen, "he wrote songs and kept up all his West Coast contacts." And whereas both his father and his uncle Charles had served a lengthy apprenticeship, notably at the distilleries, which gave them a deep understanding of the company's products, Junior skipped all that and was so disinterested in Seagram's whiskies that he never even visited the Chivas Regal distillery that was providing the company with an increasing share of its profits.

Within a few months he had been parachuted to London to head up Seagram's increasingly important operations in Europe. Typically Edgar did not bother to tell Mcdonnell, who, as the executive in charge of the whole international side of the business, was to be Efer's boss and who had transformed the international side into a major success. In London Efer struck most of the people he met as "a young man going on fifty, far from stodgy but sound of judgment." Naturally Mcdonnell was at first reluctant to accept the family's decision, but found Junior loyal, pleasant, and prepared to work hard. As Mcdonnell said to McQueen: "There were lots of things I wanted to get done that Phil Beekman was opposed to. But he was certainly not going to block any idea put forward by Junior. Having both Junior and myself make presentations on acquisitions and on strategies for running particular brands and investing was pretty tough to beat." Edgar Jr.'s first independent deal—"To give Seagram a place at the top distributional table," as his father put it—was to buy Oddbins, a quirky, new-style chain of liquor stores, which proved an ideal outlet for the whole range of the group's products, especially its wines. Moreover they got back virtually the whole purchase price when they sold the company's headquarters in Wapping in East London. Buying Oddbins was a first indication of his determination to get away from spirits, for Oddbins made its reputation by selling wines, not spirits.

By now his rise to the top was inevitable. By 1985 he was back in New York as COO of the House of Seagram, the key subsidiary responsible for the US. There he showed the pattern that was to be familiar in future situations. He sacked 15 percent of the employees in a group previously noted for its paternalist attitude. To make the change in corporate culture even more obvious, he went about the cull in a pretty brutal fashion. It was "totally Machiavellian, totally Sicilian," as Jerome Mann, one of Bronfman's *consiglieres* during the operation told *Fortune*. For, as one newly promoted executive put it, "I know that one day there may be a knock on my door and I'll be told, 'It's been fun but now it's all over.' And I know it'll be Edgar

Jr. who will be doing the telling." As *Fortune* commented, "Some insiders say that Edgar Jr. can be chillingly abrupt when his decisions are questioned." Worse for the business he took an ax to Seagram's historically independent distributors, aiming to retain only those who "treat Seagram brands importantly." Those who remained were confused because he had formed four separate operating companies to handle Seagram's range of spirits. He also dumped four of Seagram's seven advertising agencies. In his defense it has to be said that by the mid-1980s Seagram was coming increasingly to resemble DCL, once Mr. Sam's model, but by then a creaky organization relying on increasingly unfashionable products.

A year after Junior's return to New York Beekman was sacked after nine years' loyal service, his departure due less to faults in his management than to a personal tragedy. His son was an early victim of AIDS and Beekman, like so many fathers suffering the same problem, blamed himself. He was—simply—shattered and left, and was succeeded by David Sacks, though he soon recovered. In the following two decades Beekman made a substantial fortune for himself as an industrialist and investor, remaining a golfing partner of Charles's. At sixty-two years of age, seven years older than Beekman, Sacks, the man described by insiders as "Edgar's divorce lawyer" was clearly a stopgap.

Not surprisingly the 1986 *Fortune* article that included Edgar Sr.'s plans for a successor started a breach between the brothers that was soon to become an unbridgeable gulf. Their relationship had already been affected by a dramatic upheaval in Charles's previously tranquil personal life. In 1982 Charles had divorced his first wife and married a strong-minded lady called Andrea—universally known as "Andy." Charles and his first wife, Barbara, had been neighbors and close friends of Andrea and her first husband, David Cohen,* indeed Charles had been a groomsman at their wedding. When the affair broke into the open, Cohen declared his intention of suing Charles for alienation of affections. Charles met him and naturally enquired how much the irate husband was demanding. The story goes that when Charles was told the figure was $10 million, he allegedly arranged for a check for that amount to be hand-delivered that afternoon. Soon after his remarriage Charles and his new wife moved to New York, mainly because, as he put it, "Andy likes New York, I like New York." It helped that

---

* Cousin of the famous singer Leonard Cohen.

in New York he would be merely one among hundreds of very rich Jews as against the isolated position he occupied in Montreal, enabling him to avoid the limelight he so sincerely detested. The move did not help relations between the brothers. Edgar even tried to prevent Charles from having an office next to his.

In 1987 came the first step in disentangling the brothers' financial joint ventures when they sold their 38 percent holding in Cadillac Fairview—a few years earlier they had bought a substantial minority interest held by the Reichmann brothers, who needed the cash for their giant Canary Wharf development in London's Docklands. There had been a number of warning signs after the merger of the original Fairview company with Cadillac—nothing to do with the motor company. Whereas Fairview had been confined to a handful of—highly profitable—office and retail developments, Cadillac brought with it the problems inevitably associated with its portfolio of a host of much smaller residential units. These involved a disproportionate amount of management time—indeed at one point Kolber had to move in as CEO of Cadillac. There were inevitable problems, political as well as financial, with attempts to raise rents and sell at least part of the portfolio.

Typically the brothers did not tell Kolber in advance of their intention to roll up but left the delicate task to one of their lawyers. Kolber had shown an unhealthy independence when they had proposed that he should be succeeded by one of the family. To which Kolber replied firmly that he had seven deputies, any one of whom could have succeeded him perfectly adequately. The failure to tell him directly was a severe blow to the pride of a man known by then, in Newman's words, as "the only non-Bronfman Bronfman." Nevertheless he was at least allowed to conduct the negotiations. Kolber asked for a 1 percent negotiating fee—about $12 million—to be paid to his charitable foundation. Phyllis had already sold her shares but Charles and Edgar agreed; Minda's family objected and characteristically the gentlemanly Charles put up $6 million of his own money to fill the gap. Kolber's negotiating skills were worth far more than $12 million, for he managed to extract a price nearly double the market value when he started negotiations, giving him a profit of $100 million, while the brothers shared $1.3 billion. Their timing was perfect: In October 1987 the stock market had collapsed and investors were scrambling to get into supposedly safer investments like real estate. Supposedly is the operative word; within a few years rents at the key Toronto-Dominion Centre had plummeted by 40 percent and in 2002 Kolber and Charles's son Stephen bought back Place Montreal Trust, one of their major investments, for less than a half of the amount it had cost to build.

Eighteen months later came the long-expected decision to promote the thirty-four-year-old Edgar Jr. to the position of COO. Junior's rise to the top was hastened by David Sacks's health problems. He had bypass surgery, and when he returned he was a changed character, unable to cope psychologically with the strains inevitable in managing a major business, especially one where the "controlling shareholders felt that they could interfere whenever they chose." In his new role Junior behaved with the calm, charming assumption of the prince charming, giving him the total, and almost totally unjustified conviction that he was entitled to do what he wanted with his inheritance. He was immensely ambitious; aiming, as at least one well-placed observer believed, to be the single most important businessman in the country, though not in the liquor business, which he so despised. As his successor as head of Seagram USA, Willie Petersen, a South African and former Rhodes scholar, told McQueen: "Edgar relished deals. He found the day-to-day running of an operation less appealing. It was the creative side that always enthused him: the advertising, the label design, the aesthetic elements of what we were doing, deals, combinations, acquisitions, plotting on a grander canvas."

Whereas his father and his grandfather had been prepared to listen to those around them Efer was increasingly surrounded by yes-men. He became heavily reliant on hordes of consultants, the traditional refuge of insecure or incompetent managers. In the "corporate reengineering," his choice, the Boston Consulting Group, was largely the result of a dinner Efer had had with Jack Welch, the fabled head of General Electric, who had boasted of the way he had sacked one hundred thousand people— nearly ten times the number of Seagram's employees. Unsurprisingly, as one veteran puts it, "Unlike his father he was disloyal to established people." He brought in people from outside the liquor business at vast salaries—and often then had to pay them even larger redundancy payments. He brought in psychologists, and while not himself politically correct had to clean up his own act when he ensured that the staff behaved in an appropriate fashion. He was never more than a part-time COO, and the strict standards for which Seagram had been renowned naturally slipped. Previously, for instance, the eagle eye of the company's legendary treasurer, Harold Fieldsteel, had ensured that any problems with stock levels had been quickly attended to, but no longer. For Efer seemed increasingly unin-volved in day-to-day management, to the extent of not knowing, indeed seeming to not care, about the salaries paid to even his most senior execu-tives. As one old-timer put it, "He was simply uninterested."

In 1991 he totally restructured the company. The bulk of the operations—wines and spirits, accounting for over three-quarters of total sales—went to Ed Mcdonnell, his mentor in London ten years earlier. The beverage group, under Petersen, consisted merely of the much smaller, re-cently acquired and obviously disposable, soft drinks companies. Mcdon-nell's promotion came because of his success in transforming Seagram's international operations into a major contributor of profits—of which three-fifths came from Europe alone. Sensibly enough Efer wanted Sea-gram to be associated purely with premium brands, as it had been in his grandfather's day. In 1988 he cut out twenty-five non-premium brands, which represented a mere 8 percent of sales and 4 percent of profits. These included the US rights to Burnett's Gin and Four Roses—which was still a blend. In 1992 he went one further, selling no fewer than twenty-three high-volume low-end brands, including Ronrico rum, Kessler and Calvert whiskies, the Leroux cordial business, as well as Wolfschmidt vodka.

The sale—to American Brands, best known for Jim Beam bourbon—was an implicit admission of failure in attempting to challenge Bacardi in white rum and Smirnoff in vodka as well as an acceptance that it was use-less to try and sell any brands of blended whiskey apart from 7 Crown and Crown Royal and, above all, Chivas Regal. But the sale did emphasize one success, that of Seagram's Gin, which had become by far the biggest seller in the country. Nevertheless by that time Seagram's portfolio did not in-clude any of the world's fastest growing spirits brands and although the sale did result in record profits for 1993—on lower turnover—they did nothing to point to future success. Nor did the purge do anything to solve Seagram's fundamental problem, the continuing slide in sales of the blended Ameri-can whiskies—apart from Crown Royal—on which the firm's fortunes had been founded, let alone help them cope with the implacable trend towards lighter spirits, notably vodka and Bacardi—as well as the increasing success of "straight" whiskies, bourbon and Jack Daniel's.*

In 1988, thanks largely to David Sacks, Seagram had spent $1.2 billion

---

* Although technically a Tennessee whiskey, it is always thought of as a bourbon.

on buying Tropicana, a highly respected brand in the orange juice business. But Junior's erratic management style—which involved frequent changes in management—combined with competition from Minute Maid, owned by the even mightier Coca-Cola corporation, ensured that Tropicana could never live up to the demanding levels of profitability that Seagram was used to in the spirits business. Luckily six years later Pepsi-Cola bought the brand for $3.3 billion. Edgar also lavishes great praise on his son for developing Seagram's line of coolers, including an advertising campaign featuring Bruce Willis—a piece of marketing that obviously interested him far more than the historic Seagram business. At an estimated promotional cost of $100 million, Seagram's line of coolers became a serious force which, however, proved a passing phenomenon rather than a permanent factor in the drinks market, for the coolers sold only a fifth of their original projected figures. As McQueen put it, "Seagram had bought leadership in a fad category with few prospects . . . men avoided the product and women preferred Chardonnay." But orange juice and coolers were merely diversions from the main arena.

Even the group's increasing foreign interests—as opposed to international sales of Chivas Regal and the group's champagnes—could never be more than inadequate palliatives given the sheer size of the problem posed by the decline in Seagram's core liquor business. It helped that in 1981 they had bought Wilson Distillers in New Zealand and Continental Distillers in Australia three years later, in the process acquiring pole position in the spirits market there, as well as joint ventures in promising markets like Korea and Thailand. So far as wines were concerned, Seagram had already bought a major stake in such promising firms as Montana, the leader in the then-tiny New Zealand wine business, and Saltram, a medium-sized Australian wine producer, after failing to buy Hardy's, one of the industry's giants (the chairman, Tom Hardy, had reacted by saying, "If they think it's worth that much I think we should keep it for ourselves"). But in the Far East their efforts were hampered because they did not own a brand of cognac, far and away the favorite spirit among the Japanese and the Chinese, not only in China itself, but, more importantly, among the "overseas Chinese" scattered throughout Southeast Asia from Taiwan to Singapore.

Edgar had always argued that the Bronfmans were a rich family because they didn't throw their money away, but with their purchase of Martell they did so in dramatic fashion. The Firino-Martell family, which had controlled this historic business since it was founded back in 1715, played both bidders, Seagram and Grand Metropolitan (which owned IDV), very cleverly against each other. Both were keen because they didn't own a major cognac brand at a time when the future for France's greatest brandy seemed limitless because of the boom of the late 1980s in the Far East in general and, more particularly, in Japan, a part of the world where Seagram was weak, and relied on partnerships. The decision to engage in a bidding war proved a divisive issue. At first Junior declared that the price was too high and so did the chief financial officer and Ed Mcdonnell. Moreover Edgar remarks how, if David Sacks had been around, he might have opposed it, "which could well have made it impossible for me to persuade Charles." In the end Efer came round, because cognac, the biggest gap in the Seagram portfolio of brands, was such a major seller in the Far East.

So Efer and another rising star, Steve Banner, like Sacks a former partner in Simpson Thatcher, upped the bid to $922 million, thirty-eight times earnings. The price was clearly absurd, and so was Edgar Sr.'s statement in his book, published ten years later, that "Never for a moment has anyone connected with our firm regretted the acquisition of Martell." I see very little, if any, evidence for his statement that "Sales have exceeded our forecasts and most important, so have profits," for Edgar's sense of timing could not have been more wrong. The disaster was the result not only of the collapse of the Japanese market immediately after the purchase, but also of the dramatic slump in the sales of a brand that had been number one or two in the cognac market for well over two centuries but whose market share had halved by the time Seagram sold Martell in 2001.

Junior found some consolation in his personal life. He and Sherry had divorced amicably and he continued to see a lot of their three children, for he was a devoted father. In late 1990 he met a beautiful, rich, well-connected Venezuelan girl, Clarissa Alcock, and apparently fell head over heels in love with her, though cynics allege that his choice was influenced by his desire to find a more suitable trophy wife than Sherry had been. He duly showered Clarissa with flowers and asked her to marry him three times—the last time agreeing that it would have to be she who would have to propose. His devotion was shown by two gestures. The first was in the lordly Bronfman style. While he was living in Manhattan before he married Clarissa, Seagram bought a French couturier, Hervé Leger, who was renowned for his clothes' bandage-like silhouettes, essentially to provide dresses suitable for her slender figure—the purchase always lost money and in 1998 was virtually given away to a Los Angeles design firm. The other tribute was more personal, a song that showed the romantic behind the ruthless businessman:

> I wish I wasn't breathless at the way you move
> I wish I wasn't blinded by the lightning when you do
> I wish you couldn't reach me in the place in my heart
> Belonging only to you.

He was waiting for her to propose, and in 1993 she stammered out a proposal at the bar of the Carlyle Hotel in New York. In February 1994 the Jew and the Catholic were married—by a priest and a rabbi—in Caracas. It took them two further years to rebuild a house on one of the smartest blocks on the Upper East Side of New York. Peter Rose, Phyllis Lambert's favorite architect, duly came up with a spectacular space, the interior hollowed out to allow for a soaring atrium dominated by a life-size Nigerian fertility statue.

The previous year, and largely thanks to Mcdonnell's wooing of Vin & Spirit, the Swedish state wine and spirits monopoly that owned the brand, Seagram acquired the worldwide rights to sell Absolut vodka, the only real challenger to Smirnoff. Absolut was a brand that owed everything to its image and carefully crafted advertising and virtually nothing to any particular quality. The deal was an admission that Seagram had badly missed the boat. Until 1993 Absolut had been distributed worldwide by IDV who also owned Smirnoff, and V & S received only half the profits. So Vin & Spirit was naturally keen on a deal with Seagram, and Mcdonnell was greatly helped by the arrogant—and sometimes boorish—behavior of the IDV executives responsible for the brand. As the negotiations progressed he brought in Efer, who worked as hard and as effectively as he was to do when negotiating with Matsushita two years later. IDV veterans claim that the terms of the new deal were far from generous, and after acquiring the brand Seagram could do little more than keep up the momentum, for sales had already climbed to well over three million cases a year in the United States alone before the takeover. By early 1994, the thirty-nine-year-old Junior had completed his rise to power, succeeding his father as CEO of Seagram. Not surprisingly father and son went in for a touch of the bella figura in their offices, which included a whirlpool bath, sauna, and other executive trappings.

In 1991 the Bronfmans started a serious search for diversification away from the drinks business, and it was not only rational considerations but also the two Edgars' love of show business that led them to media, then becoming an increasingly fashionable sector. They soon found a natural target in Time Warner. Cynics like Ken Auletta believed that Edgar Jr. "wanted a bigger playpen: one offering Hollywood's most profitable studio, pay-TV company Home Box Office (HBO), record group, and publishing company; such magazines as *Time*, *People*, *Sports Illustrated*, and *Fortune*; a position as the second-largest owner of cable systems; and keys to a mammoth entertainment and information library." Efer was working through Michael Ovitz, the most important agent in Hollywood, a man who, by a strange coincidence, was the son of a salesman who had worked for a Seagram distributor. According to McQueen, Ovitz had already briefed the Seagram board on the entertainment business and was certainly responsible for introducing the Bronfmans to Herbert Allen, Jr., the leading investment banker to the sector and a key player in the many deals in the entertainment business during the 1990s. As early as the spring of 1993 Seagram had bought 4.9 percent in the group, thus signaling its intention to repeat its previous success with DuPont by buying a big enough stake in Time Warner to "consolidate" the profits, i.e., include its proportion in its own accounts. This had proved particularly useful for Seagram, whose profits from liquor were not looking too healthy in the '80s. But on this occasion the situation was very different from that leading up to the purchase of the stake in DuPont.

The combined Time Warner business, which in those innocent days was considered the eight hundred–pound gorilla in the media forest, had been created by one Steve Ross. His career had started as the manager of family-owned funeral parlors and parking lots but by the time of his death from cancer in 1992 he had assembled the biggest media business in the United States. He was, says Connie Bruck, "handsome, charismatic, and irresistibly charming to many whom he courted. And he was gifted—in his intuition about people, in his facility with numbers, and in his ability to cut deals so deftly that the other side often left the negotiating table blissfully unaware of having been taken."[3] During his last illness he was persuaded to name as his successor not Nick Nicholas, his co-chairman, but Gerald Levin, who had risen to fame by masterminding the success of Home Box Office. Levin had been a brilliant student—his Hebrew was so good that at the age of thirteen he would occasionally conduct services at his family's local synagogue. But clearly he was never going to welcome an outsider barging in on a kingdom he had so recently and so ruthlessly conquered, especially as he was obviously struggling to fill the boots of a much more considerable predecessor.

All the time the Bronfmans were accumulating more stock in Time Warner, bringing their stake to just under 15 percent—an important level in a group that, unlike Seagram, did not have a controlling group of shareholders. It did not help their efforts that Paul Desmarais, a leading Canadian businessman who was also a director of Seagram, had also bought three million shares for it appeared, wrongly, that he was in cahoots with the Bronfmans. As a result the two Edgars were perceived as aiming at complete control of Time Warner. Worse, there was a recent precedent of a situation in which an investor had gained control of a prize media asset without buying the whole company. Everyone at Time Warner was afraid of a repetition of what had happened to CBS in 1986 when Lawrence Tisch of Loew's Corporation had gained effective control of the network although he owned a mere quarter of the equity. The situation was not helped by Edgar Sr.'s blundering, which soon helped scotch a deal that required the most delicate diplomacy to soothe Levin's natural fears. For Edgar Sr. made it clear that Seagram wanted the same sort of deal as with DuPont, with a couple of seats on the board, although he tried to limit the damage by emphasizing that it would be a "passive investor." The board of Time Warner simply did not believe him—if only because before buying their stake in DuPont the Bronfmans had attempted a full takeover of St. Joseph Minerals. The directors' apprehensions were reinforced by newspaper articles that Edgar would replace Levin with Mike Ovitz. Moreover the stock market didn't much like the idea—one analyst, John Wakely of Lehmann, said markedly that "I'm being asked to invest in Edgar Bronfman Fund Management Ltd." To make matters worse, one major institutional investor, US West, which had a bigger stake than Seagram, was not represented on the board. They and other major investors were obviously going to be unhappy with any such deal.

So in January 1994 the board of Time Warner unanimously adopted a "poison pill" defense, providing that any bidder with more than 15 percent of the stock would have to pay a hefty bonus for the remainder, unless the bid were in cash. This would have cost $30 billion or more—clearly beyond the reach even of the Bronfmans' purse. Seagram was stymied, for to allow its share of Time Warner's earnings to be included in its balance sheet under a system called "equity accounting," Seagram needed to own more than 20 percent of Time Warner's equity—at 25 percent their stake in DuPont was well over the minimum. So the Edgars gave up and made a modest profit by selling Seagram's stake a couple of years later when Time Warner's stock started the upward move normal among media stocks in the last years of the century. So, just as the investment in DuPont had been at least partly the result of opposition to the purchase of St. Joe, which would have proved a disastrous one, so the infamous purchase of Universal in 1995 was—again at least partly—the consequence of the refusal of a possible partner, in this case the Time Warner board, to behave in a sensible fashion, a failure that was to lead to a disaster that engulfed both sides.

Sixteen

A UNIVERSAL PANACEA

The whole empire was sacrificed on Edgar Jr.'s obsessive desire not
to be a mere coupon-clipper combined with his inherited sense of
shame at being involved in the liquor business.
— LEO KOLBER

THE FIRST FATAL STEP IN THE DECLINE AND FALL OF THE HOUSE OF
Seagram came the year after the failure of the link with Time Warner.
It involved the exchange of the stake in DuPont for control of MCA/Universal, a mixed bag of film studios, record companies, and theme parks. To
Junior, DuPont was "a boring business." In the words of *BusinessWeek*, he
was unwilling to accept "the company's creeping transformation into an investment fund in corporate drag." He was not alone in his attitude. In the
last five years of the twentieth century many other CEOs sold solidly profitable businesses or loaded them up with excessive debt to to pay for more
modern, "exciting," and almost invariably disastrous investments, generally
in the world of media, including, and especially, the fashionable electronic
sector.

Junior had another motive, to try to get out from under the long shadow
still cast by his grandfather. Junior himself admitted that it was his "sense
of financial security [that] made it possible to be 'brave,' to go out and try
new things and be 'different'"—it was typical of the family's attitudes to ignore the fact that his adventures also involved the other shareholders in
Seagram, who by the 1990s owned two-thirds of the stock. For some years
the very success of the DuPont investment had overshadowed the rest of
the group's activities and analysts would ignore even the best results from
the liquor business, for DuPont was the reason why many investors were
still supporting Seagram's shares—a development that naturally disheartened executives in the liquor business. The combination of a steady but

unexciting basic business and an increasing flow of dividends from DuPont suited not only nonfamily shareholders but also Charles who—like his uncle Harry sixty years earlier—was looking for a quiet life. But Edgar Jr. had a gut need to sell the stake in DuPont, even though Kolber proposed financing any future purchase from a combination of DuPont dividends and greater borrowing.

Edgar Sr. was inclined to support his son's desire to get away from the existing structure, and not only because of their shared obsession with show business. He could use the excuse that he had become unhappy with a change in the management at DuPont. Worse, he had discovered, rather late in the day, that DuPont's Conoco subsidiary had been negotiating a joint deal with the ruler of Dubai to develop a large new oil field in Iranian waters. This was especially awkward for Edgar as president of the WJC and as a believer in the doctrine that Tehran was the "head office" of Islamic fundamentalism. These unquantifiable factors helped Junior when he presented the case prepared by Goldman Sachs for selling the stake. It was reinforced by belief that the stock could not be expected to do better than the S & P 500. This was based on advice from Junior's favorite, Boston Consulting Group, who had divined that the price of oil would go down and that DuPont would also be hit by expensive bills for environmental cleanups. Charles was more conservative, his attitude was simple, that "as long as we had DuPont, we would be protected generation after generation." But Edgar was gungho for growth.

Nevertheless the deal was done, largely by Junior, and relied heavily on the way DuPont saved Seagram a billion dollars in tax. According to his father, Junior "drove a hard bargain" but even he was forced to add that "I wasn't exactly ecstatic about the price." It was $36.25 a share, a 40 percent discount on the market price, though the tax scheme more than made up the difference and the deal ended by giving Seagram $7.7 billion in cash plus warrants to buy 156 million DuPont shares at a fixed—albeit very high—price.* The sale was the culmination of an extraordinary success story based on Mr. Sam's original investment of $50 million in Texas Pacific thirty years earlier.

---

* Seagram's advisers managed to treat the money it received from DuPont as a dividend rather than a capital sale, thus attracting a far lower tax burden. Goldmann did this by allowing DuPont to grant Seagram warrants to buy the same number of shares, albeit at a price that meant that they were unlikely to be cashed. But in 2003 the IRS forced Vivendi, by then Seagram's owners, to pay a total of $2.7 billion in back tax and interest.

By now Edgar Sr. was a truly nonexecutive chairman, with Edgar Jr. as CEO. Both of them obviously already had a clear idea as to where to invest the money. For many years they had been eyeing the diversified entertainment group MCA/Universal, but in 1990 it had been bought by the Japanese electronics giant Matsushita. MCA/Universal had been built up by Lew Wasserman, the most extraordinary figure in the post-war history of Hollywood—quite rightly Connie Bruck entitled her masterly book on him *When Hollywood Had a King.* In some ways he resembled Mr. Sam. Both were self-made men whose parents had emigrated from czarist Russia. Both had hoped to become lawyers but had had to start work young. Both had minds like walking computers, both had enormous energy and vision, both relied on a small band of ultra-loyal executives, both possessed boundless charm deployed when it suited them, and appalling bouts of anger, many of which were tactical. But there the similarity ended, for Wasserman was far colder, less emotional, more ruthless, less sympathetic than Mr. Sam. As the network executive Don Durgin told Bruck, Wasserman was "a very attractive man. I didn't like him, because he was such a shark—but it was a shark you almost had to admire as he circled you." Symbolically the headquarters he built was a forbidding edifice, its color resulting in the nickname "the Black Tower." Moreover Wasserman had been closely involved with the Mafia for most of his forty years in Hollywood through the lawyer Sidney Korshak, the mob's Hollywood ambassador. "They were joined at the hip," wrote Connie Bruck.

Wasserman had started as an agent working for the legendary Jules Stein of the Music Corporation of America—invariably known as MCA.[*] He came into his own with the arrival of television, for he was virtually the only person in Hollywood to foresee its potential importance. He also invented the "packaging system" by which agents were able to sell helpless studios a package comprising a whole slate of their clients, not just actors but directors and many of the technical crew as well. By the 1970s he had sold the agency business and had not just built up a total dominance over the production of TV films and above all TV series, he had also acquired Universal Studios at a knockdown price. After a bad start when he hoped to make films on an assembly line basis similar to that normal in television,

---

[*] The only person who ever dared to mock at MCA was Billy Wilder. In *Some Like It Hot* the two musicians played by Tony Curtis and Jack Lemmon are looking for work and breeze into an office labeled MCA. The only occupants are two frowzy women drinking gin from the bottle.

he was saved by *Airport*, whose producer, Ross Hunter, was sacked after Hunter had claimed—rightly—to have saved the studio. But Wasserman then had the sense to employ talented producers like Ned Tanen and David Selznick and David Brown with hits including *Jaws* and *ET*. He then transformed the Universal studio lot into a highly successful theme park, its visitor appeal based on the glamour attached to any Hollywood studio.

But by the end of the 1980s Wasserman was aging and he and his anointed successor, Sidney Sheinberg, decided to sell out. They found an unlikely buyer in Matsushita, the Japanese electronic giant. In selling out, as Wasserman himself said, "It wasn't the price that was wrong, but the deal itself." In fact it proceeded from the same reasoning that led to the disastrous mergers in the media business later in the decade. For Steve Ross had set an earthquake moving; even Wasserman was afraid that he simply didn't have the financial muscle to survive in a sea where the sharks were getting ever larger. Matsushita itself was following in the tracks of Sony, its smaller but far livelier competitor, which had bought Columbia Studios the previous year.

Sony, like the Bronfmans, had used the "super-agent" Michael Ovitz to help them with the bid. In 1974 he had left the leading William Morris Agency with a number of colleagues and started a competitor called the Creative Artists Association. He was, if it seems at all possible, even more aggressive in his packaged deals than Wasserman, the man he recognized as his master, and over the two decades after he founded CAA Ovitz had become the most hated man in Hollywood. He had modeled himself on Wasserman, hoping to repeat his trick of transmuting power as an agent into dominance of Hollywood. But Ovitz lacked the older man's streak of genius, of intuitive understanding. As Nikki Finke put it, after his downfall, "his power was such that it took real courage" for both show business executives and journalists "to lay bare the profound and lasting effect that Ovitz had on Hollywood for twenty-seven years through threats, intimidation, bullying, blacklisting, and destabilizing."[1]

The sale of MCA/Universal to Matsushita took only a few weeks to complete, at a price—$66 a share—far lower than Wasserman and Sheinberg had hoped, though even Sheinberg received $113 million.* Moreover

---

Wasserman owned five million shares bought at an average price of three cents and would have received $327 million, but to avoid capital gains tax took preferred stock instead, providing him with an annual income of $28.6 million for life.

it was based on a total cultural misunderstanding. The vendors had assumed that they would have access to unlimited funds from their new parent, that, as Bruck puts it, Matsushita "would be a kind of corporate sugar daddy." But the new owners were hit by the Japanese recession, which lasted the whole decade, and in any case their cautious, notoriously conservative corporate culture would never have allowed the company's employees in Hollywood any financial latitude—typically, the Japanese would not allow them to buy either CBS or NBC, even though major TV networks were crucial elements in any entertainment group pretending to be comprehensive in its "distribution"—as opposed to "content," the other buzz word at the time.

By 1995 Matsushita was keen, bordering on desperate, to sell MCA/Universal as quietly and quickly as possible, a disposal that could be made without loss of face because the executive who had negotiated the original purchase had retired. Not surprisingly Ovitz came back on the scene as a secret negotiator. Within a short time Junior had made two ultra-secret trips to Matsushita's head office in Osaka and concluded a deal on his own ("alone was alone" he told Connie Bruck[2]). The deal was so secret that even Lew Wasserman heard about it only from the newspapers. In this it was totally different from the normal run of such affairs, generally leaked during discussions that invariably involve hordes of overpaid lawyers, accountants, and investment bankers. Although Matsushita was a publicity-shy and willing seller, Junior could rightly be proud of his successful acquisition of 80 percent of MCA/Universal for $5.7 billion—allowing for debt payments—about the same as the Japanese had paid five years earlier, and, as he said, "below auction value." The sale, together with Sony's attempts to hive off Columbia Studios, showed that the Japanese had realized, rather late and expensively, that their corporate cultures, marked by consensus and lack of urgency, could never cope with the demands of the movie business.

For Matsushita it wasn't an important deal—as an MCA executive, Blair Westlake, told McQueen, "Washing machines was probably a bigger product line than the film business." But it was an undeniable triumph for Junior, recognized as such within the industry when he was chosen to make the opening presentation at the industry's most prestigious event, the summer gathering of moguls in Sun Valley, Idaho, assembled by Herb Allen, the investment banker. For most people agreed with the judgment of *Forbes* magazine that Junior had secured a bargain. Matsushita had retained

Universal's $3 billion in debt as well as its 20 percent interest. As a result, according to *Forbes* anyway, the Japanese had financed the bid by a handy $4.4 billion. What's more, Junior had minimized possible losses from Universal's white elephant movie, *Waterworld*, which was costing $175 million, by making sure that he would be landed with only $50 million of the cost, ensuring that it would not be a loser—well, not a major one anyway. And by *Forbes'* reckoning both Universal—including its film library and the record division run by the legendary Dave Geffen, which were each worth over $2.75 billion—resulted in a total value of $9 billion. For Edgar Sr. the clinching point was that "we now control MCA which was never true of DuPont. Even if we had, I knew I could never manage DuPont. I don't know enough about the chemical business. On another level, I didn't have the feeling for DuPont that Edgar has for MCA." The turning point in the family history came at the same time as the death of the indomitable Saidye, who survived her "Baby Face" by over twenty years to die at the ripe old age of ninety-eight while her sister Flora celebrated her centenary, for the Rosners were clearly a long-lived family.

Yet the sale of DuPont and purchase of Universal broke the unspoken rule of thirty years: that the family could do what it liked—even invest in Paramount and MGM—with its own money, but did not gamble with the funds that belonged to Seagram itself. Yet in the switch from DuPont to MCA/Universal they totally ignored the interests of outside shareholders, treating Seagram as purely a family business. Even so, the non-executive directors were mute throughout. They had been personally selected, largely by Charles, as the cream of Canadian business and would certainly have followed his lead had he chosen to fight. But it just wasn't in his nature. Not surprisingly the announcement of the deal sent Seagram's shares down by nearly a fifth to $26.75.

The episode ended with a telling conversation between the two brothers. Predictably, Charles was, as an associate put it, "more interested in finding a safe investment that would protect the family fortune." By contrast, for Edgar, "buying MCA presented an enormous opportunity for my son." When Charles said, "I thought as we got older we were supposed to get closer and the better friends," he was clearly thinking of the breach represented by the MCA deal. To which Edgar asked the brutal question, "Did you ever say no?" "No, I didn't want to start a family feud"—the ghost of Allan and Mr. Sam still hung heavy.

In any event although Seagram's shares rose by 50 percent during the bull market of the late 1990s those in DuPont more than doubled, a rise that would have provided Seagram with around $9 billion in capital gains. If the Bronfmans had held on to their stake until 2003 it would have been worth $12.5 billion, so the sale of the stake led to a net loss to the shareholders of $3 billion—not including the dividends. From an investment point of view it exchanged a sure and growing source of income, the very basis on which the stock market valued the company, for an uncertain future in the dicey world of show business, and this basically on the whim of an overage adolescent. Crucially—and unremarked by most commentators at the time or since—it demonstrated to a startling degree the extent to which the family still regarded the company as a personal fiefdom. They—and their handpicked band of thirteen loyal if "distinguished" outside directors—totally ignored the interests of outside shareholders, who by then accounted for two-thirds of the company's shares, a proportion that was steadily increasing over the years thanks to a steady trickle of divestment by family members. Yet to the family—and even to the furious Kolber—the exchange was regarded as being the same as switches in the family's personal investment portfolio.

When he retired from the board at the end of 1999 at the age of seventy, Kolber analyzed the results of Junior's maneuvers. First was that "they didn't have to sell DuPont to buy MCA, it could have been financed out of loans and the dividends from DuPont." And when Junior responded that DuPont "was just a commodity play" Kolber exploded: "Some commodities: Nylon. Dacron. Teflon. Textron. As it turned out the stupidity of it was breathtaking." Moreover Hollywood was the "lowest margin business this side of fast food, with a lot higher maintenance of the help. Kids flipping burgers did not have agents, did not come with entourages, and did not travel in private jets."

He was not alone. One columnist in The New York Times wrote of "the Bronfman Follies"; another article carried the headline "What Shiny Toys Money Can Buy" and went on to assert that the deal was designed to provide Junior with a "playground." An even more key point was made in another report saying that Seagram's wine and spirit business was "fighting to stay afloat." But it was "Lex," the much-respected financial columnist in the London Financial Times, who provided the most damning critique of the deal. After noting that "there is zero industrial logic in a drinks company buying into Hollywood" the commentator went on, "It would be better—" and he could have added more responsible—

"to sell his family's large stake in Seagram and invest that in Hollywood direct."

Both Edgar Sr. and Jr. had assumed that Ovitz would take over MCA—even though Wasserman, after telling Edgar that "your son hit a home run" had added that if Ovitz became CEO he would leave the board. Ovitz's greed for power and money had prevented him from taking the top spot at Columbia following Sony's takeover. But Junior was so keen to employ him that he even accepted Ovitz's outrageous financial demands, which, it was said, added up to $250 million,* demands that Charles felt bold enough to veto. This left Junior dumbstruck—although Wasserman said that this was the most positive news he'd heard in a long time. "Frankly," Junior told a meeting of executives, "Ovitz was Plan A. I don't have a Plan B." By that time Ovitz had a much bigger target in his sights; to become number two at Disney. But only a few months after he had been hired, Michael Eisner, Disney's ruthless boss, got rid of him at a cost of $140 million after a bitter row that rumbled on in the courts for nearly a decade.

In any event Ovitz suffered worst in a classic case of "time wounds all heels." In 1998 he attempted to create his own inter-media group, bringing together his old fiefdom, the agency CAA, a TV production company, and Internet outlets. Ovitz invested $150 million of his own money in the project, only to see the enterprise collapse into the hands of Jeff Kwatinetz, a minor player in a world in which Ovitz had been the Demon King. Ovitz then became totally unbalanced, blaming his downfall not on himself, but on Hollywood's supposed Gay Mafia, led by such arch-demons as Barry Diller and David Geffen.

Junior promptly asked Geffen to find a replacement while continuing to spend enormous sums on stars for films that proved disasters—and others that were never made. Most spectacularly he paid Sylvester Stallone $60 million for three movies. For the failure to agree terms with Ovitz somehow persuaded father and son that a single, unqualified thirty-something could run two world-scale businesses, Seagram and MCA, simultaneously. As David Olive pointed out, "Unfortunately Edgar Jr. was never able to commit to either booze (it doesn't help that his favorite tipple is mineral water) or to entertainment. One day, the most important thing in the

---

* Bronfman's generosity had started when Edgar Sr. sent him a case of the fabled 1961 vintage of Chateau Lafite to thank him for his help with the takeover.

world to him was a terrifying new ride he helped design at a Universal theme park in Florida. But a month later, his colleagues could be forgiven for thinking Edgar Jr. had no interest in amusement parks, such was his complete fixation in transmitting digitized movies over the Internet."[3]

The Bronfmans inherited a lot of solid assets that could have been re-dynamized after a decade when Wasserman and Sheinberg had rather rested on their laurels, followed by five years during which Matsushita had refused to invest in them. The assets were a mixed bag. Most troublesome were the theme parks. Lew Wasserman had for once got it wrong, for the idea was not easily exportable and relied too much on the glamour of the Hollywood image. By the second half of 1999 the parks were losing at a rate of over $40 million annually with attendance consistently below estimates.

Junior established himself in L.A. with a splash, buying a legendary beach house, Number One Malibu Colony, which had been built by Bing Crosby with his royalties from "White Christmas" and which had subse-quently been owned by such luminaries as Robert Redford. But this was largely a gesture, for Junior spent most of his time at 375 Park Avenue. His first step to obliterate the past was to remove the name MCA from Wasser-man's infamous head office—the Black Tower—and to ask the coolest of ar-chitects, the Dutch Rem Koolhaas, to design a new headquarters featuring an openness that would be a complete contrast to the closed world of the Black Tower. Not surprisingly the project was abandoned three years later.

The rejuvenation process was not helped by Junior's open contempt for what he described as a "dumb town." "He seemed to feel," wrote Bruck, that "belittling his predecessors made him bigger." He spent the next few years systematically denigrating everything about the previous manage-ment, arguing that it was a business in long-term decline, scorning the idea that much of the problem sprang from Matsushita's blockage on expendi-ture. Junior then went in for a total purge, including all the infrastructure, the back office, accountancy, legal, pensions, and human resources execu-tives who form the framework of any serious business. They were, one for-mer executive told Bruck, "tainted with the disease. The disease was the way Lew did it." Junior's analysis was not unreasonable. Most companies that have been run in a highly personal way by long-serving chief execu-tives like Universal—or Seagram for that matter—need a thorough spring cleaning to inject more orthodox management techniques when the founders have finally left the scene. But Junior, always anxious for advice, called in two more sets of management consultants, the usual tribe of ignorant adolescents trying to impose standard formulas totally unsuitable for the movie business. As Tom Pollock of Universal told McQueen, "He wanted to show himself as a strong, tough, money-minded manager to Wall Street." The cost was stupendous, reckoned at $200 million, half of which went to his old favorites, Boston Consulting Group. In management theory these outlays should have resulted in savings five or ten times that amount. Needless to say they didn't.

His hirings and their attitude were naturally greeted with horror. They were based on a simple, and superficially attractive, thesis: He wanted to treat the movie business as if it were like other industries, and not to depend on the boom-and-bust, literally hit and miss, mentality that has been the prevailing philosophy (if you can call it that) since the studio system had broken down four decades earlier. As David Plotz put it, when—he did not say if—Edgar Jr. fails in Hollywood "it won't be the failure of a romantic. It will be the failure of someone much less interesting: a businessman." To put it more kindly, his—supposed—professionalism as a businessman was not the quality required in Hollywood. His natural sense of superiority allowed him to think in public, saying that he might hand over the marketing and advertising function to the liquor people. He was jeered at even when he made a perfectly sensible suggestion, that the price of admission to a movie should be geared to the cost of making the movie—something that had been common throughout Hollywood's history.

For when the bean counters at Seagram looked at Hollywood's way of doing business they were horrified. As one senior financial official put it, they saw that the Hollywood executives were "a bunch of phonies" and gasped at the financial structure. Universal was committed to making around a dozen films a year, costing around $50 million each to produce and a further $40 million each to market, in exchange for half the income from exhibition. This involved takings of at least $180 million for each film. No wonder to orthodox financial executives "the only sensible investment in Hollywood is in a film library"—indeed Wasserman's first great coup had been to buy Paramount's library for a mere $50 million, a sum he recouped tenfold within a few years. At the extreme, Bruce Hack, the former Seagram executive who was appointed CFO, was overheard screaming over the phone that Universal didn't "even have a corporate chart—can you believe it? They are brain-dead out here, just brain-dead." In a town where, as William Goldman so memorably remarked, "no one knows anything," Junior and his cohorts seemed to know less than nothing.

After a time, wrote Bruck, quoting an old Hollywood hand, "the taking of Edgar is now a cottage industry." He was merely one in a long line of outsiders given the standard treatment: "Dazzle them," goes the old mantra, "get them to invest as much money as possible, and then drive them out as soon as they are broke." His first mistake was being too generous to the previous regime he had sworn to remove. He provided Sheinberg with $300 million to set up a production company called the Bubble Factory, which soon burst leaving a loss of $150 million. Sheinberg promptly went out to attack the way Junior had, allegedly, destroyed Universal—he called the sackings "ethnic cleansing." Clearly Junior was in a panic through his inability to hire Ovitz. Instead he hired Frank Biondi, who had formerly worked at Home Box Office and Viacom, granting him an employment package that was pretty amazing even by Hollywood's elevated standards, including as it did a clay tennis court complete with an underground watering system to keep the playing surface in tip-top condition, and a screening room costing a cool $2.1 million. In Bruck's words, Junior's team contained "a marked preponderance of people who had either no experience of managing a giant corporation or no experience in running any facet of the entertainment business." Not surprisingly streams of executives came and went with monotonous regularity—and fat payoffs. As head of the studio he chose Ron Meyer, an affable ex-Marine who had been Ovitz's Number Two, who had played soft cop to Ovitz, hardest of cops, an appointment that was greeted with disbelief by the cognoscenti.

Nevertheless in the longer term Meyer's willingness to let control go to competent executives, notably Stacy Snider, in charge of filmmaking, returned Universal to the big time with hits like *The Mummy, Meet the Parents, Erin Brokovich*, and *Gladiator*, and in 2001 Meyer and Snider were made Man and Woman of the Year by *Variety*. But Junior still had to cope with the big beasts in the Hollywood jungle. In particular he had to do a deal with a major power broker, Dave Geffen, one of a trio, with Steven Spielberg and the former Disney boss Jeffrey Katzenberg, who had founded DreamWorks, a major supplier to MCA. The deal cost MCA well over $54 million—estimates vary—but resulted in largely unprofitable films. Connie Bruck quotes a (necessarily anonymous) executive as saying that Junior was like a party piñata: "Hit him and money comes out."

Junior's hopes were aborted through two disastrous mistakes, both connected with Barry Diller. Junior's admiration for Diller, a key father figure, was unbounded. "A unique talent," he gushed, "of which there are only a few in a generation." The record of "Killer Diller" had been extraordinary, culminating in the way he assembled the Fox empire for Rupert Murdoch, including a studio, 20th Century Fox, and a totally new TV network. But Murdoch was never going to allow anyone else to take real power, as he apparently told Diller, "There is only one principal in News Corporation." Not surprisingly Diller left Fox in 1992, apparently swearing that he would never work for anyone else, but the period with Murdoch had proved to be the high point of the career of someone later described as "a mogul in search of an empire."

Although Diller did a number of shrewd and lucrative deals in the following decade, bad luck, and a refusal to pay over the odds for a company, transformed him into something of a "nearly man" in the media world, while brasher, less talented, less realistic figures forged ahead. To his eternal regret he had been outbid by Sumner Redstone of Viacom in an attempt to buy Paramount Pictures and had gone back, effectively, to square one, assembling Home Shopping Network, an unimpressive, totally unglamorous bundle of assets that, as the name implied, was a pioneer in Internet shopping. His realism, his lack of the egomania-cum-megalomania required to become a true mogul, prevented him from creating his own major media empire, though it did enable him to assemble a very large fortune, which may have been his main object all along.

Junior had managed to regain control of Universal's cable and domestic television assets, including the USA cable network, after a lengthy legal battle during which he had managed to wrest complete control from MCA's previous partner, the redoubtable Sumner Redstone of Viacom, albeit at a cost of $1.7 billion. Yet in October 1997 he ceded control of all these assets including Universal's domestic TV production and distribution business to Diller's HSN for a mere $1.2 billion in cash and $3 billion in paper. Moreover it soon became clear that Junior did not understand the USA television setup, for Universal's TV subsidiaries included two popular cable channels, USA Network and Sci-Fi Network, as well as a production arm with programs as popular as *Law & Order* and *Jerry Springer*. The deal demonstrated Junior's dependence on "father" figures. After the sale to Diller, all Universal retained was a 49 percent stake in the merged company—renamed USA Networks—and the promise that he could recover control at an undefined date—which Diller believed could be as long as thirty years in the future. Somehow Junior persuaded himself that the deal was a great one, for he claimed, "It's innovative, no one's ever done it before." To everyone else in Hollywood it looked like disaster. From the 1950s on it had been—and remained—axiomatic that studios needed control over TV outlets. "After all," one studio head told Bruck, "TV and motion pictures are similar creative processes, and the distribution is intermeshed." But Universal, alone of the major studios, ended up without a TV operation of its own. "By separating TV from movies, it violated the fundamental laws of synergy."

The deal was not only against the—sensible—orthodox view, it had several other results. First, Junior—in true Bronfman style—had not told Frank Biondi in advance; second it gave the impression, as Bruck puts it, that "he had been worsted in a deal"—a fatal mistake in the macho Hollywood jungle. The failure to tell Biondi was a major tactical error—a piece of lordly indifference to outsiders and their feelings typical of the family— as well as an insult since he had restructured the company and sold off the TV and cable businesses in which Biondi, formerly of Viacom, was a seasoned veteran. (His reaction was that "you're selling the best asset we have, and you're selling it cheap.") More fundamentally it worried the rest of Universal, for people started to ask whether they would be next, given that the deal totally undermined the only real reason for any group as diverse and sprawling as MCA/Universal, the "synergy" supposedly available from utilizing the brand to cross-fertilize the businesses.

Junior then went on to ensure that Seagram got the worst of all worlds. From the beginning it had been assumed even by well-wishers like *Forbes* that he would need to acquire a TV network to take full advantage of the enormous asset represented by Universal's film and television libraries. But he was so obsessed with retaining his 49 percent of USA Networks that he wouldn't let Diller buy NBC in 1999 (he had the right to veto any deal involving more than 10 percent of the shares in USA Networks). This step would have complemented the Diller Universal TV empire, and his refusal was a classic case of the Bronfman need for control as well as refusal to spend up to $8 billion. This was disastrous: "Anyone with that piece of Barry Diller should make use of it," said a major deal-maker. Worse, it dashed Diller's perfectly legitimate aspirations to use USA Networks to achieve his lifetime goal of controlling a major integrated media operation and thus naturally infuriated a man "whose anger has never been slow to fade," as *BusinessWeek* put it. The two did not meet for a whole year. Nevertheless the same year Diller was appointed to the Seagram board, and he and Junior remained friends, nominally at least.

Music had always been Junior's dream. As he told Bruck, "We'll never be number one in publishing. . . . We'll never be number one in TV. . . . We'll never be number one in theme parks. . . . Only in music can we be number one." His first step was to buy a half-share in Interscope, a record company specializing in gangster-rap stars like Death Row and therefore cold-shouldered by other record companies. It proved a smart buy, but besmirched the image of Universal Music (soon after the purchase Death Row's impresario, Marion "Suge" Knight, went to jail).* In this instance Junior's lack of concern for official opinion served him well. But he failed to clinch a more important deal, his attempt to buy the British music group EMI. A friend of Junior's told Bruck, "Edgar has only one idea: it's buy EMI, buy EMI, buy EMI. Owning USA Networks was never about making TV work. It's been about his being able to sell it . . . to get money to buy EMI. And if he gets it it will truly be the Music Corporation of America—even though he's changed the name." In any event he failed—even though Edgar Sr. sent Sir Colin Southgate, EMI's chairman, a bottle of one-hundred-year-old Martell cognac.

One of Junior's shrewdest hirings had been in the person of Doug Morris, who had been sacked from Warner Music, to take charge of MCA music, known at the time as the Music Cemetery of America. Morris was the only subordinate with whom Junior felt entirely comfortable; they talked the same language and Junior felt, rightly, that he had something creative to contribute. Moreover the sense of participation gave him a sense of power unequaled in the rest of his empire. As McQueen put it, "Here he could be king and command recording artists, like minstrels in a medieval court, to appear live onstage to serenade him."

Having turned the division around Morris was ready for more. In 1998 Junior spent $10.4 billion on buying Polygram, a major record company, from the Dutch group Philips, at the height of the boom in media-related stocks, leaving Seagram with an enormous burden of debt. The reason he gave was that the acquisition made Universal Music what Junior rightly claimed was "the greatest music company in the world," responsible for one in four of the world's record sales, and gave him a stable of artists ranging from Willie Nelson and Jimi Hendrix to Eminem. The combined

* In early 2005, Death Row was involved, though not charged, when one of its affiliates, headed by one Irv Gotti—who had renamed himself after the famous mafioso—was accused of money laundering for a major drug dealer.

group was a good fit, since Universal's sales were concentrated in the US, Polygram's internationally, and Universal had no classical music labels while Polygram had no fewer than three. However the acquisition involved sacrificing dozens of less profitable artists as well as whole labels like A & M and Geffen, beloved of aficionados for the way they nursed non-mainstream talent. As Al Cafaro, the sacked boss of A & M put it, "It's a Wall Street world now." Not that Wall Street was happy, since sales had peaked in 1996 after vinyl discs had been replaced by compact discs. He then spent $100 million on another trendy label, the hip-hop kings, DefJam.

Junior promptly went into his usual job-cutting, saving an estimated $300 million. One of his most savage cuts came from Polygram Film Distributors, which had been one of the biggest in Europe, thus ending the dream of an independent European film major created by Polygram's ventures into filmmaking, which were losing money. Junior was unable to auction the business, so he had to sell the film library for a mere $235 million and fold the rest of the business into Universal. He then had to be involved in the music industry's relatively successful but expensive battle against pirates like Napster exploiting the Internet to record music and distribute it free.

For Junior the strain was exacerbated by the automatic opposition Charles was mounting to every move. This questioning had got badly on his nerves. As he said, "When you're trying to transform a company, and you have a major owner who does that reluctantly and makes his reluctance known, it makes your job more difficult, to be sure." Apart from reliance on management consultants Junior also fell for another delusion prevalent in the late 1990s. Previously investors had judged corporate earnings by the profits they had earned after interest, depreciation, and other basic expenditures had been taken into account. But Junior, like many ambitious CEOs at the time, relied on the delusion, increasingly widespread in the latter years of the 1990s even among supposedly sophisticated investors and their advisers, that Earnings Before Interest, Tax, Depreciation, and Amortization (known as EBITDA) was a legitimate measure of a company prospects. This was not only a valuation system far removed from financial reality but a complete reversal of the financial conservatism that had marked all the family's businesses for seventy years.

By the end of the 1990s the group's revenues were $12.6 billion, with losses of $126 million in music and $206 million in film. Universal's theme parks brought in $45 million, but even though Junior spent an inordinate amount of time and effort on a minor element in his empire it remained a distant number two to Disney, although within a few years they were at least regularly profitable. So the group relied almost entirely on the $552 million profits from wines and spirits to balance books badly upset by the massive borrowings required to buy Polygram. Nevertheless, noted Kolber bitterly, "Junior was oblivious to it." By the millennium the rift between Edgar and his son and Charles and his allies like Kolber was already deep. Despite Seagram's increasing reliance on a bailout from the drinks business Efer simply had no time to bother about it, but nevertheless would not give up control. One obvious contrast came with Junior's attitude to packaging. Whereas his grandfather had worked obsessively on every detail of the design of every bottle, every label, Junior casually approved new packaging for some major brands in the course of a flight—in a private jet, naturally— between New York and Los Angeles.

Inevitably the drinks business suffered, not just from his neglect, but also from being treated purely as a cash cow, with ever-increasing and ever more unreal profits targets. The "reengineering" that resulted from the Boston Consulting Group's efforts had cost over $100 million and resulted in such idiocies as renting of "the Ark," an office block in London shaped like a pregnant whale and so totally unsuitable for offices that, though newly built, it was due to be pulled down. It did not help that in 1995 Ed Mcdonnell resigned, to Junior's obvious relief, simply because he was fed up. Typically he was awarded a handsome leaving present, in his case rights to the Philippine market, then losing money. He went on to found a flourishing group, based at his home on Hilton Head Island, notably selling wines in the West Indies. Under his less independent successor, Steve Kalagher, sales and profits continued to rise, but the hidden costs were enormous. Investment was difficult if not impossible.

To make matters worse the men responsible for distilling and blending at Martell—and their brethren at Chivas Regal—had to accept the increasingly unrealistic projected sales figures being provided during the 1990s by the marketing department and so were forced to build up everincreasing stocks at enormous expense—by the time Martell was sold in 2001 it had enough brandy for eleven years' sales in stock, nearly three times the normal level and a huge burden for Pernod Ricard, the French group that bought the brand in 2003. (By contrast the whiskey stocks proved useful when Chivas launched its eighteen-year-old whisky, a step opposed by Edgar because they already had a twenty-one-year-old in Royal Salute.) But in some cases the pressure, which included discounting—previously a no-no at Seagram—on a wide scale, was self-defeating. One of Junior's worst mistakes deeply damaged sales of Chivas Regal, the group's pride and joy—and biggest profit earner—in the United States. Presumably as a result of obeying the rules of "managerial correctness," he put world marketing into the hands of a new company, Chivas Brand, run from London. But this created appalling tensions between the brand's managers and the old-timers in the American distribution system. The situation was exacerbated when Junior discarded Doyle Dane Bernbach's long-running advertising campaign, replacing it with an ever-changing series of invariably uninspired advertisements. As a result, by 2000, sales of Johnny Walker Black Label, which as late as 1985 had been a mere three-quarters of those of Chivas, outsold the Bronfman's pride and joy by over a tenth.

Junior also told the liquor group to raise $1 billion by selling investments to feed Universal's hunger for capital. Some of the results were sensible, like shutting a number of distilleries, including the two historic and thus aging sites at Waterloo near Toronto and at LaSalle. The closures left Seagram with only one major distillery, at Gimli in Manitoba—near its raw material—but having to buy in straight whiskey. A further cost-cutting exercise involved the abandonment of Barton & Guestier's showpiece bottling plant outside Bordeaux and the running-down of the brand. But the worst move was the sale of its two most important brands of champagne, Mumm and Perrier-Jouet—the latter highly profitable because of substantial sales in the United States through Chateau & Estates. The new owners, Tate Hicks Muse, a New York private equity firm, which paid $300 million for the brands, had to invest heavily in the aging and inadequate production facilities that had contributed so heavily to the decline in the quality and sales of Mumm. It did not help that Seagram had copied the label for use on Cuvée Napa, its much cheaper brand of sparkling wine from California, and thus confused buyers. But Seagram had sold badly; Tate Hicks sold the brands a couple of years later for a substantial profit.

Of course it would have been sensible, especially after the takeover of Universal, for Seagram to have merged with its great Canadian rival, Hiram Walker, to counteract the increasing power of British groups like IDV. Several attempts were made, the most promising in 1986 in conjunction with the Reichmann family of property developers. This would have enabled Seagram to fill key holes in its portfolio, notably with Courvoisier cognac and Beefeater premium gin. The idea was that Seagram would guarantee that the Reichmanns would get a proper price when they sold some of Hiram Walker's other brands, notably Ballantine's Scotch whisky, which clearly Seagram could not buy because of monopoly considerations. But the deal died and the Reichmanns went away to build their dream development at Canary Wharf in London; and Hiram Walker was bought by the British Allied Domecq. Later Seagram tried to take over Allied Domecq, but failed because of the fear of Allied's chief executive, who was widely viewed as incompetent, that he would be sacked.

The final blow came with the failure of a proposed merger with IDV, an idea first suggested in a conversation in a Seagram jet after a conference. This was vital to what remained a company still largely reliant on steadily declining brands like VO and 7 Crown. In 1994, sales of Jack Daniel's, the symbol of "straight" rather than blended whiskey, overtook those of 7 Crown for the first time. Even Chivas had reached a plateau of four million cases, albeit a very profitable one. But the merger proposals fizzled out. They seem to have broken down over Absolut vodka, the question of control, and Edgar's bella figura. Vin & Spirit, the Swedish owners of the Absolut brand, had the right to veto any change of distributor and refused to allow IDV to have anything to do with the brand—not surprisingly given IDV's natural concentration on Smirnoff, the market leader. To make matters worse the IDV management made it clear that Edgar and his son could no longer enjoy their regal lifestyle at the company's expense. But the fundamental problem was that both sides firmly believed that they would be master in the new organization. Unfortunately IDV's case for supremacy was far the better, for their major brands—notably Smirnoff and Baileys Irish Cream—were storming ahead. Moreover, IDV was not only bigger but had had a far more successful record over the previous three decades. Yet although their executives were prepared to cede control, the Bronfmans were not really prepared to give up their rights—as one well-placed observer put it, "They wouldn't give up brands so the discussions got lost in a maze of arguments about the arrangements for joint distribution. They realized that the combined firm would end up with more accountants than salesmen."

IDV promptly merged with Guinness to form Diageo, which became by far the biggest drinks company in the world, and Seagram was left out in the cold as number three in the drinks business thanks to the recovery of Allied Domecq. Moreover the failure of the merger with IDV convinced the industry that Seagram was not for sale. But the outlook was grim. In October 1998 Seagram's debt was downgraded by Moody's "because of the volatility of the entertainment sector," a decision that probably had Mr. Sam, always so proud of his company's credit rating, turning in his grave.

Seventeen

THE FRENCH CONNECTION

I'm not going down in history as the one Bronfman who pissed
away the family fortune.
— EDGAR BRONFMAN, JR.

THE AVALANCHE THAT LED TO THE DOWNFALL OF THE BRONFMAN
dynasty was set off by the panic typical of the fevered financial atmosphere of the times. The totemic event came on January 10, 2000, with the
announcement of the merger of the Internet firm AOL with Time Warner,
an event which, in theory anyway, had no direct connection with the
Bronfman family. But, said one director, "It was perceived as changing the
landscape and terrified everyone remotely connected with the media in
whatever form; magazines, TV, movie studios, cable systems." For "convergence" between every aspect of the "content" and "distribution" sides of
the business had become an ultimate—and in the end appallingly costly—
buzzword. As Jo Johnson and Martine Orange put it in their excellent account of the saga that destroyed Seagram, "Levin shaved off his mustache
and removed his tie, [Steve] Case [of AOL] put on a suit. The message was
that the distinctions between the two worlds—the 'old' traditional media
represented by Time Warner and the new economy represented by AOL—
would soon disappear."[1] The orthodox view at the time, expressed by a major shareholder in Seagram was that "we are going to a world of vertically
integrated companies where only the big survive." Junior went one further:
"We're going to get eaten alive here," he told John Borgia, Seagram's head
of human resources. At least one Frenchman understood the meaning of
the deal. "Nothing will be the same again," said Jean-Marie Messier, CEO
of Vivendi, "AOL and Time Warner are the first to understand that the
new and the old economies must merge."

Indeed the fall of the House of Seagram was perhaps due as much to Gerald Levin as to the Bronfmans themselves. Back in 1994 he had rejected the chance to protect his group by allying himself with Seagram, and six years later he had thrown the whole media world into turmoil by Time Warner's merger with AOL, and in doing so engendered enormous losses for everyone, not least his own shareholders. In 1994 Levin had been afraid of the family's influence, five years later he was even more frightened by the apparently unstoppable rise of the grossly overvalued Internet companies, above all AOL. His fear was exacerbated by the ludicrous forecasts made by a handful of influential "analysts." I put the description in quotation marks for in reality, they were snake-oil salesmen who had lost sight of the figures and acted basically as front persons for the investment banks where they worked, eager to sell the stock involved and arrange any merger going. When he was presenting the case for merger Levin started the softening process by getting Mary Meeker of Morgan Stanley, queen of the tribe, to address his executives and warn them of the deluge to come. In both cases fear proved a bad counselor.

For the Bronfmans the general fear inspired by the merger was embodied in the Napoleonic[*] figure of Jean-Marie Messier of the French group Vivendi. Not surprisingly, it took someone very much out of the ordinary to ruin the House of Bronfman. Messier was a unique phenomenon, a one-off product of an elitist system itself unique in the world. As Johnson and Orange put it, "Without his vision and personality—a strange blend of French technocratic arrogance, wannabe Hollywood showmanship, and investment banker charm—Vivendi Universal would never have come into existence." Nevertheless I disagree with their belief that without his weaknesses it might have survived. For one thing his empire was based on the French market—a major disadvantage in an increasingly Anglophone world, for another it was bitty, with none of the basic strengths required—TV networks or major film studios. In the event even Messier had to march to a drumbeat set in the United States.

Messier belonged to the tiny elite that dominates France's political system. The vast majority of ministers and the, often more influential, senior bureaucrats are all graduates from ENA (the Ecole Nationale d'Administration) the most exclusive and influential of the handful of the country's

---

[*] Like Napoleon he was small, in his case only five feet seven inches tall.

Grandes Ecoles. These are all highly selective as opposed to France's universities, which are open to any qualified high school graduate. Messier was a provincial, the son of a chartered accountant in Grenoble in Southeastern France. A brilliant student, he was offered a place at the Ecole Centrale, an excellent school but not the best. At the second attempt he was admitted to the Polytechnique, founded by Napoleon as a school for engineers, but which had blossomed into a nursery for France's elite. He then soared even higher, as one of the fewer than a hundred French-born applicants admitted every year to the ENA, founded by General de Gaulle in 1945 to provide France's top administrators. This caste—the "Enarches"—remain supreme within the relatively sheltered public sector, but once they venture into the private sector, as they increasingly did in the 1980s and 1990s, they came across equally able graduates from other elite institutions like HEC,* the top commercial school and the misleadingly named engineering superschool Ecole des Mines; and even a handful of total outsiders who had never been to any of these institutions but who had some knowledge of the realities of industrial, commercial, and financial life. Unlike the Enarches these were executives who had often managed or built up major international companies.

At ENA the provincial, petit bourgeois Messier was socially and culturally insecure but compensated by his prominence in the classroom discussions that formed an important part of the curriculum. Indeed his interventions were too frequent for some of the professors. But he graduated sufficiently near the top of his class to become an *inspecteur des finances*, the even tinier group automatically admitted to the inner sanctums of the French administration. Messier was different, he was virtually the only Enarch to combine the intellectual superiority instilled by the school with the sort of megalomaniac attitude found in the other overly ambitious chief executives who played such a major role in the world's business scene in the late 1990s. He also, crucially, became a member of A3E, one of the small dining clubs that group France's elites.†

Messier was spotted and put to work devising the privatization program being implemented by France's center-right political parties to undo the nationalizations of the socialist government of President François Mitter-

---

* Hautes Etudes Commerciales.
† At this point Messier started to style himself J2M.

rand. Messier, still only thirty, soon saw that the program was run by the finance ministry under a future prime minister, Edouard Balladur. As one of his advisers Messier built up a network of leading businessmen who needed his help and thus gave him the contacts he later required when assembling his business empire at Vivendi. In 1988 the right, and with it Messier, was turned out of power. But by then his reputation was such that he received seventeen offers of employment. He chose Lazard Frères, the biggest player in the country's investment banking community. Messier worked incredibly hard on innumerable deals—he acquired the nickname of Robocop—and cemented his relationships with the heads of France's major businesses, men who as PDG ("President Directeur Général") exercised as much power as their American equivalents, the chairmen and chief executive officers of major corporations.

But Messier knew that he could never aspire to run Lazard, a family firm, and by 1994 was looking out for a top job. He found one in the unlikely form of Société Générale des Eaux. This was an unwieldy conglomerate founded in 1853 to provide French towns with water and sewerage networks. Over the years it had become a veritable business octopus in many towns and had accumulated a great deal of property, as well as a major stake in CanalPlus, France's major pay-TV network. But it was vulnerable: first because its long-term chief, Guy Dejounay, was aging and, inevitably, had been deeply involved in the municipal political corruption endemic in France, and which was increasingly under attack. Thanks to his contacts the thirty-seven-year-old Messier became Dejouany's successor in November 1994.

The only opposition came from Jacques Calvet, PDG of the Peugeot Citroën motor group, who spoke for the—often highly effective—men who ran France's major corporations and against the "Enarchs" who were encroaching so insidiously into the industrial and financial world. "How," he asked, "can anyone think of entrusting a group with two hundred thousand employees to someone who has never managed more than his own secretary?" As one of the Bronfman directors put it, "Messier was a deal maker, it was all he knew," and added, "How can you trust a man who wrote his autobiography before his fortieth birthday?" To an outsider commenting after the event it is not surprising that within a few years Messier, who had been the consummate rainmaker as a civil servant and investment banker, created a hurricane that destroyed him, crippled his group, and with it any hopes that the French might have of playing in the international media league. The only parallel in Europe—there were of course far more in the United States—is with Germany's Bertelsmann, run by Messier's friend Thomas Middlehoff who also entertained major international ambitions—though later he was dismissed and the group saved by the Bertelsmann family.

From the beginning of his reign Messier behaved totally unlike any other French company chief. He claimed that he was a visionary and that "it was necessary to give an image, ambition, enthusiasm . . . it is easier to represent such a vision through a man." His ego was such that, as Rupert Murdoch put it, Messier had "never met a journalist he didn't give an interview to"— Messier himself admits that he had encouraged a cult of personality. It helped that his inheritance was one of complete autocracy. Dejouany had been a dictator, hating meetings: "Three is a demonstration," he would say when more than two people entered his office. So it seemed perfectly logical for Messier to bring in what he called his "dream team" headed by another *inspecteur des finances*, Guillaume Hannezo, as finance director. Hannezo, disorganized, his shirt-tails everlastingly hanging out of his trousers, the very opposite of the traditional Enarch, was deeply loved by the staff for his "mad professor" image, but increasingly found himself totally unable to control his boss. Nevertheless Messier's first steps seemed orthodox enough, raising considerable sums from the sale of various businesses to reduce the debt load. But from the beginning Messier was insecure, insisting on a grandiose new head office and seizing any opportunity to assert his status.

Messier was clearly never going to be content with the group's core businesses. Nevertheless he first showed his willingness to pay over the odds in 1999 when he bought the leading American water supply business, US Filter, for $8 billion, and was forced to write off over half of the purchase price within three years. But from the first, if only by renaming the group as Vivendi, he was clearly intent on building up a major media group to challenge the American domination of the sector. The idea of a national champion capable of taking on the Americans was not by any means a novelty in French business. The best parallel is with Jean-Yves Haberer, the Enarch who had been chairman of Crédit Lyonnais, a publicly owned bank that had crashed spectacularly a few years earlier, one of whose major disasters was to back a former waiter, Giancarlo Parretti, in a disastrous bid for MGM. But Haberer had the excuse that he was acting under the orders of President Mitterrand who simply instructed him to build the biggest bank in Europe. He did, at a gigantic cost to the French taxpayer.

Messier started by some sensible steps: In pursuit of his first aim to be number two in the booming telecommunications business in France he did a deal with the SNCF, the state-owned French railway system, to lay fiber-optic cables beside the railway tracks. But Messier had to retreat from a highly promising sector, mobile phones, because he did not have the funds to invest in SFR, which owned Cegetel, the cell phone network the group had owned since the 1980s. He had to bring in new shareholders, including British Telecom and the German Mannesman group, which had undergone a spectacular transformation. Historically it was known as one of Germany's biggest engineering groups, but in the late 1990s it had built up a commanding position in the cell phone business in Germany. The introduction of new shareholders left him, as so often in the future, with a minority holding—in this case 44 percent, in strict refutation to the sensible, if vulgar, French saying, *être minoritaire c'est d'être con*, to be a minority is to be, shall we say, an arsehole. He was also the unhappy owner of a mere 24.5 percent stake in British Sky Broadcasting, the increasingly profitable satellite broadcaster controlled by Rupert Murdoch.

Messier could easily mop up Havas, a pillar of French-language advertising and publishing. Unfortunately CanalPlus, a key brick in the group's future—although at the time Vivendi owned only a minority stake of 49 percent—had weakened its prospects when its chairman, Pierre Lescure, had to overpay for a major rival NetHold, going into losses in the late 1990s. By then the Lex column in the *Financial Times* was warning that "Vivendi had switched from restructuring mode . . . to predator before proving that it can squeeze a good return from the core business. The group remains relatively unfocused and has issued a slew of new paper." By contrast Seagram's share price had trebled to over $80 during 1999, though the market then cooled dramatically enough for it to plunge below $40 in October before rising again on the hope of a merger. Moreover, the tide seemed to be turning in favor of the decision to swap DuPont for Universal in the media frenzy of the times when, as one commentator put it, "old-fashioned stocks like DuPont (and Caterpillar and Eastman Kodak) were losing out in a big way to any company offering a glimpse of a brighter new world."

It was Junior who set the ball rolling, for Messier, although interested in a deal, had assumed that "there was no reason to think that Edgar was looking for partners." But Junior had lost his nerve, even though the various parts of Universal were coming together. Unlike Rupert Murdoch and

Sumner Redstone of Viacom he was not prepared to ride out the storm in cyberspace, and not engage in deals motivated by fear. But there was one increasingly urgent reason for a deal. Seagram was now only in third place in the drinks business and its media business was entirely content-based, a major disadvantage at a time when the ideal was held to be a balance of content and distribution—an imbalance greatly increased by Junior's sale of control of Universal's television interests to Barry Diller. Junior had already been seduced by the belief that technology was going to revolutionize the world of media, a credo he had proclaimed to a Seagram conference the previous October.

After a first—secret—meeting between the two during a fashion week visit to Paris by Junior and Clarissa, Messier claims that Junior said, "Your strength and our strengths seem to go together," for Messier seems to have mesmerized him as Ovitz and Diller had done a few years earlier. By then Junior had apparently abandoned a more limited idea of a deal involving only CanalPlus. But, in the words of Alec Berger, an American-born corporate strategist working for CanalPlus, "When Edgar [Jr.] took it to the next level, all of a sudden it became a financial megamerger deal. It became more political than capitalistic."

At the same time Messier opened the way to a deal with Seagram when he abandoned his attempt to take over Mannesman, controller of such an important cell phone network in Germany, leaving the field open to Britain's Vodaphone. His reward came at the end of January with an agreement with the wily Sir Christopher Gent of Vodaphone to launch Vizzavi, Europe's biggest Internet start-up with a budget of over $1.5 billion, designed to compete with the likes of Yahoo! and Wanadoo. It was riskier than them because it would not be charging subscribers and would rely completely on advertising for its income. Nevertheless as a portal it covered the field, being suitable for wireless devices, personal computers, and interactive television. The announcement was greeted with a hysterical storm of approval, above all from the so-called analysts. Even *The New York Times*, which warned that "Vizzavi barely exists," felt that "the general concept behind Vizzavi is solid." There was only one important dissenter, Hans Snook, the visionary marketeer who created Orange, most successful of cell phone start-ups, who said bluntly, "It looks like a Yahoo! me-too. You can't win with a me-too product." And indeed Gent's motives remain obscure, for all his efforts were devoted to building up the world's largest cell phone company and Vizzavi was an expensive distraction. Perhaps he was hoping to involve Messier sufficiently so that he could lay his hands on Vivendi's key stake in Cegetel.

Such was the temper of the times that, even though Vizzavi would be entering a crowded field, the announcement had an electrifying effect on Vivendi's share price. The reaction to Vizzavi, which after all was only an idea behind a project, was a perfect example of the mood of unreality that had taken over at the time. By then "analysts" had forgotten all about assets, or profit and loss, they were selling dreams. When Messier complained in his book that the market had exaggerated its importance he was right—though at the time he did less than nothing to douse the analysts' enthusiasm. Within two months of the announcement the shares had jumped 130 percent to E141, six times their level when Messier had arrived, for analysts valued the Vizzavi project at a cool E40 billion (then around $40 billion). This of course provided Messier with the—grossly overvalued—currency he required to take over Seagram. And he needed to pay in shares because in doing so the Bronfmans would not be liable for any tax, always an overarching concern in the minds of the family.

The talks, basically between Messier and Junior, went on throughout the first months of 2000 and within a short time the participants were already concentrating on price, as if the principle of the deal was already decided. In public Junior was prefacing his speeches with false apologies that he would not be announcing Seagram's merger with—and would then name every likely and unlikely group in the media world. In fact Messier was the only real suitor; all the other possible buyers, like Rupert Murdoch, found Seagram too expensive and were afraid that the important music business would be permanently affected by illegal downloading from the Internet. On March 8 Junior lied to a meeting of executives from Universal when he declared to general applause that "the company is not for sale." The talks soon involved Brian Mulligan, Seagram's finance director, as well as both Hannezo and Pierre Lescure, the guiding genius behind CanalPlus. On Wednesday, March 22, 2000, after six months of preparations, and just as markets were topping out all over the world—and with them Vivendi shares, which had peaked at E141 on March 10—JMM and his team presented his ideas to eight members of the Bronfman family and their advisers from Morgan Stanley. Lescure gave Johnson and Orange a dramatic account of the presentation. "This was his big act. He was absolutely calm, clear, and convincing. He explained everything about the new economy . . . I had never heard him articulate his vision so convincingly. . . .

With his strong accent, but speaking fluent English, he was at his very best, smiling but not too much, and polite, telling the family how delighted he and his French team were to be received by them in New York."

The response was everything he could have asked for. According to Lescure, Junior was especially effusive: "He looked so satisfied, so happy, finally he had done something that looked like it was going to please all the different members of the family. . . . Jean-Marie," he gushed, "if you were a US citizen, I would tell you to run for president." But then Messier had been talking to a willing audience, none more so than Junior, with his disdain for the family liquor business. Messier had also probably underestimated the effects on the family of the decline in Seagram's reputation and its stock price in the last five years of the twentieth century after repeated rumors of abortive mergers, with such as Disney and News Corporation, resulting in a rise in the share price a mere quarter of that enjoyed by AOL Time Warner. Moreover the board had been softened up by a presentation emphasizing the necessity for convergence by its longtime investment bankers, Goldman Sachs, whose chairman John L. Weinberg and his son John S. Weinberg had been directors successively for over a generation. And as the bankers could have pointed out, by that time they had run out of alternative partners; as one insider put it, "Messier was the only horse willing to pay up for it [Seagram]."

Junior rationalized the decision to sell when he told Vicky Ward,[2] albeit after the disaster, that "we were going to sell Seagram at some point because my father has seven children and twenty-two grandchildren. And we don't have any special voting rights"—a frequent precaution against takeover in family-controlled companies that Mr. Sam had never bothered to introduce because the idea that Seagram would pass out of the hands of the family would never have occurred to him. As one analyst put it later, "I happen to think the Bronfmans are cashing out." The Seagram shares had fluctuated wildly between $26 and $64 over the previous eighteen months, and the final terms of the merger valued them at a 40 percent premium to the pre-bid price. The newly merged VU was valued by the market at a cool $100 billion, only a little below the AOL Time Warner figure of $113 billion. Edgar Jr. obviously welcomed the opportunity not to be the boss—"the toughest thing for Edgar," said his elder brother Sam, "is this whole sense of responsibility." By accepting what he had, naïvely, supposed would be a real job as number two in the merged firm, Edgar would be relieved of that burden and, crucially, would retain control of Universal's enormous music business, his real love.

Edgar Sr. agreed that it "was the best way to take care of the next generation." Even Charles Bronfman seemed satisfied, but then he was far less involved than he had been. The previous year he had garnered $400 million by selling 15.5 million shares, over a quarter of those he owned or controlled, allegedly for "estate planning reasons," thus reducing his stake in the family business from nearly 16 percent to under a tenth. As Lescure put it: "He did not comment. He did not say a word, but I had this feeling that even this little man with his narrow and suspicious eyes was more than a little impressed." Moreover, for reasons Messier would not have known about, both brothers were ready for a deal: They were looking for release from the chains that had bound them together for the previous forty years through their joint ownership of their stock, while they—and most obviously Charles—remained desperately anxious to avoid the arguments that had torn the previous generation. The get-out was perfect: Had they sold their third stake in the market it would have sent a totally negative signal, as well as being an obvious act of abdication. Then there were the terms: not only because of the price—which valued Seagram at an eye-opening $34 billion, as against $13 billion at the time of the DuPont sale. In theory anyway the new group, to be called Vivendi Universal, with no mention of Seagram, would join the other members of the Big Five, headed of course by AOL Time Warner, CBS Viacom, Walt Disney, and Rupert Murdoch's News Corporation.

Only two members of the family expressed regret, publicly anyway. From his quasi-exile in California, Sam said, "It's in our blood, it's where we came from." For Phyllis Lambert, who had already given 750,000 shares, the bulk of her holding, to the Canadian Centre for Architecture she had established in Montreal, the deal merely proved that Junior was as out of touch with the reality of everyday life as he had always been. But even to her—the least involved of the family—selling Seagram was like a death in the family. "I mourned all summer," she told a television interviewer, "I really mourned. I mourned to see something that was built and responsible and had a great sense of culture go up in thin air." They were joined by the veteran drinks commentator S. I. Stone.[3] He saw it as "one more nail in the coffin of family capitalism. Seagram has been nearly as synonymous with Bronfman as Ford has been with Ford. . . . Bronfman's position remained unique—as large as their empire grew, in an era when holding even 10 percent of a large company's stock ensured family control, the Bronfmans retained 24 percent of Seagram's voting stock." But there was one major difference between this deal and the one that had created AOL Time Warner a few months earlier. The Bronfmans—well, Edgar and Junior anyway—really believed that it would work whereas Steve Case, the chairman of AOL, had foreseen that AOL was grossly overvalued and that its share price would plummet within the foreseeable future without a merger.

But there was one major complication that further weakened the value of the combined group. The Bronfmans were not going to accept the deal while Vivendi owned only 49 percent of the major pay-TV channel, CanalPlus, a key outlet for Universal's films and TV series. So, while buying Seagram, Messier also had to pay the excessive price of $15 billion for the rest of CanalPlus. He had also to give Pierre Lescure the overlordship of all Vivendi Universal's media interests, in which he would have charge even of the Hollywood studios. This was ridiculous, and not only because Meyer and Snider were on a roll—in 2000, box office receipts on Universal's films had exceeded $1 billion for the first time. Yet Lescure's only real experience had been within the highly protected, highly subsidized French market, where CanalPlus had been responsible for the production of most of France's largely unexportable, mostly self-indulgent, films. In its only venture into Hollywood, CanalPlus had lost out badly through investing in Carolco, described by Orange and Johnson as a "mega-budget, spare-no-cost producer of so-called 'event films' . . . Carolco is blamed for ruining the economics of filmmaking in Hollywood." It duly filed for Chapter 11 bankruptcy proceedings in 1995. As Junior put it—too late—"Pierre is a wonderful guy, but he didn't know his ass from his elbow when it came to the US." Fortunately Lescure never interfered in the Hollywood business and Messier bought peace at Universal Studios by adding at least $50 million to the $40 million Junior had provided to retain key executives a few years earlier.

Messier had succeeded because he had taken full advantage of the rise in his shares. As one banker told Johnson and Orange in what could have served as a text for most of the deals struck at the time: "If you double the value of my currency, I don't mind overpaying . . . Messier was paying with shares that were fundamentally overvalued because of the hype surrounding Vizzavi. He had at least $20 billion of Vizzavi in his share price." For only overvalued currency could have matched the seemingly excessive demands being made by the Bronfmans. After more negotiations that lasted until the middle of June, Messier applied what was termed a "collar" to provide what turned out to be totally inadequate possible compensation for the sellers against any loss resulting from a substantial fall in the bidder's share price—such was the wildly manic temper of the times that neither partner in the AOL Time Warner deal had thought such a provision at all necessary. Nevertheless, in hindsight, many bankers were shocked that the deal did not provide for any really substantial fall in the share price—nor for the ability of Seagram to walk away from the deal if the share price collapsed. But clearly the family was desperate for the deal.

In terms of the value of Vivendi's shares at the time, Messier paid $35 billion for Seagram, of which around a third would go to the Bronfman family. He also took on $8 billion worth of debt, a total price justified only by Messier's wildly optimistic valuation of Seagram's assets. And, of course, the valuation depended on what the market thought of Vivendi's shares. By the end of June the shares had dropped by a fifth, triggering the "collar," which increased the allocation from 0.7 to 0.8 of a Vivendi share to the Seagram shareholders. This meant that each Seagram share was worth $77.35.

The deal marked the end of Seagram—for the merger was based on the assumption that Vivendi Universal would sell the liquor business for between $8 and $11 billion. The deal was badly received: "The industrial logic for combining Seagram and Vivendi is pretty spurious," sniffed *The Wall Street Journal.* "What Messier is doing is downright scary," wrote *Business-Week,* for he was "betting he can turn a hodgepodge of media assets into Internet gold. He has to do it fast." This did not worry Messier, who waved some fancy valuations for the group's assets, including a residual value of $20 billion for Universal Music, where, he predicted, world music sales would more than double within a few years thanks to the new distribution possibilities offered by the Internet. And his credo remained intact, claiming that only his group and AOL Time Warner were building the direct relationships with customers required in the new Internet age. Indeed his empire, with sales of $23 billion in its media business in 2000, would be only just smaller than Disney and much bigger than any other media group, AOL Time Warner with income of $36 billion of course excepted.

On the surface the Bronfmans had secured a number of safeguards. Messier would be chairman of the combined group, which would be headquartered in Paris, while Junior, who for five years had been chairman of two major businesses, had to be content with the vice chairmanship with an undefined role in the entertainment side of the group. The Bronfmans would have four other seats on the twenty-member board, one for Edgar Sr., one for Charles, and two for their representatives, providing that they retained 75 percent of the 7.7 percent stake owned by the family, and in return promised not to oust Messier or try a takeover. Unfortunately the board was even more dysfunctional than Seagram's had been and the language problem accentuated the atmosphere of mutual incomprehension among what was inevitably an ill-assorted bunch of directors. As McQueen points out, "Directors could use either English or French. Simultaneous translation was provided through headphones, but the translation was slow and sometimes inaccurate." Typically at a meeting before an AGM, "Messier spent thirty minutes explaining Vivendi's cash flow using a complicated chart. At the end of the presentation no one was any the wiser in either language."

Messier invariably referred to the deal as a takeover, although at the time Junior told *BusinessWeek* that it was "best characterized" as "a merger of near equals." To which the magazine added, "'How near?' is the question." But those who knew of his overwhelming passion for music noted that, in theory anyway, he would be in charge, not only of the Internet operations, but also of Universal Music. For, publicly at least, he was confident. It was always assumed, he said, that it was the third generation of an entrepreneurial business that is supposed to destroy it, yet "I'm assuring the future of the generations to follow." He even claimed that "there were two decision-makers at the company—Jean-Marie and myself." But Junior did not help the position when he remarked at one of the road shows promoting the merger that "the best thing about owning an entertainment company was selling it."

The deal was concluded at the worst possible time for Seagram. When Junior had bought the studio, it enjoyed a tenth of Hollywood revenues, a figure that had fallen to 4 percent in 1998 but had recovered very strongly once Meyer and Snider had hit form—remember that it takes two years for a movie to be approved, produced, and exhibited. In 2000 their box office revenues reached over $1 billion. By then Meyer had become profoundly cynical about Messier. "Did people really take Jean-Marie Messier seriously? No," he told an interviewer, "but we're a cynical town where numerous people come and go...it takes time to establish credibility in Hollywood."

There could be no pretense at cost-cutting in the combined group. Edgar, naturally proud of the way he had slimmed down both Universal and Polygram, continued to complain that Messier had never done the same—not realizing that he was simply uninterested in an activity as boring as management when there were deals out there to be done. To Messier the only hope for the future lay through those fashionable mantras, synergy and "convergence," combined with the magic being introduced through Vizzavi's all-singing all-dancing portal. Moreover the European and more especially the French market were heavily protected, and the merger offered a unique opportunity for Seagram's films, TV series, and music to gain access to these valuable viewers through the many "pipes" available—pay TV, mobile phone, and Internet portals. (That is if all the pipes proved viable.) Indeed some onlookers were ecstatic. One analyst identified VU and the British group Reuters—which joined the walking wounded during the first years of the millennium—as "long-term winners in the pan-European media industry."

Junior was soon disabused of the idea that he would be a genuine number two overseeing the Internet and music operations. Messier's condescension made it clear that, as he told *Fortune,* "I think Edgar feels better being number two than number one. . . . He is free to say anything, knowing he doesn't make the final decision." Junior soon realized his helplessness when Messier bought Barry Diller out of USA Networks for $3.2 billion, valuing the whole enterprise at an absurd $15 billion, four times the value when he had done his deal with Diller. As he told friends, "This is insanity. People are going to start thinking these are my decisions." But, as McQueen points out, and like his uncle Charles, he was "congenitally unable to have a confrontation . . . the best he could muster were mild rebukes that Messier did not take seriously." Messier's perception of his supremacy—and his arrogance—was symbolized by his attempt to remove a Mark Rothko painting, *Brown and Black in Reds,* a star item in the art collection so painstakingly assembled by Phyllis Lambert, from the Seagram building to his apartment on Park Avenue. When the Bronfmans protested he simply moved it to his office.

But by the second half of the year the tide was turning against the whole media sector and with it the previously fashionable EBITDA measure always favored by Junior when calculating profits. This had favored Vivendi, able to consolidate the whole profits from Cegetel while owning only 44 percent of the shares. The whole structure was badly designed to appeal to investors, especially Anglo-Saxons used to coherent businesses. By contrast the new VU was a rambling combination of wholly and partially owned companies and numerous minority shareholdings, a structure familiar in continental Europe but unknown in Britain or the United States, where the discount normally applied to conglomerates would be increased because of the messy structure. Not surprisingly, by July 13 the Lex column was describing the merger as without doubt "the most heroic act of value destruction this year." Terry Smith, a particularly dyspeptic British commentator, criticized Bronfman for his "almost comical" focus on EBITDA, as if the interest burden he had taken on while building Seagram from a drinks company into a media business was somehow unfair. As he pointed out, Seagram's profits to March 31, 2000, valued by EBITDA at $285 million, were reduced to a $1 million loss at operating level by a more orthodox profit measurement. Moreover this was before allowing a further $278 million for interest charges. By the end of the year a commentator on *Les Echos*, a French financial daily, was wondering whether Messier would follow the same disastrous path as Haberer had done with Crédit Lyonnais a decade earlier, while Ron Meyer had let the cat out of the bag by saying that the—as yet totally unproved—Vizzavi "is clearly the future of the business whether it works or not."

Within the group the idea of synergies so energetically promoted by Messier seemed at best vague, at worst nonexistent—the Boston Consulting Group estimated them at a few million dollars, way way below the promised $220 million. It did not help that as in other dictatorships the organization was chaotic. As the head of Vivendi Environnement, the long-forgotten rump of the group Messier had inherited only a few years earlier, put it, "No one was interested in cooperation, so we talked only about acquisitions." Messier made matters worse by boasting at the end of the year that VU had "zero debt, we are rich." In fact VU was lumbered with a burden of over $25 billion, nearly four times the level at the end of 1998 before Messier's acquisition binge had gotten under way. And as a result within eighteen months the whole group charged ahead with reckless abandon into near-disaster. Nevertheless to the ordinary Frenchman the deal seemed more and more like a French takeover, a symbol of Messier's claim to be the supreme representative of France triumphant—*La France qui gagne*.

Eighteen

THE END OF "L'AFFAIRE"

I've got the unpleasant feeling of being in a car whose driver is
accelerating in the turns and that I'm in the death seat.
—NOTE SENT TO JMM BY GUILLAUME HANNEZO AT THE END OF 2001

IT SCARCELY NEEDS REPEATING THAT THE FIRST YEARS OF THE
twenty-first century marked the end of virtually all the dreams connected with the media business, above all where the new electronic media
were concerned. Nevertheless the disaster that overcame VU accounted
for a sizeable proportion of the $240 billion estimated losses by major me-
dia groups between 1998 and 2001. Yet in this debacle Messier and the
Bronfmans were merely one of a whole tribe of sufferers. The Bronfmans
are reckoned to have lost $3 billion, probably the largest loss ever sustained
by a single family. Even so, the Bronfmans lost less than had Ted Turner
from the problems at AOL Time Warner, for most of the $9 billion he re-
ceived when he sold CNN to Time Warner had continued to be tied up in
the group's stock. He lost at least $5 billion. In fact, proportionately, the
Vivendi disaster was not substantially worse than that endured by shareholders in other companies that had led the charge during the late 1990s.
Vivendi's shares dropped 84 percent and those of AOL Time Warner 78
percent in the three years after their mergers were first announced. Moreover Messier was only one of the many CEOs who were evicted during
2002, a year in which the "old media" represented by Time Warner—and
Universal for that matter—triumphed over the electronic upstarts. But
Messier was the only major European victim, much bigger than Thomas
Middlehoff, who had tried to transform the German group Bertelsmann
into a major media player but was stopped by the controlling family before

too much damage had been done. Messier's downfall was also unique because it exposed a fundamental divide at the summit of the French power elite.

After the Seagram deal Messier's megalomania, never very far below the surface, took over completely at a time when the other hungry beasts in the media jungle were sated with their acquisitions. His previous explanations that deals provided "convergence" or "synergy" grew ever less credible, they were simply labels attached to purchases that caught Messier's ever more whimsical fancy. The former J2M had blossomed into J6M (Jean-Marie Messier, *Moi-Même Maître du Monde*—"Me Myself Master of the Universe"*). For the two deals, Seagram and CanalPlus, had totally unhinged him. As one banker close to him put it, "He stopped listening after Seagram." His belief that he was not merely *a*, but *the* only Master of the Universe led him to systematic trickery later exposed by the SEC—whose condemnations related purely to his activities in 2001 and the first half of 2002. Messier was so confident that he had refused an offer of E30 billion by RWE, a powerful German utility group, for the "old" businesses in water supply and other muncipal services, now known as Vivendi Environnement, final proof when the story leaked out that he was interested in size rather than profits.

His ambition, he declared, was that VU should become "the world's preferred creator and provider of personalized information and entertainment and services to consumers anywhere, at any time, and across all distribution platforms and devices." His ideas were truly global. "We will neither be apostles of US cultural domination, nor of *l'exception francaise*," he declared. But by now his values were clearly American—he even revealed his pay—a mere $3 million—and the bonus attached to it, a decidely un-French attitude. The already problematic financial situation worsened when it emerged that CanalPlus, besides losing over $600 million a year, had brought with it a number of off-balance sheet commitments, to everyone from a film studio to the organizers of Formula 1 motor racing. It was the media commentator Michael Wolff who best summed up the transformation from an ENA nerd to Master of the Universe in a now-famous description. Walking with his son, who remarked, "Look at that guy!" Wolff saw:

---

* He took the name from the name of the puppet representing him in the French satirical program *Les Guignols*.

languorously moving up Madison Avenue, a small man with a coat cast cape-like over his shoulders and the most pleased-with-himself expression I believe I have ever seen on an adult, whom I recognized to be Jean-Marie Messier (I doubt if anyone else recognized him). He occupied a wide swathe of the sidewalk, with a strut to the left and then a strut to the right, nodding and smiling, or rather bestowing blessings on passers-by (who gave him wide and incredulous berth). He seemed to see himself as some combination of religious figure and maestro—his idea, I suppose, of an American mogul.[1]

Like his transatlantic equivalents but notably unlike even the most autocratic of his French brethren, Messier was spending the company's money on a truly Hearstian scale. The biggest expenditure was on an apartment on Park Avenue, so convenient for the office he said, the cost of which exceeded its $17.5 million "budget" by $1 million, an expenditure naturally concealed from everyone else. Messier defended the outlay, claiming that it was "simply a reflection of my double professional life, in Paris and New York," and that in any case the purchase was initiated by Junior. More relevantly he points out that the sale of many of what one could call the "imperial adjuncts" to the Bronfman regime—three planes, the London townhouse, a helicopter, and a "training center" in Virginia—fetched five times as much as the cost of housing him.

By the end of 2000 Vivendi's shares had dropped by a third, reducing the value of the bid to $57, against the $77 at the time of the offer—a fall that did not deter Messier. Moreover the first symptoms were appearing of the disease that was to topple him eighteen months later. *The Economist* later summed up JMM's downfall as the result of the way he "repeatedly concealed from the board, and his managers, the complicated and precarious deals and transactions he was carrying out, not to mention the company's debt position, which ultimately brought Vivendi to the edge of collapse." The SEC later alleged that December 2000 marked the start of his fraudulent activities. In fact it was JMM's attempt to live up to a boast he made after the merger that the company "would generate annual EBITDA growth in 2001 and 2002" that started the rot, forcing him into a downward spiral of exaggerations and downright lies—a classic case being the, largely false, quarterly profits announcements in July and October 2001 that cheered up Vivendi's share price.

The first sign of the "Messier disease" came in January 2001 with the purchase of a major stake in Maroc Télécom, the monopoly telephone op-erator in Morocco. He had made the first investment in 1999 but didn't tell anyone about the second, and much bigger, stake, even Junior, who was naturally furious—and his anger would have grown if he had known that JMM had made a commitment to supply E1.1 billion additional capital. In the course of 2001 the situation grew worse, with investments like the $1.2 billion he poured into Elektrim (Telco), the Polish equivalent of VU's Mo-roccan investment. Almost every week came a new initiative—including Houghton Mifflin, last of the great Boston-based publishing firms, bought for $2.2 billion. For, suddenly, the publisher's educational books were going to be a major plank in the new Vivendi. He also continued with his unfor-tunate habits by paying $1.5 billion for a mere 10 percent stake in Echostar, the American satellite television company. Indeed, during a year when other groups, however ambitious, had stopped buying he averaged a deal a month. By 2001, as the media/telecoms/dot.com bubbles were burst-ing all around him, "Messier was the last big spender in cyberspace," as Johnson and Orange put it.

But his biggest commitment, which came just after Junior's resignation, was to pay nearly $12 billion to buy the majority stake in Barry Diller's USA Networks. Diller, who had been unable to achieve either of his two aims, to control a studio or a TV network, because he was not prepared to overbid, was clearly cashing in his chips. As Michael Wolff put it,[2] his cau-tion "made Diller, in an age of excess, seem like the last prudent man." The "prudent man"—who had vowed never to work for anyone again—ended up as chairman and chief executive of Vivendi Universal Entertainment, without a salary but with 1.5 percent of the stock, with the right to sell it back for a minimum of $275 million. Moreover Diller retained USI with its valuable, if mundane businesses like Ticketmaster and the Home Shop-ping Network. At this point Meyer and Snider revolted and negotiated pay increases of over $10 million apiece. For Hollywood could never take Messier seriously. Indeed some of his attempts to fit in were rather pathetic—he even learned a few words of Yiddish, trying, for instance, to distinguish between *kibbutz* and *kibitz*.

If Vivendi's financial position had not weakened after 9/11 he would have bid for the major French holiday group, Club Med. The next month came a more specific blow when the first bad news from Enron put the spotlight on any ambitious, heavily indebted group run by a high-profile, autocratic chairman. Junior immediately spotted that it represented a global shift, with boards having to take increasing responsibility. His reaction came the following month when he told Messier that he was resigning his operational role as chairman of the music division. This was not unexpected: Messier had systematically sidelined Junior and at executive board meetings would call upon him to discuss music when there were only five minutes left. Messier's reaction was that of the classic betrayed Jewish entrepreneur wailing, "How can you do this to me?" In fact he cried and said that "I take this as a personal failure." In public, however, the decision was glossed over, although, as Johnson and Orange put it, "The fulsome mutual praise" involved in the announcement "confirmed many people's suspicions that all was not well at Vivendi Universal." By then JMM had spent $50 billion and the shares were starting to suffer from a "Messier discount."

By May 2001 most of the Bronfman family had taken advantage of the end of a ninety-day lockout period to get rid of their shares. Phyllis was one of the first to sell and Flora, Saidye's still-sparky nonagenarian sister, was easily persuaded that her idiot great-nephew had sold the family business to a loser. For their part the Edgar side of the family sold over $1 billion worth of Vivendi stock—covering their actions with Edgar's assertion that "Vivendi Universal has got off to a very fast and successful start." But Charles, always indecisive and everlastingly obsessed with potential tax bills, waited and eventually sold much of his stake at near the low point of $12 a share. This confirmed the wry remark by the investment banker Herbert Allen, Jr., that, "I've seen more money lost by people trying to avoid taxes than any other single issue." Junior's reaction was brutal, that "one of the things that appear to be difficult for the Charles side of the family to do is to accept responsiblity for its own decisions. They should have sold all their positions for $65 or $70 a share." The family still owned 52.5 million shares as late as September 2002, worth $630 million, and representing 6.1 percent of the total after selling $2.25 billion worth, and remained Vivendi's largest shareholders.

But the Bronfmans' anxiety to sell put pressure on Messier's desire to maintain the share price through regular share buybacks. He was forced to buy 1.6 percent of the company from the family for $1.3 billion. Not surprisingly these purchases—which amounted to $11 billion over two years and amounted to nearly 10 percent of the company's total capital—were never presented to the board, a major failure that was to lead to trouble after he was deposed, for the purchases greatly added to Vivendi's already considerable indebtedness. The pace increased after the Enron debacle, for, as Johnson and Orange point out, Vivendi had all the hallmarks of a future victim: It was "large, complex, acquisitive, and audited by Arthur Andersen," the major auditing firm driven into oblivion by the Enron disaster.

Cash was becoming tighter than ever with hopes of reducing the debt burden resting on a speedy sale of the historic Seagram liquor business. It could have been sold in the summer of 2000, immediately after the takeover, for Donard Gaynor had assembled a powerful group of investors with the blessing of the Bronfman family, although Charles, who still says, "I'd love to still be in the liquor business," became increasingly detached as the VU share price fell, taking with it millions of his dollars, and withdrew from the syndicate Gaynor had assembled. He and the other senior executives involved were backed by Lehman Brothers as well as two of Seagram's major partners, Vin & Spirit and Kirin, the brewers who were still their partners in Japan. The group bid a healthy $8.2 billion, but were repulsed by Morgan Stanley, the bank acting for VU. At first Morgan Stanley simply did not believe that the bid was serious, and when it was firmed up they disliked the idea of losing face, and in any case had told the VU board that the business was worth at least $9 billion. There was a subtext, that perhaps they hoped to divide the business and ensure its sale to two of the major international drinks companies interested in Seagram, who might well provide banking business in the future.

It did not help that the bankers seemed to know very little about the drinks business and above all did not understand that if Seagram were divided up the world distribution rights for at least three major brands—Absolut, Mumm, and Perrier-Jouet*—would be up for grabs, thus greatly reducing the value of the business. To make matters worse they seem to have assumed that Vin & Spirit would have had nowhere else to go, even though every liquor group in the world was queuing up for the opportunity to take on such a star brand as Absolut. The bankers were probably supported by Junior, afraid that any new management would certainly have showed him up by performing more effectively than he himself had done. Selling the historic heart of the family business to a number of groups prevented any direct comparison with his own management record. The result was that the business was—eventually—sold at below the estimated value of between $8 and $11 billion. A joint bid by Diageo and the French

---

* Seagram had retained world distribution rights following the sale of the two champagne brands.

Penod Ricard group brought in a mere $7.7 billion after tax. Inevitably, because the purchasers already possessed such strong positions in the international liquor business, the sales were delayed for nearly a year until December 2001 by antitrust and monopoly authorities on both sides of the Atlantic. The delay obviously reduced Vivendi's projected cash flow.

Messier's growing problems were not only financial, for he ended the year with a gaffe that turned the whole French cultural establishment against him. In response to a question at the press conference he had called to announce the deal with Diller, Messier claimed that "as we all know and as we all understand, the Franco-French *exception culturelle* is dead." By now Messier was so out of touch with his native country that he simply did not understand the waves the remark would cause, nor the gulf it exposed between the two cultures, French and American, he was hoping to bridge. The immensely powerful French cultural establishment was immediately up in arms, and not only for intellectual reasons, since CanalPlus still financed over two-thirds of French films and Lescure was an "untouchable," a key figure in the establishment. It did not help that Messier was right, the "exception" was a philosophical front behind which the French cultural elite could finance a mass of usually self-indulgent and unappealing films. But by the time that the attack had gained momentum Messier had abandoned Paris for Park Avenue in more senses than one.

By 2002 VU was clearly on the slide, for its debt, which had been a mere E3 billion at the start of 2000, had risen to over E21 billion and Messier was living in what Ronald Reagan once memorably called "la la land." Yet in early 2002 he still seemed a heroic figure in the eyes of the world's business leaders. Indeed he was acclaimed at the World Economic Forum in New York* when he staged a concert featuring artists from Universal Music as eminent as Bono and Peter Gabriel. In January 2002 *Fortune* magazine summed up Messier's plight in a sardonic note. "Facing increasing criticism from his countrymen for his profligate lifestyle and abandonment of traditional French culture, Vivendi Universal CEO Jean-Marie Messier decided in January to pose for a series of photographs in *Paris-Match* in which he rode on his corporate jet, took skating lessons in Central Park, and relaxed in his New York City office in front of the Mark Rothko painting." The

---

* It is normally held at the Swiss ski resort of Davos but moved to New York as a gesture of solidarity after 9/11.

photo opportunity involved was part of a media campaign, badly needed after a bungled share placement had set the share price plummeting. The credit rating agencies had already put the group under surveillance "with a negative outlook" but Messier was saved by the greed of the group's investment bankers, Deutsche Bank and Goldman Sachs, both obviously hoping for further business. This led them to take up a tranche of fifty-five million shares and attempt to place them on the market. They couldn't, not without taking joint losses of over $650 million* and leaving the market with a considerable overhang of sell orders. The placement had raised $3.3 billion but shares valued at $73 the previous year were being sold at below $60. At the same time, as luck would have it, AOL Time Warner then issued a profit warning.

By this time the group's head office was spending over $300 million a year—over $1 million a head—what with chartered jets, flights on Concorde, and consultants. Unfortunately Hannezo's finance department remained grossly undermanned, totally incapable of satisfying the increasingly complex financial reporting requirements of both French and American authorities. Hannezo's deputy was heard to remark that "anything less than $500 million doesn't interest me." But it was the announcement of the group's results for 2001 that set in motion Messier's departure. Until then, as Messier points out in his book, the shares had done as well—or rather less badly—than the other overhyped media stocks. It did not help that publication had been preceded by a row between Consob, the French bourse's newly active regulatory authority and two of the partners of the small French firm that was VU's joint auditor with Arthur Andersen.

The results presented to the directors on March 5 were so bad that the meeting can be seen as a turning point in Messier's fortunes. After writing off $16 billion goodwill from overpriced acquisitions VU announced a loss of $13.6 billion, the biggest ever by a French company, surpassing even the record set by Crédit Lyonnais in the early 1990s—though a mere bagatelle compared with the $54 billion AOL Time Warner had written off earlier in the year. Although Messier had assured the directors that the group was free of debt, in fact the total amounted to $29 billion—a figure increased by $8 billion a few months later after Messier's departure had led to a gen-

---

* The real figure emerged only later that year after Messier's departure.

eral spring cleaning of the accounts. It did not help that the figures were largely impenetrable. As always the tetchy London analyst Terry Smith provided the sharpest comment: "We could get enough from the published numbers, even if they were incomprehensible, to know that they were pissing money against the wall." As the SEC later alleged, "The earnings release was materially misleading," the position was worse than Vivendi had stated "because of its inability to access the earnings and cash flow of two of its most profitable subsidiaries, Cegetel and Maroc Télécom." These "substantially impaired Vivendi's ability to satisfy" the debts and other obligations resulting from its many acquisitions . . . Vivendi borrowed against credit facilities to pay the dividend"—it had also used Cegetel as a cash cow, much to the fury of the other shareholders.

A management get-together at the northern French seaside resort of Deauville a fortnight later did not help—one senior executive, Michael Jackson, reflected the general mood when he said that people came away "unfortunately feeling worse about the organization they work for, that it was chaotic." Barry Diller rallied to Messier's support, rebuking the management for their obsession with the price of the stock, but this merely echoed the old Hollywood saying that "no one needs an enemy who has [someone like Diller] for a friend."

The first to spot the discrepancies had been Sam Minzberg,* the lawyer who was representing Charles's interests and who had been on the board of Seagram as well as being president of Claridge Inc, which managed both Charles's personal fortune and his charitable activities. In his book Messier reserves a special hatred for Minzberg as one of the two major conspirators who, together with Claude Bébéar, plotted his downfall. By this time Minzberg was not taking Messier altogether seriously, signing his own memos as S1M mocking Messier's JM6. As he says, "By then I could see that the emperor had no clothes, although everyone else thought that he was wearing Armani." At first Junior had not taken much notice of Minzberg's criticisms, but after the March board meeting his attitude changed—although he did not play nearly as important a role in Messier's downfall as the American press claimed later that year. As Junior said, Minzberg "just did his homework. He went through the figures and said

---

* He was a partner in the firm that had been advising the family for three generations, which had merged with a Toronto firm to form Davies, Ward, Phillips & Vineberg.

what Messier said just wasn't true. I paid very little attention to it at the beginning and suddenly realized: Oh my God, we've got to get this guy out. He lied to me, he lied to everybody, and that's putting it charitably. But his lies were invariably ones of omission. He would tell you something that was technically the truth, but would leave a misleading impression"— Junior frequently used the term "Clintonesque." Nevertheless as Minzberg told McQueen, Junior, while "not a fool, believe me . . . was more of a gentleman than I am."

But Minzberg continued to feel isolated and as time went on naturally grew increasingly agitated—"It's painful swimming against the tide," he told me, "and sometimes one loses control." He obviously upset the French, used to frigid formality at board meetings, and Edgar Sr., still not convinced of Messier's guilt and not really involved in the business, merely pretended that Minzberg was some wild boar out of control. His attitude was obviously influenced by the fact that Minzberg was his brother's representative, not his. (Later he apologized to Minzberg for his earlier doubts.) But Messier did not help himself by blaming the groups' troubles largely on CanalPlus, trying to divide and rule by separating Lescure and his deputy Denis Olivennes. They were furious, and were further enraged by JMM's demand—first expressed in a newspaper interview and not to them directly—that CanalPlus eliminate its losses within two years. In fact this was not unreasonable given the size of the chain's debts—over $5 billion— and losses of $700 million a year. But the demand triggered an e-mail from Lescure and Olivennes to the employees complaining of Messier's "Stalinist" management techniques. Olivennes resigned and Lescure was sacked after refusing to be pushed upstairs to an honorary position, a step that led to a headline "Canal Putsch," a strike by the whole of CanalPlus's staff, and a not unreasonable revolt against Messier as a symbol of irresponsible international capitalism.

The Anglo-Saxons were not alone in smelling problems. In late March analysts at Crédit Lyonnais sent out a long, hard-hitting research report entitled "The End of an Exception" and suggested that Messier could, indeed should, be fired, a note that resonated right through the markets.[*] But the board was divided, not only by nationality. The Bronfmans were in a

---

[*] Messier tried to blacken the name of one of the analysts involved, Edouard Tétreau. Messier claimed that Tétreau had once been fired for getting drunk and peeing into his boss's fridge. But Tétreau's boss, Jean Peyrelevade, simply and literally told Messier to go fuck himself.

different situation from the French non-executive directors. "They didn't have a financial interest," says one director, "with the Bronfmans their own money and credit was involved." Nevertheless three of the French directors announced their intention to resign, influenced by new legislation broadening directors' responsibilities. They included the honorary chairman of the major French bank BNP and, rather later, Bernard Arnault, the chairman of LVMH-Moët Hennessy and an old friend of Messier's, who did not sit on any other board as a non-executive. "The others jumped ship," says one insider, "but Arnault ducked the decision by simply not turning up to board meetings." This allowed Messier to use his proxy until he was persuaded otherwise by a nasty letter from the Bronfman camp. Messier's efforts to recruit suitably high-profile replacements were notably unsuccessful. The most vehement refusenik was Michel Pébéreau, chairman of France's biggest bank, BNP Paribas, and a major lender to Vivendi. Yet in his book Messier claims that the bankers "soon realized that apart from short-term difficulties, Vivendi Universal's situation was healthy and its shares quality ones." In reality Messier's only banker supporter was Marc Viénot, the septuagenarian former chairman of another major bank, Société Générale, and, crucially, chairman of Vivendi's audit committee.

Many commentators have complained of the length of time it took to get rid of Messier following the revelation of the results for 2001, though in fact it took only three months, not an unreasonable time given Messier's apparently impregnable position. The allegedly drawn-out process was attributed to a culture clash between the French and American directors—Junior went so far as to allege that anti-Semitism was a factor in the "delay." The Bronfmans believed, wrongly, that the French assumed that their opposition to Messier was based on a desire to seize control. In fact the French were simply determined to find a French solution to ensure that assets deemed vital to the country did not end up under foreign control. Nevertheless the French non-executives, as close to Messier and as loyal as their equivalents at Seagram had been to the Bronfmans, protected the interests of VU's shareholders far more effectively than their Canadian and American counterparts had done. For their part the Americans fully realized that they needed a French champion, and one, moreover, who had credibility with the French business establishment. But without any prompting from anyone a volunteer appeared, Claude Bébéar, and by the end of May Minzberg was proposing that he take on the chairmanship—"I tried hard to get the French on board," he says. Bébéar refused the poisoned chalice but nevertheless played the crucial role in Messier's downfall, as much by the credibility he brought to the opposition as any direct action on his part.

Throughout his life Bébéar had been a major exception to many of the rules governing French business, in fact he was rather like a highly effective "good ole' boy," an avid hunter and a sports fanatic—albeit with a very un-midwestern love of wine and the finer things of life. He had studied at the Polytechnique, but had graduated in a lowly position thanks to an over-active social life and his love of sport, above all rugby football. He then went off to Rouen, a small city in Normandy, to join an obscure insurance company run by a friend of his father's. It was as if a graduate of Harvard Law School had gone off to practice in Peoria. But Bébéar was ambitious and, unlike other graduates from a "Grande Ecole," realized the necessity of acquiring a professional qualification—in this case that of an actuary—to do his job properly. By 1975 he had become chairman of the company, which he renamed Axa. His first major triumph came in 1991 when he took over the loss-making Equitable Life, the fifth-largest American life in-surer, which he restored to profitability. Some years later when I asked him how he'd done it he replied simply, "We looked more carefully at the fig-ures than anyone else." By the mid-1990s Axa was a world group, with a major presence in Britain as well as the United States, and dominated the French market thanks to the takeover of UAP, formerly France's largest life insurer. After retiring—nominally at least—in 2000, Bébéar had time on his hands and was, perhaps, a little bored. By early 2002 he was becoming worried about any repercussions in France of the ever-growing shadows over American media groups, inevitably inviting comparison with Vivendi. This was intolerable for someone who had proved so triumphantly that French business could conquer the American market. Moreover Bébéar had been suspicious of Messier since 1994 when Messier had promised to join a company associated with Axa, but had joined what became Vivendi without telling him.

Bébéar's worldwide success proves the absurdity of the charge that JMM's downfall was the result of a narrow-minded, "Franco-francais" con-spiracy, an accusation widely made in the American press. Messier's fury against him was uncontstrained. In a classic case of pot-kettle he says, "When speaking of megalomaniacs, M. Bébéar is not far from the throne," claiming that his rancor dated back to Messier's days working with Edouard Balladur and at Lazards. Bébéar's intervention was triggered by a trip he and a group of friends had taken to Edinburgh on March 23 to watch an international rugby match between France and Scotland. They used one of Vivendi's private jets, an Airbus A319, which had been fitted up in suitably regal style, complete with a bedroom at the back. All the passengers—apart from Jean-Pierre Rives, a retired hero of French rugby—were major businessmen in their own right, but never dreamed of having a private plane; it was simply not "the done thing" in ordinary French business circles, where the bosses were content with power and had no need for the trappings favored by their—probably less psychologically secure—American equivalents. They naturally agreed that the aircraft was a sign that Messier was behaving as if he owned the company and had lost any sense of reality. Messier made matters worse when he denied that Vivendi owned the plane, and that it was merely leased to the group when required. In fact it belonged to a subsidiary.

Within three weeks Bébéar had gone public—in a way typical of a French insider. During the interval of a performance of *The Barber of Seville* at the Bastille Opera House he told Henri Lachmann, chairman of a major electrical manufacturing group and a fellow rugby enthusiast, "Henri, the situation is becoming dangerous. As a board member it's your responsibility. If you don't do something, it's the whole Paris stock market that's going to suffer." Within twenty-four hours the whole French financial world had heard and understood the message: that Bébéar had entered the ring against Messier. And he had plenty of allies. Lachmann, as well as two other directors, Bernard Arnault and Jacques Friedmann, were members of an exclusive dining club, Entreprise et Cité, founded by Bébéar and his friends, mostly industrialists whose businesses had flourished in the international arena.

By then the press was thoroughly enjoying what were clearly going to be Messier's death throes. The most accurate articles were by Jo Johnson in the London *Financial Times,* and Martine Orange in *Le Monde,* France's most respected newspaper. The idea of honest journalism is rare in France so, not surprisingly, Messier was convinced that it was all a plot, that the Bronfmans were behind the *FT*'s attacks and that Lescure was behind *Le Monde*'s comments. Worse, he still assumed that VU's financial problems were merely seasonal, transitory. In return Messier enlisted the influential right-wing daily *Le Figaro* to defend his corner. But he went even further by accusing Minzberg of telling the *FT* that he wanted to get rid of Messier.

At that point Minzberg blew his stack. "By then I had become convinced that Messier was a liar," he told me.

By contrast the French political establishment—in the middle of a presidential election campaign—was terrified that were Vivendi Environnement to be taken over by a foreign company the details of its long involvement in municipal corruption through its water supply contracts in most of France's major cities might be revealed. Messier, at his best in adversity, went to see Bébéar in his office, famous for its luxury—and its collection of hunting rifles. Bébéar refused outright Messier's offer of a seat on the board, and listened coldly to his explanation that he had been introverted since the age of twenty and was living out his adolescence, replying simply that "it was a bit late to live out such a crisis while at the helm of a major group." Bébéar—not for nothing was this leathery figure known as "the old crocodile"—told him bluntly that no one had any confidence in him anymore. Nevertheless Messier later claimed that Bébéar had supported his strategy.

The next act in the drama, Vivendi's Annual General Meeting, came a week later, on April 24. It had been preceded by a board meeting and lunch where awkward questions were asked for the first time. Most importantly Arnault and Minzberg queried whether Vivendi could afford the cost of $1 billion of the dividend Messier was proposing. But at the AGM Messier was at his persuasive best, cajoling the seven thousand shareholders, tempting them with the dividend, and ignoring the fact that the stock price had fallen from E61.50 to E38.20 in the first four months of the year. He was backed by Viénot who affirmed, in answer to the only serious question asked at the meeting, that, in his opinion, Messier's "strategic choices have the unanimous backing of the board"—a statement in direct contradiction to the opinions expressed by Junior and Minzberg at the board meeting earlier that day. Nevertheless the meeting delivered a major blow—and one that was virtually unprecedented in French business history—by rejecting Messier's proposal to grant over E2 billion worth of stock options to the group's executives. Worse, it soon became clear that three major banks, BNP Paribas, Société Générale, and Crédit Agricole, had all abstained. The next day Messier had breakfast with Arnault and Albert Frère, an influential Belgian financier. They told him, in effect, to cool it and to stay in Paris. "The house is burning. Don't go back to New York. Stay in Paris, this is where things are happening."

The next couple of months were filled with maneuverings. The share price and Vivendi's credit rating were remorselessly sliding—by May the shares had fallen to a mere fifth of the March 2000 level and the debt rated at only just above junk status. By then Messier had acquired a new nickname, JPLM—*juste pour le moment* (just for the moment), and Bébéar had come out into the open. In a radio interview he had declared that Vivendi had "a strategy and a decision problem." But that did not help: When he tried to persuade the French board members to oppose Messier they took fright at their new legal responsibilities and preferred to resign. Messier survived a stormy board meeting in New York partly because Minzberg became too persistent and aggressive in his questioning. He simply did not understand the veil of courtesy that invariably exists within a French board meeting where the prevailing motto is *Cher ami, cela ne se dit pas*—roughly equivalent to "my dear fellow, one simply does not say things like that." Simon Murray, the one director who was neither French nor part of the Bronfman contingent, was particularly offended. He is best known for *Legionnaire*, his best-selling book about the five years he had served in the French Foreign Legion. More relevantly he had gone on to gain an MBA from Stanford. Subsequently, in the course of a varied and distinguished business career, mostly in Hong Kong, he had co-founded a major mobile telephone business in the Far East. So he had been a logical candidate for the board in Messier's earlier, saner days.

But all the time Vivendi was in increasingly urgent need of cash injections. Thanks to support from Deutsche Bank—and in direct contradiction to what they had said the previous month—Messier and Hannezo were able to use a stake in Vivendi Environnement to raise enough cash to survive. But time was running out. By lunchtime on June 24 the share price was down to E18, below the E23 level at which they had stood when Messier had taken over seven and a half years earlier. The next day Arnault finally resigned, persuaded by his advisers that remaining on the board would expose him to possible legal action. Junior promptly asked Messier to resign and repeated his demand at a breakfast the next day. At the board meeting on June 25 the directors were faced with an analysis of the group's financial situation presented by Goldman Sachs. In the absence of a major bond issue, clearly impossible given Vivendi's lowly credit rating, the group would have to file for bankruptcy within three months. Goldman was not alone—Citigroup had prepared an even more pessimistic estimate.

Unfortunately Junior's demand, like Minzberg's earlier criticisms, had been expressed so brutally that Simon Murray and the remaining French directors could mount a successful veto to plans to eject Messier before finding a successor. In line with French company law the board would now disperse during the summer, indeed for ninety days, a period during which only the chairman could convene another meeting. This was clearly intolerable, and the situation, as so often, was aggravated by news from Wall Street, this time the revelation of a massive accounting fraud at Worldcom. Yet the next day Messier confidently told a group of skeptical analysts that he "would be pleased" to run the company "for another fifteen years." He claimed that it had "around E3.3 billion in unused credit lines"—even though this was implausible, given Vivendi's desperate condition.

But by now the vultures were hovering ever closer. As Alain Minc, a major guru of French business put it, "France Inc. took over." Two major banks, BNP Paribas and Société Générale, (the largest lender to Vivendi) refused to help following visits by Lachmann and Friedman to their chairmen, both members of Bébéar's dining club. By then Junior and Minzberg were urging that a successor had to be found as quickly as possible. For, as Minzberg says, "If it hadn't been for Bébéar's credibility Vivendi would have gone into bankruptcy." Nevertheless it remained a distinct possiblity; Charles Bronfman was not alone in saying, "We must put in someone to get rid of Messier." It was Junior who flew to London and won over Simon Murray who had remained passionately loyal to his friend until Junior persuaded him to abandon him. Apart from helping to soothe the British and American banks involved this was virtually his only contribution to ousting Messier despite the family's claim to the contrary. They were backed up by Barry Diller, who claimed that "Edgar is the unsung hero of the whole story." But then he had made more money out of the drama than anyone else, so could afford to be generous, as was his habit when talking of people whom he had bested in a deal. In reality since the business was French, the majority of the directors and shareholders were French, and most of the debts were owed to French banks, any solution to the Messier problem had to be essentially French with the Bronfmans marginalized, a situation to which they were totally unaccustomed.

Bébéar's candidate was one of his rugby-and-wine-loving friends, Jean-René Fourtou. He was an obvious choice. He was a management consultant who enjoyed sorting out difficult situations as a corporate fireman. In the previous two years he had successfully overseen the peaceful and successful merger of two proud pharmaceutical companies, the French Rhone-Poulenc and the German Hoechst, into a new group, Aventis. He had the reputation of being quiet but shrewd. A friend who worked for him told me, "He always asked the question you dreaded at any meeting, but can be generous with his praise." Also, as a semi-retired sixty-two-year-old, he had no need of further glory. That evening the French board members were convened by Bébéar, who persuaded them of the need to oust Messier immediately and replace him with Fourtou. The directors who were delegated the ungrateful task of demanding that Messier summon a special board meeting were Henri Lachmann and Jacques Friedmann.* Messier reportedly went berserk at the request, blaming Bébéar's desire to become the godfather of French business, President Chirac, and the "Hollywood moguls who had encouraged the Bronfmans to use their 'bootlegger' methods."

The end was in sight. Despite the hasty sale of the remaining shares in Vinco, its construction subsidiary, VU was about to have its debt reduced to junk status. On the evening of June 30 Messier accepted his fate. But there was one last twist in the story. To ensure his departure Messier demanded—and received from Viénot and Junior—a $21 million package, four times his total remuneration for 2001. This demand was ironical, for in his autobiography he had criticized the former chairman of the oil group Elf Aquitaine for the golden handshake he had negotiated to ensure his departure. Two days later Messier convened a meeting of all the staff at the head office and was cheered to the echo. This was not all that surprising for the French have always reserved their greatest admiration for leaders who have ruined them, like King Louis XIV and the emperor Napoleon Bonaparte. But there was another twist; objections by the more Enarch-minded members of the board to the appointment of Fourtou, who was, after all, not one of them. They put forward a medium-ranking banker, Charles de Croisset, but he demanded a fantastic financial package to take on the job. Bébéar was coopted to the board in his absence—in Botswana, where he told Fourtou, "I've killed a buffalo, have you killed yours?" He duly returned and Vivendi was saved.

After the takeover Junior had reflected that Vivendi suffered from two enormous weaknesses: "First that we were early, far too early, and that's the

---

* Friedmann was used to such a task, for he was known as "the undertaker" because he had done the same with a number of chairmen of state-owned companies in the past.

same thing as being wrong. Second, value creation is all about execution and we did not execute the merger." So far as the Bronfmans were concerned the final outcome was summed up by the realistic Kolber. "Looking to unload debt and maximize shareholder value," he wrote, "Junior sold Seagram, including its heritage liquor assets, to Vivendi for $34 billion in an all-stock deal, from which the family was supposed to realize $6.5 billion. Vivendi stock, which traded at $83 when the deal was made, sank to $11 two years later, when Charles was still holding most of his. In the end Junior traded 25 percent of DuPont and control of Seagram for about 8 percent of Vivendi, ending up with less than 5 percent after various Bronfman positions were sold off." As David Olive pointed out, "The current misery of the Bronfmans is deeply personal. Professional managers like Jerry Levin left with their personal fortunes, if not their dignity, intact when their failed convergence schemes led to their ouster. Not so the Bronfmans, who not only lost several billions but also, and to them far more shaming, the company they had inherited from their father and which they had sworn to preserve." As Edgar Sr. said, "The real disaster is bad judgment," but in this verdict he continued to believe that his second son had converted Seagram "into something that was really dynamic."

As for Messier, he persisted in believing that very little of the disaster was his fault. Moreover he was the only one of the many tycoons ejected that fateful year who, thanks to his rigorous education, could produce his own defense within three months of his departure. The result, Mon Vrai Journal[3] ("My True Story"), includes not only his version of the VU saga but also a general analysis of capitalism's problems and his solutions for them. He defended himself by pointing out, quite correctly, that the shares of every similar company, not only AOL Time Warner but such apparently solid groups as Deutsche Telecom, had crashed in the first half of 2001. But most of the book is a ridiculous account of how his departure was all the result of Evil Forces, ranging from hedge funds to credit rating agencies, as well as not a few nefarious plotters. Not surprisingly top of the list were the directors who had ousted him, whom he calls "pyromaniac firemen." But there were plenty of others, including journalists on the Financial Times, which "behaved more like a tabloid than a respectable paper," and Le Monde, which allegedly hated him because while at Lazard's he had thwarted their efforts to buy L'Express, a leading French news weekly. The list also included President Chirac—who probably genuinely did dislike him because of his earlier close connection with Chirac's great rival

Edouard Balladur. In general he accused his opponents of having typically French "xenophobia and archaism." He seems to have believed that he was merely a victim in a soap opera, for he uses the word *Dallas* a lot, as though he had been surrounded by a horde of would-be J. R. Ewings. Some of the book is frankly ridiculous, for he even claimed that the French way was that of consensus as opposed to the dictatorship of American CEOs. And in full victim/martyr flow he claimed that his departure was only for the sake of the shareholders and the employees, which I suppose in one sense it was. More legitimately he could claim that just as VU had been merely one of the fallen idols of the media/Internet craze, so he was only one of the many bosses—including of course Gerald Levin and Steve Case of AOL Time Warner—who took the blame for the mania. But, apart from outbursts like this, a cold day had dawned for VU, as it had for so many other fallen stars of the media world.

Nineteen

THE AFTERMATH

INEVITABLY AND DESERVEDLY, IT WAS MESSIER WHO CAME OFF worst from the debacle, though Hannezo, a far less culpable figure, also suffered. In defeat as in victory their fortunes followed those of AOL Time Warner. The SEC had already moved in to investigate the irregularities in numerous AOL deals that had been revealed by Alec Klein in *The Washington Post*. In December 2003 the SEC turned its attention to VU and threw the book at Messier and Hannezo, alleging that they had "committed multiple violations of the anti-fraud, books and records, internal controls, and reporting provisions of the federal securities laws." According to the SEC, they had "reported materially false and misleading information about its 'EBITDA' growth and liquidity in its SEC filings and public releases," including VU's "liquidity and cash flow positions." As a result the pair were ordered to return any profits they had gained from their illegal acts. Messier was banned for ten years and Hannezo for five years from any directorship, while Vivendi itself was ordered to pay $50 million to "investors harmed by the fraud"—unlucky souls who presumably included the Bronfmans.

But the French police were even tougher. It soon became clear that they were on his track. So it was no surprise that in June 2004 Messier was arrested and charged with manipulating the share price in September 2001, when markets were in turmoil after the events of 9/11, by buying back shares in the two-week "closed period" before the group's results were announced—and that he went on to purchase more shares while he was announcing the results on September 25. The warrant also covered his alleged concealment of the additional investment pledged in Maroc Télécom. French justice always moves at a glacial speed and it was only in January 2005 that Messier was placed "under investigation"—the next step could be a formal charge. At the same time there was an extraordinary development when two FBI agents flew to Paris because paintings found by the French authorities in Messier's Paris apartment were suspected of being four of the most valuable items stolen from the Isabella Stewart Gardner Museum in Boston in November 1990. The "Messier" paintings included a Vermeer and two Rembrandts, supposedly smuggled out of Boston to end up with a German industrialist.

Messier's old firm, however, recovered surprisingly quickly. With the support of France Inc., Fourtou pursued a sensible divestment policy, even though his inheritance was an almost inconceivably complex and sprawling mess. He also had to renegotiate (i.e., cancel) the golden goodbye Messier had managed to extract to punish the directors for dismissing him. More importantly he inherited a debt burden of $20 billion, with an urgent need to raise half that sum in the immediate future to avert a cash crisis. And, as the representative of France Inc., he had to ensure that none of the major French assets were to be sacrificed. By comparison, AOL Time Warner was in a far worse state. After the departure of Gerald Levin in January 2003 the stock had fallen by three-quarters, the group's debt burden was $24 billion, and Levin's successors had to write off an awesome $54 billion in its asset values. But the new chairman, Dick Parsons, saved AOL Time Warner, largely by abandoning the doctrine of synergy, requiring each division to justify its own results, while Fourtou's success was accomplished largely by transforming VU into a largely French-based conglomerate with little or no connection between the group's component companies.

Indeed by 2004 Fourtou was even able to declare a dividend, albeit a small one designed as much to mark the group's recovery as anything else. Surprisingly, virtually alone of all the fallen giants of the post-Enron era, VU's accounts did not have to be restated. Even the hostile Minzberg agrees that "Hannezo was honest, every dollar was accounted for, all that was wrong was the puffing of the share price." The assets included not only the original water and sewerage businesses but also three thousand other subsidiaries that ranged from a seven-hundred-strong chain of gift stores that dominated the US market for vibrators, a Citrus Technology Center near the Three Gorges Dam on the Yangtze River in China that aimed to produce the perfect orange, two football clubs, a brand of bottled water, as well as Messier's $18.5 million Park Avenue apartment and a leaky palazzo, while the art works were as various as the Hearst collection, though not as valuable.

For many former Seagram executives the single worst result of the Vivendi deal was the dispersal and sale of the works of art that had formed an integral part of 375 Park Avenue. Naturally Phyllis Lambert in particular was heartbroken. "These collections," she said, "are really part of the heritage of New York." In 1979 Seagram had sold the building to the Teachers Insurance & Annuity Association for $85.5 million, from whom Seagram leased the office space it needed.* Nevertheless Lambert had retained, as she put it, "The same high standard of control over the interior, the furnishing and the artwork as before," helped by the fact that it was classified as a "Landmark Building." Yet everything in the collection, which amounted to twenty-five hundred items, sculptures and photographs as well as paintings had to go—including the Rothko painting *Brown and Black in Reds* that Messier had tried to hang in his New York apartment. But the star of the show was saved. The enormous curtain that Picasso had painted for Diaghelev's production of the ballet *The Three-Cornered Hat* was deemed to be an integral part of the building and therefore could not legally be removed from a Landmark Building.

Inevitably for VU the cost of what sometimes amounted to a "fire sale" was enormous. Some investments turned out to have been total disasters, and none more so than Vizzavi, supposedly the Great White Hope of the group. Vivendi's half-share was soon sold for $143 million—a mere hundredth of its alleged value two years earlier—to its partner Vodaphone, which promptly absorbed the operation in its own organizational structure. Bargain hunters included Rupert Murdoch, whom Messier had described as just "a smiling dinosaur"—he picked up Telepiu, the Italian pay-TV operation, for $870 million, half the price originally agreed. The stake in Echostar communications had to be sold back to the company for $1.066 billion—a loss of $400 million in less than a year. More important were the assets which France Inc. wanted to retain. One of the key French

---

* There are two explanations for the deal: That Seagram was short of cash as a result of the 1970s slump, or that it was a gesture of spite by Edgar Sr. against his father.

ones was Cegetel, the mobile telephone company. Clearly Vodaphone, the (English) partner, was not going to be allowed to buy VU's stake in so important a French asset, and in the summer of 2004 VU was granted a valuable tax concession enabling it to consolidate its stake in the group. So far as the media interests were concerned the French retreated within the fortress labeled *exception culturelle*, ensuring that the precious French publishing businesses, including dictionaries and Vivendi's enormous stable of French magazines, went to a French buyer, as did Vivendi Environnement. By contrast non-French "cultural" assets were disposable—the publisher Houghton Mifflin went to a private equity house at a loss of over $600 million.

But the biggest problem was the American entertainment interests. Fortunately, seven years after Seagram had bought them they had been transformed into (relatively) star performers. *Forbes* reckoned that their 2002 income would be $700 million, double that in 1998, while Polygram was slated to earn $1 billion, double the figure before Junior bought the company—both figures a validation of Junior's management skills, at least in business sectors in which he was interested, a success overshadowed by the sale of Seagram to Vivendi. Right through 2003 a tangled set of deals were proposed. They involved a dozen or so major American media organizations, an incomparable cast of "usual suspects" like Kirk Kerkorian of MGM who made a low early bid of a mere $11.5 billion, Sumner Redstone of Viacom, Martin Davis, formerly of 20th Century Fox, John Malone of Liberty Media, Barry Diller—and Junior. He found backing, not only from his father, but also from a number of serious financiers, including the Blackstone Group, another private equity firm, Thomas H. Lee, as well as Merrill Lynch and a substantial debt financing facility from the Wachovia Bank, the fifth largest in the United States. His offer, of up to $13 billion, turned out to be a loser, but, as Ron Snyder said at the time, "The most important part of it was that Edgar gained his credibility back on Wall Street and with the private equity groups. It was not easy."

The battle lasted the whole year, a delay due to Fourtou's desire to get a price close to $15 billion—and the reduced pressure to sell following the successful disposal of so many other subsidiaries. So Fourtou could play the field, weighing up the numerous combinations of bids at his leisure. A sale of the majority of the assets would trigger payments to the Bronfmans of nearly $700 million and, unsurprisingly, Barry Diller had ensured that he would benefit by up to $1.3 billion in the event of a sale of USA Interac-

tive. Finally in October 2003 Fourtou sold 80 percent of VU Entertainment for $13.8 billion in cash to a surprising winner. It was the industrial
giant General Electric, which at first had been hesitant over committing
the necessary funds. At the time its only major media asset was NBC,
which Junior had prevented Diller from buying for Universal. Among
other advantages the deal allowed GE to make savings of between $400
and $500 million, and to create the integrated group Barry Diller had
dreamed of six years earlier. Although GE—in the shape of Bob Wright of
NBC—was firmly in charge, both Meyer and Snider survived the inevitable purge. Indeed Meyer could not conceal his satisfaction. "We've
been rescued," he trumpeted, "I can't even describe the difference. We're finally around a company that's in our business." The longest-lasting legacy
was a rumbling row between Diller and Vivendi over the tax situation and
the alleged breach of contract left by the messy partnership between
Vivendi and Diller's USA Interactive. Finally in July 2004 a US court ruled
that Vivendi was liable to pay a tax bill of $600 million—albeit payable
over a twenty-year period. Eleven months later Diller's company sold its
stake in VU Entertainment for a cool $3.4 billion, partly in return for
abandoning his lawsuit.

Fourtou's steady nerves enabled Vivendi to emerge at the end of 2003
with a loss of only $1.4 billion, a 90 percent reduction on the 2002 figure,
and debt was down to $14.2 billion despite an investment of nearly $5 billion in Cegetel/SFR whose profit had leaped by nearly a third in 2003. By
the end of 2004 Fourtou had reduced the debt even further, to a mere E3.1
billion, not much more than a tenth of the burden he had inherited little
more than three years earlier, while the remaining businesses were making
steady progress. Unfortunately in early 2005 a shadow fell over Fourtou
and his finance director, Jean-Bernard Lévy. In line with his habit of not
remaining more than a few years in any particular job, Fourtou had
planned to move at the end of the year to the position of chairman of the
supervisory board with Lévy actually running the company. But their plans
were disrupted when they were accused of insider trading by the French authorities because Fourtou's family foundation had been one of the biggest
purchasers of a convertible bond VU had issued in late 2002 when they
were allegedly aware that VU's position was far more promising than they
had yet told shareholders.

Following their sale the liquor businesses were greatly refreshed by their
new owners. The changes were less apparent with the brands acquired by

Diageo, like Captain Morgan and Crown Royal, which had become a major brand, Chateau and Estates, and the remaining California vineyards. Sam was given a two-year contract to run the wine group including an office at his home, two hours' drive from the winery, but once this expired he left the group, the last member of the family to do so. By contrast the brands bought by Pernod Ricard were in a much worse state, having been totally neglected by Junior and requiring major doses of tender loving managerial care. But by 2004 Chivas Regal was growing at a "handy pace" well above the market while Royal Salute was pounding ahead at a rate of 40 percent a year, and even 100 Pipers was making a comeback, selling over three million cases worldwide. Pernod Ricard's efforts included exploiting the names of Chivas Regal with an ultra-premium eighteen-year-old Gold Signature and a Royal Salute fifty-year-old, brand extensions showing how well Mr. Sam had laid their foundations. Martell was in such a dreadful state—in fourth place in the cognac league after two and a half centuries at, or very near, the top position—that a revolution was required. The firm had eleven years' sales in stock, three times the level it needed, and production was scattered over five sites. The most painful step the new owners had to take was to cut back severely on its purchases of wine and brandies. Worst affected were growers in the Borderies, a small part of the Cognac region but the source of the nutty brandies that had historically formed the key to the quality of Martell's products. And when Pernod wanted to follow the other major cognac firms by shutting its bottling operations in the center of Cognac itself the workers went on a—fortunately short-lived—hunger strike, but Pernod kept its nerve, realizing that the comeback of the oldest major firm in the business would be a slow one.

And what of Junior—whose mismanagement, or rather lack of management, had done such damage to Martell, and all Seagram's other brands for that matter? He first went out and consoled himself by spending $50 million on 40 percent of Asprey & Garrard, a venerable London-based luxury goods business, which was also the royal jeweler. It had fallen on hard times after some years in the hands of the eccentric younger brother of the sultan of Brunei and was planning on turning itself into an international brand at a cost estimated at $200 million. But this investment was merely an appetizer. Edgar and Junior finally resigned from the board of Vivendi on December 3, 2003, by which time the *Financial Times* could call Junior "the official idiot of the entertainment industry." This—widely expected—step came a month after Junior's bounceback as part of a consortium that bought Warner Music—the Wall Street cred he had gained through his failed bid for Universal proved invaluable. For Junior, now nearing fifty, this was an important statement of the way he was proposing to spend the rest of his working life—in the business that had been his first love since his teenage years.

Junior and his partners were taking advantage of the urgent need of AOL Time Warner to reduce its debt, and so formed part of a year-long gavotte that involved four of the world's five major music groups—the only exception, ironically, being Universal Music, then still firmly in the hands of Vivendi. But Sony, Time Warner, and the German Bertelsmann group were all anxious to merge in the light of the crisis created by the "imperial overstretch" of media groups around the millennium, compounded by the arrival of the Internet as a—sometimes free—new means of distribution. In addition the British firm EMI, the only independent group, appeared in dire need of a partner. The situation, however, was confused because of the domination of the Big Five, and any combination would infallibly be subject to close and lengthy scrutiny by antitrust authorities, above all in Europe—as indeed proved to be the case with the combination of Sony and Bertelsmann's music interests.

This complication provided an independent bidder like Junior with an opportunity, which he took when Time Warner abandoned talks with Bertelsmann in favor of—equally fruitless—negotiations with EMI. So Richard Parsons of Time Warner opted for the $2.5 billion offer made by the group assembled by Junior, even though it was $300 million below the potential value of the EMI bid. Junior put $250 million of his own money into the bid. But the offer was headed not by him but by Thomas H. Lee Partners, a private equity group based in Boston that provided much of the financial muscle. Lee himself is a professional contrarian who had made his name and his fortune by buying Snapple in 1992 for a mere $135 million and selling the brand two years later for a cool $1.7 billion. Lee went heavily into the Warner Music bid with $650 million of its own money, and brought in other serious investors including the mysterious media entrepreneur Haim Saban as well as Bain Capital Fund, which put up a reported $350 million, and Providence Equity Partners, which contributed $150 million. The group had its problems—the Quadrangle group backed out as did Saban, who in the end returned but did not invest much, so Junior had to invest a further $50 million.

The bid was timely because the music industry had finally got its act together and was making progress in containing the impact of recordings over the Internet. In addition the risk element in the bid was less than appeared at first sight since Lee had understood the value of Warner Chappell, its music publishing subsidiary, which held the copyrights for a vast library of songs, ranging from *Rhapsody in Blue* to *Winter Wonderland*. It alone was worth at least half the bid price. In addition there was considerable scope for cost-cutting. Warner had laid off nearly a third of its sixty-five hundred employees in the previous three years, but one shrewd analyst believed that "WMG has delayed cost-cutting in 2003 due to attempts to find a suitable merger partner to share in the cost reduction savings." The bidder knew how costs could be cut; by shutting offices in low-priority regions like Latin America and merging labels—a step that would inevitably involve reducing the firm's roster of artists. But the seller also got a good deal, and not only because it did not involve the considerable and time-consuming "regulatory risk" inevitable in a deal with another music group (shades of the protracted sale of Seagram's liquor interests three years earlier). Parsons liked the music business and was happy that his group could retain a fifth of the company if it chose. He also insured his group against a future merger of Warner with another music business. In that case Time Warner would be entitled to 19.9 percent of the merged company.

When Junior relinquished his executive role at VU he said that he "wanted to do something on his own. I didn't want to work for anyone. It didn't matter who it was." After the Warner purchase he repeated this mantra, saying that: "If you are ever going to put your eggs in one basket you had better control the basket." But as Scott Sperling, the Lee partner responsible for the purchase, remarked, "We have an investment that is not Edgar alone. There is a management team that is deep in this company." The key figure was Roger Ames, the well-respected chairman of Warner Music, who had obviously been against a merger with another company. "The deal with Edgar is, he does a good job or someone else comes in to do a good job." Throughout his business life, Junior's greatest single aim had been to control his own music company, and when, at first sight, he achieved his goal, he was not in control, he was merely an employee. His relative lack of power was the cost, which he regretted only occasionally, in public at least, of having been allowed by his father to destroy the family business. Edgar Jr. naturally pursued his usual policy: He cut a thousand jobs and scrapped a number of labels. As a result the company was emerging into—albeit tiny—profit when it was floated in early 2005. Unfortunately, although the owners managed to recoup their investment, the stock, originally scheduled to be offered at between $22 and $24 a share, was eventually priced at a mere $17 and did not rise above that level in the first months of trading. As so often during his business career Edgar's moves attracted criticism, most obviously from the record label's biggest band Linkin Park, its only entry in the top ten, who accused the owners of "fleecing" their bands to the detriment of the artists it had under contract.

Not surprisingly the collapse of Vivendi Universal ensured that the gulf between Edgar and Charles, which had started to open nearly twenty years earlier, became permanently unbridgeable. "It's very personal between my brother and myself," said Edgar, "I think he holds a real grudge." Psychologically it was Charles who suffered the most permanent damage. When asked whether he missed Seagram, he replied, "Totally." And like many wealthy people any loss panicked him. After the sale Kolber heard Charles complain that he would have to make cuts in the staff of Claridge even though he was still worth well over $2 billion. As Kolber wrote, "In my entire life, I had never heard Charles, or any member of the Bronfman family, say anything like that." Yet Charles remained a Bronfman in his social expenditure. His seventieth birthday party—held in 2001 before the final collapse of VU—was celebrated by a cruise down the Italian coast in a luxury liner, the *Sea Goddess*, accompanied by seventy of his closest friends.

Despite his earlier move to New York, Charles remained a Canadian citizen and an ardent patriot—though not to the point of paying tax. In 1994 the Charles and Andrea Bronfman Foundation established the McGill Institute for the study of Canada with a C$10 million endowment. This was three years after he had allegedly succeeded in transferring over C$2 billion of his own money out of the country, in what Newman calls an "infamous transfer" that avoided a capital gains tax bill of C$700 million. Initially revenue officials opposed this piece of tax evasion but were overruled by their seniors in meetings for which no minutes were prepared. The transfer was supposedly oiled by a donation of C$100,000 given by Charles and Kolber—a former "bagman" for the Liberals—to the then prime minister, the Conservative Brian Mulroney, in one of the biggest contributions to his second election campaign, ostensibly because of his pro-business stance and his support for Israel. In 1996 Canada's auditor-general criticized the "advance tax rulings" involved in the transfer, saying that they "may have circumvented the intent of the law." The auditor's criticism led George Harris, a social activist living in Winnipeg, to sue Revenue

Canada. But the Canadian justice system moved too slowly. In 1999 a judge allowed the suit to go forward but in 2001 time ran out for contesting the transaction while the loophole involved was closed. The whole affair aroused enormous public interest, for although the beneficiary was never named everyone assumed that it had been Charles.

Despite the collapse of the money tied up in the family company the brothers did not, financially, suffer too badly because they had accumulated so much capital through other investments. According to *Forbes* magazine's annual surveys, Charles's fortune had risen from $2.6 billion in 1996 to a peak of $3.7 billion at the height of takeover speculation three years later, and was back to $2.7 billion by 2003, although it had improved by $200 million by the end of 2004. For the first time this put him ahead of Edgar—albeit only by $100 million. For Edgar's fortune followed a similar curve, his wealth rising from $2.7 billion to $4.3 billion between 1996 and 1999, before falling to (I must *not* write "a mere") $2.5 billion in 2004. Moreover even at the end of 2004, Edgar was one of only fifty entries in the first *Forbes* "four hundred richest" list back in 1982 to have been in every list in the subsequent twenty-two years. The total assets of the extended Bronfman clan—including all the descendants of Echiel's eight offspring—are impossible to calculate but are certainly more than any other family in the liquor business, the Browns (of Brown-Forman) or the tribe that owns Bacardi, which adds up to $8 billion. Proportionately, the biggest losers were the many senior managers whose savings, and indeed their pensions, were almost exclusively tied up in Seagram stock. They often lost millions of dollars, although no member of the family is on record as sympathizing with their plight.

If the Bronfmans had held on to their shares in "boring" DuPont they would have kept up with their fellow billionaires. Relatively, of course, both Edgar and Charles had fallen in the *Forbes* magazine rankings between 1996 and 2004, Edgar from 125th to 186th richest in the United States, and Charles from third to seventh in Canada. There the tortoise, represented by the Thomson Group, founded by Roy Thomson, had overtaken the Seagram hare. Roy Thomson's son Kenneth, though never rated very highly, ensured that the fortunes of the Thomson family rose steadily between 1996 and 2004, with Kenneth's fortune skyrocketing from $7.4 to $17.9 billion. But then the Thomsons have had the sense to leave the management of their groups very largely to professional managers. So have the Westons, another family of "quiet Canadians" whose family wealth is now reckoned at $9.9 billion. In contrast to the Bronfmans, the—relatively less wealthy—Ricards and Browns of two family-dominated liquor companies, Pernod Ricard and Brown-Forman, have flourished largely because the families involved are fully aware of the limitations of the family's capacities. If a member of the Brown family wants to join the business he or she has to get two degrees, a masters as well as a bachelors, thus ensuring that, as one of the family told me, "They may be stupid but they won't be lazy." But the Bronfmans' control freakery prevented any such policy.

Over the years Charles had become increasingly involved in Israel, which became his second home—it helped that Andrea was a member of a powerful Anglo-Jewish family that owned a house in Jerusalem. Indeed by the twenty-first century, thanks largely to his remarriage, his loyalties had clearly switched away from Canada and Montreal. He took to spending half the year in New York and the other half in Jerusalem, though he still claims that "I'm a Canadian and a Jew and that's it." Sadly, his beloved wife, Andrea, was killed in a traffic accident in Manhattan, in January 2006.

Charles's involvement had already become much deeper after his godson, Leo Kolber's son Jonathan, and thus almost a family member, had emigrated to Israel in 1989—the only member of the clan to take this crucial step—and naturally became Charles's partner in Israel. The move was easier for him; Jonathan's mother had lived in Israel and, with fluent Hebrew, had worked as a translator there before she had met his father, so he was far more closely linked to the country than his father—or any of the Bronfmans for that matter. But they remained committed. As *The Jerusalem Post* noted at the time, "Although his ownership of Koor makes him the largest foreign investor in Israel, billionaire Charles Bronfman's biggest gamble is on the future of the Jewish people"—thus demonstrating a legitimate alternative to Ben-Gurion's absolute position, accepted by Jonathan Kolber, that all Jews should emigrate to Israel. The Israeli government recognized their commitment when Charles and Jonathan were made honorary citizens of Jerusalem, the first North American Jews to be so honored.

Charles and Jonathan had played the market shrewdly. They had helped build up Super-Sol into the biggest supermarket chain in Israel, selling out their investments in the boom time of the late 1990s and buying a major stake in a big food company in 1991 when the market was depressed at the time of the first Gulf War. When he sold out, for $45 million, Charles reinvested the money so successfully that he sold the new investments for $500 million, using the money to buy Koor Industries, one of Israel's largest conglomerates, formerly the pride and joy of the country's powerful union movement. But they had problems with Koor, Israel's largest employer, where Jonathan was CEO. In the early years of the twenty-first century Jonathan was forced to "downsize," firing six thousand people.

But Junior's father, and his aunt Phyllis Lambert, had used the capital their father had left more creatively than in mere investments. In the decade after the opening of the Seagram Building Phyllis Lambert completed her education in architecture and lived both in Paris and in Los Angeles. She claims that "originally I had no intention of returning to Montreal," but after her father's death did so, mainly to be near her mother. When she returned she immediately made an impact. Although she was involved in some of Cadillac Fairview's massive real estate projects, including one designed by van der Rohe, she was a regular critic of most of them: "We were urban guerillas," she told me, "putting up placards at some of Cemp's projects." Not surprisingly she greatly upset the precise, businesslike Leo Kolber, most notably after she had demanded the appointment of a design chief at the company. Kolber refused but agreed to a meeting. He assembled his top managerial team from all over North America on a date to which she had agreed. She never turned up. Kolber blew his stack and the brothers ensured that she would no longer have any contact with the company. But the protests continued. "What was I supposed to do?" asked Kolber rhetorically. "One of my principal shareholders was demonstrating against me, though not refusing any of her dividends."

More positively she had already been responsible for the establishment of the Saidye Bronfman Centre in Montreal, which received a major award, and had helped in the restoration of the historic Biltmore Hotel in Los Angeles, a project that sparked off the transformation of much of the city's downtown. Later she also worked with Edgar to help save the Ben Ezra Synagogue in Cairo. This is part of an extraordinary complex, which Edgar had heard about on a visit to Egypt on WJC business, and which includes early buildings celebrating the three great monotheistic religions, for it is also the site of a Coptic church and the earliest mosque built in Egypt.

When she returned to Montreal to live in a converted peanut factory in Old Montreal, its historic heart had largely been saved from development by the all-powerful Mayor Jean Drapeau as part of the preparations for the 1967 Universal Exhibition. But the city's hundreds of dignified nineteenth-century graystone buildings remained under threat and were being steadily demolished. "I kept on returning to photographs of the graystone buildings," she says. "I was studying buildings as they relate to their time." So in 1975 she bought Shaughnessy Hall, one of the most distinguished of nineteenth century mansions, and four years later created the Canadian Centre for the Study of Architecture. Over the years this has involved assembling a major collection of architectural drawings and photographs—in doing so she created a new market for them—and a study center that has involved building a new wing—in graystone naturally—onto Shaughnessy Hall. The CCA, which she connected with the Whitney Museum in New York to avoid any hint of parochialism, is now probably the best equipped such center in the world, though to the outsider it reflects the cool and detached mentality of its founder.

Phyllis has collected honorary degrees from no fewer than eighteen universities as recognition of her efforts in urban regeneration, and in 1997 her record reached a climax when the World Monuments Fund gave her the Hadrian Award, "For an international leader whose sponsorship of cultural activities has advanced the understanding, appreciation, and preservation of world art and architecture." This is an honor given over the years to such notables as the Prince of Wales, Lord (Jacob) Rothschild, and the Aga Khan.

Edgar continued in the presidency of the WJC into his seventies. But in the early years of the twenty-first century he had to cope with a crisis within the WJC after a small clique had mounted a campaign to oust him for alleged maladministration. Above all, the rebels, who included his former close associate Elan Steinberg, seized on the letter—on private writing paper—Edgar had written to President Bush criticizing Ariel Sharon. The power of the letter was increased because the co-signatory was Bronfman's close friend Laurence Eagleburger, Henry Kissinger's faithful deputy for much of his career in the foreign service and, albeit for a very short period, secretary of state. In the end Stephen Herbits—who had returned from the US Defense Department—rode to the rescue and, as a newly appointed general secretary ensured that the troublemakers were removed.

By then Bronfman's presidency of the WJC had led him to contemplate the future of Jews outside Israel in the light of his own religious odyssey. When Edgar was first elected to the presidency he asked Rabbi Soloveitchik, "the preeminent sage of Jewish life," for advice. His reply, "Jews were not here just to fight anti-Semitism," struck deep, for Edgar had realized the largely hidden, and thus more dangerous, threat posed by assimilation, expressed above all in the way so many liberated young Jews "marry out." So he naturally perceived a part of his role as "keeping Jews Jewish." "The ultimate problem in Judaism," he told Morris, "is not what happened fifty years ago, but what we are doing to ourselves, which is assimilating and opting out of our Judaism. It is a silent Holocaust."

In Israel Edgar found that there was an underlying assumption that "with rate of assimilation ever rising, the Diaspora is doomed." At times he agreed. "Our more recent history," he wrote, "is not as it was in the past: we have not just left the Pale of Settlement to come to America (or elsewhere) to be better Jews but, in effect, to escape our Judaism." So far as American (and Canadian?) Jews were concerned, "For too many years we have expressed ourselves, not by learning Judaism and the pride that comes from that, but by writing checks for Israel and feeling pride in that country and its mighty army. We face extinction in the diaspora, that's the real threat." His background helped him to understand the problem. As a result, since the mid-1980s he has made considerable, and usually successful, efforts to reclaim for Judaism his seven offspring, who had by then often "married out"—to Catholics, Episcopalians, and in the case of his son Edgar, to a black Buddhist actress followed by a Catholic; marriages that had naturally ensured that their children also needed reclaiming for Judaism. For he had found another mission, he would speak on campuses, saying that "you have to make it cool to be Jewish. . . . I feel a calling to do this, people want something spiritual, something that brings meaning to their lives."

During the aftermath to the Messier debacle he naturally suffered a period of depression but—while nearing his seventy-fifth birthday—he embarked on a major crusade. His first object was to counter the increasing tide of anti-Semitism in such unlikely countries as France—where President Chirac had told Singer that Jews were the cause of anti-Semitism in France and everywhere else. He also continued to try and protect the many small Jewish communities in the world. This was a task that still needed undertaking even though, as Singer points out, "When the WJC was founded in 1936 nine out of ten Jews in the world lived in inhospitable environments. When we started the percentage was down to a half. Now it is a mere 10 percent." Some, like those in Argentina, had been near implosion under the effects of political and financial upheaval.

Above all Edgar has tried to ensure that Judaism became inclusive rather than exclusive; in Herbits's words he "didn't want Jews to turn in on themselves," he wanted to tap "convert power," to bring within the fold the many millions of Jews proud of their racial heritage but who had married out, and their children as well. "Our slogan," he told the *Jewish Chronicle*, organ of British Jewry, "should be to include Jews who self-identify as Jewish. The great secret of Jewish survival is Jewish pride. . . . My answer to 'who is a Jew' is anybody who wants to be"—a stark challenge to the orthodox belief that only those whose mothers were purely of Jewish blood had any right to call themselves Jewish. Unfortunately, and typically of his ability to shoot himself in the foot, he added that "the whole concept of Jewish peoplehood, and the lines being pure, begins to sound a little like Nazism, meaning racism." Not surprisingly what Oliver Hardy would have called "another fine mess" provided Edgar, and thus Stephen Herbits, with a major cleanup problem, and reduced the impact of Edgar's otherwise brave and sensible remarks.

His view was backed up by the leading British journalist Jonathan Freedland in the *Jewish Chronicle*. "There is something oddly self-defeating about the current Jewish approach which tends to count out rather than in. While other peoples would regard a marriage 'out' as the potential recruiting of new people, the partner and any future children, our starting assumption is that we have 'lost' a soul. The result is a demographic crisis, our numbers shrinking as close to 50 percent of Jews outside Israel choose to marry people not born a Jew." Edgar is trying to assert the supremacy of Freedland's belief that "we are much more than just a faith; we are a culture, a civilization, a people." Unfortunately Edgar's attempts to induce the Jewish establishment, most obviously in Israel but also throughout the world, to accept a wider definition of Jewishness that has nothing to do with the Jewish religion and would include anyone with a significant proportion of Jewish blood, is almost certainly doomed. Nevertheless there is a head of steam about his efforts, which parallel those of people trying to revive Yiddish, the language of the Diaspora, as against Hebrew, the long-lost language that became the official language of what might be perceived as the imperialist Israelis.

In their very different ways he and his sister have both shown the indomitable spirit and iron will of their father, the most remarkable man ever thrown up by the liquor business. And both are leaving legacies worthy of the man, albeit nothing to do with his own achievements. Phyllis will be remembered for the Seagram Building and for the CCA while Edgar will leave the WJC, a symbol of a new-style, aggressive style of Jewry, unafraid to tackle the world. Their father, despite himself, would have been proud of them and their achievements. But he would, inevitably and rightly, have told both of them that their achievements would have been impossible without the massive fortune he accumulated. He could also have boasted— and I would have agreed with him—that at least three of the brands he created, Crown Royal, Royal Salute, and of course Chivas Regal, are increasingly recognized as both pioneering efforts and leaders in their category.

But he could have gone on to boast that his legacy to the industry was far more than a handful of brands. It included the very concept of a worldwide group covering every type of wine and spirits from every corner of the globe—Bordeaux, California, Scotland, Puerto Rico. But the real uniqueness was not just industrial, it was also, and far more profoundly, social as well. It lay in the idea that drinking hard liquor could be respectable, a belief unthinkable before Prohibition, and while the years when alcohol was officially banned in the United States had the perverse effect of making alcohol fashionable, only he, Mr. Sam, went on to make it socially acceptable. He did this, not only through promoting the genuinely reliable quality of his offerings but, more importantly, through his campaigns for moderation. If today the whole world is responding to the cry "drink less but drink better," this is due in large measure to Mr. Sam.

NOTES

ONE: MR. SAM, NO ORDINARY MONSTER

1. Weir, *The History of Distillers Company, 1877–1939*, 289.
2. Robertson, "Samuel Bronfman," ms. in McClellan Archives at McMaster University.
3. Newman, *Bronfman Dynasty: The Rothschilds of the New World*, ix.
4. Marrus, *Samuel Bronfman: The Life and Times of Seagram's Mr. Sam.* An honest and invaluable book, of particular value in the early chapters of this work.
5. McQueen, *The Icarus Factor.*
6. MacLennan, *Like Everyone Else, But Different!*
7. Introduction to *Plain Talk! Memoirs of an Auditor-General*, by Maxwell Henderson, 81.
8. Bronfman, *Good Spirits.*

TWO: YECHIEL AND HIS TRIBE

1. Vital, *The Origins of Zionism*, 511.
2. *The Whiskey Man: The Balmoral Hotel-Bronfman Saga.* A booklet issued in 2003 by the City of Yorkton.
3. James Gray, son of an alcoholic and not surprisingly a confirmed prohibitionist, wrote the seminal book, *Booze, When Whiskey Ruled the West*, published in 1972, that provides an excellent account of the Bronfmans' career and problems. Indeed, the Bronfmans' involvement was the magnet that originally drew his publishers to the subject.
4. Cook, *The Regenerators: Social Criticism in Late Victorian English Canada*, 178.
5. Chidsey, *On and Off the Wagon.*
6. Asbury, *The Great Illusion*, 114.
7. Hunt, *Booze, Boats, and Billions.*

THREE: THE HARRY YEARS

1. Thompson, *The Harvests of War.*

FOUR: THE PROHIBITION BUSINESS

1. Lacey, *Little Man*, 55.
2. Herzberg, *The Jews in America*, 195.
3. Willoughby, *Rum War at Sea*, 15.
4. Coffey, *The Long Thirst*, 179.
5. Hunt, *Booze, Boats, and Billions*, 54.
6. Birmingham, *The Rest of Us*, 153.
7. Kelly, *The Making of a Salesman*, 148.
8. Summers, *Official and Confidential*, 254.

FIVE: THE ROAD TO RESPECTABILITY

1. Wilson, *Scotch: The Formative Years*, 205.
2. Eisenberg, *Meyer Lansky, Mogul of the Mob*, 107.
3. Brebner, *Canada: A Modern History*, 425.
4. Neatby, *William Lyon Mackenzie King*, vol. 2, 133.

SIX: GREAT EXPECTATIONS, GREAT DECEPTIONS

1. Kefauver, *Crime in America*, 238.
2. Kelly, *The Making of a Salesman*, 149.

SEVEN: CROWNING GLORY

1. Blum, *From the Morgenthau Diaries*, 110.

EIGHT: A TRULY CANADIAN JEW

1. Graham, *Earth and High Heaven*.
2. Davies, ed., *Anti-Semitism in Canada*, 137.
3. Bermant, *The Jews*, 70.

TEN: NOT JUST DYSFUNCTIONAL, DISINTEGRATING

1. *Vassar* alumni magazine, February 1959.
2. *Vanity Fair*, October 2002.
3. *The New Yorker*, September 13, 1958.
4. *Harper's Magazine*, July 1970.

ELEVEN: THE GENERATION GAP

1. Kolber, *Leo: A Life*.

TWELVE: CROWN PRINCE

1. Lloyd, *Well It Seemed Like a Good Idea at the Time*, 196.
2. Newman, *The Titans*.

THIRTEEN: TIME FOR BUSINESS

1. "Gentleman's War?" *The Economist*, December 22, 1984.

FOURTEEN: KING OF THE JEWS?

1. Bronfman, *The Making of a Jew*, 61.
2. Bower, *Blood Money*, 324.
3. Singer interview with Yad Vashem online magazine.
4. Interview, Jerusalem Institute for Public Affairs, November 2, 2003.
5. Gitelman, *The Jews of Russia*, 286.

FIFTEEN: CLOWN PRINCE

1. McQueen, *The Icarus Factor.*
2. *The New Yorker*, June 6, 1994.
3. "Bronfman's Big Deals," 66, *The New Yorker*, May 11, 1998.

SIXTEEN: A UNIVERSAL PANACEA

1. "Vanity Too Fair," *LA Weekly*, April 2004.
2. "Bronfman's Big Deals," 66, *The New Yorker*, May 11, 1998.
3. *The Toronto Star*, July 6, 2002.

SEVENTEEN: THE FRENCH CONNECTION

1. Johnson and Orange, *The Man Who Tried to Buy the World*, 46.
2. *Vanity Fair*, October 2002.
3. Stone, in *Beverage Business*.

EIGHTEEN: THE END OF "L'AFFAIRE"

1. Wolff, *Autumn of the Moguls*, 72–73.
2. *New York* magazine.
3. J. M. Messier with Yves Messarovitch, *Mon Vrai Journal*.

BIBLIOGRAPHY

Allen, Frederick L. *Only Yesterday: An Informal History of the 1920s*. New York: Wiley, 1997.

Allen, Ralph. *Ordeal by Fire: Canada 1910–1943*. Garden City: Doubleday, 1961.

Allsop, Kenneth. *The Bootleggers: The Story of Chicago's Prohibition Era*. New Rochelle: Arlington House, 1970.

Anctil, Pierre. In *Anti-Semitism in Canada*. A. Davies (ed.), Waterloo, Ontario: Wilfred Laurier University Press, 1992.

Asbury, Herbert. *The Great Illusion—An Informal History of Prohibition*. New York: Doubleday, 1950.

Bermant, Chaim. *The Jews*. London: Weidenfeld & Nicolson, 1977.

Birmingham, Stephen. *The Rest of Us: The Rise of America's Eastern European Jews*. Boston: Little Brown, 1984.

Bliss, Michael. *Northern Enterprise: Five Centuries of Canadian Business*. Toronto: McClelland & Stewart, 1987.

Blum, John M. *From the Morgenthau Diaries: Years of Crisis 1928–38*. Boston: Houghton Mifflin, 959–67.

Bower, Tom. *Blood Money: The Swiss, the Nazis and the Looted Millions*. London: Macmillan, 1997.

Brebner, J. Bartlett. *Canada: A Modern History*. Ann Arbor: University of Michigan Press, 1960.

Bronfman, Edgar. *Good Spirits*. New York: Putnam, 1995.

———*The Making of a Jew*. New York: Putnam, 1996.

———*The Third Act* (with Catherine Whitney). New York: Putnam, 2002.

Bruck, Connie. *When Hollywood Had a King*. New York: Random House, 2003.

Chidsey, Donald B. *On and Off the Wagon*. New York: Cowles Publishing, 1969.

City of Yorkton. *The Whiskey Man: The Balmoral Hotel–Bronfman Saga*. Yorkton, 2003.

Coffey, Thomas. *The Long Thirst*. New York: Norton, 1975.

Cook, Ramsay. *The Regenerators: Social Criticism in Late Victorian English Canada*. Toronto: University of Toronto Press, 1985.

Eisenberg, Dennis, Uri Dan, and Eli Landau. *Meyer Lansky, Mogul of the Mob*. New York: Paddington Press, 1979.

Gitelman, Zvi. *The Jews of Russia*. New York: Viking, 1988.

Graham, Gwethalyn. *Earth and High Heaven*. Philadelphia: JP Lippincott, 1944.

Gray, James. *Booze: When Whisky Ruled the West*. Toronto: Macmillan, 1972.

Henderson, Maxwell. *Plain Talk! Memoirs of an Auditor-General*. Toronto: McClelland & Stewart, 1984.

Heron, Craig. *Booze: A Distilled History*. Toronto: Between the Lines, 2003.

Herzberg, Arthur. *The Jews in America*. New York: Simon & Schuster, 1989.

Hunt, C. W. *Booze, Boats, and Billions: Smuggling Liquid Gold*. Toronto: McClelland & Stewart, 1988.

Johnson, Jo, and Martine Orange. *The Man Who Tried to Buy the World*. London: Viking, 2003.

Kefauver, Estes. *Crime in America*. New York: Doubleday, 1951.

Kelly, Philip J. *The Making of a Salesman*. New York: Abelard & Schuman, 1965.

Kolber, Leo with L. Ian MacDonald. *Leo: A Life*. Montreal & Kingston: McGill–Queen's University Press, 2003.

Lacey, Robert. *Little Man*. Boston: Little Brown, 1991.

Leacock, Stephen. *Wet Wit and Dry Humour*. New York: Dodd Mead & Co., 1931.

Lloyd, Sue. *Well It Seemed Like a Good Idea at the Time*. London: Quartet, 1998.

MacLennan, Hugh. *Like Everyone Else, But Different!*

Marrus, Michael R. *Samuel Bronfman: The Life and Times of Seagram's Mr. Sam*. Toronto: Penguin, 1991.

McQueen, Rod. *The Icarus Factor*. Toronto: Doubleday Canada, 2004.

Messier, Jean-Marie with Yves Messarovitch. *Mon Vrai Journal*. Paris: Balland, 2002.

Neatby, H. Blair. *William Lyon Mackenzie King*. Vol. 2, 1924–32. Toronto: University of Toronto Press, 1963.

Newman, Peter C. *Bronfman Dynasty: The Rothschilds of the New World*. Toronto: McClelland & Stewart, 1978.

———*The Titans: How the New Canadian Establishment Seized Power*. Toronto: Viking, 1994.

Pacult, F. Paul. *A Double Scotch*. Hoboken, New Jersey: John Wiley, 2005.

Pinkus, Benjamin. *The Jews of the Soviet Union*. New York: Cambridge University Press, 1988.

Richler, Mordecai. *Solomon Gursky Was Here*. Ontario: Viking Markham, 1989.

Robertson, Terence. "Samuel Bronfman." 1969 ms. in McClelland Archives at McMaster University.

Smith, Amanda, ed. *The Letters of Joseph Kennedy*. New York: Viking Penguin, 2001.

Summers, Anthony. *Official and Confidential: The Secret Life of J. Edgar Hoover*. New York: GB Putnam's Sons, 1993.

Thompson, John H. *The Harvests of War: The Prairie West, 1914–1918*. Toronto: McClelland & Stewart, 1978.

Vital, David. *The Origins of Zionism*. Oxford: Oxford University Press, 1975.

Weir, Ronald. *The History of Distillers Company 1877–1939*. Oxford: Clarendon Press, 1995.

White, Theodore H. *The View from the Fortieth Floor*. New York: William Sloan Associates, 1960.

Willoughby, M. *Rum War at Sea*. Washington: Treasury Department, 1964.

Wilson, Ross. *Scotch: The Formative Years*. London: Constable, 1970.

Wolff, Michael. *Autumn of the Moguls*. New York: Flamingo, 2003.

ACKNOWLEDGMENTS

THIS BOOK WOULD NOT HAVE BEEN POSSIBLE WITHOUT THE HELP OF A great many people. My old friend Professor Trevor Lloyd deserves special thanks for his hospitality and his patient efforts to guide me through the thickets of Canadian politics. Val Smith, another friend first met back in 1948, supplied me with the true figures for liquor sales in recent years from his publication, the *International Wine and Spirit Record*. Louise Chinn was endlessly patient in trying to track down the many obscure characters in the story. Jimmy Lang, Colin Scott, and Art Dawe kindly guided me through the intricacies of whiskey distillation. Michael Levine eased my path to meeting Charles Bronfman and Phyllis Lambert. Professor Michael Marrus, the official biographer of Mr. Sam, was generosity itself, while Gilles Bengle kindly arranged an instructive tour of the Bronfman-related sites in Montreal. Discussions with Stephen Herbits greatly helped me in disentangling the later history of Seagram and clarifying the character of Edgar Bronfman, Sr. Peter Max Sichel provided me with many insights into the world of American Jewry. At St. Martin's Press, Sean Desmond proved to be a truly professional editor, a rarity these days, and one whose efforts helped me greatly to improve the book.

He—and I—owe a great deal to Christina MacDonald, most scrupulous and tactful of copy editors, and to Julie Gutin, who coped magnificently with the problems inevitable in producing a book three thousand miles from a—sometimes tetchy—author. Ben Hart was terrier-like in his pursuit of illustrations.

The many other people who helped me unravel the tangled tale of the Bronfmans included Dr. Dorian Hays, Tom Jago, Jack Keenan, James Espey, Sir George Bull, Ivan Straker, Leo Kolber, Samuel Minzberg, Rabbi Israel Singer, Vince Ficca, and John Magliocco, as well as the many interviewees who do not wish to have their names mentioned. Thank you all.

INDEX

A3E, 267
A & M, 260
Aaron, Barney, 18, 24, 50, 52, 133
  operations on Rum Row, 59
Aaronson, Jan, 151
Abbott, George, 67
Abram, Morris, 220
Absolut, 202, 263, 285
Adenauer, Konrad, 214
Alcock, Clarissa, 241–42
alcohol
  attitudes changing towards, 90–91
  blending of, as art, 113
  demand for quality of, 112
  distribution difficulties for, 93
  drinking habits changing of, 201–2
  economic dependency on, 31
  government control over, 29–30, 87,
    110–11
  licensing of, 93
  market changing for, 172–73, 200
  methyl, 92
  nationalization of sales of, 33
  railroad freight's role in transport of, 40
  smuggling into US of, 38
  tax revenue from, 52
  wholesaler's licenses for, 34
Alexander II (czar), 20
Allan. See Bronfman, Allan
Allen, Frederick Lewis, 55
Allen, Herbert, Jr., 243, 250
  on tax avoidance, 284

Allen, Ralph, 81
Allied Domecq, 263
Allsop, Kenneth, 90
American Brands, 239
Ames, Roger, 306
Anctil, Pierre, 118
Andrea. See Bronfman, Andrea
Andrews, A. J., 16
Anglia TV, 185
Anti-Defamation League, 217
anti-Semitism, 83, 87, 119
  in Canada, 27, 124
  in Canadian financial community,
    73–74
  Edgar's opposition to, 213
  in Montreal, 118
  in Quebec, 118–19
  in Russia, 20
  at Trinity College School, 153
  World Jewish Congress fighting, 216
AOL, 275
  Time Warner merger with, 265
AOL Time Warner, 273–74, 280, 297–98,
  300
  debt reduction needed by, 305
  profit warning by, 287
Arbatov, Georgiy, 221–22
Arnault, Bernard, 290, 292–93
  Vivendi board resignation of, 294
Arthur Andersen, 285, 287
Asbury, Herbert, 28, 91
Ashkenazi emigration, 118